Studded with Diamonds

Studded with Diamonds and Paved with Gold:

Miners, Mining Companies and Human Rights in Southern Africa

Laurie Flynn

BLOOMSBURY

First published in Great Britain 1992
Copyright © 1992 by Laurie Flynn

The moral right of the author has been asserted

Bloomsbury Publishing Ltd, 2 Soho Square, London W1V 5DE

A CIP catalogue record for this book
is available from the British Library

ISBN 0 7475 11551

Typeset by Hewer Text Origination Services, Edinburgh
Printed in Great Britain by Clays Ltd, St Ives plc

'If you are advertising any product, never see the factory in which it was made . . . Don't watch the people at work . . .

   'Because, you see, when you know the truth about anything, the real inner truth – it is very hard to write the surface fluff that sells it.'

Helen Woodward, advertising copywriter, *Through Many Windows* (1926)

CONTENTS

Introduction: Another Blanket

Strange though it may seem, the blanket is an item of special significance in the mining industry of southern Africa, particularly in Lesotho – the landlocked country surrounded by Natal, the Orange Free State, the Cape Province and Transkei – where so many of the miners come from. At once a badge of status or occupation, a source of warmth when sleeping, and a fine winter coat against the cold and rain, the blanket comes in a bold variety of patterns and colours embodying images of royal crowns, golden eagles and mine headgear. The blanket is as flexible as the migrant miner has had to be in adapting to the myriad rules and regulations of the mine compound where he eats and sleeps.

The blanket folds and stores easily when the miner is below ground and has no need of it because of the remorseless heat in which he works, winning gold, diamonds, platinum, zinc, vanadium, coal and asbestos from a hostile environment. Then when the miner comes off shift and must avoid cooling down too quickly in the cold night air, he plucks his blanket from a pile, wraps it around himself in an instant and pins it in place.

Besides the wide range of purely physical uses, the miner's blanket also fulfils an important psychological function in the turbulent atmosphere of the mining compounds, the huge, anonymous, men-only warehouses where black mineworkers live in enforced separation from their families. In these places, closer in spirit to prisons or mental hospitals than anything that could be called home, the blanket acts as a shield, protecting the individuality and independence of the migrant worker who has left his birthplace for the South African mines, where an aggressive hierarchy rules his life.

In the winter of 1981 I stayed in a motel on the road from a mine at Heuningvlei on the edge of the Kalahari Desert to Havelock, a mining community which nestles in among the generously forested hills

1

of Swaziland. There I read *Another Blanket*, a report published by a South African church organisation called the Agency for Industrial Mission, which was the result of some remarkable research by a group of Christians concerned about the conditions and human rights of the 700,000 migrant black mineworkers who are the key to South Africa's wealth and industrial development.[1] To record the experiences and understand the feelings and frustrations of the miners, black theological students were carefully trained as participant observers and then placed inside the closed mining compounds of the Rand and the Orange Free State. The young priests lived in the hostels, submitted to the mine acclimatisation system (where people have to spend hours, sometimes for several days, running on the spot inside a high-temperature heat chamber), ate the food and experienced the rigours of working underground. At the end of their stay they were debriefed professionally; the transcripts of the debriefing sessions were then edited and published as *Another Blanket*.

The report displayed an unusual journalistic sensitivity for human feelings and aspirations and as I read it into the dawn of the eastern Transvaal, many things fell into place for me. I realised that by looking, as I had been doing, at worrying conditions in the asbestos mines I had only examined the edges of a much larger industrial fabric which shaped the lives of millions of people throughout the southern African subcontinent. *Another Blanket* suggested that the grave injustices of apartheid were not the sole responsibility of the Afrikaners. The report made clear the mining industry, with its insistence on pass laws, oppressive labour controls and cheap labour, had played a central role in devising the structures of racial discrimination. Furthermore, when the architects of apartheid came to draw up their plans for the permanent subordination of black labour in South Africa, it was to the mining industry which they looked for a working model.

In subsequent weeks I resolved that I would use my time and energy as a television reporter to investigate the links between the wealth of London (where much of the mine financing was arranged) and the rural poverty of southern Africa. I began to look at the circumstances in which British businesses secured hegemony over diamond extraction and at the methods employed to try to seize control of the Rand after gold was discovered in 1886. I began to identify the mechanisms by which the wealth of Namibia was kept from its people for seventy years despite promises that the country was being held in 'sacred trust' for them. I began to examine the behaviour of multinational companies after the formal introduction of apartheid and detected worrying patterns of behaviour. It seemed as if, in the drive for financial return, the companies became blind to moral considerations.

I began to research the safety and accident record of the mining industry and found that one human being died for every single ton of gold mined. This changed radically my feelings about the advertising slogan 'Gold is for lovers', which is employed by the South African International Gold Council to promote the sales of engagement rings and wedding bands throughout the world.

I also found that the real causes of major mine disasters were not being probed properly. As my investigations continued I decided that, while I would have to poke about in record offices, company reports, government archives, land registries and the like, it was essential not to lose sight of the deep, almost incredulous sense of hurt felt by the miners themselves. And over the years my mind has often returned to *Another Blanket* and to one part of the report in particular – the 'Lifela' or recitation chanted by Basotho miners as they cross Mohokare, the Caledon River, the border with South Africa, on their way to another contract in the mines.

Lesotho, now I leave you with your mountains where I used to run,
I am going to the white man's place – the table-land,
Keep our children so that they may grow up on your sides as we did
    ourselves.

I am leaving you in Lesotho. I will never see your men with your
    beautiful mountains,
I am going to the white man's place – with electricity,
I am leaving all the dark places here but I still prefer the mountains
    of Lesotho.

Mohokare, now I assume another blanket now that I have crossed you.

Perhaps this is the last time that I cross you here,
And if ever I have the chance of crossing you again,
Wash me clean, Mohokare, and make me a pure man.
Make me a man who is fit to go to heaven; cleanse me from my sins
Because I am going to the dangerous place where I may lose my
    life . . .

But now that I have crossed you, all the evil things I have done,
May they move with you and go down.
In crossing the river I become a new man,
Different from the one I was at home.
Now that I am on this side, I am in a place of danger
Where I may lose my life at any time.
So prepare me for death.

In the summer of 1990, while preparing this book, I returned to Lesotho, the landlocked country of the blanket, to its capital Maseru and then north into the hills to Tsime. I was going to meet Matseko Lejalla, the widow of Tebalo Lejalla, a miner who did not make it back across the Caledon River. Tebalo was one of 177 men who died in an avoidable fire at Kinross gold mine in September 1986. Kinross had a special resonance for me. I grew up in the Lothians across the water from another Kinross in Scotland, and I remembered that there had been a similar, avoidable disaster in my own country twenty years before. And on the night before the Kinross fire, I had been at a celebratory banquet.

The Gold One Hundred Centenary Banquet was held with considerable style in the ballroom of the Johannesburg Carlton Hotel and brought together the main players in white South Africa's world of gold: captains of industry, bullion dealers, financial journalists, investment analysts, white politicians and visiting dignitaries from the world of precious metals and high finance in London, Tokyo, New York and Geneva. The entrance to the ballroom had been remodelled for the occasion, with styrofoam panels and discreet lighting turning a nondescript hotel doorway into a replica of an underground gold mine. The effect was heightened by two black men dressed as miners, who were guarding the entrance.

Both men wore shorts and mine shirts, knee-pads and boots, their black skin glistening in the intense light; they sported miners' safety helmets with built-in safety lights switched on to spotlight everyone who passed them. One carried a pick over his shoulder, holding it threaded through his folded arms so that it would not fall to the ground; the other carried a shovel. The carefully calculated result was momentary alienation in the guests, halting animated conversations and preparing them for what came next: a mountainous cascade of golden coins spilling on to a mine truck, no less effective for being achieved with the assistance of bulk purchases of chocolate coins from Johannesburg confectioners.

Before long the 600 guests were seated and the master of ceremonies called to order this skilfully constructed hyper-reality of food, of wine, of gold. Then the State President of the time, a sturdy, bumptious-looking man called P.W. Botha, slid into place at the top table to a growing volume of polite applause. At this, the few black people present, whose role was to wait at table, nervously spaced themselves out around the room and drew the mask of stillness over their faces. The centenary banquet was under way. First there was a brief address of welcome, then a toast to the Republic of South Africa by the Minister of State for Mineral and Energy Affairs, Mr Danie Steyn. Then the food was served – smoked salmon and angel-fish mousse, cream of asparagus soup, mango sorbet, roast sirloin of beef with mushroom sauce.

In the gap afforded by the mango sorbet I remembered an unpleasant document given to me by one of South Africa's more mischievous mining journalists.[2] A confidential report from the Human Resources Laboratory of the most powerful body in southern African mining, the Chamber of Mines which is the employers' grouping, it focused on the use of offal in feeding the hundreds of thousands of black miners who dig South Africa's gold. Written by Peter De Vries, one of the Chamber's leading sociologists, the report concluded, 'the main problem is not with offal itself but with the way it is cooked'. In many mines, the author noted, the cooking arrangements for offal were so poor that:

  – it was not washed properly – dung and stones were found in the intestines;
  – it was kept too long and allowed to rot thus causing diarrhoea;
  – it was not cooked with the correct spices;
  – it was not cooked enough.

The banquet ended with strawberries romanoff and sufficient replenishment from one of the many bottles of South African wine to dull my thoughts of Mr De Vries and his memorandum. Then Mr Botha, who had recently thrown many foreign journalists out of his country and crushed dissent in the townships by declaring a 'national emergency', was on his feet, delivering his centenary message about the metal that paid for his soldiers and bought their imported equipment. 'There is an old proverb', he began with what he could scarcely have imagined was originality:

Silence is golden. I considered applying that truth in this case. However I appreciate the invitation to be your guest, together with Mrs Botha.

In spite of the fact that I never owned one gold share, I appreciate the value of this bright yellow metal to our country ... Gold has many qualities. Over the decades it has served as a symbol of stability, contributed its share as an important instrument of civilisation, although we must admit that many a tragedy was caused by the lure of gold.[3]

That same evening, 120 miles away on the high veld east of Johannesburg, in the compound dining halls serving the number two shaft at General Mining's Kinross gold mine, 177 African miners from Lesotho, Malawi, Swaziland, Pondoland, the Transkei and the Ciskei were having supper before commencing the last shift of their lives. The next morning I was on my way to the scene of the tragedy.

Given that I attended the Johannesburg banquet the night before the disaster and then later met the people left to wrestle with its tragic consequences, I would like to dedicate this book to the memory of Tebalo Lejalla and the 176 other miners who died at Kinross. The book is also dedicated to Matseko Lejalla, Tebalo's widow, a warm, generous and remarkable woman, who is pictured on the back cover, to the family's beautiful children Ntsoke, Tseko, Malebotho, Mpempe and Malani, and to all those whose lives have been mangled by a mining economy which for a century or more has always valued things above people.

Acknowledgments
I would like to thank all those generous people who have given help, inspiration and support to this study of mining companies and human rights in southern Africa. My parents, Vincent and Ann, have shaped it in more ways than they will ever know. Judith Condon has tolerated my interest in mining when I was at home and put up with anxious periods of absence as I dug deeper into South African mining realities through the 1986 emergency and the hard times which obtained before the release of Govan Mbeki, Walter Sisulu, Nelson Mandela and others in 1990.

Special thanks also to Ewan and Rosanne, young people whose intelligence and sense of justice is a constant source of inspiration; and to a long list of people whose work, friendship and personal kindness lightened the burden of investigation in a range of agreeable and even extraordinary ways. To Jean Leger, Marianne Felix, Luli Callinicos, Neil White, Eddie Webster, Jim Jones, Charles van Onselen, Belinda Bozzoli, Francis Wilson, Richard Spoor, Lindy Wilson, Dunbar Moodie, Davitt McAteer, Gordon Brown, Ingrid Brown, Moketse Mphole, Gabriel Hlaele, Marcel Golding,

INTRODUCTION: ANOTHER BLANKET

James Motlatsi, Cyril Ramaphosa, Ben Ulenga, Justice Sello Tsukulu, Phiri Lelingoana, Lineo Nketu, Romila Patel, Phil McCowen, Laurence Dworkin, Brian Tilley, Hans Brandt, Nyana Molete, John Hendy, Fiona L'Arbalestier, Anthony Zwi, Paul Benjamin, Debby Zwi, Clive Thompson, Mark Stephens, Halton Cheadle, David Knopfler, Shula Marks and Neil Andersson – my thanks for everything. Thanks also to those presently or formerly at Granada TV who ably supported these investigations in one way or another – Simon Berthon and Paul Greengrass, John Coates and Steve Bolton, David Odd, David Woods, Phil Taylor, Lawrence Jones, Howard Somers, Alan Ringland, Oral Ottey, Roland Coburn, Celia Dougherty and Michael Gillard: you were a pleasure to work with.

I would also like to extend my thanks to Tom Paxton for permission to quote from his song 'Dogs at Midnight' (copyright © SBK Songs); and to Liz Cowen for editing the manuscript; and to all at Bloomsbury, especially Mary Tomlinson, Liz Calder and Nigel Newton.

One day soon I hope to be able to add a South African government to the list of thanks and acknowledgments. But I can't do so yet for a simple reason. Since I first started poking about in the realities of the subcontinent's mining industry, South African governments up to and including the present mildly reformist one have put obstacles in the way of the free flow of information. They threatened some camera operators and deported others, impounded cameras, film stock and video tapes, stopped and searched cars, questioned people who gave interviews and in a bid to sabotage a television film on De Beers, the diamond-mining company in which the government owns shares, informed all members of the crew, myself included, that we were no longer welcome visitors to the country.

Although I have written repeatedly to the new State President, F.W. De Klerk (himself a former minister of mines) and to other members and representatives of his government, detailing my reasons for wishing to return, legal entry is still being resolutely denied. Successive applications for a press visa to continue investigating safety conditions in the mining industry and repeated appeals to ministers and high officials are all turned down without explanation.

It should be noted at the outset that the South African mining industry is the richest in the world and exceptionally highly concentrated. Six great mining houses dominate the industry and the South African Chamber of Mines. They are Anglo American, which together with the De Beers' diamond mining company is run by the remarkable Oppenheimer family; then there are General Mining-Union Corporation (Gencor for short), the company through which Afrikaner business obtained a share of the mining industry; Rand Mines, part of the Barlow Rand conglomerate (in which the Oppenheimers have a minority share); Johannesburg Consolidated Investments (JCI or Johnnies for short) which the Oppenheimers control; Gold Fields of South Africa, formerly a British-controlled company which Anglo failed to take over in 1989 and which as a result came under the control of the tobacco millionaire Anton Rupert and his associates; and, finally, Anglovaal, controlled by the Menell and Hersov families. All the companies are quoted on international stock exchanges and British and American institutions and shareholders hold very significant portions of their stock.

Writing this book has involved the generous help of many South African citizens. But mistakes and misjudgments are my own responsibility and I will do what I can to put them right in the interesting years to come: interesting because the international community stopped being mesmerised by the mineral wealth of South Africa in 1990 and finally withdrew its support for the South African system of apartheid. A new beginning is now in sight and it is no exaggeration to say that what happens in the mining industry will be decisive for the country's future development.

Mining is by far the biggest employer of industrial labour in South Africa and its main generator of wealth. While some social forces want to change little and want little to change, there is growing recognition of the need for serious reform. With reform there is at last a prospect that the cruelty of the migrant labour system can be undone and the mineral wealth of the country can, for the first time, begin to be used for the benefit of the entire population.

LAURIE FLYNN
London, January 1992

1 The Life and Death of Tebalo Lejalla

Matseko hadn't expected to see her husband back in Lesotho until Christmas. He had taken a contract as a migrant miner in South Africa and had no right to take his wife or family with him. Since his last visit home she had thought of him from time to time, what he was doing, who he was with. But she had grown used to these protracted absences and had learned to drive her worries from her mind as she did the household work, cared for the children and tended the little plot of land outside the rondavel, the traditional, circular, stone-built family house with sun-baked mud on the walls inside and out and thatch on the roof. Sometimes when she was a little anxious, Matseko went out of doors to look out over the hillside and take in the view down the valley below. But most of the time, when she was inside, she listened to the radio, a source of comfort as she went about her business. She was indoors and the radio was playing that morning when the urgent tones of an emergency announcement suddenly interrupted the soothing diet of township soul, Lesotho evangelical church choirs and traditional Basotho folk music which flowed from the set she kept on the kitchen cabinet. She turned from where she was cooking on the powerful Dover Wellcome stove to look directly at the radio as soon as she heard the worry in the announcer's voice. There had, he said, been an accident at one of the South African gold mines, Kinross on the far east Rand. By this time, days after the disaster, the mine owners, Gencor, had finally assembled some serious approximation to a death list. The mention of Kinross made her anxious because it was where her husband Tebalo was working as a development worker, constructing new travelling ways and opening new mining faces below ground.

Matseko grew markedly more anxious as Radio Lesotho began its tabulation of the Basotho dead. Since her family name Lejalla clustered comfortingly in the middle of the alphabet, there was hope amid the tension, hope that her husband had cheated death. But not for long. As the announcer hit the surnames beginning with the letter L, the hope died suddenly and irreversibly and gave way to an intense feeling of sickness and dread. LEJALLA, Tebalo, each consonant, each letter on the announcer's lips was a new corkscrew to the heart and at the end of her husband's naming Matseko felt overcome. She sat – or rather slumped – down on the floor, gave way momentarily to her nausea and then began to gather herself for the ordeal of telling the children, at least those of them who were old enough to understand that they would never see their father again. Rallying herself required intense concentration, single-mindedness, to the exclusion of all else. As a result Matseko scarcely took in the second part of the announcement – that the government of Lesotho had arranged for all the Basotho corpses to be delivered to Maseru and that all widows should attend a national service of remembrance. The announcement closed with music, appropriate and sombre, and then the radio played on.

That same morning the best part of 500 miles away in Johannesburg, Derek Keys, the new chief executive of Gencor, the powerful Afrikaner mining company which owned the stricken mine, faced the most difficult moment of his life. With the death list, however unsatisfactory and incomplete, now made public, it was his job to open a press conference at which taxing questions would be asked about the company's safety record. Mr Keys and other Gencor executives had to defend the company's reputation. In the well-appointed room in the company's Johannesburg head offices Mr Keys declared himself 'humbled by the sacrifice others had had to make in pursuit of common goals' and told the dozens of assembled reporters, including myself, that a trust fund would be set up to help the widows and children of the 177 dead men.

Neither Matseko Lejalla nor any of the other widows in Lesotho were ever visited by company officials. Direct company contact with the relatives of the dead seems to have been limited to the families of the five white miners who died in the tragedy; people who also needed all the comfort and support that Gencor and the South African mining world could give them. The white families lived near the mine in the purpose-built and racially exclusive mining town of Evander. The rest of the widows, children or parents of the deceased, different in skin tone, were prevented by law from living with their husbands near their places of work. As a result the next of kin of the 172 black miners lived in remote locations scattered throughout southern Africa; and, so far as I have been able to ascertain, while their rural isolation and

10

poverty meant they were more not less in need of help, they were offered no comfort or assistance of any kind in their time of greatest grief. If they were lucky, like Matseko, they heard the news of their husbands' death for themselves on the radio. But in other cases in Lesotho, the Ciskei, the Transkei, Malawi and Mozambique, and the other sending areas where black workers were recruited for Kinross, they heard the news in garbled form, by word of mouth from an agitated neighbour, relative or friend.

'There was no physical messenger, no letter, no explanation, no help, no nothing,' Matseko recalled. 'And because of this it was a doubly hard and difficult time. I can't understand why they didn't come, or why they didn't help.'[1] She shook her head to dispel the painful memory of those moments when she first heard Tebalo was dead at the age of forty-one, and the days and weeks that followed when she was trying to find money to feed her four children, now there would be no more remittances from the mines. For two months after the disaster Matseko didn't receive any money from Gencor, one of South Africa's biggest and most profitable companies. 'Without Tebalo's mother who gave us the few rands she could spare, these would have been hungry times as well as hard ones,' adds Matseko matter of factly.

To date Matseko and her children have still never received a visit, a letter or a word of explanation from Gencor about what happened to Tebalo and 176 other men on that day in September 1986 when they lost their lives in South Africa's worst-ever gold-mining disaster. From the District Labour Office in Butha Buthe, Matseko now draws a small pension of about £25 a week for herself and her children. This is paid by Rand Mutual, the South African Chamber of Mines' insurance company. From time to time payments stop for a month or two without explanation. When they resume, there is no back pay and again no explanation. Some time later she received a lump sum of £2,250 in compensation. Since no one has ever come from Gencor to explain things, Matseko still doesn't know if the pension is hers as of right, whether it will continue for life or whether it will be terminated at the end of five, ten or fifteen years. And she has heard nothing from Derek Keys about the Kinross Trust, which the company set up in the immediate aftermath of the disaster. Matseko's only succour apart from her pension has come from her family and her neighbours, people who have not forgotten about proprieties or acts of kindness or generosity which they perform in the quietness of the countryside, away from the bright lights of press conferences and the mass media, as the simple personal duty of one human being to another in any society worthy of the name.

STUDDED WITH DIAMONDS

After the service in Maseru, Tebalo's corpse was brought home in a vehicle loaned by the government and driven by his brother. For most of the way from Maseru the road is tarmac but just beyond Butha Buthe at the turn-off towards Tsime haHlasoa, Tebalo's birthplace, it becomes sand or mud, depending on the season. Either way it is treacherous and slow, with great scars and ruts giving way to huge pot-holes which seem sizeable enough to swallow any vehicle, including a makeshift hearse. After what feels like several miles of difficult terrain, the road flattens slightly and passes through arid fields where mealies grow and cattle forage in the hope that hungry humans have missed a grain or two on the sun-dried cobs. And then the road reaches its summit and goes downhill into Tsime across the fording place of water which gives the district its name, the shiny place of water, in the Bushman tongue. Here the rocks glisten as if they had been freshly painted with limitless supplies of marine varnish. And here, where strong berberis-like bushes glow with orange beneath the green and slender elegance of a clump of aloe trees, the body of 41-year-old Tebalo Lejalla had come home. After the ford it was only a matter of carrying the coffin a few hundred yards, up the incline and along the path to the lightly fenced, squared-off piece of land looking down into the valley that the local chief Hlasoa had allotted the young miner as his new home when he and Matseko married in 1973.

The coffin stayed at the house for a few hours while relatives were invited and the local priest of the Lesotho Evangelical Society prepared the funeral oration. In accordance with the dead man's wishes that he should be buried on his own small plot of land, the funeral service was performed in the garden of the rondavel; and the burial mound was placed there too, fifty paces from the door of the house through which Tebalo passed dozens of times each day when he was at home. Today his orphaned children often play near by and no one worries that the occasional thistle or strong thatching-grass is sprouting on the cairn. In their own way these help to mark the grave and the passage of time since the hours of sharpest pain in September 1986.

From time to time Matseko walks slowly by the mound in pensive mood. But not very often – for she is a philosophical woman from a philosophical people who seem to accept death when it calls. Talking with me inside the single-roomed circular house, Matseko is frank about her feelings of sorrow and loss. But she is also at pains to demonstrate that the cycle of life continues and renews itself in the feeding of children, the visiting of friends and neighbours and the endless business of the day. 'Not all the rain falls on one roof,' she reminds me when I ask her tactfully how she is making out. Her inner strength and dignity are evident in the way she punctuates her thoughts with essential activities, making tea for us, putting her youngest child to the breast, feeding us generously, squatting on the floor to wash dishes. Then momentarily her stress shows through as she pauses between task and conversation to take a long and obviously calming pinch of *ugwayi* or snuff.

While Matseko found it relatively easy to begin to talk about the loss of her husband, it was much harder for Nmangaweze Lejalla to talk about the loss of a favourite son. Yet at first it had seemed as if the conversation would, as discussions about death go, be relatively straightforward. Nmangaweze had come down from her own rondavel away in the hills on the other side of Tsime to talk with Matseko and the stranger from overseas who was interested in mining accidents. At first she seemed relaxed and willing to talk freely. She listened with pleasure as Matseko spoke of Tebalo, the second-born of Nmangaweze's seven children and her favourite. Soon she began to talk of him herself, wistfully and nervously, saying how much she missed him and how kind to her he always was. But before long it became clear that Nmangaweze, a slender, dignified old lady, wizened like a dark olive left in the sun, was troubled by the experience and had something else weighing heavily on her mind. All of a sudden she no longer wished to talk and explained in something of a fluster that she had to depart in search of a lost horse. The horse which she had borrowed from a relative in Butha Buthe to do some ploughing, had disappeared along with one of her nephews, and she must leave instantly, she repeated, because otherwise her nephew might cross into South Africa with the horse to go to Qwagwa, the bantustan or dumping ground for people like Nmangaweze who, though Basotho, were born on the other side of the South African border near Bloemfontein.
As Matseko was explaining that it was hard for her mother-in-law to speak of her dead son, Nmangaweze disappeared from the rondavel, promising to talk further about Tebalo's childhood at a later date. A little later, from neighbours living next door, Matseko got word that we should drive up the road to pick up Nmangaweze, take her to the police station in Butha Buthe to report the missing horse, and perhaps even travel with her to break the bad news to its owner, but in any event talk to her on the way. When we arrived at the meeting place, Nmangaweze had gone off to a neighbouring village to consult a local wise man about the whereabouts of her horse. Thanks to his calming influence and sound advice she was as pleased to see us as we

13

were to see her, and as we bumped along the road she began to talk about her dead son, her marriage and her life. Tebalo was, she said, 'the favourite of all the children, a sweet baby, hungry for the breast, always anxious for more food in the early days but also as he grew in years, especially kind and helpful with the domestic work, feeding and caring for the other children and tending the animals'.[2]

'In these qualities', she declared bluntly, 'he was a welcome contrast to his father, a man spoiled and broken by the mines.' Her husband Ranakeli Lejalla had recently died and her sorrow had been lessened by the low ebb their marriage had reached over many years. While it had been good when they were first together, it was no life at all once the cycle of migration to the mines of South Africa set in. Then her husband was away all the time, for months and years on end, a typical migrant worker, bored and lonely at the mine, losing himself in drink and dreams he could ill afford and able to visit his family for only a few days or weeks a year. 'In the early days', she said, 'I was proud of my husband. He was a man of some spirit and independence, and he was well remembered for this. The northernmost part of the village of Tsime was named after him – Tsime na Ranakeli, the part of Tsime beside Ranakeli's house. This section of the village is some way from the main settlement, high into the hills away from the main road towards the snow-capped mountains called Thaba-Telle.

'Before Ranakeli decided to build his family rondavel there, no one had thought of expanding the settlement in that direction. So because of his initiative the newly inhabited area became known as Tsime na Ranakeli.'

To get enough money to build the house and support his family, Ranakeli frequently had to leave Tsime and Lesotho, cross the borderline and work in one of the mines in South Africa. As the conversation continued later outside the car, a friendly local schoolteacher Ntlebere Francis Thabisi, who taught Matseko's children, took it on himself to provide clarifications, background and footnotes to the story.[3] Up until the mid-nineteenth century, he explained, the Basotho lived a secure and settled life in an agricultural economy. With the arrival of colonists in the lands near by, the country even experienced a welcome agricultural boom and became for a while the bread basket of the Orange Free State. But the discovery of gold, coal and minerals below the ground in South Africa changed all that and Ranakeli's generation, and his father's before him, were pulled away from the land and integrated into the cash economy of the mines. They became oscillating migrants, living in the countryside and travelling to work away from home on tough, enforceable contracts which might last as long as two years. With its

14

fittest manpower exported, some of its richest lands confiscated by South African farmers, and a fateful mix of mono-cropping and drought, Basotho society entered a long period of uninterrupted agricultural decline. This in turn increased the country's dependence on the mines and on South Africa still further. In this way the British protectorate of Basutoland, created by the great Basotho King Moshoeshoe, was transformed into a vast labour reserve for the mines, with recruiting stations in every district. Men like Ranakeli were pulled to Johannesburg or the Free State to work below ground; women like Nmangaweze and children like Tebalo were left behind to cope as best they could on the meagre wages husbands and fathers sent home from the mines.

Like many others working away on the mines, Ranakeli Lejalla was illiterate, which meant that he could not write to Nmangaweze. During his long absences on contract in South Africa he was lonely and, like the vast majority of miners caught in this unnatural existence, sought friendship and comfort in the black communities and locations near the mine. This compounded the difficulties of sustaining meaningful family relationships in Lesotho and cost a lot of money. 'This', explained Nmangaweze, 'caused bitterness and serious problems when he returned home on his annual week or fortnight of leave. In one way I'd be glad to see him but I would also be questioning and angry that he had not written or sent money for weeks. With so little time at our disposal and such tensions in the relationship, the time we spent together became very coarse.'

It was her son Tebalo's kindliness and good sense in dealing with this situation when it became, as it sometimes did, a screaming battleground, that endeared him to his mother. 'He would try to protect us from one another and from our problems. Even at quite an early age, he tried to calm us, to help us put aside our conflicts. In the end because he had to work as a shepherd he spent more and more time away from the house. He was living with his grandfather whose cattle he tended and we lost his restraining influence. In time Ranakeli became an increasingly bitter and angry man, who responded to my criticisms and worries in an unkind way. Sometimes he would show me pictures of another woman, saying how much more beautiful she was than I. He would say she was his lady back at the mine. I did not know for sure whether this was true but that didn't mean it upset me any the less. Tebalo would always comfort me after an incident like this. And as he grew older and my marriage became more and more of an empty husk he always tried to help me with money and advice and food and clothing for the other children.'

15

If her husband Ranakeli was lost to the mines for all but a few weeks of the year, Tebalo too spent increasing amounts of time away from home. Like so many boys in Lesotho who should have been at school full-time, Tebalo was often absent. There was work to be done as a herdsboy, looking after his grandfather's cattle. This took up endless days and nights, especially if one of the cattle strayed and had to be tracked and found, which provided a useful excuse for non-attendance at school and was one that Tebalo used even when it was not appropriate. One way and another, according to his mother and his wife, he spent too much time wandering the hills looking after or looking for cattle. His education at Muela primary school suffered. In the end Tebalo missed so many classes he could not move on from primary to secondary education, which limited his ability to control his life. Like his father before him, Tebalo was only semi-literate and could not communicate with his wife by letter when he was away from home. As a result Matseko too felt deprived of information, neglected and kept in the dark, a typical 'widow of the Reserves' in the description of the perceptive South African writer Phyllis Nantantala, even when her husband was alive.

'At first', said Matseko, 'none of this mattered in the slightest. We were both young, happy and in love. I had grown up some way away from Tsime. My sister died as a young child, my father worked away at the mines and my mother in the end abandoned us, unable to take the strain. I was brought up by my aunt and sent every day of every term to school at Qualo. It was during an athletics match between my school and Tebalo's that I met him for the first time. We were married in 1973 when I was seventeen. The gap in our ages didn't seem to matter. We were so happy together. We had a relatively good start you see. Marriage can be very difficult for some women in Lesotho even today. In the old days women like Nmangaweze were chosen by their would-be husbands, brought to the family rondavel and more or less flatly ordered to stay. My marriage with Tebalo was not like that. We met and courted a little. He went through initiation school; twice I think he went off to the mountains with the tribal elders to be taught customs and tradition and, through circumcision, to be initiated into adulthood. He loved those times where the old ways were remembered and passed down the family lines. In preparation for marriage Tebalo had also gathered quite a serious amount of money. He got this by working at the Vaal Reefs gold mine in South Africa. It was so far as I could gather a hard place but he was young and fit and managed to save, so in the early days we had no financial worries. Later when he was away I would become very nervous, worrying what might happen to him, who he would be mixing with, what he would be doing.'

Tebalo put in two contracts at Vaal Reefs, the biggest mine in South Africa and quite possibly the world, employing 40,000 men digging ore and smelting gold. In most countries this one gigantic mine would have developed around it a town the size of Sheffield to house, feed, educate and entertain all the miners and their families. But it was the explicit policy of the mining industry and after it of successive apartheid governments that black miners should not be able to live with their wives and children. If they were allowed to build cities in the mining areas, the reasoning went, they would soon throw up their own civic associations, businesses and trade unions and the white population would be outnumbered and deprived of their monopoly of economic and political power. So like his father before him Tebalo, in order to care for his family, had to wave them goodbye. Like most miners, Tebalo seldom spoke to his wife or his mother about what went on at the mines in which he worked. These were usually such troubled and hurtful places that any conversation beyond details of place names and wage rates only tended to emphasise how degrading the mines were and how powerless the miners.

At the Transformation Resource Centre library in Maseru I met Rakali Khitsane, a former schoolteacher who now works as an accountant managing the TRC's finances. Unable to generate enough income by working as a schoolteacher, Rakali had taken two contracts from the Employment Bureau of Africa, working both times at the same mine as Tebalo. Rakali spoke in tones of pained humour about his experiences there. Ntate Rakali, as his friends and colleagues call him, is a tall, fine-looking man with a serious face that bursts into the sunniest of smiles when he decides to speak freely. 'I went to the mines very much against my will,' he told me, 'out of hard economic necessity. I disliked Vaal Reefs from the very first. I had grown up in a farming area near Mohales Hoek with my father working at Vaal Reefs and Welkom gold mines on a contract that allowed him home to plough in the ploughing season. At Vaal Reefs I soon learned how the oxen felt in the morning when we put them in the yoke. At Vaal Reefs I was treated exactly like a beast of burden and knew instinctively that this was no proper place for any human being.

'When you get to the mine, no effort is expended on explaining things, on helping you to get your bearings and feel at home in this huge, disorienting place. Instead, as if by some miracle, you are supposed to know your way around. On your second day you are taken to the acclimatisation chamber.

17

If this is your first contract you have no idea what this involves. You strip naked in this desperately hot room, you wrap a towel round your waist and then for four hours at a time you run up and down a set of concrete steps. You don't even know what this is for if you're a newcomer and all you hear is a never-ending series of barked commands, shouting and swearwords, directed at someone, directed at you. At the end you feel terrible, shattered, empty. But there is worse in store when you go underground.

'You go down and down and down in the mine cage with almost no idea where you are going and what you should do. It's only when you get to the working place itself that you really begin to understand the danger involved. First it's hotter, far hotter, than the acclimatisation chamber. In fact the heat is stifling, unbelievable. You feel you cannot breathe. You sort of slip in and out of consciousness and then, at last, you reach the heading where you are to work. You survey it for yourself and see that the hangings are not protected. The flaws and faults are only too visible and yet it is your job to work in this threatening place, to disturb and conquer it before it conquers you. This creates incredible tension. On my first day underground I began to feel as if I had taken some terrible cocktail of alcohol or drugs. I was nervous and excited and frightened, so frightened, all at once. More and more as I got through the day the heat was getting to me and in truth I was going a little crazy.

'I asked, I begged to be taken out of there. The white miner just ignored me but I persisted and in the end spoke to the shift boss. He sneered at me and shouted, "These old people. I don't want old people – they're stubborn." I somehow made it to the end of the shift and then demanded to see the doctor who had found that I was fit for underground work. He was kind in his way and changed my grade and said I was fit only for surface work. I became a clerk in the acclimatisation chamber. At Vaal Reefs, such a huge mine, it was a very, very busy place. I would start with the first batch of a hundred to a hundred and fifty men at three o'clock in the morning and work them through until seven a.m. Then a second shift would come on from eight until twelve noon. It was non-stop running up and down those concrete blocks until you dropped. You were allowed only a very little water, a sip at best. In the chamber itself, it was so hot every single part of your body would drip sweat until all the moisture in your body was gone, or so it seemed. Your tongue would sweat, your private parts, even your finger and toenails would sweat until their liquid content was discharged. Looking back on it now, it seems clear to me that acclimatisation was a form of manipulation or even torture. It was this sense of wrong that made me grow to hate the place and everything to do with it. The rest of the mine was scarcely any better. Underground you could be insulted or assaulted by white miners. In the compound if you lost your pass or card, there was a flood of abuse and you could lose a day's pay or even your job.

'I've never been in war but I have read about wars and I used to call Vaal Reefs a concentration camp. I don't know if I was exaggerating. But I don't have any other word for it – a concentration camp. All the time it was like being locked up inside a border post. It was control, control, all the time control and manipulation. To sleep you were packed in rooms; to eat you were forced to stand in lines; to get to work you were like cattle in the crush. At no point was there any privacy, any choice, any room for discussion. It was a hateful place.'[4]

Like Rakali Khitsane, Tebalo Lejalla lasted no longer than two contracts at Vaal Reefs. But this gave him enough money to live with his new wife, buy seed and pay for some ploughing to be done on the little bit of land that was available to him for subsistence farming. Tebalo's hopes for farming were never matched by the yield and next he resolved to try another form of mining, working in the Liqhobeng state diamond diggings two days' walk from his home at Tsime. His partner in the physical work of digging for the diamonds was his mother, Nmangaweze, and while they never made serious money from this activity, it produced some sort of a wage for the family to live on.

Matseko and Tebalo's family was growing. They had their first child Ntsoke, a girl, in 1975 and their second Tseko, a boy, in 1978. Like many fathers, Matseko explains, Tebalo felt slightly displaced by the arrival of his children and their demanding ways. This, joined with growing money worries, brought some tension to their lives. In 1982, with the arrival of a third child, Malebotho, another baby girl, Tebalo decided that he should take a new contract from The Employment Bureau of Africa (TEBA) and earn some more money from the South African mines. He was assigned to a company called Roberts Underground Construction, a subsidiary of Gencor, and put to work in a specialist team charged with developing new underground roadways at a gold mine on the far east Rand called Kinross. The Scottish name of the mine flows from the strong involvement of British finance in the South African mining industry. Kinross, like the other mines next door Bracken and Leslie, was developed by the Union Corporation, a company which after the Second World War established strong British connections with a senior director, Brendan Bracken, who had been Winston Churchill's minister of information and propaganda during the Second World War.[5] Union Corporation later merged with General Mining, the Afrikaner mining house, to form one of the big six of South African mining, the General Mining Union Corporation.

Gencor is still reluctant, years after the disaster, to let journalists inspect the mine or visit the compound where Tebalo lived. But you can see the grim, regimented contours of the compounds as you drive along the main road east of Johannesburg, past Benoni, Springs, Leandra and Bethal. Then, starting out of the veld, come the Kinross A and B compounds fenced in with cement walls and barbed wire and their names and block numbers picked out in paint on the corrugated iron roofs for easy identification from the air by military helicopters. Kinross Mine was first incorporated in November 1963, when Tebalo was eighteen years old. The sinking of the original shaft system began in October 1964 and was completed in March 1966.[6] The ill-fated Number Two shaft was added early in the 1980s to work new ground and to improve hoisting techniques in what was by then an exceptionally productive mine, at which every month the miners blasted, drilled and hauled 175,000 tons of ore. This in turn was hoisted to the surface and put through the gold extraction process. The result of all this effort in the twenty-one years before the disaster was some 200 tons of gold and a profit of 400 million rand or £100 million.

Some indication of conditions at Kinross was given in a pioneering 1977 International Labour Organisation report researched by African graduate students during their holidays and written up by the Dutch ILO official, Fion De Vletter.[7] The report noted that because of conditions in the Kinross compound 'one is deprived of the opportunity to do private things'. The lack of privacy even extended to the toilets:

> The ablutions are centralised and up to about 100 metres away from some of the rooms. The design of the toilets allowed for no privacy and this was something novices were not used to . . .
>
> As you enter the toilet you can see all the people who are releasing themselves exposed . . .
>
> Breakfast consisted of teas, soft porridge without milk and minced meat or soya beans . . . Food seemed particularly bad on Unicorp Mines [Kinross and Winkelhaak] . . . The most disliked manner of preparing food is the mincing of entrails and mixing them with various kinds of vegetables . . .

The ILO report also revealed that complaints about harsh discipline were 'particularly common on the Kinross and Winkelhaak Mines'. 'All miners abhor the misuse of power by the compound policemen who when they caught somebody for any offence . . . handcuffed the man to the central pillar in the room next to the stove for the whole night before his case was heard the next morning.'

From what miners at Kinross have said, little had changed inside the compounds between the writing of the ILO report and Tebalo Lejalla's arrival at the mine in 1983. Tebalo's life in the compound was subject to a virtually endless list of rules and regulations, relating to what food would be available in the canteen and when; how much toilet paper he would be issued with for a month; what time he would have to rise to start the journey to work; which racial group he would be able to ride with in the mine hoist; how he should address white miners and foremen; what work he could and couldn't do; which toilets on the mine encampment were for whites only and which ones were for blacks; what rights if any he had to invite friends to his dormitory room; what food he could buy from the mine store to supplement what was almost certainly an inadequate diet.

In addition there were penalites for being late to work, questioning instructions, losing your pass, or coming into the compound after hours. The compound had little in the way of social provisions, such as libraries, leisure entertainment, or facilities for unmanaged and spontaneous activity. All the time, above ground as well as below, in and out of working hours, the miners were being watched. Mining compounds had first grown up in the diamond mining industry in Kimberley and were essentially military or police institutions run on authoritarian lines for the benefit of the mining companies. The food they provided was in theory scientifically planned and highly nutritious. But the circumstances in which it was cooked, the use of untrained staff, the inevitable burgeoning of corruption inside closed institutions, ensured that on delivery the food was often poorly presented, tedious or even grossly substandard. Miners like Tebalo sought release from this totalitarian universe, and from the massive tensions of working underground, in a variety of ways: in music and dance, in drink and visits to the nearest black location where, in the shebeens or illegal drinking dens, they could relax and possibly find the company of women.

While Tebalo was at Kinross, Matseko began to worry about him, and when he did not write she would sometimes travel across the border to visit him at the mine. The fact that she was allowed to do so was evidence of the limited reforms some mining houses had adopted after the riots and other explosions of stress and protest that had taken place in the 1970s. The more Matseko came to know about Kinross, the more she worried. For anyone with eyes to see it was a cruel and unnatural way to live, the outgrowth and embodiment of a society which sought to hold the majority in permanent subjection. Yet in some respects there were reasons to be hopeful. By the mid 1980s, at the time of Tebalo's second contract, the National Union of Mineworkers was becoming firmly established in South Africa and even at Kinross, much to the chagrin of the white mine bureaucracy and the white miners, whose commanding position in the work process had hitherto been protected by a thoroughgoing ban on black union organisation. Like hundreds of other Kinross workers, Tebalo hoped for change to the system, change which would bring him better pay, more responsible work and perhaps even the right to live near his work with his family. He joined NUM and for the first time had a taste of freedom, of what it meant to express your thoughts freely, to list your grievances and be treated with dignity and respect.

In July and August 1986 hopes were running high among black miners throughout South Africa. Union organisation, outlawed for a century under British colonial rule and the long years of apartheid, had grown by leaps and bounds after the National Union of Mineworkers was founded in 1982, and at last there was the prospect of genuine bargaining with the Chamber of Mines. As the miners at Kinross went to work on the morning of 16 September, national wage negotiations had been taking place and the black miners' union was hoping decisively to narrow the ten-to-one gap between what black miners earned for doing the work and what whites were paid, often for standing around shouting at them. In Kinross's complement of 4,000 workers who went below on the early shift that morning, Tebalo and his fellow development workers travelled as usual in racially segregated groups, the blacks going down at the less convenient time and waiting for the whites to arrive. That morning too there were the usual everyday tensions associated with climbing into a cage and dropping more than a mile below ground to go to work; and there was the intense, unending heat. As they began their work, some of the tension dissipated in the activity of mining, the cutting, blasting and drilling or in Tebalo's case the shaping of a new development. In all respects but one it was just another day in the life of the Kinross Mine.

There was a problem that morning in the main haulage-way of the mine. The ore was supposed to flow through to the hoist for onward transmission to the surface. But a rail on the main tramline had buckled, probably due to rocks falling from the roof, and if it wasn't mended quickly the mine could lose a whole day's production of gold. For a South African mining company this was an unwelcome prospect at any time, particularly on a day like this when the gold price was high. So an emergency welding team headed by a white miner was sent down to carry out a running repair. With a cutting torch powered by oxy-acetylene, they were to cut into the rail, remove the buckled section and float in a replacement.[8] Once it was welded in place this would allow the all-important flow of gold to resume. Unfortunately neither the mine management nor the white miner, who alone under South African law were allowed to make decisions about mining safety, had paused to think about what they were doing or what the consequences might be if something went wrong. Yet, because of a set of blinkered business decisions taken six years earlier, the risks were high and the consequences tragic.

In all gold mines people have to cut and blast and drill in confined spaces up to two miles below the surface of the earth. This is a dangerous and hostile environment where great care has to be taken. But even after the shafts have been sunk, the roadways drilled and blasted, the underground environment is still far from stable and things are always going wrong. At Kinross in 1980 management had had a familiar problem: rocks falling from the roof of the main haulage-way on to the railway track below had paralysed the flow of ore through the mine, reduced the quantities of gold the mine could smelt and upset head office. Gencor managers and head-office executives decided to solve the problem by lining two-thirds of a mile of the underground tunnel with a coating of polyurethane foam. This decision, taken on short-term business grounds, would lose 177 miners their lives six years later, causing a minor incident underground to escalate first into a serious fire and then into South Africa's worst-ever gold-mining disaster.

In deep and dangerous mines like these, a variety of techniques is used to minimise the problem of falling rocks. The roofs of the roadways are kept painted and then covered in wire mesh. At particularly tricky points a cement skin can be floated in; and if necessary whole roadways can be gunited or covered in a layer of cement. This is what should have been done at Kinross. But as Gencor head office executive Con Fauconnier was inadvertently to disclose to a press conference after the disaster,[9] Gencor had decided not to use cement guniting and instead installed a thick coating of polyisocyanvrate foam. Mr Fauconnier explained the reason for this decision: guniting involved the transport and use of bulky machinery in the mine's main artery, which had immediate implications for production

23

and profitability, for it meant that the ore being dug would have to stay underground rather than move through the mine for final hoisting to the surface and processing into rough gold. To avoid interrupting production Gencor management made a different and in the event disastrous choice. Instead of using gunite, they went for polyurethane foam, which can readily be delivered to the problem area in handy cartons, frothed and expanded with air and then blown on to the roof of the roadway like ready-made cream being squirted on a trifle. The compelling short-term advantage was that no cumbersome machinery need disrupt the flow of ore through the mine while the coating was put in place. But the foam is highly combustible. It ignites easily and burns like a forest fire; and when it burns it gives off a deadly cocktail of toxic gases, including cyanide, which make it impossible for human beings to breathe. The foam is dangerous enough above ground or inside a house, where in a variant used as a cheap filler for the furniture industry it is an acknowledged killer, but its use in the confines of a mine tunnel thousands of feet below ground is a recipe for disaster.

The foam was installed below ground along 490 metres of a tunnel known as 15 cross-cut north using various sub-contractors, including Rockgrout Construction and Aerofoam Industries. For six years Gencor's luck held. Then on 16 September 1986 Frederick Viviers, the white miner in charge of the welding team, cut into the buckled rail on the main haulage-way with his welding torch. The flames from the torch could easily have ignited the foam on their own, but the torch and bottle set was poorly maintained and the acetylene cylinder was defective. As a result it caught alight and ejected flames. The flames in turn ignited the foam lining of the tunnel, which was soon burning along its entire length. The resulting inferno created a huge release of noxious gases. Driven by the artificial wind that went through the mine to help with ventilation, the toxic fumes soon spread everywhere underground.

Some miners fled for their lives, among them Frederick Viviers. Kisisi Mathumbi was the senior black miner with the welding team. After the disaster he told me what had happened. 'The white man fastened the oxygen bottle to the torch and started doing his work with the bolts and the fish plates. He finished with the bolts, but as he put the torch off, the red bottle burst into flames. The white man did nothing. As soon as he saw the fire, he dropped the torch and ran away. The four people with me, saw that the white man was running away, so they ran too.

'I was left alone as his team leader. I was trying to get the bottle, but I was burning because the bottle was so intensely hot. The fire had now spread to the sides and even the pipe-covering along the mine tunnel began to burn, adding to the problem. I was on my own now. I threw down the bottle and then ran for my life. I found steps and went up to section 7, where by sheer luck I found the underground manager for number one shaft and told him what had happened.'

For miners like Tebalo Lejalla, who were working downwind of the incident that morning, there was to be no escape. The toxic fumes spread through the workings. As they breathed in the fumes their lungs ceased to function and they choked to death trying to summon the strength to escape. For hours after the fire no one in the mine management seems to have realised how grave the consequences of the accident were to be. The welding ignited the foam at 9.25 a.m. Ten minutes later the mine management were informed what was going on and sent in rescue and fire-fighting teams. By 11.30 the death count was thirteen and the first of the injured began to arrive at the hospital near by in the mining town of Evander. By noon hundreds were on the surface with worrying tales of the carnage down below. By 5 p.m. the first public statement was made to the South African Press Association; but even this gave little indication of the extent of the catastrophe. This only became clear at 8 a.m. the following morning when at a press conference at the mine stunned Gencor officials disclosed that the death toll had risen to 170. In the course of the rest of that day seven more bodies, including those of two men who had gone down to help with the rescue, were found and brought to the surface. By the end of the day with 177 dead South Africa had experienced its worst-ever gold mining disaster. Among the 177 deceased was Tebalo Lejalla, aged forty-one.

Three days after the disaster Gencor's chief executive Derek Keys called a press conference at Gencor's Johannesburg head office to express his thoughts. 'I wish to take this first public opportunity, on behalf of the board and all fellow employees of the Gencor group, to express our shock and deep regret at the tragic loss of life and suffering involved in the Kinross disaster,' he stated. 'We extend our loving sympathy to the bereaved. We pray for the full recovery of the injured.'[10] At Kinross events in the wake of the disaster showed little evidence of such sensitivity. Several days later there had still been no proper briefing sessions to explain what had happened or discussions at which the thousands of deeply troubled miners who survived could ask questions, express views or seek medical and psychological help. Instead the mine concentrated more effort on dealing with government and the press than the uninjured survivors of the incident and the 4,000 other miners who had to come to terms with it.

In short Gencor was no more successful at managing the aftermath of the disaster than it had been at ensuring a safe working environment underground. As a result an aggrieved mood built up inside the compound which suddenly propelled miners from depths of sorrow to heights of anger and then back again. Faced with this situation most business organisations would have difficulties, but for one run on strict, authoritarian, apartheid lines like Gencor, the difficulties were insurmountable. The company had neither the human and political skills nor the democratic spirit to help it respond in a generous and supportive way. Instead the bureaucracy carried on along its usual path, causing first further offence and then open rebellion among the younger miners. An early bone of contention was the company's memorial service for the victims. Staged less than a week after tragedy struck, this was Gencor's attempt to put the disaster behind it and resume something like production as normal on the mine. The service backfired and led to an outburst of elemental rage from younger black miners.

Even before the service they felt that the company was in too much of a hurry to get the mine back into operation and had reneged on a pledge that the mine would be shut for a full week before normal work was resumed. But this was as nothing compared to the insensitive way the memorial service was organised. It was planned without consultation with the people who had suffered the overwhelming majority of the losses and without inviting the black miners' union to send representatives. The service was conducted in Afrikaans, with the all-white members of mine management and Gencor head office staff lined up like school prefects. The minister from the Dutch Reform Church had no connection with the black miners and delivered his benediction in Afrikaans. Black miners do not speak Afrikaans as their native language and its use in such situations has strong connotations of racial dominance. Many of the black miners felt the management had been insensitive in organising the service, feeling instead that they should have been allowed to take the lead. Ignoring the cautions of their union leaders, who had said they should simply stay away, a group of young miners decided to give free expression to their feelings.[11] As the Reverend Nel struck up in Afrikaans, one of them called out insistently, 'Speak Fanakalo', the esperanto language of command employed by the mines to allow white foremen to instruct black miners. Then in the distance singing and chanting was heard as migrant miners began a display of toyi-toying, the protest dance that has come to

26

dominate recent South African political history. They moved closer and closer to the service, and in defiance of renewed entreaties from NUM shaft stewards moved in around the preacher himself, venting their anger at the way they and their dead comrades had been treated.

Despite everything, the Reverend Nel kept extraordinarily calm and tried to continue preaching; but in the end his voice was drowned by the chanting miners, and his flower-covered podium swept aside. Then the miners proceeded to the catering area which Gencor had provisioned with drinks and sandwiches for its guests. There they gave vent to their disgust at the occasion: moving along the line of trestle tables, they commandeered the food and drink in a display of raw anger. At this the mine management withdrew, a sensible decision because any attempted reassertion of their lost authority might have provoked a riot. As they moved away, it fell to Hazzy Sibonyani, NUM's national safety officer who had just arrived, to calm the scene and urge the miners to find another way to give expression to their anguish.

The miners' grievances, however indelicately expressed, were real enough. Their resentment, already considerable, would have redoubled if they had known what was going on behind the scenes over the post-mortems of dead black miners. From the beginning of the disaster, blacks and whites were treated differently. The fifty injured whites brought to the surface on the day of the disaster had been rushed by ambulance to the well-equipped Evander Hospital near by. The hospital was kept closed to blacks, who were the overwhelming majority of the victims, dead or alive. Black survivors were ferried by mine buses and lorries to another hospital, further away and much less well equipped. There, at Kinross's sister mine Winkelhaak, distressing scenes unfolded. Hundreds of injured and disoriented black miners could not be accommodated inside the hospital, so they were deposited on the lawns outside to await treatment. The hospital, in scenes reminiscent of the chaos at the Hamidya Hospital in the Indian city of Bhopal eighteen months before during another terrible industrial disaster, was overwhelmed and could not cope. It soon ran short of urgent medical supplies and was reduced to phoning Johannesburg for emergency rations, which were sent out along the Rand by car. Hospital staff then drove out to meet the supply cars half-way, collected the supplies and drove them back to Winkelhaak.

Before they were buried the apartheid system inflicted one last degradation on the bodies of a number of black miners. At Kinross the five dead white miners were post-mortemed normally and properly, but no such elementary courtesies and human rights were afforded to the black

27

miners. Because they were black, their bodies were not sent to Diepkloof, the Rand's premier mortuary; instead they were post-mortemed in a haphazard way at various ill-equipped locations. Later for *World in Action* we gave the first indication of what had gone on at Kinross after the bodies were brought to the surface:

> To get at the lungs of the dead colleagues of these black miners, mortuary assistants worked as if on a production line, using industrial bolt cutters to open up bodies.
> The corpses of the dead were piled high without ceremony or respect.
> This week, one surgeon, still angry at what he saw, lodged an official complaint with the government.[12]

Gencor officials rushed to deny the report. According to Gencor officials (quoted in the *Star*), the British television film on Kinross 'appeared to contain a number of unsubstantiated and biased statements'.[13] Bruce Evans, Gencor's chief executive for the gold and uranium division, said the allegations about the way autopsies were carried out were 'blatant untruths'. Harry Hill, a Gencor corporate communications executive, also angrily denied the report and again insisted that it contained 'blatant untruths'.[14] Another Gencor statement said: 'We find it distasteful that anyone should go to such lengths to sensationalise this tragic accident and cause further distress to the families of the victims.'[15] And there the matter would have lain but for the actions of the National Union of Mineworkers and their legal advisers, the Johannesburg firm of Cheadle, Thompson & Haysom. Anticipating that the situation after the disaster might also be problematic, they had retained the State pathologist of Namibia, Dr J.B.C. Botha, on a watching brief. He was the 'unnamed surgeon' in the *World in Action* report who was so angry at what he saw of the post-mortems that he lodged an official complaint. In his report to NUM, which the union released as a result of the controversy, he wrote as follows of autopsies on thirty-three victims, all black, performed at the Springs mortuary on 22 September:

> The bodies had not been adequately preserved prior to autopsy and in many decomposition had already commenced. I do not know where the bodies had been stored as the Springs mortuary has to the best of my knowledge, only refrigeration facilities for 24 bodies.
> The bodies were stacked on top of each other in four piles on the floor

because of the inadequate space available. This resulted in post-mortem injuries which were at times exceedingly difficult to distinguish from ante-mortem lesions.

The mortuary is inadequately equipped for the performance of autopsies. Skulls are opened with an agricultural bow-saw as no electric saw is available while bolt cutters are used to open the thorax as cartilage shears have not been provided.

The scale provided for weighing organs is both obsolete and broken while the mortuary staff are expected to weigh the bodies on an antiquated scale, calibrated in pounds and ounces, of the type used to weigh bags of grain.

No specimen containers were available for the taking of blood or tissue samples.

Dr Botha concluded by expressing his deep disquiet: 'The Kinross mine accident was of national importance and may have far-reaching consequences for the South African mining industry. I therefore find it inexplicable that the post-mortem examinations of the victims were not performed with more thought and coordination.'[16]

Dr Botha then outlined how the situation should have been handled. All the bodies should have been transferred to a central point with adequate facilities. The Diepkloof mortuary was a modern facility with room for up to 600 bodies. If there had been any serious post-disaster planning then all the dead would have been sent there. Dr Botha also insisted that a State pathologist should have been appointed to supervise and co-ordinate the autopsies. Full details of the body positions when they were found underground should have been given to scientists conducting the autopsies, along with blood samples from all the victims instead of a random few. This would have enabled systematic analysis of the toxic gases in a variety of victims from a range of different positions inside the mine. And, he added, routine tissue specimens should have been obtained from all bodies in case detailed histological examinations were required later. This information would have helped doctors monitor the long-term health risks for those 2,000 miners caught underground and exposed to toxic fumes who managed to get out alive.

No such thoroughgoing disaster-management scheme was initiated. Instead the awful truth about what had happened to the 'non-white dead' was flatly denied by Gencor officials, who spoke of 'blatant untruths' and of finding it 'distasteful' that 'anyone should go to such lengths to sensationalise' the tragic aftermath of a mining disaster. When our report was confirmed by Dr Botha, Gencor executives made no apology for misleading the South African public. Instead Bruce Evans conceded that his information about the post-mortem had been 'incorrect'.[17]

Eventually, days after the disaster, Gencor's list of the dead at Kinross was more or less complete. The lists of company numbers were at last matched with the full, individual names of almost all the black miners. The names of the dead white men were on it from the beginning. Now only five people remained who were known to the company only by their Christian names, together with their company numbers and the number of the clock they punched. The bodies were on their way home, Tebalo's and others to Lesotho, some to Transkei, Ciskei, Mozambique, Swaziland, Pondoland and all the other areas where men had to leave their families in order to feed them. Back in Tsime, near Butha Buthe, Matseko Lejalla had heard the news on the radio and had told her three oldest children, Ntsoke, who was ten at the time, Tseko, seven, and little Malebotho, aged three and a half, who could scarcely begin to understand what had happened or what death meant. The youngest child of all, Mpempe, was only four months old when the blow fell and never knew his father. Naturally Matseko did her best to shield her children from the stress and pain of death, but this was not easy because she had another problem which almost always befalls the widows of victims of industrial accidents, particularly in places like southern Africa where there is no welfare state. Matseko had no money.

Not long after Matseko heard the news, Nmangaweze Lejalla, Tebalo's mother, was informed that her favourite son was gone: 'Three of us were digging trenches for water pipes at the chief's place,' she told me. 'They came with my husband, Ranakeli. As he approached I grew very anxious. The old man could not hold back his tears and I knew that something was very wrong. Finally he managed to let the news cross his lips and I learned that I would never see Tebalo again.'

As the families of the 177 dead miners made their arrangements to bury their loved ones, tension inside the mine compound at Kinross was reaching previously unknown levels. The mine manager had promised initially that no one would have to go back to work for the rest of the week, but he was over-ruled by head office and the miners felt they were being forced back to work in breach of a solemn promise. In this difficult situation, NUM's local organiser Tshediso Mothupi moved to organise the union's own memorial ceremony to reduce tension and mourn the dead. Tshediso

Mothupi looks more like a reggae musician than a South African mining union official. In his late twenties, slender of build and gentle of gesture, he has a magnificent set of jet-black dreadlocks. Atop of them, night and day, he wears a bright yellow safety helmet covered in stickers which announce the imminent arrival of justice and freedom in South Africa. Tshediso cannot be separated from this helmet, even in those few hours after Kinross when he managed to flop down for a short sleep in the tiny union office in the black location near Secunda.

Such was the continuing atmosphere of crisis and disorientation that still surrounded the mine on the morning of the union's memorial meeting for the dead of Kinross that no one quite knew what to expect. I felt sure I would be ahead of Tshediso for once as I reached the little office in the community centre where NUM was based. But he and his colleagues were already hard at it at 5.30 a.m. chattering down telephones, fixing things with the local police and military commanders, and producing makeshift posters for display at the football ground where later in the morning NUM would pay its last respects to the lost ones of the mines. The meeting was scheduled for 10.30, but from 7 a.m. onwards miners started arriving from all over the region. They congregated in the church hall near the union office, in silence at first. This was soon to be broken. The singing began near the back of the hall with one young man less daunted by the situation than the rest of us. 'Huchene mahucheche,' he sang out, pausing to see if there was a response. 'Huchene mahucheche,' answered a few others, hesitantly at first. Quickly the soloist made his call again – this time bringing a serious response. Within minutes a spontaneous service of remembrance was under way, continuing uninterrupted for the next three hours. The singing was complemented by a slow and dignified dance, again begun by a few isolated individuals, then taken up by others. Soon different parts of the hall began to compete with one another. In affirmation as well as lamentation chant followed chant and song followed song, lifting the spirits of those who had already collected inside the hall and drawing hundreds, even thousands, more to gather in the street outside. The singing went on for hours, spreading out to include all those in the street who had initially come just to listen. It grew in beauty as well as in volume, at once an anthem of sorrow and a hymn of praise, giving vent to unashamed, unlimited sorrow and simultaneously expressing hopes of better things and better times to come.

At around 10.30 the call came to leave the hall and walk quietly to the football stadium, where the meeting was to be held. The crowd filed out, turned the corner, and there on the larger boulevard that led along to the stadium came face to face with the South African government's way of marking the occasion: tanks lined each side of the road, with their pill-box hats, turrets and gun vents open and a variety of weapons poking through. Below and behind them in the street were hundreds of infantry men in full riot gear, accompanied by the greatest display of savage dogs it has ever been my privilege to encounter. The thousands of miners swept past this phalanx of white State power in silence and entered the sports ground. Before the meeting could be called to order by Tshediso and Cyril Ramaphosa (then NUM general secretary and now Secretary of the African National Congress), the South African Air Force put in a brief appearance, buzzing the crowd with a succession of helicopters, which added storms of dust to the sinister soundtrack they laid down as background. Then as Tshediso began to speak the public address system spluttered and broke down.

During the not insubstantial period of technical difficulties, more singing began and I copied down the statements on the posters and banners spread everywhere around. The first to catch my eye was one which stated simply: 'Since Johannesburg was born one hundred years ago, 80, 000 workers have been killed in the gold mines. So while others celebrate we remember our comrades who have died lonely deaths deep down below.'

Others, less poetic, announced, 'Gencor, a safe work place is a right. Negotiate with NUM.' 'We demand safety stewards.' 'We want the right to refuse dangerous work,' and 'We are forced to blast so we can get the stof [the stuff or gold ore] out.' One, which was all the more affecting for its understatement of what had been going on, said, 'My brother is with me, carrying his pick and shovel. On his feet are heavy boots. Every day he sees men die in the mines.' As I finished reading it, a brown Datsun car sped into the stadium and pulled to a halt on the far side away from the platform. Out stepped a tall woman dressed in flowing African dress. She was warmly greeted by Cyril Ramaphosa, who then introduced her to the audience. It was Winnie Mandela, who 'speaks for the jailed and exiled leaders of the ANC'. As this announcement was made the audience gasped at the daring of it, bringing a recently unbanned person to a probably illegal gathering during a state of national emergency.

Mrs Mandela said, 'I bring you deep sympathy from our leaders, and from the mothers in the township and from the rest of the long-suffering people of South Africa. This is just the beginning of a long struggle. You are the power, the labour of this land. It is through your efforts and sacrifices that the great, golden wealth of South Africa is produced. And then once it is above ground it is spent and used and consumed on soldiers and weapons and tanks and tear-gas to keep you in your place. They have kept you like cattle, penned in compounds away from your wives and children and any normal kind of life.

'In at least two countries, this polyurethane foam may not be used in mines of any kind. But here in South Africa in the richest mines of all there is no such prohibition. Why, I ask myself, why? And again and again comes the same answer. It is because they do not care for our lives, that we have lost 177 of our brothers. And besides all this there is tragedy and violence in the townships. This is real suffering and we have suffered long enough.'[18]

Winnie Mandela's was only one of a succession of short and powerful speeches which dwelled not only on suffering and injustice but pointed to a day of reckoning that would come soon. For his speech Cyril Ramaphosa decided not to use English but Sesotho and Xhosa. At the end of the meeting Mrs Mandela and her brown Datsun disappeared as suddenly as they arrived, chasing back along the road to Johannesburg and its even more populous black satellite Soweto. As the crowd ebbed away, we helped to retrieve as many of the posters as we could, ferrying the mementoes of fallen men back to the union's tiny office. Once inside, Tshediso looked happier, relieved that the memorial service had passed off without the chatter of guns from the South African army or police, a man renewed and with enough energy to help the troubled miners of Kinross in the weeks and months ahead. As ever there was plenty for him to do – within a fortnight, there were two further outbreaks of fire at Kinross. The fires were small in size but large in symbolism because they broke out once again on the ill-fated level 15, where disaster had struck before. Thousands had to flee for their lives. These further fires caused Ramaphosa to reiterate his call for a full public inquiry into the disaster 'with the participation of international safety experts as proposed by the European Community's foreign ministers' and to underline once again that workers' lives 'were continually being endangered because of management's neglect of safety standards'. Kinross, he stressed, had been a predictable, avoidable disaster. The loss of life was needless and inexcusable and arose from the deformed way in which the mining business had come to conduct itself in the colonial context of South Africa. Eight hundred miners died in the country's gold mines every year, he pointed out.

The life and death of Tebalo Lejalla is the story of just one of that number; the sorrow of his widow Matseko, her children, Ntsoke, now aged sixteen, Tseko aged thirteen, Malebotho now nine and Mpempe aged six, and their grandmother Nmangaweze, only an indicator of the immensity of pain left behind by the mining companies in their remorseless harvesting of a nation's wealth. Today in Lesotho, Matseko, one of many widows, renews her life. With the 9,000 rand (£2,250) compensation she has had so far she has built a new breeze block and cement building next to the rondavel, in which she and her family eat, wash, sleep and relax. Matseko is proud of her achievement in the face of adversity. 'I came back from Springs in South Africa with the compensation cheque full of energy and decided I would build something for the children. This new house is built with modern building materials, breeze blocks, a zinc roof, metal windows with glass inside. I am proud of my achievement. The miners' union has promised to help the widows develop some employment through co-operatives. I hope that this will happen. If not, when I get the extra compensation the union says we may get because of the company's failures, I will use one thousand rand to go to Durban or Johannesburg and stock up for trade as a hawker. What I have now is sufficient only for survival. With more money I could plan ahead and be sure that my children can finish school. Without more help I will not succeed in keeping them at school.'

In time Matseko felt comfortable enough with me to turn the conversation to what had obviously been bothering her since the intensity of grief had first subsided. 'No one has ever come from Gencor,' she reiterated, 'and, as a result, none of us knows anything about what happened to our husbands on that day in September 1986.' Since the South African government has gone to considerable lengths to avoid having a proper public inquiry into the country's worst gold mining disaster, there was no official report I could give Matseko. So I told her in my own words what had happened at Kinross, how dangerous material had been put in to stop rock falls, how a welding team had been sent in to do a repair and yards of foam had caught fire and 177 men died as a result. Matseko sat silent, then at the end shook her head and repeated again, 'No one came from Gencor. No one bothered to tell us what had happened to our men.'

Shortly before I left I asked Matseko if she had a photograph of her late husband. 'Tebalo's passport never came back from Kinross,' she replied, 'so I have no photograph of him.' Then she added, 'In memory of our time together you will take away the plate on which I served you food.' As I got ready to leave the Lejalla rondavel, and Tsime, the shining place of water, she said she had good hopes for the future. Finally, outside the front door, she pointed to her son Mpempe. 'He is my picture of Tebalo, so like him in every respect. I would like to be sure he will never be a miner.'

2   De Beers and Human Rights in Namibia

The cruelty of the southern African system of migrant labour began with tokens of love. In 1867 the first reports of rough diamonds being found between the Orange and the Vaal rivers began to circulate. Then in 1869 the sale of the Star of Africa, an impressively large diamond, convinced the doubters and soon there were 5,000 diggers, dealers and speculators combing the area.[1] By the early 1870s the mines at Kimberley were under way, a morass of competing claims worked headlong downwards in defiance of elementary considerations of planning or safety. It fell to a ruthless vicar's son from Bishop's Stortford in Hertfordshire to rationalise the brutalism of the unfettered marketplace. In its place Cecil John Rhodes brought amalgamation and large-scale production under strict controls, a system achieved in coalition with the Rothschilds and other finance and mining men who understood that serious money could only come from the assiduous promotion of monopoly. From the beginning Rhodes's business dealings were unorthodox and sailed close to the wind. Rob Turrell reasons – on the basis of convincing evidence presented in his recent book – that Rhodes sabotaged rival pumping equipment at the mine to increase his power and income in the early days.[2] Later, once he and his allies had taken over, the shares of the De Beers' Consolidated Mines became the brightest shooting star in the firmament of Victorian values and colonial business expansion; and thereafter he had no special need to engage in such routine criminality. With his mastery of De Beers he could buy up leases and concessions and sell them on to his own publicly incorporated company at a handsome premium; and with the spiralling value of De Beers' shares there were enormous opportunities for stock jobbery and insider trading. In January 1885 a single De Beers' share fetched £3 10s in the market; by March 1888 the same share would trade for £47.[3]

From the beginning an intense, aggressive, racial capitalism was being moulded in Kimberley and the Cape by Rhodes and his associates. Black claimholders, independent diggers and dealers were marginalised and later formally barred from any meaningful stake in the industry and the great mine was turned into a closed shop worked by convicts and contract workers whose freedoms were, to say the least, curtailed. They were housed in poor conditions inside a closed compound, Rhodes's 'monastery of labour' in the inimitable phrase of his cheerleader and apologist, *The Times* correspondent, Flora Shaw.[4] At the end of their contracts blacks were subjected to anal examination to ensure there was no informal redistribution of wealth achieved by the swallowing and secretion of gemstones. As for the convicts, at the end of each stretch their arms were strung up above their heads and locked inside a special glove for days on end. Their defecations were then monitored and the stools picked apart to see if they contained diamonds. Later modifications included even more aggressive searching methods, which were applied to all black workers, and the invention of an automated machine for washing and probing human stools.[5] The South African mining compound, essentially British in design, had been born.

In its organisational ethos, it embodied an arrogant, degrading and undemocratic view of man. Indigenous peoples, conveniently classified as 'primitive', were seen as muscular machines who, ostensibly for their own good, were to be shackled to the corporate engines of a civilisation which proclaimed its superiority over all aspects of their culture. In his perceptive book *The Character Factory – Baden-Powell and the Origins of the Boy Scout Movement*, Michael Rosenthal examines how the imperial mission disguised the crudity of colonial expansion and turned it into a dream fulfilled. He describes the development of a 'specialised rhetoric to turn the unpleasant facts of conquest and exploitation into the burdens assumed by a selfless nation altruistically dispensing the glories of its civilisation'.[6] The specialised rhetoric was not the only form of public discourse. Sometimes the guardians of Britannic expansion spoke in a coarser tongue. 'The native labourer is to us what the Irish labourer is at home – the hewer of wood and the drawer of water,' wrote the *Daily Independent* in its leader column of 12 October 1880.[7] By the time gold was discovered in 1886, the die was cast. Thereafter a vast industry based on the exploitation of the richest spot on earth would stamp its racial mould across a subcontinent according to a more or less unvarying pattern of discrimination, monopoly and authoritarian power.

After the death of Rhodes, others came forward to carry on his mission to monopolise diamonds, among them Sir David Harris and Sir Ernest

Oppenheimer. At a secret conference in Cape Town in 1930, they joined with the South African government, itself a major owner of diamond claims and a principal beneficiary of the industry through income tax and export revenues, to reinforce the intricate monopolistic arrangements whereby diamonds are kept in scarce supply and carefully filtered out into the market-place to keep prices extravagantly high. In Windhoek I found a copy of the minutes of Sir Ernest and Sir David's secret sessions with the South African minister of mines. They set out the rules by which the diamond game has been played ever since.[8]

Sir David was particularly frank: 'For goodness' sake,' he pleaded, 'keep out of the newspapers and Parliament the quantity of diamonds that can be produced and put on the market. If you do not, it will alarm the whole trade.'[9] Sir Ernest also spoke bluntly. 'I know the problems of that coast very well. We own or have options on nearly all the farms there ... The £300,000 [investment] also means this – no prospecting on any of our farms. We own 250,000 morgen of ground there and we give the undertaking that we shall not prospect.'[10]

'I am certainly the last one who wants it to be known what is taking place,' he added.[11] 'The syndicate as syndicate does not exist. There is no such body corporate. There are a number of independent firms but they are not linked together. We have not a constitution binding us together. We are like the British empire there.'[12]

Besides the landlocking of mineral resources to ensure that prices could be raised, other restrictive practices were introduced – to cut wages and weaken the bargaining power of the native mine labourers Sir Ernest needed to unlock the wealth of his Namibian diamond deposits. From the moment he and his partners acquired full control of the deposits in 1921, Oppenheimer's companies were involved in the development of a system of migrant labour which cruelly restricted the rights and freedoms of tens of thousands of Namibians, mainly Ovambo migrant workers from the country's northern province. Some of the cruelty has been ascribed to the isolation of the Namibian diamond deposits and the early rush to exploit the discoveries. And certainly these were in an exceptionally wild and lonely part of the planet.

It was an accident of nature and the sands of time which laid down this precious gift to mankind – lonely beaches encrusted and impregnated with the finest gem diamonds in the world, millions of them like sparkling stars that had fallen from the sky. Created by vast volcanic eruptions deep inside the earth, the gemstones were propelled to the surface through the same gaps or pipes from the earth's core that had seeded Kimberley and the lands between the Vaal and the Orange rivers. But over the centuries the Namibian gems went on a truly extraordinary journey. Thrown into the Orange river by seismic disturbances, they tumbled and trickled downstream, to be deposited finally in the Atlantic Ocean at Orangemouth, where the river met the sea. Multitudes of them were swept out from the land and then, by another quirk of nature called the Benguela current, they were reclaimed by the tides and laid down on marine terraces and beaches in between tonnes of sand, sea shells and seaweed.[13] The first diamond was found a few miles inland by a black railway worker on the German colonial railway between Luderitz on the Atlantic Ocean and Keetmanshoop, the point on the map where the line turned north to make for the colonial capital, Windhoek. The railwayman, Zacharias Lewala, had worked in the diamond mines at Kimberley and when he found the first gemstone, he turned it over to a shrewd German inspector of the permanent way called August Stauch. Herr Stauch staked huge land and mining claims as a result of Mr Lewala's discovery and became rich and famous.[14] Mr Lewala by contrast died a poor man, but his discovery set off an explosion of mining enterprise as German colonists hunted high and low for diamonds.

In some places, like the little valley Idatal, no work was involved. Gems were simply found lying on the ground, fallen apples beneath a tree. Elsewhere vast quantities of sand had to be sifted in the harsh desert sun, often for a small return. The colonists sheltered themselves from the conditions by building fine houses, dance halls, bars and restaurants, and even a casino in the boom town of Kolmanskop near the port of Luderitz. Then in 1915 Germany lost control of its colony in the Namib desert; South African and British troops moved in to control the territory, supervise the mines and cut off Germany's supplies of diamonds.

In the wake of war Ernest Oppenheimer spotted a spectacular business opportunity to obtain a monopoly over the production and sale of Namibian gems and to make himself the king of diamonds. Oppenheimer was a financier with strong political connections in Britain and America. Conveniently he also had good contacts in Germany, the land of his birth, and in South Africa, his adopted home, where like his role model and predecessor Cecil Rhodes he pursued an active political career. Oppenheimer warned the German owners of the diamond concessions that they would lose everything if they didn't come in with him. He also pointed out the contrast if they were to merge with his business associates in the Union of South Africa. Their wealth could be protected inside his complex of companies, the Anglo

American Corporation of South Africa. Next he persuaded the new South African prime minister, Jan Smuts, and his Cabinet to endorse his portfolio of problematic land and corporate titles and sign over to him an area three times the size of Wales. Inside this Sperrgebiet or Forbidden Zone he was given exclusive access and mining rights for fifty years. The rent for this huge private colony, from which he could exclude all visitors, was £130 a year. When I visited the Sperrgebiet for the first time in 1987, the fifty-year lease signed in 1921 had neither expired nor been equitably renegotiated. The rent was the same and the no entry signs were still in place.[15]

In a final master stroke, Oppenheimer and his business associates persuaded the South African administration to sign away for nothing valuable profit-sharing rights the government had just acquired as a result of years of work by those German colonial officials who had some notion of the public interest. These rights would have given Namibia a half share in the billions of pounds worth of profits the Oppenheimer companies have since taken from the Sperrgebiet. All this would have been over and above the diamond tax revenue and export duty gathered in by the State.[16]

At first Consolidated Diamond Mines of South-West Africa (CDM), as the Oppenheimer company was called, operated in the desert fields around Kolmanskop, and the company built a mining compound there for the black contract workers it brought from Ovamboland in the north of Namibia, or from British Bechuanaland, now Botswana. Colin Newbury, in his book on the history and politics of diamonds in southern Africa, has noted the reluctance of the Ovambo people to work in the harsh conditions prevalent in the mine. 'By 1923', he writes, 'over half the labour force of 5,000 consisted of outside recruits from northern Botswana, who suffered a high mortality rate . . . with scurvy or tuberculosis.'[17] These were not the only causes of death. De Beers' accident records show that the mining equipment was often poorly laid out and this produced a crop of injuries. Company Number 2507, Brecht Poiolo, for example died on 18 July 1924 when, in the course of trying to free some machinery, he was sucked into the diamond recovery plant and buried alive in sand.[18] The place where he had been standing was subsequently fenced off, a precaution that should have been taken before any human being was allowed to work in such an exposed and dangerous place. There were other deaths in the early days. One group of black labourers was so dissatisfied with the food, accommodation and working conditions that they attempted to escape from their contracts by walking across the desert.[19] But only the company and the diamond police have ever had any accurate maps of the Sperrgebiet and the men soon died from thirst, hyperthermia and exhaustion. In those early days in the desert, not everyone could be housed in the main compound. Some workers had to process gravels or dig sampling trenches in isolated locations well away from the main compound. If they were white, they were treated well, transported in and out, or accommodated in comfortable tents. But if they were blacks different standards applied and they were housed in bizarre cement structures resembling a telephone box set on its side and without a door. A few of these can still be seen in the desert, poor and degrading shelters to quarter the human oxen of the diamond mines. In the compound there was a harsh set of rules which removed from the individual workers any meaningful control over their lives. The rules covered bedding, the issuing of food, approved methods of cooking, washing, the lighting of fires, the drawing of dry rations, the manner of address to foremen and other white company officials, attendance on sick parades, provisions for body searches and a host of other matters from restrictions on the consumption of alcohol to permitted forms of recreation.[20] These rules applied only to 'Native Labourers'. Since Sir Ernest's rules were backed by government proclamation and given the force of law, anyone who broke the rules was in breach of contract and faced not only harsh internal company discipline but could be brought before a court, fined and even, in some cases, imprisoned.

In 1928 new and infinitely richer deposits of diamonds were discovered at the extreme southern tip of the Sperrgebiet, on the north bank of the Orange river and along the lonely marine terraces in the direction of Luderitz. Accordingly, after the Depression of the 1930s and the Second World War, the company's centre of operations shifted south and Kolmanskop was left to become a ghost town, with the desert sands slowly reclaiming buildings and invading the barrack-like dormitories of the original mining compounds. As the great economic boom of the 1950s got under way, demand for diamonds in Europe and America reached unprecedented heights and the Oppenheimer mining companies decided to engage in a major expansion of the mine and lay down a company town at Oranjemund, with neat family houses, shops and schools for some of their employees. A bridge was erected across the Orange river, and entry to the mine effected from the South African side across the Sir Ernest Oppenheimer Memorial Bridge.

The new town was in a country ruled by a League of Nations mandate, assigned to Britain and then reassigned for its government and development to the Union of South Africa, part of the British Empire of Nations. With the coming of apartheid in the 1950s a unique opportunity arrived to make a stand and ensure that the company town grew up in accordance with the spirit of the mandate, a 'sacred trust' to promote the welfare of the 'less developed peoples'.[21]

De Beers' main business partner in the diamond cartel was the white South African government, and the company's continuing franchise to mine the fabulous beaches of Oranjemund depended on prolonging the symbiotic relationship between itself and the South African State. As a result, where it might have been resisted and the resistance been justified in terms of international law, apartheid was enthusiastically introduced by De Beers inside its company town in the middle of the desert. Worse still, the option of passive resistance was not even seriously entertained by Africa's greatest business house. Throughout the 1950s, 1960s and 1970s, therefore, the contract workers from Ovamboland were penned in single-sex compounds and denied all rights to social life and union representation, which were guaranteed to whites. They were also effectively shut out of town life. They were not allowed into the retail stores, the cinema or the clubs for whites, all of which belonged to the company. Everything, from water supplies to toilet facilities and the provision of food and health care, was segregated. At the company-owned post office there were separate counters for blacks and whites, and in the supermarket blacks could not enter through the front door but had to go round the back and wait to be served.[22]

De Beers' personnel files contain eloquent testimony to the feelings of the Ovambo miners about their employment conditions. In 1971 and 1972, before the Soweto rising, before the strikes in Durban and before the riots on the South African gold and coal-mines, the Ovambo contract workers launched a remarkable protest action. At mines, farms and other workplaces throughout Namibia, then a South African colony, the Ovambo people joined the campaign for a peoples' contract, withdrawing their labour and returning home to their families in the north of the country until changes were made. At a great meeting at Oluno, Ondongwa on 10 January 1972, their grievances against the injustices of the contract labour system were set out in a series of speeches and documents, which rank alongside any other twentieth-century distillation of the need for human rights and dignity.

The migrant labour system, speakers explained again and again, was a modern form of slavery. There was no meaningful individual contract between employer and employed. Instead Ovambo men could only leave their designated 'homeland' in the north for another part of the country if they had taken a contract. The contract took the form of an agreement between an individual and a labour-recruiting organisation belonging to the mining companies, including De Beers, and supported by the colonial State. But there was no equity in the relationship and the contract forms were rubber-stamped in multiples of four people to save paper and minimise legal and administrative charges. The people taking contracts had no say whatever in any of the terms and conditions.

When the peoples' contract dispute began, De Beers' intelligence agents brought senior managers at Oranjemund an extensive report of the meeting at Oluno.[23] The report itemised the many injustices and restrictions on personal freedom in the system of 'Kontrak' which, the report stressed, the Ovambo had christened 'the Draad', the fence or prison. The system meant that people were not free to change jobs in pursuit of better wages or conditions. If they left their jobs before the expiry of the term of contract they were in breach of master and servant and pass laws and could be rounded up, jailed or even forcibly returned to their employer. The contract was so restrictive that they could not even return home in time of family sickness or emergency. The Draad was feared and hated for another reason also – the degrading system of token medical examinations that went with it. This was a humiliating ritual in which the Ovambo, a proud people with their own values and cultural traditions and their own authority system which stressed respect for elders, were forced to strip naked by the hundred in the open air, then bend over to have their anuses examined for tuberculosis and any other signs of disease. Such examinations had little to do with medical care but were part of the ritual subordination of black Africans by colonial officials and whites working for foreign-owned mining companies. In one particularly moving section, De Beers' agents reported how the authors of the peoples' contract tried to summarise the epic scale of the injustices involved:

> Every person is perfectly created by God, but the contract system leads to complete indifference to human value, which was created by God himself.
>
> The contract system had changed the so-called homelands into a slave labour market . . . This slavery has resulted in Ovambo compounds in the form of a prison, with one entrance and sharp pieces of glass cemented on top of the walls, and inconvenient hard beds, made out of cement which cripples the people.[24]

At the CDM mine there was widespread support for the peoples' contract; and in addition to the many generalised grievances about the

Draad, the miners at Oranjemund also identified a range of problems specific to the mine. These included poor pay, bad food, lack of privacy in hostel rooms, lack of training and leisure facilities, not unimportant in the middle of the desert. In response to this pressure some concessions were made by De Beers. New contracts of employment were drawn up, and some improvements offered on pay, though the accompanying telexes from Anglo American in Johannesburg, who acted as consulting engineers to De Beers, made it plain that the company had decided to offset the costs of boosting African wages by sacking people.[25]

On the key issue of compassionate leave, the company did nothing. Privately the general manager, G.Y. Nisbet, noted 'the tremendous disappointment that nothing new emerged concerning compassionate leave'.[26] In April 1972 Nisbet and some of the other local managers persuaded the Anglo American Corporation architect's department at Fox Street in Johannesburg to take a look at the hostels in which the men had to live. In a memorandum dated 14 May 1972, the architects reported that they had made a number of interesting discoveries: 'even at CDM the ordinary labourer had no way of informing management of his legitimate complaints or problems ... A very interesting piece of information ... was that the Ovambo at home never eats where he sleeps. A very firm request was made that dining halls be erected adjacent to the kitchens in each hostel.'[27]

The report also noted in passing that library facilities were inadequate, not unimportant when there was no television service in the area; and that toilets were grouped together often at distances from the dormitories so considerable as to be extremely inconvenient. The nature of the report, and continuing pressure from the migrant miners themselves, seems to have convinced the local Oranjemund management to keep pressing for serious reform. In October 1972 De Beers' local Namibian managers prepared another confidential report which set out the local company's justification for increased expenditure on hostels and housing for blacks. The document began with some self-serving remarks about how facilities at Oranjemund had 'always been superior to those of all the other companies and authorities in South-West Africa'. 'But', it added,

> although the facilities were acceptable to the Ovambo in the past, it is evident that many of these have become outmoded.
>
> The exposure of the Ovambo to white civilisation over the years has changed his attitude, mode of dress and living standards. The facilities and amenities at the hostels have not kept pace with this development. As

mentioned at the June board meeting it is essential that corrective action be taken to remedy this situation.[28]

The report then proceeded to indict De Beers' and Anglo's priorities and management practices. Hostel rooms were unsatisfactory because there were ten people per room. These numbers made normal living and privacy of any kind impossible. Inside the rooms windows were set at ceiling level as if in a prison. The windows did not open. Instead there were only crude, wooden air vents at the top. Because of their design the miners were unable to see the outside world. This was a serious deprivation because, due to the difficult local weather conditions (sand and dust storms and intense heat during the day followed by cold at night), the miners seldom, if ever, had the opportunity to sit outside.

Worse still the miners were living, eating and sleeping in the same room, an inordinately unhealthy state of affairs. Reading and writing was impossible at night due to a centralised system of lighting controlled from the administration block. The furniture in the rooms was unsatisfactory, comprising bare, prison-like tables made of steel and two wooden benches. There were no dining halls. The mine kitchens for blacks were obsolete. Steam cookers, fish friers, tea- and coffee-making equipment were all ancient and worn. Floors were unhygienic and broken. No beer was brewed and, by contrast with whites, blacks were not allowed alcohol of any kind. The toilets and washing facilities at Uubvley, Oranjemund and Affenrucken hostels were gravely inadequate and there weren't enough of them. Inside the hostel lavatories people had to defecate in public since there were no partitions, cubicles or doors, only a production line of unprotected lavatory pans. The urinals were badly worn and difficult to clean. The number of washbasins was severely inadequate. Walls were damp and floor finishes slippery. There were no mirrors. At the sports field, blacks stood in the open while whites had access to a covered stand. There were no toilets for blacks at the sports ground. In the hostel blocks there were no reading rooms. The store facilities for blacks were appalling, with long queues for a pitifully narrow range of supplies.[29]

The local De Beers' managers were also becoming increasingly anxious about wage levels. White wages were continuing to grow at an estimated 10 per cent per annum and black workers were being left further and further behind. The diamond mine, one of the most profitable mines in the world, was still paying them poverty-level wages. In 1974 John MacKenzie, the general manager at Oranjemund, decided to try to do something about the overall situation and drafted a CDM company charter to summarise appropriate goals and objectives. The draft caused great anxiety at Anglo/De Beers' head office, with the British De Beers' director P.J.R. Leyden and his boss Julian Ogilvie Thompson detailing their many worries about it. The two men flatly opposed the proposal to increase the number of black and coloured employees housed in married quarters as a key corporate aim.[30]

MacKenzie redrafted the charter, softening the clauses complained of and then resubmitted his document to Anglo American's Main Street, Johannesburg head office and waited for a final reply. Dated 30 December 1974, this ordered him to delete any reference to increasing the number of black and coloured employees housed in married quarters. Another positive clause which had stated that a key objective of the company was 'to improve living conditions of employees through the continual upgrading of amenities and standards of communication' was the subject of a wrecking amendment and became a bland injunction to maintain 'adequate living conditions for employees'.[31]

By 1976 Anglo began turning the screw at the mine, and asked for cuts in mine housing budgets. This meant that even CDM management's modest plans for modification of the hostels and a few token houses where some senior blacks could live with their families came under threat. Next MacKenzie was asked to house eligible black families in truly minuscule houses, in a separate 'township' called Oranjemund West, a prospect which worried him deeply and was to become a recurring problem in the years ahead. As a result of the financial pressures, while the appearance and rhetoric of change were daily more abundant, underlying injustices continued to fester.

In 1979, even as the process of political change speeded up in Namibia, the grievances of the migrant workers flared up again. On 15 April one of the 1,100 men living in De Beers' North Hostel killed himself. Simson Haggaya hanged himself in his hostel room after he had been refused compassionate leave, even though he had had a mild heart attack and was thoroughly depressed. He was told that he could only return home after twenty-eight days, as provided for in the new, model contract of employment. As the news of Mr Haggaya's death spread through the five hostels, there was consternation. Even though the workers had no union, a right still denied them by CDM, a growing number refused to go to work. They demanded a proper inquiry into the suicide and asked for the personnel officials who had treated Mr Haggaya so unsympathetically to be moved to other jobs.[32] With feelings running high, the men in each hostel began to list their particular grievances. Overall food quality was still poor. There were regular shortages of meat, vegetables and even bread in the more remote parts of the massive mine. Some of the hostels were overcrowded. And in one hostel an empty tube of poison had been found inside a bag of mealie meal, much to the consternation of people in the hostel whose mealie-pap porridge was made from what they feared might have been contaminated meal. For once the mine manager agreed to visit the hostels and speak directly to the men. He made some concessions and then warned that if they did not return to work and accept company rules and regulations, they should pack their bags and get ready to leave.[33]

Later that year the general manager J.O. Richards was wrestling with further cost-cutting measures which resulted from De Beers' persistent refusal to make sufficient funds available to sort out the housing and hostel problem once and for all. In a powerfully worded telex to Anglo American and De Beers, now publicly showing its faith in the future by building a prestigious new office block in Windhoek on which no expense was spared, Mr Richards explained once again why it would not do to cut back on size and space availability for black family housing at the mine. 'It is discriminatory, highly emotive and political dynamite,' he reminded Africa's greatest business organisation,

> to refuse them the right to have their own children with them on the grounds that the houses we have provided, and are going to continue to provide, are too small for their families.
>
> The Anglo American Corporation housing standards presumably are for segregated townships in South Africa. In Oranjemund we must be careful not to lay ourselves open to accusations of establishing in 1980 segregated housing in Namibia.
>
> The siting of the Oranjemund West shop, the new club and the cinema-gym will appear to strengthen such accusations and our position is not really defensible as white CI employees (of comparable grade to the blacks being offered smaller houses) are housed in larger houses in the established town area. Further it is inconsistent to have integrated schools, clubs, sport etc and segregated housing areas.[34]

The list of human rights' infringements and grim conditions at Oranjemund belies the manipulated images of De Beers' unforgettable worldwide advertising campaigns. These present diamonds as flawless and incomparably beautiful, miraculous firestones evoking the deepest and most lasting emotions that human beings have for one another. Here on the immense coastal beaches, where the bed of the sea is virtually indistinguishable from the floor of the desert, the company that finances the 'Diamonds are for ever' campaign was for many years engaged in the exploitation of the people of an occupied country. Denied the right to vote, to freedom of speech and assembly, denied even the right to move about their own country as and when they chose, and prevented by De Beers from having decent food, proper leisure facilities, washing facilities and toilets with a degree of privacy, and denied the human right of visiting home when family members were seriously ill, the dominant images of diamonds for anyone who has examined conditions in the mine are not those of romance and human love and affection but of cruelty and injustice, inhumanity and greed.

For Gordon Brown, once a senior member of the management team on the mine, the behaviour of Anglo American and De Beers, the twin Oppenheimer companies which have ruled the destiny of Namibia's diamond fields for the past seventy years, is all the more worrying because the mine where this epic tragedy of wealth and poverty was played out was, in all probability, the richest and most profitable mineral deposit in the world. Over the years it has been a treasure trove for De Beers and Anglo American, returning enormous profits, which in many senses have financed the extraordinary growth of Anglo until today, inside South Africa, it controls assets equivalent to perhaps as much as half the value of all the corporations quoted on the Johannesburg Stock Exchange, while beyond its shores it is the greatest mining house on earth.

Brown, a loyal company servant whose experiences at Oranjemund turned him into a whistle-blower who openly criticised the system, puts it this way: 'Oranjemund is a phenomenally rich mine. The present value of diamonds sold since its inception is in the region of £5,000 million. The working costs are extremely low and revenue has been extremely high because of the high quality of the diamonds. This gives a very high profit margin. I would say that CDM is one of the most profitable mines in the world; the bulk of the money has just been taken out of the country, with no reinvestment in regional development. The profits were simply sent across the border to Kimberley and Johannesburg. There they provided the basis for the exponential growth of Anglo.'[35]

Brown adds his own evidence to that embodied in the company's internal documents:

'At the mine itself living conditions for the whites were very good, as they would need to be in such a lonely, isolated place. But as you will understand the majority of the people who lived and worked at Oranjemund were not whites. In the period 1920–70 conditions were very, very poor, and only began to change after the major strike in 1971 when the Ovambo people started their campaign against the contract system. They worked a ten-hour shift in the open air, with only a twenty-minute break for lunch. Lunch was really a misnomer. They got a flask of cold tea and half a loaf of brown bread, which they ate where they were atop an earth-moving machine or in the bed rock gullies where they were sweeping for gem diamonds.

'They lived isolated from their loved ones, in atrocious single-sex compounds. There were no proper dining-room facilities, the workers had to collect their meals from the mess in metal buckets then take them back to their rooms and eat out of those buckets in the dormitories. Sporting and recreation facilities were virtually non-existent for blacks – there were one or two dirt soccer pitches and a few dartboards, but certainly nothing comparable to the conditions that the whites had. At the world's richest diamond mine, the majority of people who worked there were simply being exploited, and De Beers grew very, very rich as a result.'[36]

When I finally gained access to the CDM just before Christmas 1989, I was surprised to find that many of the migrant workers still lived in the monotonous surroundings of six-bed dormitories. There was one refurbished block, which was all most visitors were shown. Here some serious shopfitting had gone on and the grim, institutional surroundings had given way to one- and two-bed units with some recreational space. The African workers had finally been allowed to build a Sand Hotel, an interesting collection of shebeen bars where they could drink and talk with their friends in circumstances relatively free from the eyes and ears of those in authority. But, in general, progress has been painfully slow, constrained above all by the watchful eye of Anglo American's diamond services division in Johannesburg and its refusal to sanction serious expenditure and finance fundamental reform.

While I was visiting the mine, I learned about one of the company's pet projects – a new chair for Stellenbosch University, the top Afrikaner institution in the Cape. It is to be called the Harry Oppenheimer Chair for the Study of Human Rights. For thirty years Henry Oppenheimer was chairman of both Anglo American and De Beers. Among various confidential documents relating to the Namibian mine which I have come across is one that all students at Stellenbosch should be given access to – the 1976 report of a visit to Oranjemund mine by Anglo American's medical consultant, Dr J.L.C. Whitcombe. In the course of his tour of inspection, Dr Whitcombe decided to cross the Orange river and take a look at conditions on the company's Beauvallon Farm, where produce for the mine was grown. Dr Whitcombe was appalled by what he saw and on his return to Johannesburg he wrote a particularly tough, confidential letter which set out what he saw and how he felt about it. Dated 9 September 1976, it is a worrying example of what appears to be a gap between what Anglo said in public and what it practised in private throughout the years that Harry Oppenheimer was in control.

I visited the married quarters on the farm and wish to place on record that in my opinion these are completely unsuitable for conversion into single quarters ... Over the years one has gained the impression that because the coloured workers have not made a fuss about their appalling living conditions, no effort has been made to house them properly ...

I have also visited the school. I understand that a new school is planned and is to consist of three classrooms, although four are really needed. One class is being taught in the so-called 'Club' Recreation Hall where there is no cleaner and where the lavatories are filthy so that children have to be sent to their houses when they wish to be excused.

There is no adequate storage space in the school so that the house occupied by the headmaster and his wife ... has a room full of books and equipment for the school. One of the female schoolteachers lives in a one-room hovel to which has been added a corrugated iron 'room' which is used for cooking purposes.

There is a stand pipe some distance from the house and of course there is no bathroom. The lavatory is about 20 metres away from the house. She is married and has a small child.[37]

3   How to Steal a Country

In the spring of 1985 Africa's greatest business organisation, the De Beers–Anglo American mining group, was engulfed by an unprecedented crisis. The company, which had avoided investigation in Europe and America by weaving such an artful web of interlocking offshore companies that it was effectively beyond the reach of any single national jurisdiction, became embroiled in a major scandal in its own backyard. A white South African judge engaged in a routine local government corruption inquiry decided he could not ignore information about the mining industry which had been brought to his attention and began to lift the curtain of secrecy which has surrounded the Namibian diamond industry for most of this century. As the judge dug deeper, allegations of grave corporate misconduct ricocheted round the municipal courtroom in Windhoek, Namibia's capital city where he held his hearings. The legal drama culminated two years later in the publication of a voluminous report, which devotes 300 pages to mining in Namibia and key chapters to De Beers' behaviour concerning the diamonds of Oranjemund, the nation's principal economic asset.[1] The report accused De Beers of plundering the world's richest diamond mine and taking out huge profits ahead of Namibian independence, thereby deliberately shortening the life of the mine and greatly reducing its remaining profitability. The report, which based its analysis of De Beers' behaviour not on circumstantial evidence but on swathes of top-secret mining documents leaked to the Commission from a source inside the De Beers' organisation itself, is one of the most devastating assaults on the reputation of a major corporation since Ralph Nader took on General Motors.

De Beers' problems came at the end of a sixty-year period in which the company had been able to do more or less exactly as it pleased in

50

Namibia. The country had no independent government and its southern half was essentially a private colony run by De Beers on behalf of the South African State, the company's main business associate in the world diamond cartel. For more than half a century after the Versailles Treaty in 1919, De Beers had total control over Diamond Areas One and Two, a land mass three times the size of Wales and one of the world's most beautiful – and bountiful – desert wastelands. Only the company and the Diamond Police had proper maps, indicating where water could be found amid the vast expanse of the desert. The entire area was fenced off with electronic sensors. Marine and airborne patrols ensured that anyone who entered without permission would be swiftly caught. Some of these regulations might have been necessary to stop diamond smuggling. But the company lost sight of any need to legitimate its activities or exercise its monopoly power with some element of caution or restraint and turned an entire province into a private corporate kingdom frozen in time. Even the South African Police throughout the area were in De Beers' pocket – the company paid all salaries and expenses and ran the legal system as if it were a wholly owned subsidiary.[2]

To protect its monopoly and shroud itself in secrecy the company developed a special corporate security division. Its main job was to search the miners at the end of their contracts to ensure they had no gemstones hidden in their luggage or secreted in some part of their anatomy. Every time someone crossed the Sir Ernest Oppenheimer Memorial Bridge, they went through the De Beers' memorial X-ray unit in which their bodily parts were screened. Tight control was kept on the movement of cars which, once brought into the mining area, could never leave again. It was the same with the company's earth-moving equipment. When equipment went out of service or broke down it was quarantined indefinitely in the desert to ensure that no diamonds reached the outside world inside a shipment of scrap metal.[3] Outside the mine the De Beers' securocrats had a branch office in the port of Luderitz. From there they kept a watchful ear and eye on the thinking of the local population and, as leaked internal documents show, fought remorselessly to preserve their monopoly power.

In Luderitz, one of the loneliest towns on the coast of Africa, one consolation was the pleasure of the beach. But much of this was closed off as part of De Beers' Sperrgebiet or Forbidden Zone. The town council took up the issue and asked for Agate Beach to be excluded from the zone and incorporated in the town lands. The move was part of a campaign to build a future for the town based on tourism now that De Beers had stopped bringing mine supplies in through Luderitz and switched its business to Port

Nolloth across the border in South Africa. But the CDM management and
their security advisers were deeply troubled by moves to gain public access.
On 9 May 1972 the CDM general manager G.Y. Nisbet set out his worries
in an anxious memorandum to the Anglo American consulting engineer at
head office in Johannesburg. CDM, he wrote, was 'strongly opposed' to any
public access or development of any kind. 'The establishment of a tourist
camp or caravan park in the area would be tantamount to deproclamation . . .
any exploitation of the areas in question would result in a significant financial
loss to the company . . . this of course does not apply to individuals.'[4]

The company's restrictive stance caused more disquiet in the local
community, as CDM's Chief Security Superintendent noted in a report
of a public meeting in April which he submitted to company headquarters.
'Advocate van Zyl . . . passed some virulent remarks about the company, the
essence being that it is unheard of that one company should control such a
vast area without mining or development in large sections of it. He compares
the control of the concession to the feudal system of the Middle Ages.'[5]
The row rumbled on for years, and became aggravated due to pressure
from the government tourism adviser that as well as Agate Beach being
opened up, it would greatly help the development of the tourist industry if
Sossusvlei inland could be made accessible to the public. Sossusvlei is one
of the wonders of Namibia, a clay-pan of water surrounded by the highest
sand dunes in the world. Located inside Diamond Area Two, where De
Beers have never done any mining in all the years they kept the 20,000
square mile territory landlocked, Sossusvlei was a major tourist attraction.
But again CDM fought to keep progress and development at bay. In a letter
dated 12 November 1976 to the chairman of the Diamond Board, the mine
manager, J.O. Richards, frankly explained corporate concerns:

> The opening of Sossusvlei could create a serious precedent regarding
> pressure to open other areas in Diamond Area Number Two and in
> Diamond Area Number One, especially in Elizabeth Bay, Pomona, and
> Bogenfels.
>   Any agreement regarding Sossusvlei should be subject to no future
> requests being submitted to opening such areas where the security risk
> is so much higher.[6]

The other major goals the people of Luderitz set themselves were the
refurbishment of the abandoned diamond workings at Kolmanskop and
the opening of the private coastal road south to Oranjemund. The aim

was to create something memorable in Luderitz that would celebrate the extraordinary history of the diamond industry and simultaneously improve access routes to the town from the south so that tourists would not have to make a huge elliptical detour round the diamond area, adding hundreds of miles to any journey to or from Luderitz. In 1979 the School of Architecture at the University of Natal completed an imaginative conservation study of the town and its environs. It recommended substantial restoration of the old buildings and a range of working displays which would show how diamonds were mined, separated, cut and polished; some of CDM's fences should be taken down; the single-track railway should be put back; the casino should be restored and used for entertainment. Sadly, CDM once again resolved to stand in the way. In June 1979 the CDM chief security superintendent J.S.T. Fletcher marshalled corporate fears in a lengthy memorandum about how tourist developments would breach security defences.

> The screen of inhospitable terrain and regulation which makes this a no-go area for the general public, and thus makes possible an effective surveillance security screen, would have been cast aside.
>
> The innocent tourist – at present encouraged by the Luderitz brochure to view 'the phenomenal sand rose' would equally be inquisitive about the presence of diamonds.
>
> Finally such a facility, if granted, would permit the adherents of SWAPO in Luderitz easier access into the presently forbidden area, either to procure diamonds with which to swell party funds or to seek liaison links with their opposite numbers and sympathisers inside the mining area, unmonitored and uncontrolled.[7]

As a result of the various disputes, some concessions were won from the company. Today there is minimal access to Agate Beach and Sossusvlei has been opened to the public. But no major development has been allowed at Luderitz or Kolmanskop. Privately the company resolved that it had to seem more active in the northern part of the Sperrgebiet, but not necessarily to mine diamonds or assist the development of the area. As the CDM mining manager Melvin Foster put it in a 1981 report:

> The strategy formulated requires as a first step the establishment of a relatively minor production facility at Elizabeth Bay, thereby establishing a presence at the northern end of Diamond Area Number One at the earliest opportunity . . .

The benefits of this strategy are . . . a reasonable production undertaking can be seen to be operating in the politically sensitive north of Diamond Area 1, effectively countering the moves to declare certain areas open to tourists.[8]

The purpose appeared to be not primarily to mine diamonds, but to keep the corporate kingdom safe from outsiders. At no stage did CDM or De Beers develop their own solutions to the town's problems. It seemed that they preferred to hold back rather than promote local development because diversification threatened their monopoly power.

Inside colonial Namibia De Beers was not only the country's premier business organisation, it was also the country's biggest feudal landlord controlling a corporate Campbell's Kingdom and resisting change and development in a sustained and single-minded way. The company's writ also extended to the Diamond Board for South-West Africa, the government body supposedly responsible for regulating the diamond industry. But the Diamond Board was a watch-dog without bark, bite or even a kennel of its own. De Beers paid for all its business expenses right down to the letter heads and toilet rolls. The Diamond Board offices were even located inside De Beers' corporate headquarters in Windhoek, and De Beers deducted a nominal rental from its pre-tax profits as a business expense. The secretary of the Diamond Board was a De Beers' employee; and while in theory the Board had its own representatives at the mine in Oranjemund to check on the type and scale of production and to supervise mine planning, every one of these officials was also a De Beers' employee. In colonial Namibia there was no separation between the State and civil society. Here the tail didn't wag the dog, it was the dog. At the end of the production process, the diamonds left Oranjemund for Kimberley in South Africa, again without independent checks and there was therefore unlimited scope for abuse. In London, where the Namibian stones were sent for distribution and resale, the Diamond Board was again supposed to have its own agents. But these too were always De Beers' employees.[9]

For six decades the world's most powerful mining company held Namibia, a country without its own government, in the palm of its hand. Then in 1982 the *ancien régime* began to fall apart. The scandal started as if by accident in November 1982 when the senior South African colonial official, the Administrator-General, was faced with mounting evidence of corruption and maladministration in local government in the war-torn northern province of Ovamboland. This is one of the more heavily populated regions where

54

the desert gives way to richer and more productive land and where, for a variety of reasons, the independence of the people had not been quite so successfully crushed as elsewhere. Here in Ovamboland the skills of peasant farmers combine with the moisture of the rainy season to propagate a rich harvest. While the Ovambo people were the main source of migrant labour in Namibia, the process of colonialism never quite defeated them and they became the effective backbone of first the Ovamboland Peoples' Organisation and then later the South-West African Peoples' Organisation, which led the struggle for national freedom. In order to forestall the emergence of national unity among the black majority, the South African colonial authorities introduced eleven tiers of tribal government to enforce their authority at a local level. In Ovamboland few people bothered to participate in the contrived electoral processes that went with the system. As a result the bantustan government not only lacked legitimacy but was fragile, inefficient and bribable.

Faced with indisputable evidence of corruption, the Administrator-General decided that the situation was serious enough to warrant proper investigation. He appointed a respected South African Supreme Court judge to head the probe, Mr Justice Pieter Willem Thirion. Although he lived in Pietermaritzburg in Natal, the judge had spent some of his youth in South-West Africa and had developed a considerable affection for the country. He resolved to do what he could to root out corruption and foster rational administration in its place, an essential development if the country was ever to achieve independence.[10]

Initially Thirion's inquiry focused on a Portuguese transport contractor who had left Angola after independence for the balmier atmosphere of Namibia, where he still found it possible to turn a profit. The contractor, Antonio Alves, soon made a fortune in Ovamboland by a simple device. He submitted false bills for payment to the local government authority for work he had never done. Then, when accountants began checking his fictional deliveries of building materials against what the local government had used or held in stock, he left the country in something of a hurry. As the judge dug deeper he found that the proprietor of Tony's Transport was not the only man involved in illegal drainage of the public purse. A number of government officials were implicated or involved on their own account. One investigation of bantustan government salaries showed that eighteen people signed for a total of 179 wage packets, making them nearly as well paid as the fraudulent landowner in Gogol's novel *Dead Souls*. Surveying the scene, an enterprising architect had started building fictional structures and managed to secure payment of £750,000 for a building which did not exist. A range of government officials were also feathering their own nests by building and furnishing private houses with misappropriated public money.[11] As newspapers began to report the judge's progress in lifting the corner of a very musty carpet, two men were particularly impressed by his determination. The first was a Scots-born mining manager working for De Beers, the second a self-made Namibian businessman of German extraction who had in the past tried to do something about the extensive corruption in the national Meat Board and in the system of awarding fishing quotas in the country's rich waters off the Atlantic coast.

Gordon Brown came to Cape Town as a teenager when his father, a Glasgow doctor, emigrated from Scotland with his family in search of warmer climes. Leaving school at eighteen, Brown decided not to go to university right away, and took a job in the accounts department of a Cape Town motor dealer. By 1968 he wanted a change. He saw an advertisement for employment in Oranjemund, put in an application and got the job. 'My first job was as mining supervisor of Ovambo workers at the Alexander Bay diamond screening plant,' Brown recalls. 'It was very exciting for me being just twenty years old and being put in charge of all these people. But it was curious in a way – they all knew more than me, and while I was in charge I had to learn from them. Nevertheless I was paid a great deal more than any of them, perhaps five times as much, which again struck me as richly ironic.' After five years with De Beers, Brown had developed an enduring love of diamonds and a near obsessional appetite for the most intricate details of mining technology and history. His qualities were recognised by the company and he moved up a grade or two in the management services' division. Brown had formed a lasting respect for the Ovambo workers and their behaviour under a mine regime which operated on lines of strict apartheid; and he was one of the few whites with enough democratic instincts to make the effort to learn the beautiful Oshikwanyama language of his black mining colleagues so that a real conversation and exchange of views could take place. In June 1978 he became technical assistant to the mine manager, in charge of the mine's complex system of documentation for its mining plans and ore reserves.[12]

By 1978, after a decade on the mine, Brown was regarded as a loyal and conscientious employee, but a range of social issues had privately begun to bother him. Why, he wondered, were De Beers' black employees so badly paid when the mine was so conspicuously profitable? And why were they housed in such substandard accommodation without any pretence of recreation and entertainment when there were such excellent provisions for whites? Once aroused, Brown's curiosity wandered off in other directions. In such a big mine why were all goods and services bought in from other group companies? Why had there been no encouragement of small businesses or local enterprise that might promote lasting economic development after the mine had gone? Was De Beers' development programme in the best interests of the country? And if so why did the company drag its feet for so long about bringing proven diamond deposits into production? In all probability these mildly dissident thoughts would never have been expressed in public; but then certain highly confidential company documents started to cross Gordon Brown's desk.

These reports set out and critically evaluated various mining policies for the Namibian mine. The options ranged from a mining strategy taking out maximum profits over a relatively short term to a much slower, more balanced and orderly exploitation of the mine. Given the illegality of South Africa's occupation of Namibia and the determination of the United Nations to achieve progress towards independence, the option chosen was highly sensitive. If there was a high rate of exploitation, most of the mine's best potential would be taken out before an independent government came to power and had a chance to review the generous leasing and taxation arrangements that had been set in place for CDM in early colonial times. By contrast, if the exploitation of the mine was slower and more balanced, the remaining diamond reserves could be spread over a much longer period and the richer deposits used to cross-subsidise development of areas with a lower yield. Such a policy would alter the economic picture of the mine and, because of the very low level of authentic economic development in Namibia, vitally affect the future of the country. On this scenario, a newly independent government would have much more room to restructure the industry and ensure the fullest possible benefit to the national exchequer.

To the lay person, the documents that passed across Gordon Brown's desk were an impenetrable maze of complex information couched in the private language of the mining industry. There were endless calculations about payable and non-payable reserves, ore reserve mining factors, mining to average grade and stone size and the like. But Brown had the technical grasp to understand the options that were being canvassed and to detect in document after document persistent, alarming and, he came to conclude, significant departures from the best mining practice. What worried him most was head office's attitude to Oranjemund's seed corn. This was known in the private language of the mine as the N blocks.

The N blocks were super-rich deposits of diamonds on the marine terraces where the Namib desert met the Atlantic Ocean. There the diamonds were quite simply the finest in the world, massive in size and of an extraordinary quality. The secret documents Brown saw showed that these diamonds were most certainly not for ever, but were being depleted with alarming speed from the late 1960s onwards when for the first time in many years Namibian independence became a serious possibility.

In 1980 and 1981 the flow of highly confidential information continued and Gordon Brown began to see even more worrying projections. Some of the company's most senior local managers were making it clear that the mine was in overdrive, with more than a billion pounds of revenue being taken out in the short and medium term. Repeatedly senior mine managers returned to this theme, describing it in document after document as overmining. In one particular Life of Mine Review, the report prepared annually for the board of the Consolidated Diamond Mines of South-West Africa, the Oranjemund production manager described the mining strategy as a 'power dive', adding that 'unless we have a conscious change in strategy . . . we will power the mine into the ground and we will be unable to conduct the reclamation and clean-up operation which could extend the life of the mine by three or four years'.[13] The accompanying revenue and profit forecasts showed that the mine could well move from substantial profits to increasing losses as a direct result of the policies pursued. Since the mine would no longer be able to offset the escalating costs of mining poorer reserves against a steady but generous flow of profit obtained by taking out the highest grade and most sizeable diamonds, the mine might even close by 1992.

At this point Gordon Brown's disquiet gave way to downright alarm. He began to fear for his own future and for his colleagues' jobs and to spend more and more time discussing with his wife and his closest confidants the rights and wrongs of such a policy. Like Judge Thirion, he had come to love Namibia with its strangely beautiful expanses of desert, awesome configurations of light and land, and the delightful openness of its indigenous people. Like many other free spirits in the white population, he had become hopeful of the post-apartheid society which would result from the country's long and painful journey to national independence and had begun to hope that he could play something of a part in the national reconstruction that would follow. Now the evidence was accumulating before his eyes that his employer, the country's biggest and most influential corporation, might use its immense power of scheduling and organisation to deprive a defenceless nation of its single greatest economic prize.

This realisation precipitated a deep moral crisis in Brown's life. He spent more and more time filling in the gaps in his knowledge of the mine until it was virtually encyclopaedic. He obtained copies of many of the key documents relating to mining policy at Oranjemund and posted them on trips to Windhoek to his address in Cape Town. As he absorbed the details of the peculiar circumstances in which De Beers acquired the mining lease, the moralising side of his character came into play and he began to ask worrying questions about corporate ethics and individual responsibility. Sometimes he was profoundly depressed by the burden of his knowledge and responsibility. On other occasions he was excited and even elated by what he knew, and he began to think he might be able to help the new government run the industry on more honourable lines. All in all, by the time Judge Thirion's commission into maladministration in Namibian government got under way, he was a man on a short fuse.

By choice Gordon Brown would have stayed out of the public eye a little longer than he was allowed to. But he decided he had to share his information with at least one other person who could give him some tactical advice about how best to play his hand. He had noticed in the pages of the English-language newspaper, the *Windhoek Observer*, that a highly successful Namibian businessman called Eric Lang had begun to sound serious warnings about the hopelessly unbalanced and indebted state of the Namibian economy after all the years of apartheid. Lang was a forceful and articulate critic of the swollen bureaucracy South Africa had implanted on top of an exceptionally weak economic base. Lang thought that the only reason for such a wilful contortion of the social system as the creation of endless tribal tiers of authority was to divide the population and buy support. The situation, he believed, was out of control. With eleven tribal governments in a country with a population of one and a half million, Namibia was weighed down with an immense inverted pyramid. Each of the eleven bantustans had its own ministry of education, public works, housing and health, each separately resourced and staffed. This costly and absurd attempt to halt the momentum of national development by casting Namibian society into ethnic or tribal separation consumed some 47 per cent of the national budget, burdened the fragile productive economy with debt and, in Lang's view, could create in an independent Namibia an endless cycle of dependency.[14]

In a country where the doors of culture and learning had been barred to the vast majority of the population for so long and where there was no university, no school of economics and few if any specialist magazines, the outspoken comments of an independent businessman like Lang carried a great deal of weight. Lang had made a fortune in a range of business activities from a parts and equipment business to a successful cattle farm. But he had a strong love of country as well as an appetite for commerce and there were personal factors behind his willingness to speak out. As a young man he had seen his once highly successful father go bankrupt and Lang did not want to witness a repetition of such a tragedy on a national scale. In 1980 he had pressed for a clean up of the country's Meat Board, a State body giving subsidies and quotas to white farmers with the right political connections to the National Party establishment in South-West Africa. He had also gone out of his way to oppose corruption and the preferential award of contracts in the Namibian construction industry, and had flown to Johannesburg to complain about an allegedly corrupt employee of the Anglo American LTA construction firm. So when Gordon Brown approached him and briefed him about events at De Beers' diamond mine, Lang was appalled and decided to do something about it. His fuse was much shorter than Brown's, and, in essence, he declared war. He asked for a meeting with the Diamond Board for South-West Africa and demanded to know whether the board's officials felt they operated a system of effective controls over the De Beers' company, Consolidated Diamond Mines of South-West Africa. The officials replied that they had full and effective controls, a response which Lang found most interesting given that the supposedly independent government department supervising the diamond industry was provided with offices, secretary, and had its salaries and expenses paid by De Beers. Lang also arranged an appointment with CDM, De Beers' local company, and bluntly accused them of overmining the diamond deposit.

Inevitably Lang's impassioned rattling of the cage caused CDM to ask questions about who from Oranjemund was briefing people outside the diamond industry on such highly confidential matters as the size and quantity of diamonds being taken out of the Orange River deposits, and the effect of the rate of extraction on the life of the mine. For some considerable time De Beers' investigations proved inconclusive, with the finger of suspicion pointing at a number of people, but without any confirmatory evidence. As a result Gordon Brown held on to his job into 1983. Brown managed to remain undetected until March, by which time the terms of reference of the Thirion inquiry into governmental malpractice and misallocation of funds had been published and staff had been appointed to conduct the investigation. Then Brown started to notice that he was being excluded from company meetings he had previously attended as a matter of routine. In April he was informed that the company had decided to reorganise the office in which he worked. His job as technical assistant to the mine manager would be scrapped, he was informed, and alternative employment be offered only at Kimberley in South Africa. Brown and his wife Ingrid flew to Kimberley to look at the mine and the accommodation but decided in the end not to accept. The company then asked Brown to resign. At first he refused to go, but increasing hostility from the company and the mounting pressure on his family finally persuaded him to hand in his notice and leave Oranjemund for ever.[15]

He moved from the lonely beaches of the Namib desert to the wooded beauty of the Cape peninsula. There he built his own house at Hout Bay, walked his dogs along the beach and continued his studies of the diamond industry until his knowledge of the Orange River mining deposits rivalled Einstein's grasp of physics. Eric Lang was busy too. He had now seen copies of some of the internal documents from the mine and, while he couldn't quote from them, he felt increasingly confident of his ground. He intensified his own research into the mining industry, insisting it was ridiculous that statistics on Namibia's mineral wealth should be kept from the public on the grounds that disclosure of such information might be helpful to South Africa's enemies. Lang's intuitive grasp of the power of publicity also stood him in good stead. At a press conference he summoned on 12 October 1983 he demanded that the Administrator-General release a detailed set of statistics regarding the country's mining industry, its exports and the taxes paid by the South African and other multinational companies who dominated the mining sector. If the government did not reveal these figures, added Lang, then he would do so himself.[16] By now the Windhoek newspapers had spotted a strong and interesting story and gave Lang's every move prominent coverage. For his part Lang ensured that they had plenty of moves to cover.

On 25 November Lang was due to give a talk to the Institute of Marketing and Materials Management at Windhoek's Safari Motel. In the pre-meeting publicity Lang had made it plain that he intended to keep his promise and reveal the country's mining statistics. On the afternoon before the meeting, he received a call from the Administrator-General, Dr Willie van Niekerk, summoning him to his office. There Dr van Niekerk made it plain that he would much prefer it if Lang would neither reveal the statistics nor read out a letter from Mr Justice Thirion which he understood Lang had been sent. In a curious move that some people interpreted as a form of pressure, Dr van Niekerk told Lang that if he did not reveal certain details of his past then van Niekerk would do so.[17]

By 7.30 p.m. the atmosphere at the Safari Motel was tense with anticipation. This increased when Lang arrived at the motel to address the meeting. He was intercepted by one of the Administrator-General's assistants and whisked off to the manager's office, where further urgent consultations took place on the telephone between Lang, the Administrator-General and Judge Thirion. These continued for over an hour and resulted in Lang agreeing not to read out the letter or disclose the trade routes for the sale of Namibian minerals overseas, a sensitive matter given the United Nations Decree Number One banning the exploitation or sale of the minerals without the specific permission of the UN. When it came to making his speech, however, Lang inserted new punches every bit as strong as the ones he had agreed to pull. He opened with a candid reference to the fact that as a youth he had been caught in a diamond trap by De Beers and the Diamond Police. He had bought an uncut diamond from a policeman disguised as a dealer and had spent some time in prison for his pains. Then Lang set his audience alight by explaining that the Administrator-General had specifically ordered him to refer to this episode at the meeting. Turning the tables, Lang then said, 'I hope I have made the good doctor happy. As a one-man government in a bankrupt colony he can't have many things that make him happy.'[18]

Lang continued in similar vein. 'While it shocked me that his excellency the Administrator-General could be so petty ... it did prove to me that I am at least effective in what I have been doing the last three years. It's not been an easy task to try and expose mismanagement and corruption in this country ... The present period before independence is a most crucial one in this country, but it is also one that is marked by unprecedented corruption and the plundering of our national resources.' Turning specifically to the mining industry, Lang stated that he believed that the mining policies of one South African company – he was referring to De Beers without naming them – had shortened the life of the country's most important mine. 'I have also argued with people who say that South Africa has a scorched earth policy,' he added in conclusion. 'I am sorry to say that I am running out of arguments.'

The speech, the implied threat by the Administrator-General and the to-ing and fro-ing in the motel lobby caused a sensation in the Namibian press. Behind the scenes the effect was every bit as powerful. The Attorney-General stopped blocking Lang's attempts to get the Thirion commission to hear evidence on the lack of public control over the mining industry, and the judge resolved that he would not shy away from investigating diamonds. As if to underline the point, the judge and his investigators moved swiftly to organise an emergency session of the commission on malpractices and to issue a subpoena for Lang to appear. At the hearing a week later, Lang was cautious in the witness box, saying he could not speak freely if the court was unable to grant him and all other witnesses some degree of protection.[19]

What Lang could not do in public, he was trying to do in private. He told Judge Thirion and his investigators Martin Grote and Gerhardt Visser about the former De Beers' employee who had recently left the company to build his own house in Hout Bay. Visser, Lang and Grote flew to Cape Town and met Gordon Brown at the Newlands Hotel. Brown took them through his knowledge of De Beers' mining policies and showed them some copies of the documentation he had acquired. But he still wasn't ready to break cover and for some time he and Gerhardt Visser engaged in a complex cloak-and-dagger game of anonymous phone calls, secret meetings and expeditions to various odd places where Brown had salted away his copies of Consolidated Diamond Mines' internal reports. Today Visser recalls those months of tension and intrigue with a detached feeling of pride for a difficult job well done in circumstances that were far from easy.

Gerhardt Visser – Vizzy for short – is one of the most unusual public servants in Namibia. In 1989 he was the chief electoral officer, charged with running the elections that gave the country its first independent government.[20] He had begun to pick up electoral expertise in 1977 when the South Africans allowed the country to take a few faltering steps towards independence, before they bolted the door for another decade or more. Early in 1977, however, Vizzy was seconded to work for the Administrator-General, his main job being to investigate all known systems of elections from electoral colleges, through proportional representation to the single transferable vote and to advise on which option would best suit Namibia. But at the time the Thirion commission was set up, there seemed little hope of elections and Visser had been transferred to the Department of Justice as the deputy director. The judge then asked for Visser to work with him on the investigation and he became the chief investigating officer in charge of an increasingly controversial probe. Because of his past membership of the state security commission and his South African origins, some people thought that Vizzy would give De Beers and their business partners in the South African government an easy ride. But he too had a very strong streak of independence in his make up; he had grown to love Namibia and resent the ravages of war and colonial occupation on his adopted land. What's more he had grown up in the shadow of the diamond monopoly and didn't like what he had seen.

Gerhardt Visser was born nine kilometres from Kimberley, South Africa's city of diamonds. His father was in charge of the prison in near-by Griquastadt and as a youngster he met many people caught up in the world of illicit diamond buying and sent to his father's prison for safekeeping. Many of these people were adventurers rather than criminals and young Gerhardt revelled in their stories of monopoly power and injustice, and of how the mining giants kept many fine diamond deposits landlocked so they could dribble the gems on to the world market as it suited them, thereby boosting the prices they charged. The physical environment around Kimberley had a profound effect upon him, making him and most of the other local people, as he puts it, 'close to the earth, close to God and close to each other'. Through years of public service in Namibia, Visser grew increasingly alarmed at the wasteful and dishonest ways in which political life was conducted when it excluded the majority, and today he speaks in quiet but injured tones about the way Namibia 'has been overgrazed, over-fished, and overmined as a result'.[21]

Slowly but surely Visser and Thirion were finding their feet in the world of diamonds and metal mining. As their research progressed they found more and more evidence that there was no meaningful control over the country's most important industry. As well as the supposedly independent Diamond Board for South-West Africa being sited in premises given it by De Beers, they found that all the Board's agents checking the diamonds leaving Namibia or counting them to see if the same numbers arrived in Kimberley or London were De Beers' employees. The entire costs of running the Board, it transpired, were met by De Beers, who simply deducted them from the taxes they were due to pay. The Diamond Board secretary who convened the meetings and wrote minutes was one Stanley Jackson, but his salaried employment was as secretary to the local De Beers' company, Consolidated Diamond Mines of South-West Africa, which operated the mine at Oranjemund. As they dug further they found more and more evidence that the Diamond Board, which had been set up as an independent watch-dog, had long since been transformed into a helpless poodle which De Beers liked to keep sitting securely in its generous corporate lap.

The situation with the government mining engineer and the Inspectorate of Mines was little better. The top officials had never even heard of the Halbscheid agreement, the key controlling instrument taken over from colonial German mining law to protect the diamond fields from irrational exploitation.[22] Not surprisingly, since they had never heard of the agreement, they had never thought of enforcing its provisions or even of running the most basic of independent checks on the mine. As the investigation proceeded, Gerhardt Visser and Martin Grote began to learn about the shrewd and intelligent way diamond deposits were controlled in Namibia's nearest neighbour to the east, Botswana. There the government seemed to have a simple and effective system of checks and balances upon the activities of the mining companies and to have taken in not only huge quantities of money in the form of taxation but to have an equal share in all decision making, mine planning and development, and even a half share of the profits.[23] In Botswana, with a one-person, one-vote democratic electoral system and a black majority government, the country had invested its windfall from diamonds in free universal education and a modern health service and the country had grown by leaps and bounds. Meanwhile in Namibia, the investigators remarked, there was no remotely comparable development even though the country's diamond deposits had been the richest and finest in the world.

Judge Thirion was horrified by what he was learning about the behaviour of the mining companies and, despite growing pressure from South African Cabinet ministers to soft-pedal, he pressed on with his investigation. In July 1984 he decided to hold a week-long public hearing at which his investigators would report what they had found out so far. The mining companies would also be offered the chance to have their say. The main evidence at the hearing was presented by Martin Grote, a young economist who had joined the commission as an investigator. He had been so shocked about what he had found out about the Diamond Board that he had written a biting confidential report in which he called for its immediate abolition. Now he developed this argument in public, much to the delight of the Namibian press, which was revelling in the new-found atmosphere of openness and disclosure. Grote also spoke of his anxieties about the potential abuses in a system where De Beers controlled the mining company and sold all diamonds to another sister set of companies which it also owned, the Central Selling Organisation and its affiliates. The Namibian State had no way of checking whether it was receiving best market prices for the unusually fine quality gemstones of Oranjemund. The system whereby a large corporation could swap or send goods and services between a web of daughter companies across the globe, setting its own internal 'transfer' prices, meant that it could readily overcharge or undercharge itself, to the detriment of any country where it did business. Grote believed he had found some evidence of this with De Beers. But he did not have conclusive proof because, he underlined, in addition to controlling the production distribution and sale of diamonds, De Beers also had total control over the flow of information.[24]

When Grote's worries about transfer prices were aired in the Windhoek courtroom, De Beers decided that the time had come to put in some sort of a reply. However, the company appeared most anxious to avoid any of its executives being subjected to cross-examination under oath. This meant spurning Judge Thirion's invitation to take the witness stand. But the company worked hard to present its decision to stay out of the witness box in a more favourable light. Instead of a flat refusal, De Beers' lawyers therefore told the judge that one of its executives might be permitted to give evidence but only if the public and the press were excluded and the evidence held *in camera*. Judge Thirion felt this would be most improper and dismissed the suggestion out of hand. De Beers next sought to protect its reputation by putting evidence to the inquiry in the form of a letter from executive director Doug Hoffe. But this manoeuvre backfired and infuriated the judge, who stated that the letter was a collection of unsupported statements. Without information or analysis it was, he noted, 'an insult to even the lowliest form of intelligence'.[25]

The judge's difficulties in getting witnesses to take the stand were compounded by the web of corporate secrecy in southern Africa. National security legislation meant that almost any vital information could be classified as having strategic importance and then kept from the public domain. At the end of his week of public hearings Thirion was thoroughly depressed and more or less ready to give up. Adjourning his probe indefinitely, he stated from the bench that he was 'sick and tired of having to ask people's permission all the time',[26] and added that unless something extraordinary happened this would in all probability be the last session of his inquiry. At this mining company directors in Namibia and South Africa breathed a collective sigh of relief, reasoning that their time of trial and investigation was now over. But the judge's plea was as shrewd as it was despairing and before long he was assured of evidence of such quality that his inquiry would continue for several more sessions and culminate in an explosive report.

The basis for the next sensational development was laid in a routine enough way mostly by the passage of time. Gordon Brown had now more or less finished building his new house and was ready to come out in the open. This was not an easy decision for him to take. His feelings of vulnerability had declined but not entirely disappeared after he left De Beers. He couldn't be sacked any more, he reasoned; but he feared that his house might be burgled and his copies of documents stolen. A calm and physically fit man, he was not given to paranoia, but he was tangling with some of the most powerful people in southern Africa.[27] Furthermore Thirion's chief investigator, Gerhardt Visser, had repeatedly warned that it could be dangerous to stay in the background too long. Openness, he argued, was Brown's best defence. Eric Lang also encouraged his friend to go public and in the end Gordon Brown decided to follow their advice. With Brown willing to go into the witness box, the judge at last had something out of the ordinary and he accordingly arranged to hold more public hearings in June and July 1985. At one of these Brown delivered his evidence quietly in the course of a three-hour special session. He explained that he had worked at the mine for fifteen years, had risen slowly up the ranks and come to work at the right hand of the mine manger as his technical assistant. He saw all the mine plans and he began to see documents that called into question the life expectancy of the mine. When he started to refer to internal company documents, De Beers' legal advisers reminded the court that the documents in question had been 'stolen', and the man who introduced them in evidence was, by implication, a thief. A good many judges, particularly in Britain or South Africa where the law of confidence protects property at the expense of the public interest, might have closed off the evidence on this basis, but not Mr Justice Thirion. He believed that the court's job was to obtain reliable evidence and he allowed Brown's testimony to proceed and the documents to be added to the record.

Brown's documentary evidence ranged over the scientific, economic and philosophical aspects of a proper mining policy, which in a diamond mine involves working the high-grade deposits where there are lots of gemstones of a high quality strictly in tandem with the lower grades. This means mining the lower and higher value reserves in the proportion in which they occur in the payable ore-body. Having outlined the norms of good stewardship, Brown turned to give his insider's account of what had been going on at Oranjemund. He showed there had been significant overmining in both the stone sizes and the grades or quality of the gems extracted. He carefully reviewed the Oranjemund mining statistics and showed that overmining in stone size continued from the early 1960s to the late 1970s, when regression occurred because the most profitable deposits were by then mined out. As for overmining by grade or quality he calculated that it had taken place in every year of the fifteen he spent on the mine, except one. In addition to overmining on stone size and grade, he explained to the court, De Beers had also selectively mined those deposits with the lowest working costs. In his evidence Brown was at pains to make the story accessible to the general public. He likened the mine to a sponge cake with lots of cream on top. Under normal circumstances people would take out a slice at a time, a piece of cream along with the appropriate piece of sponge. In the case of overmining, he said, the cream is all scraped off the top.[28]

I interviewed Brown about his analysis in the park below the Tinten Palast, the Palace of Ink built by the Germans to administer their colonial rule. In the shade of palm trees which surround the building which now houses Namibia's democratically elected parliament, Brown explained the essence of De Beers' mining strategy.

'The overmining took place on the upper terraces and the N blocks which were those series of beaches situated furthest from the sea. That's where the richest blocks were in terms of grade and stone size. There was a central block between the two beaches. Now that was of lower grade and that was left behind while the company concentrated on taking out the ore reserves furthest from the sea.' Brown explained that the policy shortened the life of a mine because when you concentrate on taking out the richer portions there are many marginal areas which have to be left behind. 'They are no longer economically viable, because you have no rich ore to offset them against,' he said. By this overmining, he calculated De Beers had pulled forward one billion pounds worth of revenue and taken it before independence. The net result, he estimated, was a shortening of the mine's life by fourteen years.[29]

Brown supported his testimony to the Thirion commission with bundles of secret company documents. Among the first he produced was a thick 1968 report to the CDM general manager, D. Borchers, by his assistant, Theo Pretorius, and a team of researchers. The report is replete with references to overmining. On page one of the foreword, the general manager refers to 'the overmining of the high-grade large diamond size ore reserve blocks in the southern area in order to maintain the carat production call. This exigency produces an average stone size well above the average ore reserve size which in turn reduces the average size of the remaining reserves.'[30] On page two the general manager records his alarm at the way the mine is headed and the 'vicious circle' in which it is locked. On page three he underlines that 'the over-depletion of the larger stones can never be rectified'. On the next page he reports that overmining in 1966, 1967 and 1968 of the precious

N blocks, the finest diamond deposits of all, was running at from 219 to 326 per cent. If the mine carried on with these policies, they could be mined out within three years.[31]

A 1981 life of mine review drawn up by the production manager and produced by Brown in court called unequivocally for a change in policy, without which 'we will power the mine into the ground'. Instead of mining for maximum profit, the production manager insisted, the mine should revert to mining to average grade. An earlier report dated 31 January 1980 and written by the mine's operations research manager also outlined the various options being considered. These ranged from carrying on with maximum depletion until the end of the mine's life, overmining until 1985 then suddenly reverting to a proper policy of mining to average grade and a third, middle-of-the-road option of shifting from intensive mining and mining to average grade in 1983.[32] Gordon Brown produced sheafs of documents which mentioned, quantified, analysed, footnoted, warned, worried about and generally underlined the company's deep involvement in overmining areas of its leased diamond deposit. After he had concluded his evidence, the company made no attempt to suggest that any of the documents were forgeries or to rebut his calculations about the speed and extent of overmining. Instead it kept its head down and hoped the crisis would pass. Eventually of course the court hearings came to an end and the massive publicity in the Namibian press subsided for a while. Then CDM bought some advertising space in various papers and magazines to deny the slurs on its corporate character, slurs, it should be remembered, which resulted mainly from extracts of its own secret policy documents being read out in public.

As Judge Thirion prepared to complete his interim report, on the mining industry in general and the diamond industry in particular, De Beers' public relations department put out a series of 'Fact Papers' which purported to set the record straight. In a meticulous series of responses Brown showed the tenuous basis of these 'facts'. In February 1986 the unelected interim government announced that the report would be published, and on Friday 7 March 1986 it was finally published, again to sensational publicity in the southern African press. The report is a lengthy, well-crafted and in parts devastating indictment of the lack of control over mining companies in Namibia. The companies, the report shows, were having tax holidays, exporting huge mining samples, sending out blister copper and lead containing significant quantities of precious metals which they never declared to customs and then profitably refined abroad. The companies were paying ludicrous land rents, keeping poor, defective or even contradictory records, and avoiding serious inspection or regulation by the State. But of all the sections of the mining industry that he brought under scrutiny, Judge Thirion reserved his most withering criticism for the diamond industry. The Diamond Board was, he said, a complete sham.[33] There was no control over the mining or export of the country's most precious asset and the diamond mining company obtained its hold over tens of thousands of acres of the richest diamond deposits in the world for an annual rent of £130, a rent, what's more, that had not changed in nearly seventy years. And while the State took in a derisory rent from De Beers for the land, it was paying another De Beers' company a royalty that amounted to tens of millions of pounds over the years because the company claimed tithes and tax shares inherited from the days of the German Empire. Worst of all, although the German Empire had worked hard to develop a system of equitable controls over the industry, including a vital Halbscheid or 'Half Share' agreement, the South African government apparatus completely failed to supervise the mining of the Oranjemund deposits or run even the most elementary checks to see if De Beers was abiding by its obligations and keeping to best mining practice. Reviewing the bundles of documents produced by Gordon Brown, the judge spelled out the consequences of this failure on the ground. It meant, he concluded in no uncertain terms, that the company had overmined the deposit, thereby shortening its life and greatly reducing its future profitability. This had been done deliberately, he stated, again citing De Beers' internal documents, to meet excessive production targets set by De Beers' Central Selling Organisation, the monopolistic single channel for selling diamonds run by De Beers from London.[34]

4   De Beers between Private Deeds and Public Relations

The drive on the tar road from Keetmanshoop to Luderitz is one of the most remarkable in the world and full of surprises. At first the desert landscape seems uniform, vast in its emptiness, lacking in trees and plants, gates and fences, hedges and horizons, the straight lines and customary visual cues which would make it graspable to the measuring, Eurocentric eye. But after a while your vision begins to adjust, the eye is able to differentiate the tough, sprouting clumps of desert grasses from the patchy scrub of tiny, undernourished trees, and even to identify the generous little succulents, stubborn in their foliage and golden yellow or sea green in colour. Their eco-systems are adapted to take moisture from the mists and winds that come in from the sea, which is just as well given that here in the oldest desert in the world there are many places where there is only fifty millimetres of rainfall in a year and some where there has been none at all throughout the twentieth century.

Off the road, away in mid-field, half-way towards the edge of the world, you see first the dappled, sanded mounds stretching off into the horizon; then your eye is drawn to small hills in the distance, wispy and tentative, an endless sandscape textured as if it were made of desert snow. Further along the road the wind picks up and starts blowing sand in from the coast, carrying it like smoke in a forest fire for miles until it reaches you. It finds every gap in the armoury of the Audi, pouring in through door-seals, heating vents and even those windows you had taken so much trouble to close tightly in preparation for its arrival. Before you know it the windscreen has tinted an opaque, milky white which makes it hard to see. You stop, thinking it can be cleaned off with a cloth or a brush of the hand; but the glass on this brand-new masterpiece of German engineering has been swiftly and silently sand-blasted by the Namib and will never be the same again.

71

On further examination the headlights have also fallen victim and the thick metallic paint, five coats deep according to the advertisements, has been stripped from the wings by the brief caress of the sand. *Vorsprung durch technik* has met its match and the people at car-rental return are going to have to try harder than they have ever tried before to achieve worthwhile results. As darkness falls the consequences of having sand-blasted headlights become clear. The undipped lamps can no longer cut through the night or illuminate the road. They give out the merest fraction of their former candlepower, like the final flickers of a taper held too long in the wind and rain. Then, just as you have adjusted to this feeble light, comes the biggest surprise of all. The tar road gives out all of a sudden, without a sign on the road or explanation on the map; now there are no painted lines to follow and the car is tobogganing madly in and out of the deep tracks cut in the sand by unknown predecessors who may or may not have survived. At one point the road is so treacherous that I stop the car, open the door and get out to check that I can at least see to the bottom of the tracks. No sooner am I outside than there is another magnet calling the attention of anyone with a sense of wonder – the African sky, a fantastic blackboard on which are traced thousands, maybe tens of thousands of stars, including the southern cross. And there in its full magnificence is the planet Jupiter, turning to the world and wishing it well.

Tired beyond measure on arrival in the port of Luderitz, I reminded myself that I owed this journey and many other fascinating drives in Namibia to Consolidated Diamond Mines' public relations advisers. If it hadn't been for the many obstacles they put in the way of my documentary on the Thirion Report and the diamonds of Oranjemund, I would have been able to cover these distances by scheduled flights without attracting the attention of the Diamond Police. I would have avoided all the lengthy journeys, but missed the sky, the fireworks and the fun.

The opening move in my bid to make a programme about Thirion had been to contact Neville Huxham, the high-powered head of public relations in the diamond services division of the Anglo American Corporation in Johannesburg. He passed me on to one of his more junior colleagues, Rob Hudson, to whom I explained that I was preparing a documentary for British ITV on the economic and political situation in Namibia as it approached independence. I added that since there had been so much public discussion about the diamond industry, I would like to negotiate access to the mine and hear what the company had to say about overmining and Gordon Brown's documentary evidence. Mr Hudson was lavish with his charm, the main

72

tool of his trade, but agreeable none the less. He reminded me of De Beers' and Anglo's strong corporate commitment to freedom of inquiry and declared that while he would have to consult, personally he could see no insurmountable obstacles to a decent working relationship and access to the mine. He asked where I was staying – so he could get back to me; and then, almost as an aside, said, 'How did you come in to the country – as a tourist or with press accreditation?'

This set alarm bells ringing and I thought about changing hotels or leaving town post-haste. I was discussing the problem later in the bar of the Hotel Braamfontein with Marcel Golding, Paul Benjamin and Jean Leger, then respectively press officer, legal adviser, and safety adviser of the NUM, when the receptionist summoned me to the telephone. I took the call, which was from the chief immigration officer at Jan Smuts Airport, who said in a commanding tone, 'You must not leave the hotel. I will be with you shortly.' Since no one in officialdom other than Mr Hudson knew where I was staying, the thought occurred that he had contacted one of De Beers' friends in customs or state security in the hope that intervention by them would save him from refusing an interview about the Thirion report and access to the mine. Although the immigration officer warned me in no uncertain terms that we must not film on South African soil without a permit, he seemed a likeable and independent person. Over a beer or two we discussed my dilemma and what I attempted to describe as his. He was being got at by De Beers, I suggested, and used by the company to ensure that, for all the talk about freedom of inquiry, the unforeseen circumstances which they had quietly arranged could bring a welcome halt to the unwelcome film we proposed to make. From his response and his willingness to continue the conversation it seemed the immigration officer didn't much relish his task. He answered and even seemed to enjoy my friendly banter and he seemed like a man with something approaching democratic convictions. When he got up to stand his round I examined more closely the topmost of the sheets of paper he left lying on the table. On about the fourth handwritten line below my passport details were the words 'Myn Huis'. I have no detailed knowledge of Afrikaans but a few weeks of reading bilingual South African company reports had familiarised me with these words – mining company, or mining house. When the customs man returned with two beers I told him I couldn't help noticing these interesting words and wondering what, in present circumstances, they might mean. He laughed and replied 'You have seen too much and I have said too much. It is time for me to go.' He then sank most of his beer and got up to leave. 'One last warning, a friend to a friend. If you film in South Africa without a permit we will throw you out of the country. You do understand that.' I assured him that he had made himself crystal clear, as unequivocal as say the Pope on abortion, or Dr Hendrik Verwoerd on integrated public toilets. He laughed again and was on his way.

The following day I flew down to Cape Town, a city in such a magnificent setting that it can blind the eye to the multitude of injustices within its boundaries. Reaching Hout Bay, one of its many seaside suburbs, after a drive through wooded, hilly country, I met Gordon Brown again and tried in a few days to finish my course in the tangled history of the Namibian diamond industry. Every now and then, in response to some request for clarification of this point or that of company policy, Brown would climb in his truck with one or other of his dogs and disappear for an hour or two to retrieve a document from one of the many caches around Cape Town where he had secreted his copies of De Beers or Consolidated Diamond Mines files. In the course of a few days with Brown, I became astonished at the sheer mass of documentary evidence he had accumulated and began to feel that his case was a powerful one, which, despite everything that had happened, it would still be most interesting to put to De Beers in the course of a filmed interview. To that end I again rang Mr Hudson at head office, sent him my regards, and told him about the visit I had had shortly after giving him my address. I also indicated that I still awaited the company's decision about access to the mine with a firm expectation of a positive outcome. Then Gordon Brown and I drove to D.F. Malan Airport in eager anticipation of what promised to be a memorable flight across the magnificent vineyards and orange groves north of Cape Town beyond Robben Island on the way to a different kind of beauty, the desert lands of Namibia. In retrospect I remember the departure lounge better than the flight itself. As we got ready to board the plane the immigration officers put on another amusing little floor show in co-operation with the security police. Just as the flight was due to board, I was paged by tannoy and ordered to report to the security desk. There I was told that there were serious questions that must be put to me in a private room. Once inside the man in charge was very insistent that I should sit in a particular chair, probably for the benefit of hidden cameras. He was a strange character this senior policeman, brown and wrinkled as a walnut with eyes hidden by mirrored dark sunglasses. After a friendly enough initial chat, he suddenly slammed the brakes on his politeness and asked, putting on his fiercest look, 'Is your visit to Namibia undercover?' 'Undercover, what do you mean undercover? I booked my seat on the plane under my own name . . . ' I burst out laughing at the absurdity of it all and found, much to my surprise, that the man in charge was joining in. He was a human being again, for a second or two anyway – and then his mind climbed back into uniform. 'I want to warn you,' he said forcefully, 'if you try to re-enter the Republic of South Africa we will throw you out of the country. Is that clear?'

It was clear, splendidly clear, so much so that I could think of little else for the next two hours on the aeroplane or on the twenty-mile bus journey into Windhoek from the airport. There it took only a day to ascertain how little there was to film about diamonds if we were refused access to the mine. Now everything depended on the reaction of Consolidated Diamond Mines and what instructions they received from their head offices in Johannesburg and London. In Namibia the head gatekeeper was Clive Cowley, the Public Relations Manager for CDM, a man with a fine view of Windhoek from his tenth-floor office in the city's biggest building and a blunt tone when he is declining to co-operate. Through him we finally received a written answer from De Beers to our routine request for an interview. The letter dated 11 June 1987 stated simply: 'We regret to advise you that we are unable to agree to your filming at Oranjemund, or to offer you any assistance in the preparation of film material on CDM.'

I phoned Mr Cowley and asked him if there was any court of appeal, to which he answered monosyllabically, 'No.' I asked him if 'no help' meant that we would be unable to obtain press releases, fact papers and company reports and any other company releases and publications which were already in the public domain. 'Let me make it absolutely clear once and for all,' replied Cowley, normally a man with unlimited deposits of generosity and fellow feeling. 'You will not, under any circumstances and at any time, get any help of any kind from CDM. Nothing, you will get nothing from this company whatsoever.' This was to make our investigation of the diamonds of Oranjemund rather more of a challenge.

Nowadays few popular newspapers bother to investigate the complexities of modern business life with any degree of scepticism or persistence, excusing their lack of vigilance in the public interest with explanations about the appetites of their audience, their readers' difficulty or disinterest in understanding the world of economic production. But investigative television can still lay that world bare and set out the intricacies of malpractice or intrigue in such a way that any citizen can comprehend the arcane processes by which people can be robbed with a fountain pen. It is this democratic power of television used for purposes of public service that makes it so uniquely disliked by those with power and money. However, to bring off a serious investigation of a diamond mine, it helps to have some pictures of what goes on there, of the mining town, the dredging operations, the filtering and sorting and sifting of sand, the bedrock cleaning, the working conditions of the black migrant labourers, the conditions in the single-sex hostels, and of the end to which this miracle of modern labour is geared, the diamonds themselves. In the desert lands in the south of Namibia the process is shrouded in secrecy and enclosed in the Sperrgebiet. To this Forbidden Zone all access roads are kept padlocked with admission strictly reserved for hand-picked guests, including from time to time parties of financial journalists who are flown in, given the tour, shown the percentage earning ratios, fed in the mess, and then flown out wiser and heavier men. Here in Namibia the ubiquitous wire fences are not the only protection the diamond monopoly has drawn lovingly over its private parts. Along the coast and on both sides of the private company road south from Luderitz, there are hundreds upon hundreds of electronic sensors which, when disturbed by the slightest detectable movement of boat, person or car, sound alarm signals in the security block at Oranjemund. The sensors and alarms are built in such a way that the sector of road or fence being disturbed can be clearly identified and speedily isolated. A helicopter or light plane is then sent to detain the intruders. Given their total control of a vast area, when they are only really mining along the shore, De Beers' corporate public relations department could be forgiven for assuming that refusal of access would deal a terrible, even terminal, blow to our plan for a television programme; and so it seemed for a couple of days, while we licked our wounds and evaluated our options. We could get a few coastal shots from a boat, but at immense cost in terms of the time it would take to sail to Oranjemund along what was a desolate and dangerous coastline. Having rejected an approach from the sea, we started to think about who might lend us a plane and fly us down there. At Eros Airport, we were told, there were pilots who might do the job. On the way to Eros I took another, closer look at the letter of refusal from Clive Cowley of CDM and noticed a significant new piece of information which I had missed on previous readings. According to a footnote, the letter had been copied not only to the mine manager at Oranjemund but also sent to someone else, to 'CC SAP ADM 6', which I rightly guessed was a division of the South African Police. This worried me at first, but on reflection I began to think it might be a serious mistake by Cowley; for it gave us documentary evidence of company contact with the police in their bid to obstruct the film.

At the airport we were shown into the offices of Graham van Niekerk,

76

an interesting man who was soon to demonstrate that he did not take kindly to powerful people trying to throw their weight around. We didn't tell him everything about what we were doing, but we told him quite a lot and above all we didn't tell him any half truths or lies. As a result he agreed to fly us south over the mine. On a glorious Saturday morning we set out from Eros to see what pictures of the diamonds of Oranjemund we could take from the freedom of the skyways. It was a long, lonely and exhilarating journey across the empty desert to Oranjemund by air, enlivened at first by a mad desire to see if we could spot the Schloss Duwusib castle built with imported stone by a German colonial adventurer in the middle of the desert with his American wife's money. We failed in that ambition and also in another, equally unrealistic, desire to see the wild horses of the desert, Arab mares and stallions which had escaped from the castle after the First World War and lived a magical existence thereafter, breeding and foaling and renewing the cycle of life against all the odds. In other respects, during the flight a certain realism was forced upon us. Given the size of the fuel tanks and the distances involved, we had little choice but to fly down to Luderitz, set down there at the airstrip scored in the sand, and take on enough extra fuel to ensure that we could comfortably overfly Oranjemund and return to Eros without further anxiety about fuel. On the ground at Luderitz as we worked to remove the cockpit cover so that the camera man Howard Somers had a better chance of getting pictures amid the dust and worryingly intense light of the desert, Hartmut Jungst, who ran the town's lifeline to the outside world, a shipping and fuel agency called Grindrod, strolled over and began to talk. He told us that the police had been making inquiries about us and had phoned his company to find out if and when our plane was expected. 'I got the feeling', he said nonchalantly, 'that they were hoping that I would take the hint and decline to supply you with fuel.'

Once the tanks were full we waved goodbye, taxied down the runway and were airborne once more. We flew down the Diamond Coast, looking at the lonely beauty of Bogenfels, spotting the seals from their sudden movements and imagining their high-pitched calls through the roar of the engines, and wondering at the endless miles of barbed-wire fences De Beers had introduced. Then suddenly, just as Oranjemund came into view, a bizarre desert Legoland of houses with green lawns, shops with car parks, supermarket trolleys and advertising hoardings, a church and a school, the radio began to crackle and come alive.

'This is the Oranjemund control tower. Come in please, come in please.'

'Roger, Oranjemund, roger,' replied Graham van Niekerk. 'Receiving you loud and clear.' My mind was swimming in half-remembered fantasies of wartime films when I heard with a start, 'You have no permission to land, repeat, no permission to land and you must keep above 300 feet. You are not welcome here.' Poor Graham was speechless. I'm sure he thought for a moment that he had a gang of international jewel thieves on board. But if he did he said nothing about it. In the long and worrying silence, our hearts were in our stomachs and we thought our flight to photograph Oranjemund had been aborted at the very point where the real work was about to begin. But van Niekerk was a free spirit who felt that we had played pretty straight with him. So while he obeyed control's instruction to fly higher, he carried on towards Oranjemund. The pictures we got from such a height with all the dust outside the plane and the vibration inside were never going to be masterpieces but at least we got them. After about fifteen minutes flying to and fro, picturing the mine, the sea walls, the giant bucket-wheel excavator, the streets and buildings, we turned away from De Beers' company town in the Forbidden Zone of the desert and flew home, tired and thirsty and filled with a significant sense of accomplishment.

When we met Graham again the following evening, we learned that he had had a surprise when he returned to work in the morning. The police wanted to talk to him and had asked all sorts of questions about why foreigners should want to fly across the diamond area. The insinuation was obvious – that we could be diamond smugglers or something worse and he should keep well away from us just in case. The visit caused us renewed anxieties and we began to wonder how long it would be before our rooms were entered when we were not there, our equipment interfered with, our exposed film opened to the light, and our modest achievements rendered worthless in a moment. Despite a generous intake of alcohol taken in a misguided bid to stay calm, we began to feel that our friends at CDM were now interested in doing more than just obstructing our investigation. Through their friends in the Diamond Police they might well try to sabotage the completion of the programme altogether, perhaps by having the film impounded. We began to discuss the best way of leaving the country when all our interviews were done. From David Smuts, one of the best lawyers in Namibia, we learned some further worrying information. More than once baggage containing important documents had disappeared when he left the country. Cases went into the luggage system at Windhoek International and were ticketed to Germany; but those containing sensitive material did not re-emerge in Frankfurt. Once out of sight they were, he assumed, taken off the baggage trucks at Windhoek by the secret police, who kept what interested them.

This worrying prospect forced us to make some contingency plans to take the exposed film out in Graham's light plane across the desert to the east of Windhoek into neighbouring Botswana, a Commonwealth country in which, while De Beers was a major presence, there was no South African army of occupation or police force. We finished our remaining interviews, talked to Gordon Brown again in the beautiful park near the Lutheran church and said goodbye. We cleared our film and equipment through customs, and off at the crack of dawn with our precious bundles went John Coates and Graham van Niekerk. The rest of us stayed behind to hope, pray and remonstrate if there was any trouble. We had half an inkling that De Beers and the Diamond Police would make one last move against us and had talked through what we would do. If the equipment was seized and the film exposed to the light we would simply start again from scratch, working with equipment rented from friends in South Africa. In any event the arrangement was that if there was trouble on exit, John was to ring David Smuts, who would be poised to lobby the interim government and if necessary go into court and seek an order to protect our film. At Eros Airport just as the aircraft was getting ready to taxi down the runway the radio began to crackle again and another announcement came over the airwaves. Customs clearance had now been withdrawn and the plane would now have to fly to Windhoek International before clearance to leave the country could be given. De Beers' friends in the Diamond Police had obviously been busy overnight.

Reasoning that while De Beers probably didn't have its own air force, the South African authorities certainly did, Graham and John proceeded to Windhoek International. As soon as they landed on the tarmac and finished taxi-ing to the parking position, they were met by two senior members of the South African/South-West African police. One of the two identified himself as Detective-Sergeant Geyser of the Namibian Security Police; the other did not disclose his identity but told John simply that he was on secondment from the security services in South Africa. After the formal introductions, all our hard-won film was taken off the plane and impounded along with our equipment. For a moment all seemed lost. But it had become a specialised part of our make-up to read the game in South Africa and we had anticipated that this might happen and that, if it did, a lawyer could help. John insisted on his right to telephone a lawyer and soon had David Smuts on the line. Smuts moved into action straight away. He knew his way round the Windhoek power structure as no other, which phones to ring, which doors to knock on. He begged and pleaded, cajoled and threatened, and kept on trying again and again, warning that there would be an almighty row if the interference did not stop. Eberhard Hofmann, the interim government official in charge of media and information and a man of great integrity, sided with us and underlined that from the beginning we had been frank with him about what we were doing and had been given press accreditation by his department. By lunchtime, the question of the police behaviour in seizing our film and equipment, our 'property' as Dave Smuts always called it, mindful of how much store most legal systems set by its protection, was before the chief minister and by about 2 p.m. the two officers who grounded the aeroplane and impounded the film were forced to give everything back. Graham and John then flew off to Botswana as planned, and thirty-six hours later the film was in Manchester for processing. We celebrated as we flew home, rested up a little and then began to get the programme ready for transmission. There were a few wobbles over structure and then over the vigour of the language used to describe De Beers' behaviour in Namibia. But in the end Granada's legal advisers were happy with the evidence and with the direct and unequivocal language of the script. This stated that De Beers had 'secretly been stripping one of the world's poorest nations of its main asset'.[1] The country's resources were the subject of 'plunder' and behind South Africa's military occupation Namibia had been 'robbed of its rich mineral resources'.[2] The title of the programme was also direct: 'The Case of the Disappearing Diamonds'.

The programme was not well received in Charterhouse Street, the Holborn Circus headquarters of De Beers and its central selling organisation in London. The company had resolutely declined to give us access to the mine, to let us interview anyone about its business practices as portrayed in its own internal company documents and had even persistently tried to obstruct the investigation of its activities in Namibia. None of this was mentioned in the advertisements the company now found it necessary to place in *The Times*, the *Guardian*, the *Financial Times*, the *Daily Telegraph*, and the *Independent*. These stated that De Beers was wholly innocent, had never overmined the diamond deposit or breached the Halbscheid agreement and indeed was a company whose conduct was above reproach.[3]

On the ground in Namibia much faster corporate footwork was necessary to limit the damage caused by the continuing reverberations of the judge's report and the news of our programme. But in the end on its home turf in Windhoek, De Beers and its allies in the unelected interim government finally succeeded in getting government regulation of the mining industry referred to something called an inter-departmental committee. This was mainly composed of the very people whose competence in regulating the mining industry had been criticised by the judge in his report. The inter-departmental committee produced a white paper on mining,[4] but this was never put to the Namibian legislative assembly for discussion or debate. The white paper was also accompanied by an 'Information Document'[5] which was 'laid on the table' of the assembly, a device which avoided all discussion. This was then circulated by De Beers along with a press release from the company, which claimed that the committee had completely exonerated the mining firm. The information document uses no such words, preferring more judicious formulations such as the documentary evidence being 'inadequate' and the judge's understanding of the technical issues being 'unsatisfactory'.

In fact Judge Thirion's understanding of the issues was – and is – very good, and the documentary evidence included in his report was – and is – very considerable. The life of mine documents show a power dive. The internal company documents say again and again that the company was overmining on diamond grade and stone size.

Besides the extensive documentation contained in the Thirion Report or displayed in the supporting appendices, I have also found important new documentation from De Beers' own confidential files which shows company officials discussing, planning and carrying out the overmining of the diamond deposit.. The new evidence is contained in a series of confidential internal reports, letters or telexes between the senior managers on the mine at Oranjemund and their superiors at De Beers' head office in Johannesburg.

In September 1970, for example, there was significant traffic between D.E. MacIver, the man in charge in Johannesburg, and Theo Pretorius, the man in charge of the mine at Oranjemund. At 10 a.m. on 10 September 1970, MacIver sent Pretorius an unusually important telex which opened with the following instruction: 'Urgent information required by 12.30 please.' The telex then asked: 'What could you increase your carat production to by September 1971, assuming no restriction on the plant and equipment that could be installed by that time, the working of that plant and equipment to maximum capacity, no limit on diamond size, mining the foreshore to maximum capacity and continuing sea operations with the two sea-going vessels already in use?'[6]

The telex and its 12.30 deadline caused anxiety at Oranjemund, but by 12.08 a reply was on the line. It began by outlining the best estimates of how much extra production could be obtained by responsible mining methods. Then clearly and unequivocally, one minor indication of disquiet aside, the telex gave the revised estimates of how many more diamonds could be taken out if a different and unorthodox mining philosophy was adopted.

Paragraph three read as follows:

We do not clearly understand your requirement of no limit on diamond size. If we are to continue mining to reserve then no further increase apart from the above can be expected. However if we were to overmine we would expect the following:

Increasing upper terrace mining at expense of lower terrace, approximately 5,000 carats a month less, but size increased from 0.75 to 0.85 carats/stone, no additional working cost of capital and could commence immediately.

Increasing N Blocks, approximately 20,000 carats per month increase. Size increased from 0.85 to 0.95 carats per stone. No additional working cost or capital and could commence immediately.[7]

On 2 October 1970, in his detailed reply, Mr MacIver spelled out head office's mining philosophy in no uncertain terms: 'The need to maintain an almost consistent annual stone size. M3 [cubic metres of ore put through] and total carats would seem to be of less importance than meeting the needs of the market and getting maximum profits.'[8]

Then in two extraordinary paragraphs which reach to the heart of De Beers' business methods and stewardship of the mine, MacIver asked:

What are the estimated capital requirements to enable the mining operations to be completed in say 10 years and what effect does this have on profits?

We should at this stage consider any possibility to obtain maximum profit even if unconventional![9]

From Oranjemund Theo Pretorius replied at length on 31 December 1970, enclosing a report which compared the profitability of the mine using a variety of mining policies. But in his covering letter he reached the heart of the matter: 'In all cases studied overmining increases the present value of future profits. The effects of overmining in diamond size are greater than the effects of overmining on grade.'[10]

Pretorius also explained how overmining affected the short-term profit profile of the mine, explaining that mining to average grade would give future profits to a value of 296 million rand whereas overmining would increase the figure by an extra fifty million, or about 16 per cent. In conclusion Pretorius added: 'Overmining to 25 per cent is possible but changes of a larger degree may cause mining problems and will incur additional costs ... Many other combinations of overmining are possible and a computer model has been developed which can be used to calculate the profitability of these combinations.'[11]

On 13 February 1971 Pretorius prepared another highly confidential report, 'The effects of various mining policies at CDM'. This compared three options including one which is denoted as 'the present plan'. This, the document states quite definitively, is 'to do selective mining in the larger stone size blocks throughout the mine and the continuation of foreshore mining'. The document also stated that the existing 1971 plan catered for an 8 per cent overmining and indicated that the target would go higher still, to overmining of 25 per cent.[12]

The period 1970–1 was exceptionally sensitive in the history of Anglo–De Beers involvement in Namibia. The original agreement with the Administrator-General of South-West Africa for the Anglo–De Beers' group to mine the Sperrgebiet or Forbidden Zone ran for fifty years from 1920 to 1970, and would have expired even as these decisions were being taken.[13] The lease had, it is true, been extended for periods of twenty years, once in 1940, and again in 1953. But on each occasion De Beers were given their extension of the lease by the South African government, secretly the company's main partner in their diamond cartel, and the arrangement depended on South Africa's continuing colonial rule of its neighbour to the north, the former German colony of South-West Africa.

By 1970 the United Nations was becoming increasingly determined to ensure that its responsibilities to Namibia, enshrined in the League of Nations' mandate to govern the country, were discharged in full. It had set up a United Nations Council for Namibia and was preparing to revoke South Africa's mandate. Anglo American had long operated a sophisticated corporate intelligence network and was routinely engaged in scanning the socio-political landscape for signs of turbulence and change that would affect its hugely profitable diamond business. This was the context in which De Beers was privately shaping the mining policy and taking the business decisions which shortened the life of the mine.

The next, and in an important sense even more weighty, piece of evidence about overmining comes from another highly confidential CDM document dated 1977. This too was a critical year in the progress of Namibia towards the independence which had so long been denied it. Britain, the United States, France, West Germany and Canada formed a five-country contact group to negotiate with South Africa for the country's freedom, a process which soon led to the adoption of UN Resolution 435 as a basis for independence and free elections. The confidential 1977 report is a fifty-page production study prepared by an eight-person special study group in the CDM management team. Dated 20 June 1977, the report is a review of all possible causes of production shortfall. Because of its precision and quality, the document was specifically singled out for praise by the mine's assistant general manager Mr J. McLuskie, who underlined 'the thoroughness of the investigation . . . [the] excellence and comprehensiveness of the report'.[14]

On page sixteen there is an unequivocal reference to the current overmining policy in both grades and stone sizes. It also gives detailed information on the company's extraordinarily precise knowledge of just how far in excess of average grade and stone size it was mining. Indeed in this report the targeting of bigger stones and richer ground is translated into detailed graphs which show that the company was mining in a select number of faces with grade and stone sizes way above normal.

In addition to this renewed evidence of overmining, the production study disclosed the wasteful side effects of the policy to deplete reserves. Such was the rush to boost production, the report noted, that the mine was becoming dangerously inefficient. High feed rates of ore meant poor screening efficiency; poor screening efficiency meant that diamonds were being thrown away instead of recovered. As one memorable paragraph put it: 'The tailings from the fines are only monitored by roughly hand sorting approximately half of the material. There could therefore be any number of diamonds in the fines tailings which do not get sorted.'[15]

Another paragraph noted the corporate obsession with 'throughput', quantities of beach put into the system, rather than diamonds recovered. Others dwelled on poor plant specification and design, the lack of preventative maintenance which caused breakdowns. Another lamented the dominant management style, saying that the company was 'managing according to the pressures or crises of the moment, that is reactionary management rather than planned management'. Another section of the report showed that while the company was targeting reserves of above-average grade and stone size, contradictions in measurement methods and errors in transcription when the system was being computerised, were causing immense problems.[16] With their report, the production study team on the mine were trying to sound a warning to the directors in Johannesburg and London who were fixing the high carat call. But the evidence is that while they were congratulated by their own immediate superiors in the organisation, their appeals fell on deaf ears further up the line.[17]

The management at local level changed not long after the report, but overmining continued as before. At a meeting of the general managers of all the diamond mines in the Anglo American diamond division, held at De Beers' Premier Mine on 12 and 13 January 1978, it was made plain that while Koffiefontein, another group mine in South Africa, was planning to mine to average grade, this was not to be the case in Namibia. At CDM, the minutes of the meeting record, working cost expenditure was 7 per cent over budget, with 'much of the increase due to increased carat production as a result of removing the stone size constraint' and the introduction of a three-shift system.[18]

Other CDM documents I have seen also refer to the company's policy of overmining the deposit. On 23 April 1980, for example, the new mine manager J.O. Richards wrote to the consulting engineer at Anglo American in Johannesburg that among the three life-of-mine strategies, two represented what would happen if there was a switch to an average mining policy while the third 'represented the continuation of the overmining policy'.[19]

Gordon Brown believes that these documents are further powerful evidence that De Beers, contrary to their repeated denials, over-exploited the mine. 'De Beers has deep enough pockets to enable them to buy a lot of advertising space to put their point of view. And while there is a huge gap between the company's private deeds and its statements for the purposes of public relations, people's memories are fickle. But the hard evidence of an irresponsible mining policy is very, very strong. I repeat my earlier statements that the proper thing for the new, independent government of Namibia, is to have a full public inquiry, with legal and other experts, to enable them to analyse all the company documents and hear all evidence on oath so that we can establish once and for all what happened at Oranjemund. I believe such an inquiry would obtain more witnesses and more evidence of the company's irresponsible behaviour;

it would also show that the consequences for Namibia of De Beers' strategy were devastating – the life of the mine was shortened and by my calculation no less than an extra billion pounds of revenue was taken away before independence. A poor country can do a great deal with a billion pounds.'[20]

5   The Tsumeb Take-away

The experience of the Ovambo people under the migrant labour system has found powerful expression in the work of two of southern Africa's leading artists, John Muadfangejo and Ben Ulenga. Muafangejo was a remarkable man, who died tragically young in 1987 at the age of forty-four. Born at Etunda lo Nghai, an Angolan village close to the Namibian border in 1944, Muadfangejo moved south at the age of thirteen after his father's death. Muadfangejo was virtually the only black Namibian of his generation to obtain any formal art training. Education, like most things in Namibia, was reserved for whites and Muadfangejo only cheated the system with the help of church leaders at St Mary's Anglican Mission at Odibo, who helped him train as a teacher and then, recognising his formidable talents, supported his application to study at the Swedish-funded arts and crafts centre of the Evangelical Lutheran Church in Natal.[1]

In his powerful, lino-cut filigrees of his country, its human beings, kraals and villages, animals and crops, Muadfangejo caught the vitality of the Namibian people and the extraordinary vigour of plant and animal life in an already unforgiving environment made worse by war. In his 1982 lino-cut 'They Are Meeting Again at Home', Muadfangejo pictured the routine emotional cruelty at the heart of the migrant labour system, the daily infringements of human rights which arose not from excesses on the edge of the system but from the structural violence at its heart. The work portrays the homecoming of a migrant labourer and his meeting with his partner. There is tenderness in the returning embrace between people normally separated by economic compulsion, but there is also an emotional coolness or even accusatory sadness in the rendition, which indicates that the embrace is one of comfort and relief, rather than of elation. In this Muadfangejo indicates that the reunion is transient and temporary, tinged with sadness, and soon to be followed by the renewed pain of departure.

If the figures in the foreground of 'They Are Meeting Again At Home' are sad, in the background is a hint of another Africa, unbowed and full of possibilities. Muadfangejo's work is crammed with what he termed, in the title of another piece, 'Hope and Optimism In Spite of the Present Difficulties'. Even in one of his most disturbing lino-cuts, where he pictures the physical dismemberment and fencing in of his people with a clearly marked 'Artificial boundary' absurdly dissecting the African horizon, his vision of Eden is clear and unambiguous. An intense and emotional man with deep religious feelings, Muadfangejo gloried in his use of black and white. With a handful of exceptions, these were the only colours in which he ever printed his lino-cuts and his preference for this mestizo mixture was not born of shortage of ink. In a society where black was so brutally separated from white he seemed to take pleasure in visually integrating the two colours, in comparing and contrasting them, in joining and fusing them and letting them stand together beyond all artificial boundaries.

Remembering childhood experience, the Namibian poet Ben Ulenga also focused on the emotional scars inflicted by the migrant labour system. In his poem 'Fathers' he recalls his disturbance and even resentment at the absences and returns of his father.[2]

> We do not want our fathers here
> they are strangers to us
>
> they only bring smells
> of tobacco rolls
> and sweat
> from where they spend their year
> far away from home
>
> always they talk
> diamonds
> trains
> money, mines
> gold and sand dunes
> these are the things we've never seen
> Bread!
> Dare you say Bread!

THE TSUMEB TAKE-AWAY

we all fall silent
it is not Christmas time

under fatherless moons
we burn september fires
high into the skies
for our fathers to see

now we are the fires
burning hunger smells
across the skies
do not bring our fathers here
we do not want them any more
they bring hunger
smells for us

I arranged to meet Ben Ulenga at his tiny office in the community centre at Katutura, the black township built several miles away from Windhoek to replace the old location inside the town. Besides writing poetry, Ulenga is an active figure in the political life of Namibia. A graduate of Robben Island, where he served eight years of a fifteen-year sentence for opposing the apartheid State, with the approach of independence he had become the secretary of the Mineworkers' Union of Namibia. When I first reached the office Ulenga was not available, unavoidably detained outside town in protracted negotiations to win union recognition from a company which had not yet begun to adjust to the seismic changes in the political and social environment of the 1990s. In Ben's absence, the office was occupied by two animated and worried men, Zac Basson, one of the union's organisers, and Peka Tjijenda, one of its members. Their conversation fascinated me in its progress through a gymnastic variety of languages from Herrero, Oshikwanyama and English through to the odd word of Afrikaans. The linguistic pluralism was as interesting as the subject under discussion. Peka was explaining that he was working at Namibia's latest mine, Navachab outside Windhoek, controlled by Anglo American and a valuable source of gold for at least the next twenty years.

I had seen the news flash about Navachab's first gold pour on the television news the previous evening. The report emphasised the importance of the new gold mine to the country and the commitment to the future

89

it represented from Anglo American, Africa's richest and most powerful company. Peka, however, was not impressed by the public relations exercise because, as he explained, there was no proper accommodation for black mineworkers at Navachab. Houses had been built for the whites, he complained, but for blacks it was the same old story. They were quartered in rough and poorly constructed utility buildings made of low-quality breeze blocks without plaster or adornment of any kind and with such poor engineering of services that water flowed into their rooms by day and by night. 'A mining company is not a poultry farm and we are not chickens,' Peka was saying in accented but impeccable English when Ben Ulenga walked in. An intense man, Ben readily joined the conversation and soon brought it round to his major preoccupation, conditions at Tsumeb, the copper and lead mine in the north of the country on the way to the Angolan border. 'I'm choosing my words carefully,' said Ulenga. 'Tsumeb is a terrible place. The compound is the worst of any major mine in the country, perhaps in all of southern Africa. I spent eight years on Robben Island as a political prisoner but conditions at Tsumeb are worse, far worse. Go and see them for yourself.'

Tsumeb, high in the north of Namibia, is one of the world's greatest mineral deposits. The subject of a special display in Washington's Smithsonian Institute, it contains an extraordinary range of metals, minerals and ores. There are copper and lead in abundance. The lead once blistered is extraordinarily pure and the copper is nearly as rich. Its impurities are benevolent, taking the form of important trace elements of silver and gold, accidental by-products worth millions of pounds per annum. Then there are iron pyrites, arsenic tioxide and cadmium as well as dufftite, mottramite, minetite and germanium besides other rare ores and minerals whose names are as poetic as they are obscure. There are dozens and dozens of these in the mile-deep mine, including many natural minerals never before observed or described in mining literature.[3]

For forty years the mine has been run by a syndicate of British and American mining companies in tandem with their South African allies, including Anglo American and Gencor. For the companies which are members of the Tsumeb club, the mine has been a wonderful property allowing them to make hundreds of millions of pounds without serious investment of funds. Robert Ramsey, company historian of the US mining firm Newmont, which became the main enabling partner in the coalition, has stated that Newmont's growth into a world-class mining corporation with assets of over a billion dollars was made possible by the stream of dividends from the Namibian mine.[4] He concludes,

> the Tsumeb ore body has inspired such a string of superlatives that anyone not familiar with the property may be pardoned a certain incredulity. Nevertheless it is true that few ore bodies anywhere in the world have been as high grade in as many metals, have contained so many different minerals, have presented so complex a metallurgical problem, yet have proved as profitable as has the Tsumeb ore body.[5]

William D. Banghart, a one-time Tsumeb general manager and later a board member of Newmont, has calculated that Newmont's investment, including all contributions to bring the mine into full production and after the repayment of notes of credit, was no more than £150,000. As Ramsey, the Newmont historian reports, 'Banghart says that no mine he knows of ever returned so large a cash flow for such a relatively small investment as did Tsumeb.'[6]

The name Tsumeb comes either from the Herrero tongue or from Berg Damara and means the green place. The reference is not to vegetation but to the green of a copper outcrop which discoloured like a church roof over years of contact with the moisture in the atmosphere. Because of its age Tsumeb has a special significance in Namibian history. Here, long before the arrival of mining companies from abroad, the local people mined the ores themselves and bartered them to wandering traders from the north. The Ovambo traders walked hundreds of miles south equipped with special baskets to carry the ores, which they exchanged for goods, including tools and metal work smelted from Tsumeb's output.[7]

Tsumeb's eventual encounter with modernity was effected by a mining engineer called Christopher Jones who sailed from Southampton on 7 June 1900 for the British enclave of Walvis Bay, the deep-water port near Swakopmund, which was the German summer capital. The voyage took him three weeks. The next part of his journey, the 350 or so miles from Swakopmund to Tsumeb in the north of Namibia, took him more than twice that time, travelling by ox wagon, on horse and foot.[8] Despite Tsumeb's isolation and the absence of a railway to get the ore out to the sea, Jones was highly enthusiastic about the mine's prospects. 'The mixture of ores constituting the outcrop was wonderful,' he reported to his principals. The mine itself would be dangerous and there was grave risk of lead poisoning. The wages question would need to be handled carefully because 'the boys are perfectly capable of going on strike if wrongly treated. I do not', he added, 'believe in starving hard-working men merely because it is the custom.'[9]

From the ore in sight he predicted there would be a working profit in less than five years of £390,000.[10] This was enough to inspire a burst of corporate activity in London, Frankfurt and Berlin.[11] First, the land rights were registered to a British company in Cecil Rhodes's complex of business organisations, the South-West Africa Company. Then the mining rights were assigned to the Otavi Minen und Eisenbahn Gesellschaft, or OMEG for short, an acronym which the central European mineworkers brought in to develop the mine insisted stood for the first letters in German of 'Our wages are miserable'.[12] With a light railway installed to Swakopmund to take out the ore, the mine was soon doing well, until with South African occupation of the country on behalf of the British crown, production came to a standstill for the duration of the First World War.[13] In 1920, however, the company's mining rights were restored by proclamation and by 1921 operations were in full swing again until in the 1930s the mine was overtaken first by the Depression and then by war.[14]

Under the Allied military occupation of South-West Africa from 1941 to 1944, most of the white mine staff were interned and the mine was put on a care and maintenance basis.[15] During this period A.D. Storke, a consultant engineer and geologist working for the British Ministry of Supplies, visited the mine. Mr Storke's contribution to the war effort was not so all-consuming as to prevent him from spotting the main chance. He studied the records, the machinery and the mine dumps and saw an extraordinary business opportunity. He persuaded first the British mining group Selection Trust and then the American companies American Metal Climax and Newmont Mining to form a coalition to buy the mine in 1946, when the Custodian of Enemy Property for the Union of South Africa put the mine up for sale. There were hurried investigations by a number of parties, but none of them had the insider knowledge possessed by Mr Storke. So in the end the consortium put together by Selection Trust won out with a bid for OMEG of £1,010,000.[16]

The purchasers were enchanted by the rate of return they soon began to enjoy. In the first two years they made profits of nearly £2 million just by treating the dumps of ore left behind by OMEG. The German machinery given so little value prior to the deal was found to be far from ramshackle and with a bit of imagination was soon concentrating ores and producing further excellent profits.[17] Of course there were some expenses. A town of normal family houses had to be built for white employees; roads, offices and smelting equipment had to be put in. But the entire investment came from cash flow and the development of the town, the compound for black employees, the smelter, roads and recreational facilities, were all entirely self-financing from activities at Tsumeb itself.[18] Not a cent came from America, not a penny piece from London. Instead the financial traffic was all the other way.

I drove to Tsumeb along the beautifully surfaced road north from Windhoek to Otjiwarongo. Built for military purposes and running parallel with the narrow-gauge German colonial railway lines and the telegraph poles which mimic them so faithfully, the road runs like an endless strap of liquorice through the landscape. As you travel further north the landscape begins to change, first becoming browner as sandiness gives way to signs of earth, then slowly taking on a tinge of green as you move decisively away from the ecosystem of a desert to the more moist and giving climate of the Angolan border lands, where at least once a year it rains. Just occasionally the road's progress is marked with a small strip of a town for petrol and overnight accommodation. The only other interruptions to my journey were somewhat worrying, if only to begin with. First a handsome and extravagantly hairy baboon as big as any man, who obviously liked to challenge nervous drivers, ran straight out in front of me, causing me to discover skills of avoidance I did not believe I had; then later there was the hallucinogenic vision of a group of giraffes feeding from the tops of some inviting trees. This was such a bizarre and wonderful sight that the giraffes very nearly achieved what the baboon failed to do. The car almost slewed off the road as I stared open-mouthed at the feeding animals. Like the baboon I survived and before long found myself within striking distance of Tsumeb. The road seems to climb as it reaches the mine, anticipating the leap from the enormity of the Namibian horizon to a fully fledged town with signposts, shopping parades and its own hotel. I booked into the Minen Hotel, paid a quick visit to the Tsumeb Museum and then found my way with some difficulty to the house of John and Ann Nendongo, who were friends of Ben Ulenga. Ann was a teacher of English who longed to visit Britain and hear the tongue she had studied for so long spoken on an everyday, demotic basis. John was an electrician who had missed a Tsumeb bursary to become a doctor by some administrative oversight. A man of quiet movements and beautiful manners, I was surprised to find out that in a previous incarnation he had been one of the country's amateur boxing champions. As a skilled and qualified worker at Tsumeb, he had been allowed to live with his family in a house until recently reserved exclusively for whites. But the changes, he stressed, were only at the margins of Tsumeb and affected only those few African workers like himself who had qualifications. Over a supper of fine-tasting African food accompanied by the traditional Ovambo sour-mash drink, John and Ann both vouched for the accuracy of Ben Ulenga's assessment of the Tsumeb compound. 'Tomorrow I will take you to the compound,' he told me. 'After church,' he added.

The Evangelical Lutheran church is in a fine little hall just across the road from the main entrance to the mine compound. There used to be two other buildings here and the union wanted one of them. But the idea of the union having its own office in such a prominent position did not appeal to the Tsumeb Corporation and instead of making use of the buildings they had them knocked down. The church hall is company property, which is not surprising since Tsumeb is a company town in the fullest sense of the phrase. The town grew up because of the mine and every piece of brick and mortar in it from the creamery to the crematorium pays homage to a corporation which likes to signal its presence. Outside the church hall, for example, there are scores of bicycles all carefully parked, each with a neat little Tsumeb Corporation nameplate on the front mudguard. Inside the church there are similar visual cues, with each of the fine wooden benches branded with the initials of ownership – TCL. Somehow the altarpiece and the beautiful handmade altar cloths in purple, gold and white had escaped the mark of the sponsor and my anxiety that the church service would sermonise on behalf of the omnipresent corporation began to subside. The invited preacher, it was soon abundantly clear, was an independent man who made explicit reference to the bitter legacy colonial occupation had bequeathed the land. Besides the lesson (John the Baptist in the desert) the high point of the service was the singing in which everyone joined with enthusiasm, an enthusiasm redoubled for one hymn in particular – 'Prayer because of this time'.

As he was singing, John managed to whisper its title to me, indicating that it was one of his particular favourites. During the choruses he scribbled a hasty translation of one of the verses for me:

> In this our country we have sorrow, blood is flowing,
> Oh Lord forgive us.
> Christ you are the nation's destiny;
> And for all the people
> We pray to you.

For our children,
Lead them, so they can later lead our land.

Protect those who cross the border and bring them back to the
    motherland.
Father you know us, we are oppressed, among other nations.
Oh Lord forgive us.

At the end of the service we moved out of the hall and into the street. On the
pavement opposite the main entrance to the Tsumeb compound we paused
to exchange greetings. Time and again people talked about conditions in the
compound. Daniel Elias, one of the church elders, introduced himself. A fine
man in a striped Sunday suit and with a distinguished head of grey hair, he
explained that he had first come to Tsumeb more than thirty years before
in 1958. He had worked for the company until the strike for the peoples'
contract in 1971 and after that had gone to the fishing and industrial port
of Walvis Bay for better wages. He returned to Tsumeb in the late 1970s
and had stayed ever since. He would like to stay longer and before his time
was up he would like to see changes.

'There was a strike here in 1987, after years of complaining and getting
nowhere. The men made a list of their demands. It is a shaming list and
tells you of our pain and our forbearance. Besides the pitifully low wages,
we wanted the right to live with our families and to build our own houses.
No more do we wish to be the prisoners of the compounds, the people
tucked away in sub-standard housing in Nomtsoub, the company location
built for coloured people and Herreros, where the houses are so tiny, so
roughly made, without proper windows, without toilets and bathrooms.'[19]

John Nendongo took up the story. 'In the hostel people sought an end to
the overcrowding, the bare cement floors, the squalid conditions. We wanted
the provision of electric heaters, beds, mattresses and wardrobes. We wanted
the rooms to be real rooms, with real ceilings so that our living space was not
freezing cold in winter and baking hot in summer. We wanted the food to
be real food, tasty and kind to the stomach, with fresh milk, fresh eggs and
fresh vegetables instead of the poor quality we had been forced to accept
for so long. We wanted better safety underground, proper working clothes
provided free to all, not just the whites. We wanted assurances that people
who got sick or injured as a result of their work would no longer be fired,
cast aside without any compensation as Tsumeb has done for so long. We
sought an efficient ambulance service. We are tired of the situation where

95

sick and injured people are transported to hospital by rail. In all emergencies, whether black or white, we wanted use of the company plane. We wanted also an end to apartheid and white supremacy in all facilities. We wanted better pollution control.

'In 1987 5,000 men struck when the company refused to meet with our representatives, recognise our union and deal with the men's grievances. Only 300 were taken back, the rest sacked. Union leaders were victimised. The union secretary, Ben Ulenga, was harassed and threatened with imprisonment. Yet we had an access agreement and had been on the point of obtaining union recognition when the management suddenly changed from a degree of co-operation to outright confrontation. Essentially they fought to prolong the old ways and they are still fighting to slow down the pace of change. As a result the conditions here in the compound are still deplorable.'[20]

As we moved to the compound entrance with its security gates and uniformed officials, I remembered Robert Ramsey's description of the accommodation at Tsumeb. 'The workers live in clean cool, stucco quarters,' he wrote in 1973. 'Tsumeb represents an accomplishment of which everyone can and does feel proud.'[21] We asked if we might go through and see what comforts the Tsumeb Corporation provided in its compound. But we were firmly refused. 'This is private property, we cannot let you in without permission,' explained the head of security. We retreated and began a visual inspection of the compound from the outside, walking right round its huge perimeter. Within minutes it was clear that nothing here was either proper or secure in the original, uncontaminated meaning of those words. The place was prison-like and artificial to the core, another exercise in human warehousing and social control, a human zoo. As we walked we could see the rooms had no windows, just air vents high in the walls next to the ceiling so no one could see in or out. Near by the compound walls were being extended and reinforced and new, high-tech, military-style barbed wire, a sort of endless coil of tiny but vicious razor blades stirred into a fence, was being put into spaces where the management feared people went in and out without the knowledge of security. Further round, the air vents were being modified with huge quadrangular metal grilles forming a barrier in the shape of the cross of Lorraine. These were being welded on the outside, the idea being to prevent anyone using the gap as a way in or out. Clearly, even in the new Namibia, the Tsumeb Corporation was still not enthusiastic about freedom of movement.

Just as we reached the end of the perimeter, we bumped into David

Kalimba, one of John's colleagues and assistant secretary of the Tsumeb branch of the Mineworkers' Union of Namibia. I asked him if the food was tasty: he looked at me as if I was from another planet and then described a few of the problems. There was tea, bread and jam for breakfast. But there was no question of people having the right to put in their own milk according to their taste. The bread was often old and hard, sometimes very hard. At lunchtime there was only water to drink when a bit of variety, say some fruit juices, squashes and lemonades would be nice, or even a beer or a glass of wine, as was available in the staff club for the mostly white members. In the compound the contract workers even had to buy their own cups. And if you came off shift late after working overtime, which was more or less compulsory, you were lucky to get any food at all. In general the food fell some way short of being agreeable, never mind delicious. There was no proper gravy with the rice; no fresh vegetables or lettuce. The eggs were notoriously bad and known universally as 'last year's eggs' because of the extraordinary odour they gave off when the shell was broken. 'The people who make the food are untrained,' said David, 'and there is no proper supervision.' The meat was poor. 'Sometimes I come there and I am very hungry. But the food looks so poor, the meat cut thin and so scraggy that I lose my appetite.'[22]

The 1987 strike had, David said, resulted in the provision of proper mattresses for the first time and in weekend passes and better leave. The hostel rooms were less crowded with fewer people put into rooms with twelve bunk beds. But on the bottom bunk you couldn't sit up straight and there were still concrete tables and concrete chairs. The rooms were plagued with mice, beetles and scorpions. In the compound there was one television set for 2,000 people. It was slung in a metal cage or riot grille high in the corner of the eating room. There were no recreation facilities with the exception of the one TV, which had the worst picture he had ever seen, so bad it hurt the eyes.

'When you're in there,' David said, 'they clean up around you as you sit or sleep. But the very worst thing is the toilets. They stink and are built on the tank system with no privacy at all. And I tell you you have to be very careful how you position yourself because unless you use your wits and think about balance you could very easily fall in. They say they've abolished apartheid and discrimination here. But I wonder why no whites ever use toilets such as these. I wonder how they would cope. There is a strict rationing of toilet paper too, each of us getting two rolls per month. The problem is that the food is of such a quality that you need far, far more than usual, not this

97

pitifully inadequate allocation. As a result you are using newspapers and magazines on yourself for half the month.'[23]

Denied access by security, I decided to seek an interview with the new mine manager, who had recently been brought to Tsumeb from Zambia, to ask him what he thought of the facilities over which he presided. Much to my surprise he consented to see me and even agreed that I could make a brief inspection of the compound – from the inside. 'If I keep you out,' he said, 'I know from past experience you will get a camera in for video footage or stills.'[24]

A tall and energetic man in his early thirties, young to have charge of a major mine, Peter Kinver comes from Sussex. In his neat office inside the Tsumeb Corporation administration block on the high street, Mr Kinver soon indicated what really excited him about mining. 'We use computers to enhance the satellite pictures of Namibia,' he said with understandable pleasure. 'It's amazing what information this process yields. The photographs are printed to a resolution of 30 metres, then with computer graphics they are scanned in to a resolution of 5 metres and then we look for geological faults. When we have found a promising area, we send in a helicopter so that we can carry out a visual examination of the hotspots. If these are any good, we drill them, recover the cores and find out if we have an economically feasible ore body.

'Seventeen kilometres away we've proved a ten-million ton deposit at the Tchudi mine. If we can prove more we'll have a really exciting mine. There are reserves at Tsumeb for another fifteen years. Our exploration budget is now protected, not something we can only do if we have money left at the end of the year, as was the situation until recently. Now we are looking far more to the long term. But with change coming in the country we want to wait and see before announcing our plans.'[25]

On the human relations front, Peter Kinver also talked a lot about change. 'The whole town has been deracialised,' he stated unequivocally. 'All facilities are racially integrated, clubs, tennis courts, schools, everything.' I pointed out that the appearance of change was important but that only blacks seemed to live in the compounds and only whites seemed to enjoy the comfortable houses. 'Our skilled black employees live with their families in town and we are building more houses. The hostel is for our unskilled staff. But even they could purchase houses if they wanted to.' And had the money, I thought to myself. 'Gold Fields takes the long-term approach,' he went on. 'We invest in our work force, our hostels must be of the highest standard. We have plans to upgrade the compound. We're going to have an entertainment area with electric braais or barbecues. Inside the hostel there will be a one million rand liquor outlet. There is great potential here, potential for incredible growth. At Tsumeb, Kombat and Otjihase mines all of which we own, we have now secured the foundation for long-term growth.'

Bjorn, the new compound manager, took me inside the Tsumeb hostel and showed me round. It was clear within minutes of beginning a proper visual inspection that it was built on inadequate foundations; that it was going to take a lot of 'upgrading' and that even after all the shopfitting and remodelling had been done, it would never be a comfortable or appropriate place for human beings to live in. There were concrete shelves in the hostel bedrooms, now occupied on the basis of six per tiny room instead of twelve; there were concrete bed installations, no lockers or wardrobes and no ceilings, just as the men had said. To remodel them in any substantial way might even cost nearly as much as starting again.

Seeing the Tsumeb compound from the inside it was also clear to me that Ben Ulenga hadn't used his phrase about it being worse than Robben Island for poetic effect. He believed that Tsumeb was worse. Drawing on my own store of images from Britain, the overall grimness reminded me of a Victorian prison or hospital for the mentally handicapped a century after it had been built and long after any serious money was spent to keep up the last vestiges of its original appearance. The layout and architecture were essentially punitive, an embodiment of colonial power and control. The rooms were designed to be watched over not lived in. They had no private space, no windows, no generosity of spirit. The facilities were also severely run down. In Peter Kinver's office the talk about electric braais and a central pharmacy for alcohol sounded mildly progressive. Here inside the compound it was inappropriate, the application of a strip of Elastoplast to a gaping wound in the hope that this would put off the need for serious remedial action.

Tsumeb, it was clear before we were even half-way round, was an institution in profound crisis, sliding downhill and beyond refurbishment or repair. Like the slave plantations of another post-bellum South, it should be scrapped and a fresh start made. The further I went into the compound and the closer I looked, the worse the impression became. The kitchens were tired in appearance just like the food they produced and in parts they were downright insanitary; the food was processed in batches just as the people were accommodated in batches, without the possibility of choice, taste or variety. As if to prove the point, there thundering away as we walked through

99

were giant porridge processors, merging and twisting and turning and in the end producing a tasteless and scarcely edible cement that would bind the human stomach for an hour or two. From time to time there would be some human intervention. A poorly paid, untrained and obviously alienated 'kitchen boy' would step forward to deliver a test stirring to the mealie pap, to judge its consistency and gauge whether or not it was ready. He did this in a novel way – with a large boating oar specially imported for the purpose from South Africa. Besides the pap there were other giant cauldrons of cabbage and meat stew. As a result the air all around was heavy with that strange and singular smell of poor-quality, institutional food.

Beyond the kitchens we came to the dishwashing facilities, a trough that was obviously inadequate given the number of people who were supposed to use the tiny space to clean their dishes. As for the laundry facilities, there were twenty-four sinks for 1,400 men, with cold water only and that from central points. There was one public telephone in the entire compound. Next we went to the shower rooms, which were dirty, crudely designed and built without any consideration for privacy. But worst of all, as David Kalimba had told us, were the toilets, public lavatories with people sitting in blocks of six on pans built like baths with giant baking trays slung over the top. There were no dividing walls and the miners shared odours, sounds and images of one another in varying states of excreting and undress.

I made a crude drawing of the set-up in my notebook. 'Another triumph for white civilisation,' I mumbled as I finished the sketch. My guide, Bjorn, was amused by my reaction and my obvious interest in the 'bath' toilet system, which the men spoke of with such contempt. This design was, he revealed, known in the hostel management trade by its own proper name 'the Springbok'. I paused to digest this piece of information and asked if this was an unwitting tribute to the speed and unusual dexterity of the men in using the lavatory and getting out before the flush went or they themselves fell in.

There is hope for anyone in authority who can laugh at the situation they are responsible for managing and Bjorn laughed long and loud about the Springbok. As a result my respect for him grew, although at first sight he had seemed the stereotyped embodiment of Afrikanerdom, as hard as he was humourless. Usefully built, his accent was strong and his voice guttural, as if used to command, which was not surprising given that he had worked for years as a compound manager in the South African gold mining industry. These outward characteristics had led me to assume that he was a fully paid-up, enthusiastic member of the white tribe, a tough, hard-bitten man who would do little to disguise his paranoid feelings, his opposition to reform and his hatred for 'the blacks'. But after his burst of laughter I began to see the individual behind the contra-indications. I noticed that his manner with black colleagues in the office was relaxed and courteous, at least in front of me. Before long it seemed clear that Bjorn didn't fit the white tribe stereotype; he was a thoughtful, highly intelligent man with an independent mind and a pronounced dislike of public relations' word packages. As we went round the compound, hesitantly at first, then with increasing confidence, he identified some of the critical problems. The living accommodation was sub-standard and beyond repair. In addition the rooms were dirty and no provision for cleaning the dormitories had been made in the past. The miners were supposed to do this themselves – on their day off. A cement floor in a kitchen was unacceptable – it was porous and could never be kept clean, he said. It needed to be grouted and tiled. Upgrading, he underlined, could be a waste of money and he had interceded to stop some piecemeal change, arguing that a few plastic coat-hangers and lockers in the rooms amounted to no more than an expensive lick of paint on a rotting door.

The previous compound manager had recently resigned, and Bjorn had arrived to take a fresh look at Tsumeb from the outside. His predecessor had been resistant to change, fearing and opposing it. As for Bjorn, at the end of his guided tour round the world of the Tsumeb compound, he made it quite clear that what was needed was a new start. Just before I left Tsumeb on the long drive south, Bjorn sat me down for a second cup of tea in his office. 'It's a lot worse here than I thought it was when I came,' he began. 'There is little or nothing of substance here, beyond bunk beds and food. There is no recreation, no community. The Newmont directors came from America once a year, held a meeting and took out of this place as much as humanly possible.

'People here have lost faith. They have no belief in meetings or consultations or negotiations. They've heard it all before. They've worked here, many of them, for fifteen years. They've raised this grievance and that problem repeatedly. They've asked for things, the same things, time and time again and got nothing. They just don't believe in our words any more. All confidence is gone; in essence we must begin again.'[26]

Tsumeb has other problems apart from its warehousing of human beings. The mine is difficult and wet, with men working up to their knees in water; and the conditions in the smelting plant are another serious cause for concern. In 1989 while the Mineworkers' Union of Namibia was trying to obtain a recognition agreement for its members at the mine, carefully built back up again after the best part of 2,000 of them were sacked in the wake of the 1987 strike, the new Tsumeb management persistently declined requests for a proper occupational and environmental health audit. Such an audit provides an opportunity for underlying health problems to be picked up, for equipment to be tested and machinery to be re-examined in an independent way. Denied a comprehensive audit, the Mineworkers' Union of Namibia flew in a Norwegian doctor to make a preliminary examination of the problems that arise in the course of smelting lead (which can poison the blood), copper (which can rot the teeth) and cadmium (which can gravely impair the general health of people working in or living near the plant). In May 1989 with the support of the Norwegian Trades Union Congress and the Ministry of Foreign Affairs, the doctor, Kristian Vetlesen, spent a fortnight in Namibia looking into occupational health problems, particularly at Tsumeb. He made a visit to the mine workings, which he noted were very wet, with a serious risk of flooding. His report on his visit was written up in September 1989 and sent to the union in November. 'In stopes with inadequate ventilation, the humidity together with heat creates heat stress. In the deepest part of the mine, underground rivers float. Miners cross underground rivers with water reaching breast high . . . Appropriate bridge arrangements or at least proper life jackets are not furnished.'[27]

Dr Vetlesen was denied access to the smelter, and was therefore unable to obtain flow diagrams of the smelting and refining techniques or evaluate the character and integrity of the engineering design from a pollution-control point of view. Unable to investigate the causes of Tsumeb's pollution, he began to assess the consequences, some of them very disturbing. He noted that a new filtration system had been installed in 1987, but that nevertheless people were living with their families near the smelter in an area where they were susceptible to lead poisoning.[28] He was worried about the cropping of local wood to supplement coal as a fuel for the smelter. This was done to reduce Tsumeb Corporation's costs and dependence on imports but might, he suggested, lead to soil erosion and climatic change.[29] The local water, which was pumped from the mine, had a poor taste even though it had apparently been purified of contaminants including lead, cadmium, arsenic and diesel oil.[30] Dr Vetlesen was concerned that the water was still contaminated. Local children, who were particularly vulnerable to lead pollution because they were still growing, might be drinking contaminants as well as breathing them in. This could seriously stunt both their physical and intellectual development.[31]

In the course of his visit the Norwegian doctor interviewed and medically examined a handful of Tsumeb workers. A driver from the arsenic plant reported that his work was very dusty. He had to bring arsenic-bearing ash from the smelter, mix it with coal on the floor and move it to the store. Loading the ash was particularly dusty, and when driving out, the driver often felt dizzy, tired and weak. He had a poor appetite and had lost weight during the previous three years. He was also experiencing memory loss and skin problems.[32] Another worker had been transferred from the arsenic-bag house in 1981 because of 'arsenic rash'. But he was simply being moved from the frying pan into the fire. He was reassigned to the copper plant and now removed dust from the hoppers on the boilers in poor conditions, Dr Vetlesen noted: 'forty-five hours a week, eight hours a day and five hours on Saturdays, heavy work – wears respirator with filter. Usually he brings porridge to work, washes hands, dries the hands on the working clothes. The food is ingested on the premises; there are no scheduled eating or resting breaks. March 1989, he was sent on one month leave due to excessive blood lead levels.' The man had lost ten kilos in weight in two years and experienced

Tiredness, loss of memory, confused, loss of movement control, metallic taste, abdominal pains on and off and heartburn, chest pains with blood-stained sputum . . .[33]

The clinical examination reveals an apparently confused person. Frequently he misunderstands the questions posed. There is symmetrically reduced muscular strength in the extremities; an increased fine tremor of the hands . . . the gait is ataxic and insecure. He is clinically suffering from lead intoxication. He has severe symptoms from the central nervous system, an encephalopathy.

Encephalopathy due to lead poisoning, a rare condition in adults, is often irreversible and the most severe forms may be fatal. In March he 'got out of the smoke' for one month. During this period he was on paid leave. He returned to the job without being retested.[34]

Dr Vetlesen concluded that this man, and another in a similarly parlous condition, should be immediately removed from their jobs and be considered candidates for chelation treatment, a therapy used for very severe cases of lead poisoning.[35]

Before summarising the overall results of his work Dr Vetlesen underlined that it was only a preliminary study because his access was so limited.[36] But his investigations showed that 'smelter workers are exposed to high levels of lead and cadmium. The existing occupational health and safety programme is unable to prevent serious intoxications',[37] and his work underlined the urgent need for a definitive audit of the occupational health conditions in the mine and smelter, as repeatedly requested by the Mineworkers' Union of Namibia, and just as repeatedly refused by the company.

The Tsumeb Corporation's problematic health and safety record is also evident at the company's Kombat Mine, fifty-two kilometres south of Tsumeb, where in November 1988 it had tragic consequences, with seven men dying in a wholly avoidable incident following an inrush of water.[38] Kombat had originally been discovered by the German Otavi Mining and Railway Company (OMEG). It had been exploited from 1911 until 1925, when strong flows of water stopped production.[39] The mine had reopened after nearly forty years in 1962 following the discovery of new ore bodies east and west of the old line. The November 1988 inrush began at about 3.10 p.m., when following some blasting work the previous day water seeped through the charge hole. No one checked the blast holes for seepage the morning after the blasting and no specific studies were done to evaluate the risk of an inrush of water at the mine, although a massive underground lake known as the Dragon's Breath was known to be near by.[40] As a direct result of these failures to anticipate hazards and the mine's severely defective communications procedures and warning systems, it took from 3.10 p.m. to 4.25 p.m. to warn the duty manager that a 'massive inrush of blood-red coloured water' had begun.[41] As a result of this failure a gang of one white and six black miners was allowed to proceed downwards from level 13 after the beginning of the inrush. Before they were engulfed they warned others about the water and saved many lives. But the seven men Petrus Kandera, Kativa Kandule, Johannes Katzungo, Wilson Kadumo, Johannes Njimini, Daniel Tjangano and Nils Bjorn van Bratt were never seen again.[42]

The miners' union was kept out of the immediate, on-site investigation after the disaster, but for the first time at the resulting inquest/inquiry the interests of the dead men were protected by a team of lawyers paid for by the black union, MUN.[43] For only the second time in southern African mining history the magistrate ruled that the company was criminally negligent and should have anticipated the problems that caused the seven men's deaths.[44] Besides the failure to inspect the blasting holes, to have a proper emergency plan, water gates and pumping systems and good communications, the MUN team of Edwin Cameron and Andrew Corbet pinpointed another major defect in Tsumeb Corporation's way of working. All three Tsumeb mines – Tsumeb itself, Kombat and Otjihase – were, in terms of the law, denoted as under the control of a single mining manager, Willem Hendrick Stheeman.[45] The three mines were many miles apart, Kombat was thirty-five miles from Tsumeb and Otjihase hundreds of miles away near the nation's capital Windhoek, and it was impossible for one manager to be responsible for three mines. On the day of the disaster, the company official concerned, Mr Stheeman, did not arrive at Kombat until 7 p.m. even though he had been warned about the disaster at 3.15.[46] MUN's lawyers argued strongly that such an arrangement with one remote company official in charge of three major mines was wholly against the spirit of the mining safety laws, which sought to impose clear personal lines of responsibility. The Tsumeb Corporation's arrangement where one person was responsible for three mines was an administrative and economic convenience which, they added, had contributed to the loss of seven men's lives.[47]

At the end of my visit to Tsumeb, reviewing all the evidence of skimping and cheese-paring, my mind turned again to the details of the endless stream of dividends being sent abroad while people slept on concrete-beds, ate inadequate and unpleasant food and risked their lives underground. The work of American researcher Gail Hovey came to mind.[48] Concerned about the behaviour of British and American companies in Namibia during the long years of unlawful South African military occupation, she made some precise calculations as to how much some people, already wealthy and living in comfort in the first world, made out of the poverty and distress of others. Her calculations show that by 1977 on an original investment in 1946 of 2·8 million dollars, and an additional mining and infrastructural investment of only 99 million dollars, most if not all of which was financed from cash flow and cost nothing at all, the Newmont Mining consortium had made metal sales of 1·2 billion dollars from Tsumeb. The annual average rate of return was a staggering 348 per cent from 1950 to 1970 with 90 per cent of all the wealth produced leaving the country.[49] This rate of return is anything from ten to twenty times the best rate of return a mining company would have made even in the generous business climate of the United States and was partly obtained by cutting corners, depriving people of proper food and comfort, dignity and human rights. In the same period the company contributed taxes of only 200 million dollars to the Namibian revenue, most of which was spent on keeping the African population in a state of subjugation so that the exploitation of the country could continue without interruption.

But even this does not give a comprehensive picture of Newmont's financial bonanza because, in addition to properly accounted profits, Newmont had other ways of getting wealth out of the country, and successfully managed to avoid tax payments for years at a time. Despite mineral sales of around 120 million rand a year by the Tsumeb Corporation, the Thirion Report showed, the company had paid no tax since 1980.[50] It achieved this enviable state by buying the Otjihase Mine with its manifold development costs, which it then offset against Tsumeb's profits. The Thirion Commission also fastened on to the Tsumeb Corporation's failure to report to the Namibian authorities the gold and silver content of the blister copper which the company exported for final processing in the United States. The amounts were not insignificant. In 1983 alone the copper sent abroad included 103 tons of silver worth £15 million and 247·3 kilos of gold worth at least £2 million.[51]

In its way Tsumeb is a monument to the colonial scramble for Africa, which continued even after the First and Second World Wars. From 1946 onwards the Tsumeb Corporation and its principals in Britain, America and South Africa enthusiastically exploited the mine, using a particularly harsh version of the migrant labour system. In all the years of the mine, so far as I can see, the biggest single beneficiary seems to have been one man, the geologist and mining engineer, A.D. Storke, who worked for the British Ministry of Supplies and learned enough to know that he could make several fortunes, including a generous one for himself, if he used his information to build a coalition to buy the property. Mr Storke did this and gained a 5 per cent share of Tsumeb for himself in return for an investment of just £15,000. By the time he died Mr Storke's 5 per cent of the mine had given him a dividend income of millions of pounds.[52] (His estate and his heirs continue to draw unearned income from Tsumeb up to the present day.) His allies, the British Gold Fields company, Selection Trust, American Metal Climax, and Newmont Mining, all made fortunes without effort or investment. By contrast the people whose country was turned into a defenceless colony, worked at Tsumeb in poor conditions, endured low wages, grim housing, a polluted environment and the wonders of the Springbok, that patented, trough lavatory and symbol of exploitation. This was their share, the *Uupika* or slavery that went hand in hand with the Tsumeb take-away.

6 Britannia's Fatal Shore: Consolidated Gold Fields Limited, a British Company, and Apartheid

If the institutional cruelty of South African mining began with diamonds, it was refined and brought to perfection in the search for gold. In this process one uncompromisingly British company played a decisive part. The company, Consolidated Gold Fields, was founded by Cecil Rhodes and his business associates in London in 1887; and throughout its century-long involvement in the world of South African mining, Gold Fields viewed itself as an embodiment of Victorian values, British civilisation and enterprise. The company owned the richest gold mines in the country and made spectacular profits from mines like East and West Driefontein, Kloof, Doornfontein, Deelkraal, Libanon, Venterspost and Leeudoorn. With 60,000 black miners on its payroll, the company was the largest British employer in South Africa.

During the years of grand apartheid in the 1960s, during the repression of the 1970s and the resistance of the 1980s, Gold Fields completed a cycle of profitable growth which the Johannesburg *Financial Mail* described as 'unparalleled by a mining house let alone any other group of comparable size in South African commercial history'.[1] In 1986, at the height of this profitable cycle and nearly a decade after the European Community devised a code of conduct emphasising the obligation of all foreign firms operating in South Africa to support human rights, I travelled to Gold Fields' mines on the far west Rand to inspect the compounds, sample the food and gauge the social atmosphere. Soon after I began, it became clear to me that Gold Fields, far from being more liberal because of its British links, was the worst of the major mining employers. While it owned the richest gold mines in South Africa, the British company paid among the lowest wages and was involved in systematic infringements of employees' rights on a daily basis.

107

The infringements included overcrowded rooms, poor furniture and hygiene; inadequate toilet and bathing facilities and bad sewerage in the mines' giant hostels; and bad food in the canteens. Underground ventilation was poor and there was regular pressure for production at the expense of safety. The company offered inadequate compensation to injured workers, relied on dangerously authoritarian disciplinary procedures, routinely engaged in the unfair dismissal of workers and had double standards in the treatment of black and white unions, favouring the latter while trying to suppress the former. The company also, it appeared, intimidated workers by using informers or its own private army, Gold Fields Security, and when necessary supplemented its strength by calling in the South African army and police to keep the lid on the resulting discontent.

I began the process of investigating Gold Fields' business practices on the ground at the Gold Fields West golf club about thirty miles from Johannesburg, near the company's single richest mine, Driefontein. At the golf club the atmosphere was quintessentially British with neat lawns, immaculately trimmed borders and well-set paths reminiscent of Tring rather than the Transvaal. At the clubhouse whites and blacks were evident in more or less equal numbers but in different roles. While the group chairman stated in London that he abhorred apartheid, here on the ground the company's social facilities were run on a strict apartheid basis. The whites were players and the blacks were either waiters or caddies, off-duty miners doing a favour for whites and caddying the clubs and equipment in their spare time. The black miners were dressed in beautifully laundered boiler suits with company flashes on them; and as they raced around the fairways they wore black rubber boots and miners' helmets complete with safety lights. It was an extraordinary sight and it took only a few minutes of questioning to establish that whites and blacks never played together, or ate together or drank together or urinated together or integrated in any other way.

With Gold Fields West ticked off my checklist, I drove into Carletonville, the company town Gold Fields had built to service its mining properties nearest to Johannesburg. The town was also constructed along lines of strict and unyielding apartheid, with blacks allowed into the area only as temporary 'visitors' to wash and cook for white households or trim the hedges and water the ample lawns. Gold Fields had also built the schools in the town on a white-only basis and these were an evocative sight particularly at lunchtime when the children of white miners moved around the playgrounds of the far west Rand in the full dress uniform of an English private school. Religion was organised on a segregated basis. White Christians assembled in company-funded churches which were closed to the black majority for worship. Similarly all the restaurants, hotels and bars of Carletonville were white-only redoubts. The overall atmosphere of the town was one in which the winds of change had never been allowed to blow even once since the British Prime Minister Harold Macmillan visited the area and the Driefontein mine prior to making his famous speech in 1960.

The town did not welcome outsiders. So it was something of a relief later that day to meet an intense young Basotho miner called Moketse Sixtus Mphole. Moketse and his friends Gabriel Hlaele and Justice Sello Tsukulu were to lead me and my determined colleague Steve Bolton step by step through Gold Fields' corporate heart of darkness. In the days and weeks we spent together, Moketse and his colleagues guided us with humour and a degree of controlled irreverence, which I soon realised was an essential stratagem for survival in the Catch 22 atmosphere of any enterprise controlled by Gold Fields. I first met Moketse in 1986 in a dark little room above a clothes shop in Carletonville's main street. When I met him he was one of the few black people who would venture to be seen in the town after dusk. He was involved with the emergent black National Union of Mineworkers, no longer felt isolated and alone, and had sufficient confidence to defy an important if unwritten local convention that the town was off-limits to black miners after dark. The room above the clothes shop where we met was the union's busy makeshift office, with phones ringing in one corner, the clamour of conversation in another and a secretary dealing with paperwork in a third. Moketse and his friends were at the heart of the action. Moketse was a sharp and handsome man aged about thirty-two from Tayatayaneug in Lesotho, who had been working in South African gold mines for about five years when I met him. It was soon evident that he still hadn't got over the shock of leaving his own country with its strong tradition of friendliness and independence and being compelled to live under the extraordinary rigours of the apartheid system as operated by a British company. Indeed, his experiences of racial subordination inside Gold Fields were so painful that initially he found it very difficult to talk to any white person without anxiety.

The whites he knew in the mines, another more forward friend of his later explained, were those who barked commands at him as if he were an inferior being, who ordered him to get their shovel or bring their tea and who might cuff or beat him underground if he got out of line. Understandably he worried that perhaps all whites were like those he worked with and it took

Moketse some time to relax and open his thoughts to me. In one of our initial, stumbling conversations, he explained nervously that Carletonville was named after a Canadian called Guy Carleton-Jones, who came to South Africa to find his fortune, and ended up as Gold Fields' resident director. After delivering this piece of information, he had nothing more to say; and it was only when I started to ask some very simple questions about conditions inside the Kloof compound that Moketse began to respond, slowly at first then speedily in a series of quantum leaps. Troubled by repeated failure to get him going, I asked a specific question about the quality of toilets on the Gold Fields' mine where Moketse worked. Were there still double standards in the provision and condition of toilets at Kloof? Were there doors and cubicles in the black toilets? Still there was no answer. So I asked again in a simpler and more direct form. 'Is there toilet paper in the lavatories? Is there milk for your tea in the canteen in the morning?' Moketse stayed silent, as if he was taken aback, licked his lips nervously and then laughed, loud and long. At first I thought it might be the juxtaposition of questions about milk and toilet paper that had started him off. But on reflection I could see that his laughter was clearly focused, with a separate burst reserved for each subject heading. Then suddenly his laughter subsided and he found his voice. 'Toilet paper in the lavatories . . . Milk in the morning tea? Are you serious, Mister Laurie . . I ask you, are you serious? No . . . the answer is no. No toilet paper, no cubicles, no privacy and no milk for the tea. At Kloof?' he added as if to emphasise his incredulity. Then he burst into laughter all over again. The twinkle in his eye, the friendly asides to his fellow miners, delivered in Sesotho, underlined that there was no sneering in his laughter. He was amazed that a white person should ask him such simple questions about the human ecology of a British-owned mine, and assume that Gold Fields could possibly offer comfort and convenience to its black employees.[2]

I had originally hoped to see the black lavatories at Kloof for myself. The mine was opened in 1968. The plans for it were authorised in London and the first cut of earth for the new shaft was performed by the chairman of the company, Sir George Harvie-Watt, who flew from London for the occasion.[3] But when I tried to obtain permission from Gold Fields' headquarters to enter its compounds, I received a polite but unambiguous refusal from Helene Mendes, the company's head of public relations. We would not be allowed to enter any of its properties. So we had to go slowly, building up confidence, persuading people to take time to talk in detail about their working lives, getting them to paint precise pictures of the conditions we were not allowed to see for ourselves. As Moketse warmed up, another, older man, called Gabriel Hlaele, put down a marker that he too had stories he wanted to tell. 'When he is done with Kloof, I will tell you about Venterspost, another of Gold Fields' mines just along the road from Kloof. And don't forget to ask me about the lavatories there. The Venterspost lavatories are very special.'

Kloof is the richest mine in South Africa in terms of the purity of the gold it produces, according to John Orpen, the mining editor of the Johannesburg *Sunday Star*.[4] But Gold Fields was seeking to deliver maximum short-term returns to its investors in Johannesburg and London and Kloof's development was skimped.[5] It was carried through on a budget of forty million rand, when twice as much would have made a better mine and have allowed more ore to be hauled out. But for this fact, Kloof would have been the most profitable gold mine in the world, instead of being only number two. Nevertheless Kloof is an exceptionally profitable mine, producing a profit of £100 million a year after payment of tax to the government, and promises even greater triumphs in years to come.[6] To win its riches from the earth, Kloof employs 15,000 black miners. They are housed in a grim, barrack-like and heavily guarded compound, while the white miners live near by with their families in the township called Glenharvie. The name is derived from Sir George Harvie-Watt, Winston Churchill's private secretary in the Second World War and one of a number of senior Conservative politicians associated with the British company over the years.[7] With the ice broken, I now had no difficulty persuading Moketse to continue with his verbal Cook's tour of the mine beyond the lavatories. He had few good words to say for Kloof. The facilities were poor, the hygiene inadequate, the beds hard and the food tasteless. Often there would be no meat. The vegetables were almost always overcooked. The offal was dirty and far from fresh, sometimes gritty or even stony and Gold Fields only provided two meals a day, not three like Anglo American or Johannesburg Consolidated Investments (JCI). When it came to food, Gold Fields, he insisted, undercut even a relatively old mine like Blyvooruitzicht a few miles away, where conditions were far from perfect but where the owners, Rand Mines, spent at least 50 per cent more on provisions and delivered tastier and more frequent meals. On the wages front Gold Fields was also the poorest payer, even though it had the most profitable mines. But for Moketse these problems paled into insignificance besides the physical conditions underground and the authoritarian operating procedures favoured by the company. Now that Gold Fields faced a serious challenge from black miners organised in a union, these were being intensified, he insisted.

'Kloof', he told me, 'is a hot, fiery and dangerous place. We've complained time and time again about the heat and the dangers, but nothing gets done. Other mines belonging to different companies are just as deep, but money is spent to overcome the problem of the heat. But at Kloof they just don't seem to care about our conditions. The stope or face where the ore is being mined is very, very narrow, a tight and exceptionally difficult place to work and intensely hot. The drills are big and heavy and frequently have to be worked from a crouched position leaning backwards and pressing hard against the drill handle with your feet. That's the only way you can get the strength to drill. The noise is incredible. The company does not spend money for silencers.' Underground the white miners gave the black migrants a very hard time, he said. 'They treat us like dogs. They drive us, pushing for production all the time, because of course their wages depend on bonuses for how much ore we drill out and send to the surface. They swear at us, using degrading names as a matter of course and are very hard and cruel. In this they are encouraged by the mine management.'

Something about Moketse's eyes and his use of language bore witness to the fact that despite his difficult experiences in the mining industry, he was unspoiled and trustworthy. As I questioned him closely about various aspects of the social organisation of the Kloof compound, which housed about 15,000 miners, it became clear that he was meticulously honest with a real concern to separate fact from gossip, and a desire not to exaggerate or misinform. He seemed to be fuelled by an interesting mixture of oppositional fire and deep, even religious belief in a better, more humane way of living with his fellow human beings. When Moketse described the broken-down toilets, the inadequate shower and washing facilities and the poor hygiene in the canteen yet again, I asked him if he would take some photographs. Moketse was fascinated by the idea of obtaining evidence to back up his allegations about conditions at Kloof, one of the two richest gold mines the world has ever known. We teamed him with a fine black cameraman and he volunteered to drive into the compound and snatch a few shots. Tension mounted as the day appointed for Moketse's induction into the world of photo-journalism approached. When it finally arrived hours passed without news; then the phone rang in the Carletonville office where we were waiting as patiently as our nervous systems would allow. We soon learned the bad news from Justice Tsukulu that they had been caught and turned away. What were we going to do now? We needed visual evidence; but how on earth would we get it? Once again Moketse rose to the occasion, this time with the help of a remarkable new piece of technology, the Video Eight miniaturised camera, which had only just come on the market. We purchased one of these machines, about the size of a personal stereo, which you hold in your fist rather than on your belt, loaded it up and went through a few practice runs and then Moketse was on his own. Five days later we met to retrieve the camera and view the pictures he had obtained.

The tape was as sharp as it was short, showing deplorable conditions in the dining-room at Kloof, dirty preparing tables, vile slop bins, grease-encrusted sinks and disgusting meals. The cramped and inhospitable sleeping quarters were plainly visible. But worst of all was the shower room. There were no cubicles; instead there was simply a big, anonymous room with dozens of crude shower heads poking out of the ceiling, like tulips growing downwards. Once again the design considerations were obvious – throughput, visibility and control rather than human comfort and dignity. So even in the washroom there was no privacy, no provision for storing towels or clothing. Instead, on the second richest gold mine in the world, there was the human equivalent of a sheep dip. Moketse's pictures also caught the toilets at Kloof in their full glory, broken and dirty without seats or privacy; and outside in the compound yard his pictures showed, just as he had said they would, that there was sewage backing up out of the drains and spilling out on to the ground.[8] When I saw these pictures I felt both relief and disbelief – relief that we had at last obtained pictures from inside one of Gold Fields' closed compounds and disbelief that in such a modern mine conditions could be as bad as they obviously were. As we looked at the tape again for a second and third time, more closely and analytically, I couldn't help thinking of a statement by Gold Fields' life president in London, Oundle-educated Lord Erroll of Hale who had been a member of Harold Macmillan's Conservative Cabinet before he became the chief executive of Britain's most famous private-sector mining enterprise. 'Our miners', he had stated, 'are better accommodated than I was at public school when I was a young man. When they have worked for us they are stronger, fitter, better men.'[9]

Moketse had told me a little about how Kloof management and Gold Fields' executives reacted when the black miners, feeling their way towards trade union and democratic freedoms, went on strike over various grievances in 1982, 1984 and 1985. On these occasions troops had been used and thousands sacked and sent home to the labour reserves in a bid to avoid recognition of the union. But if I really wanted to gain an insight into Gold Fields' business methods and human relations I should, he suggested, talk to David Theko Theko. David was an impressive man with a natural gift of leadership, which is why, Moketse speculated, Gold Fields had determined to sack him. I mentioned David's name to Paul Benjamin, the young legal adviser to NUM, the next time I was talking to him on the phone. He laughed and said, 'Oh, I represent him too, in a case for unfair dismissal. And I'll be seeing him tomorrow. I'll ask him if he's interested in having a talk with you.' Forty-eight hours later, David Theko Theko and I were discussing his life in Lesotho and his recollections of Gold Fields over a drink in a Johannesburg bar. He had come to the city of gold from Lesotho for a few days to sort out the final details before he collected his compensation from Gold Fields for unfair dismissal and he still couldn't quite understand how it was that the industrial court president, Mr Bulbulia, had ruled in favour of a black man rather than for the oldest mining house in South Africa.[10]

The main reason for this surprising decision, besides the intelligent way the case was presented by Cheadle, Thompson & Haysom, the union's lawyers, and the fact that the judge was a fair and impartial man, was the obvious double standard in Gold Fields' behaviour towards Theko Theko. In 1985 at the time of the national wage negotiations in the mining industry, Theko Theko was chairman of the union branch at Kloof gold mine. Gold Fields declined to match the wage increases paid by other companies. Not unnaturally this caused disquiet among Gold Fields' miners and they prepared for a strike. On 15 August, a week before the strike was to begin, David Theko Theko and another black employee, Themba Kotyana, were involved in a shouting match about the merits of strike action. The row took place in a lift cage as it moved up the mine shaft. At the height of the argument, harsh words were exchanged. Mr Kotyana twice challenged Theko Theko to a fight, a challenge which the union chairman declined, adding his apologies for the way the argument had got out of hand. Mr Kotyana later came across David Theko Theko at the mine office and assumed, wrongly, that his adversary had laid a complaint against him. He then spoke to a mine official, who advised him to initiate a complaint, which he did. At the subsequent disciplinary hearing only one side of the dispute was presented and Theko Theko was denied representation. Predictably, the hearing resulted in a decision to dismiss the union branch chairman. The mine manager confirmed the decision, which was put into effect immediately.

Theko Theko and the National Union of Mineworkers launched a legal challenge against the less than even-handed nature of the disciplinary hearing, and when the case came to court Mr Bulbulia found strongly in his favour. 'We learn from the old testament', said the judge, 'that the Pharaoh of Egypt did not deny the Prophet Moses, who was slow in speech, the right to be represented by his brother Aaron who eloquently delivered the case of the Children of Israel to the court of the Pharaoh. In this sense the right of representation is of crucial importance especially to a worker who is faced with the prospect of summary dismissal.' It was, he concluded, 'manifestly unfair to punish the one and let the other go scot-free'. Defeated in court, Gold Fields declined to reinstate David Theko Theko and insisted, as the law allows them to do, on financial compensation rather than proper fulfilment of the industrial court's order.

From the description of Kloof that David Theko Theko gave me it was clear that he could not have survived in the mine without a considerable supply of intelligence and guile. At Kloof, he explained, there was a culture of violence. A fair number of white miners carried guns and other weapons underground; and, although this was against mining regulations, nothing was done about it. From time to time one of them would threaten a black miner with a weapon. Others, whom he named, preferred straight hand-to-hand physical violence, which they directed against blacks who angered them, misunderstood their instructions or made a mistake. Although such patterns of behaviour and the identities of the individual perpetrators were well known to senior management, nothing was done to stamp out the violence; and, in Theko Theko's view, the pattern for the authoritarian culture of the mine was set at a very senior level in the company. 'Gold Fields', he told me, 'has always been very anti-union. For those of us who are active in building up the union, there may be disciplinary action or even dismissal. But this is only one part of the tough regime they impose upon the black miner. The whites run everything and wield all authority. But they do very little underground. Black team leaders and black miners do the serious work, blasting and drilling, supervising in the stopes, bringing down the bad hangings, while the whites sit on boxes and read their newspapers. The push for production of ore is very great with inducements all the way down the line, watches and cheap blankets for black workers, television sets and even brand-new cars for the whites. One day at Kloof we saw that literally dozens of new cars had been delivered in fulfilment of the bonus scheme for whites. There was great distress and anger in the mine that day, because truly it is black miners who do all the work.

'The mine management', he continued, 'are like an occupying power, working to impose their will upon us and consciously trying to keep us in our place. This came out strongly during the hearing of my case in court.' The company's lawyer spoke of the mine as being an explosive place, where without management intervention there would be grave social problems. 'Faction fighting is part of the history of mining in this country,' he told the court. 'Gruesome and macabre tales of murder, killing and looting are a common refrain. These people are mostly illiterate and uneducated. They are hundreds if not thousands of miles from home. They are superstitious and fearful. They are a tinderbox waiting only for the appropriate spark to send them into a surging flame of unrest and devastation, spreading to other mines with consequences too horrific to contemplate.'

David Theko Theko deplored this explicit head office endorsement of racism. 'It is this which has helped to inspire such cruelty and arrogance in the white miners. They do not treat us as individuals because they do not see us as individuals. They use us as a muscular force and are deeply frightened that the day is coming soon when we will be organised enough to transform the system with which they manipulate and intimidate us.'[11] David Theko Theko had a wife and four children back in Lesotho. Despite Mr Bulbulia's finding, he never got his job back again and was blacklisted on all Gold Fields' mines, a fact that neither surprised nor worried him. He would find another job elsewhere in the industry, he felt sure, and hopefully in a kinder and more considerate environment. The union would rise again at Gold Fields, he believed, for a straightforward and simple reason – conditions were oppressive.

I left David and drove back out to Carletonville to pick up Gabriel Hlaele, another man who had solid information about conditions in Gold Fields' mines. Because, outside Johannesburg, in a mining area like Carletonville, there was no bar where a black and white man could have a quiet drink together without exciting local opinion, I bought a couple of tins of lager, met Gabriel at the appointed place and then drove with him along the approach road to Gold Fields' Venterspost mine, where he lived and worked. He showed me the A and B compounds with their interminable walls and tight security around the single entrances. He described the food, the layout of the rooms, the poor provision of bedding, the inadequate washrooms, substandard cooking facilities, and then turned to the subject which really concerned him – the Gold Fields' toilets. At first I did not grasp what was so special about provisions at Venterspost. Once again, Gabriel confirmed there were no cubicles; once again there was no privacy; once again there were difficulties with the supply of toilet paper; once again the toilets were not cleaned often enough; once again white civilisation had some small room for improvement. But by now these deprivations had become a commonplace to me, a settled and expected pattern. Then the penny dropped. Here at Venterspost, it wasn't just that there were no cubicles around the lavatory pans. Here the heady mixture of a modern business, apartheid and the Gold Fields' central architects' department had devised a very special confection, deserving of a prominent mention in the annals of South African mining history. Here at Venterspost there were no individual toilet pans at all. Instead these had been fused into one vast object, a sort of gigantic goldfish tank for the collection of human detritus. As Gabriel patiently explained, the commonplace of individual pans had been done away with altogether and the lavatories arranged in sets of eight or ten, with primitive holes formed in a vitreous enamel worktop which was in turn laid over a bath-type arrangement. Underneath there was one continuous flow of water, sweeping the output of each 'individual' toilet together into a common current of human waste.

As Gabriel outlined the nature of the Venterspost lavatories for the second or third time in deference to my paranoia about getting a single, tiny detail wrong, I felt certain that no one would believe his evidence unless we obtained pictures of the offending item. I explained my fears and he said, 'I've already thought of that. One of my room-mates is very much at ease with the camera. Let's give him a film.' A few days later we met to scrutinise the results. The first prints were of conditions underground, and showed the poor wooden pit props, the confined working spaces and the generally unsatisfactory conditions. Next came pictures of the grim dormitory rooms. Then last of all were the lavatories.[12] I looked at the pictures with astonishment, and could understand why Gold Fields declined to let anyone enter their compounds. As my mind drifted off to contemplate the extent of the disregard for human comforts and human rights that Gold Fields' primitive communism of the latrine involved, I found a bizarre form of relief in imagining the meeting at Gold Fields' head office where the design brief was drawn up for these extraordinary objects. What I couldn't figure out was the purpose such a design was supposed to serve. Quite apart from the degraded conditions they embodied, they surely didn't take any less cleaning or need any less water. And then it occurred to me that the design had nothing to do with saving money or water. This arrangement was about power pure and simple, control, ease of supervision, and the denial of private space in case unrest or human sexual feelings should ever flourish there.

Gabriel and his friend the photographer could see that I was taken aback by the Gold Fields' lavatories. Gabriel told me that he too had been shocked when he first saw them, adding that he still found them deeply offensive. 'There's worse than this, you know,' he added matter of factly. 'Acclimatisation is worse than this . . . You will be aware', he began again after a short pause, 'that when you first come to any gold mine on a contract, you must be acclimatised. You are not allowed to go straight down below. You have to go to the acclimatisation chamber and there for hour upon hour, five hours a day for five days you will run up and down on the spot, stepping lively up and down a flight of five concrete steps, up and down, up and down, to the monotonous beat of a drum.'

I had read of the special fear black miners have for acclimatisation chambers in *Another Blanket*, the powerful pamphlet produced by the South African church group, the Witwatersrand Agency for Industrial Mission. But according to the Chamber of Mines the heat chambers and the acclimatisation process are the indispensable tools of responsible employers, a sort of powerful sauna devised to protect black miners from collapse due to heatstroke below ground in the stopes. But, as Gabriel was at pains to point out, few blacks feel that the system in use throughout the South African gold mines is really necessary and, even if it does have some sense to it, an infinitely more humane set up could be designed – in consultation with the miners themselves.

'Miners from the Venterspost mine', Gabriel said, 'people coming back from holiday, sickness or simply taking a new contract, have to acclimatise at Kloof's special chamber. I want to tell you a bit more about the acclimatisation chamber. I mean what really goes on,' he continued, 'not what the doctors and mine managers and the directors in Johannesburg and London say goes on, but what really happens.

'You are stripped right down, maybe with a shaggy towel around your middle to absorb the sweat, or sometimes a head-dress, like a boxer in training. You have to run up and down. But it's what happens when you collapse that I want to draw to your attention – and lots of people collapse, by the way. Then, you get your temperature taken in the medical anteroom. Of course it's not a doctor or a nurse who attends to you there. It's a medical orderly, a company employee or cog in the machine who shows you as much consideration as he would a dog.

'Now Kloof is a big mine with 15,000 workers and every day there will be fifty or more men in for acclimatisation in the heat chambers. If you faint you get your temperature taken in two places. First the mouth, then the anus. But this is Gold Fields, remember. Everything here is planned and organised along military lines with strict rules and regulations over which we have no say. I imagine that they believe it would be wasteful to have too many thermometers. I don't know. But for whatever reason the thermometer that measures the temperature in your mouth is also the thermometer that measures the temperature in your anus. And they don't throw the thermometers away, you know. There isn't a new one for every different individual. Oh, no. The thermometer goes from my mouth to my anus and then via a little dip in a dish of Dettol, into someone's else's mouth and anus.'[13]

I wanted to put Gabriel's picture of the Kloof acclimatisation system to Gold Fields' corporate executives. But they declined to comment.

Summarising his experiences at Kloof, Gabriel said, 'We don't like these conditions, you know. We don't respond kindly to such treatment. Our generation, we notice what goes on, we know there's another way. Frankly we can't quite comprehend how a British company could have treated us like this.' Gabriel's reserve and fear of whites had gone and he was in full flow. 'In Lesotho we have our own country, a member of the British Commonwealth, the former British protectorate of Basutoland. We are very poor, but we are free. It is our country and our families till the land there. It is our misfortune to be totally surrounded by South Africa, a land which has long sought to incorporate us wholesale in their system of white domination. We have avoided that fate and just about hung on to our national and political independence. But we have to come here for work, across the Caledon River into the Orange Free State and on to the Rand, near Egoli, Johannesburg, the City of Gold.

'Can you imagine how it feels to stand in line for their dirty slops of food? Can you imagine how it feels to have to strip naked in front of your elders for a medical examination of your pulse, your penis, your ears and your rectum, lined up for the careless glances of an overworked white company doctor who might as well be inspecting meat in a slaughterhouse for all the consideration he shows you? Can you imagine what it's like night after night in the uncomfortable beds in the barrack-like hostels? Can you imagine the loneliness you feel away from your wife, children, loved ones, denied the sound of a bird, a pet of any kind, watched over and manipulated, day after day and night after night? This . . . this is a system of slavery,' he stated carefully, with the emphasis on the word 'is'.

'We cannot choose which mine we go to. We cannot bring our families. We cannot even invite our friends to visit us in our rooms. We cannot have meetings. We have no freedom of speech or assembly. And all of it is so unnecessary, for these mining companies are piling up such quantities of wealth. Can you understand how the anger burns in my generation and even more so in the ones younger than me? Can you understand what our fathers and mothers went through? Can you understand that we just cannot go on living like this, that unless real change comes there will be an almighty explosion?'

Gabriel paused, silent, empty. A minute or two later he rediscovered his tongue and added that the next time he took me to view the Venterspost compound, he wanted me to look for the identification numbers and letters on the roof, positioned, he told me, so that the helicopters of the South African army and police could move in quickly in the event of a dispute and find the centre of the storm. 'Do you think it's nice being a sleeping and a sitting target,' he asked, 'with keepers all around you like animals in a zoo?'

Gabriel Hlaeie, aged forty-eight, with thinning hair, laughing eyes and a fine generous smile. An ideal witness – a devout Christian, born in Lesotho in 1942, married in 1968, with three children, he had been a policeman in his own country for some years until, with his first child on the way, he sought employment on the mines in the hope that he could earn more and provide more adequately for his family. Gabriel was married to the sister of the king of Lesotho, a family connection which should have stood him in good stead in his home country except for one fact – the then chief minister took a dislike to him and suspected him of oppositional tendencies. Like virtually every other able-bodied male in his country, Gabriel had had to leave home to support his family. He listed their names fondly, with an obvious tinge of sadness and longing as he spoke – Victoria aged seventeen, Anna aged fourteen, and Vincent aged eleven. Gabriel saw his wife and children for an average of one month a year. I asked him how much he missed his children and in a quiet way he explained he missed them very deeply, and yes in anticipation of my next question he would like to live with his wife and family in Carletonville where we stood or in Johannesburg thirty or so miles away or in a new city somewhere in between which would be built one day for the miners who wanted to live permanently in the area. Gabriel was sure that this would happen in time. For himself it couldn't come quickly enough for he was tired of living as a migrant, a foreigner denied the full fruits of citizenship by a highly profitable British company which used him as a labour input, the human equivalent of an Ever Ready battery in the power supply of white South Africa.

*   *   *

With Gold Fields refusing us access to any of their mining properties, we were forced to cultivate a much wider range of unofficial sources. One of them was a truly fearless and remarkable young man who for the purposes of protecting his identity, still necessary even today in the transition channel between the old brutalities and a new society, I will call Peter. By contrast with Moketse Mphole, Gabriel Hlaele and David Thcko Theko, Peter mixed easily with whites. Born to a family of some position and economic power in Bophuthatswana, the picture puzzle part of South Africa which the apartheid government first split into fifteen pieces and then pretended was one 'independent black homeland', Peter had started his working life in Johannesburg. Billeted in Soweto's Dube Hostel, he loathed the cramped and alienated lifestyle, the poor conditions and bad food, and resolved to find a way out. He found a job at Gold Fields' head office, where he was one of a succession of family members who had worked devotedly for the company over the years; and there he earned enough to share the rental of a little house in Soweto. Educated and highly competent, in any democracy he would have gone far. Thwarted by the atmosphere of the Gold Fields' head office, Peter found pleasures and compensations in Johannesburg and its twin town and dormitory, Soweto. He loved the cityscapes, made friends easily, liked to sit in a bar for hours and discuss the meaning of life and he took it for granted that we were trustworthy given that we had letters of introduction from Cyril Ramaphosa and from Peter Heathfield, respectively the secretaries of the South African and the British NUM. Within days of our first encounter, Peter was taking huge risks on our behalf and pointing us in the direction of interesting information, knowledgeable people and vital documents.

I still remember our feeling of amazement when he produced the first batch of confidential internal material from Gold Fields' head office. On the top of the pile was a copy of Gold Fields' closed-shop agreement with the racist White Mine Workers' Union. An inordinately lengthy and ponderous document, it contained clause after clause defining the company's interest in helping the union and the union's interest in helping the company. In return for securing the white miners' agreement to be the capos in the camps, the company conceded a classic sweetheart deal, deducting union dues by check off, using only agreed, fair and bilateral disciplinary procedures and agreeing without reservation to sack anyone who was expelled from the union.[14] I was shocked by this document for it showed that the self-same industrial relations department and board of directors who were working overtime to resist the black NUM were tucked up neatly in bed with the exclusive brotherhood of racial extremists led by Arrie Paulus.

Next in the pile was a long background briefing, Confidential Industrial Relations Report No 2 for December 1984, on 'how to deal with' the growing strength of the independent black union NUM. This, the document noted, had 'progressed from a weak bargaining party to a union with significant negotiating and industrial clout'.[15] Among the tactics suggested in this document were threats of dismissal, eviction of strikers with families from company houses, the refusal of re-engagement certificates (which black miners need to return to their jobs after a break at home), the granting of special payments or bribes to bolster support for the management, insistence that the Mine Security Force and the armed Gold Fields' Security Force would be used, a flat refusal to feed strikers although, since they lived in compounds, they had no other source of food, and a flat refusal to heed the union's plea to close the liquor stores at a time of stress and tension. The company's strategy of moving from what it called a 'soft' to a 'full blast' information campaign was clearly set out, as were details of its secret negotiations with the South African Police.[16]

Most interesting of all for journalists looking desperately for images to flesh out an investigation, was reference to a video presentation used at Kloof in a bid to unsettle the miners and reinforce the message that those who went on strike would be sacked even if the strike was legal. When we asked Peter if he could obtain a copy for us, it was clear from his reaction that he was way ahead of us and already had feelers out to see if he could get hold of a copy. The next time we met, as soon as we had settled to our table, he reached into his briefcase and brought it out. 'Here's your video. Your viewers will enjoy this,' he said, shaking his head knowingly. How right he was. The video used cruel images of hunger, unemployment and poverty in Africa to reinforce the company message that supporting the union could cost you your job. The pictures from Lesotho, home for many of the miners, were particularly shocking, and the use of images of the hungry not to help the poor, as in Bob Geldof's Live Aid, but to help the supremely wealthy mining companies, was offensive. The presenter, a black man working for the Chamber of Mines, was a curious mixture of Big Brother and Uncle Tom. 'Times are bad, jobs are difficult to get. You don't want to be one of those men who have no job and no money. Look after your job and ensure that your family never has to suffer from being hungry.' After a suitable pause for emphasis, Brother Tom added, 'Do nothing foolish, there are many others waiting for your job if you lose it.' Another pause followed ahead of the punch line. 'Think about it,' he added, with a patronising wink.[17]

Peter's value as a source was extraordinary. Supremely alert to the value of hard documentation to any investigation of a secretive corporation like Gold Fields, he was also a keen observer of the institutional tennis at Gold Fields' sumptuous headquarters in Fox Street, Johannesburg. This is a prize-winning building designed by one of South Africa's most famous architects and a shrine to corporate endeavour, made of fine materials, with a superb galleria, open-plan offices, beautiful wood panelling, splendid natural light and a prize-winning collection of pot plants. But Peter saw behind the power shopfitting. He knew the wage rates paid to the night watchmen who guarded corporate headquarters from dusk to dawn. They were, of course, incredibly low and the men had to live in Soweto's notorious Dube Hostel. Peter also knew the feeding arrangements for the porters and cleaners – they ate the refried leftovers from the directors' dining table a day later. He knew of all the loyal black clerks and employees who had been passed over for promotion in favour of blue-eyed boys with different skin tones. He remembered how blacks were forbidden to read newspapers in the office, whereas no such prohibition applied to whites. He knew the model numbers and engine ratings of the new company cars acquired for Robin Plumbridge and the other head men of the corporation and compared the tens of thousands of pounds spent on these executive toys to the parsimonious cheating that went on over industrial injury payouts or long-service pensions to people who had a tiny break in service. He knew how the British directors exercised their continuing and ultimately controlling influence in the company; he knew which security officers were sent to England for training or to purchase ammunition. Not that Peter was a cardboard cut-out 'disloyal employee'. He had wrestled with his conscience and, confronted on a daily basis by the double standards of the organisation he had hoped to serve, he had become a dissident who discovered other deeper affinities he felt he had to obey. Peter was in short an instinctive guerrilla fighter in the battle for freedom of information; and his greatest quality of all was his belief that the information should be brought into the public domain. For this, for the public interest, he was prepared to put his job on the line.[18]

At our next meeting he handed over another batch of documentation, every bit as meaty as what had gone before. A copy of the April 1984 minutes of the quarterly meeting of Gold Fields' mine managers showed that Moketse, Gabriel and David Theko Theko were absolutely right about

Gold Fields not doing enough to combat the intense heat in their mines, among the deepest and hottest in the world. The subject came up during a discussion about raising productivity, in the course of which one of the mine managers pointed out that there were all sorts of institutional and technical obstacles which stood in the way of corporate goals being realised. 'Managers', he explained, 'need support from head office when requesting capital to improve conditions. In the past insufficient capital has been allowed for refrigeration.' Many working stopes or places, the document continued, were inordinately hot, some even measuring 32 degrees Centigrade on the special Wet Bulb scale of temperature for measuring humidity as well as heat in deep mines. This was a full four degrees Centigrade above the supposed standard of 28 degrees, a dangerous and unacceptable state of affairs which made a mockery of talk about acclimatisation and heat control. Worse still, the document disclosed, 'Some mines do not have sufficient pumping capacity or water to utilise their designed refrigeration capacity.'

The ensuing discussion produced other interesting comments. 'Although planning has improved over the last few years, there has been a lack of planning in the past. . . . Group planning is five to ten years late.'[19]

Also included in the bundle were two documents relating to Gold Fields' Doornfontein mine, another highly profitable property situated towards the western end of the West Wits Line. Doornfontein had 9,000 black workers warehoused sixteen or twenty to a room. The first Doornfontein document Peter obtained for us was the public relations handout given to tourists visiting the mine to see the glamour of gold. It was a valuable compendium of statistical information relating to the mine and a touching homily to the alleged excellence of the facilities and food. 'The diet', it reported, 'is planned scientifically and has a food value of four thousand five hundred calories per person per day . . . Black employees are far better fed in the hostel than in their homes.'[20] Peter had helpfully included another confidential document from Doornfontein. Dated May 1986, this was a report to head office about the various grievances raised by workers at number three shaft. Peter thought it showed the gap between public relations' statements to white tourists and the private realities of eating in Gold Fields' Doornfontein compound.

There is plenty of food in the kitchens, but the people are blaming the cooks as they do not like the way it is cooked. Because the cooks are not properly trained, some food is spoilt and far from delicious . . .

They queried the cooking of hard porridge and fish on the same day as both are hard ... They stated that it was slavery to expect men to sit and finish everything they had taken, especially as the men have no children or dogs to help them finish their food.[21]

This last complaint referred to one of the most extraordinary of Gold Fields' many authoritarian practices. Monitors or prefects were appointed on an ethnic or tribal basis, mirroring the way the workers were housed in compounds, to patrol the canteen during mealtimes making sure the men ate everything. The capos took their authority very seriously it would seem. A number of Doornfontein miners told us that the monitors forced people on pain of discipline to eat everything on their plates, even if this was grit from the offal, discoloured or rotten parts of the fish.[22]

The Doornfontein documents also detailed another serious problem at the mine which, like the poor food, was kept quiet – cockroaches. These insects, which are a sure indication of poor hygiene, had obviously taken a firm grip at Doornfontein, which was why the management meetings were spending time on them. According to the minutes a Mr McClure suggested that the hostel should be responsible for disinfestation, not outside contractors, because this would mean that one block at a time could be decontaminated rather than everyone being thrown out of their rooms at the same time on the same day. According to the minutes a Gold Fields' company doctor called Dr Lowe joined the discussion. 'He ... said that as cockroaches did not carry disease, one should not panic about their presence, the problem of which will be with us ad infinitum.'[23]

Peter speculated whether the doctor would have reached a different conclusion if the roaches had been found in the directors' dining room at Fox Street or at the white Doornfontein club.

Beneath the document about cockroaches, which he jokingly suggested might be an accidental enrichment of the scientifically prepared diet at Doornfontein, Peter had slipped in two other documents, a photocopy of a duplicated pamphlet written for learner officials (a job category blacks were barred by law from entering) and the book-length induction module recently prepared by Gold Fields' Training Services for new white recruits. On examination, the documents showed that as a company Gold Fields was deeply involved in propagating and promoting ethnic prejudice and supremacist ideas. The two documents in use in 1986, long after the chairman of Gold Fields claimed that apartheid was a thing of the past in his company, contained the following statements:

The Bantu believes in the spirit world and performs certain rites to keep him in good luck. Nearly all these rites are accompanied by the spilling of blood from an animal like a cow or a fowl, preferably white in colour . . .

Keep off larking with him. His father would never do that and you are in the place of his father . . .

Because of him resting most of the time he is more emotionally inclined . . . Classical music does not appeal to him, he will go for jazz and soul music. If a bar is repetitive it will not bore him. In fact the more it is repeated the more engrossed he becomes. Thus repetitive jobs do not bore him. He will compose a song to go along with them . . .

The black when wanting to discuss anything of importance cannot just raise the subject and get to the point.

A Bantu will always give an answer which he thinks will please another person . . .

Being emotionally inclined the black will go for anything that will make people admire him.

He expects to be given responsibility. He is so touchy about this need that he will turn to a witch doctor to cast a spell so that he might not be deprived of it.[24]

When my colleague Steve Bolton and I first read these documents we were amazed to find such a dangerous mixture of racial shibboleths in the official training publications of any major mining company, never mind one which prided itself on its British connections, boasted of its extensive educational activities, spoke – at least in recent company meetings in London – of its 'total opposition to the political, social and economic consequences of apartheid', and announced itself as a model of corporate behaviour worldwide. But there they were in black and white. Peter was not so surprised. He had come to believe that there was a hard, cruel and authoritarian side to the business organisation whose ranks he had joined in Johannesburg. This meant, he insisted, that they not only promoted racialist ideas, but co-operated closely, very closely, with the armed forces of the apartheid State.

'Can you show us how closely?' I asked. Peter said that he would need a little time because this was an especially sensitive area. However we should take a look at Gold Fields Security and their headquarters and training camp up at the company's old Luipaardsvlei gold mine. 'Gold Fields Security, what's Gold Fields Security?' we asked in unison. 'They . . . are the heavy mob,' replied Peter. 'Anglo American won't have anything

126

to do with them, but they provide the guards and security for all the other mining companies and half the factories and offices in Johannesburg. With the state of emergency and the revolt in the townships, the police and the army are at full stretch. They have about six thousand men on their books, teams of savage dogs, armoured cars, tear gas and rubber bullets. Essentially Gold Fields Security undertake to keep the lid on in the mining compounds so that the police and the army are free to operate elsewhere. That's how I see it, anyway.'

7   Defence of the Realm: British Business and the Security of the White South African State

The operational headquarters of Gold Fields Security is discreetly located at the old Luipaardsvlei gold mine sixteen miles west of Johannesburg, and you can get to the outside edge of its ample training grounds, barracks and supply centre more or less directly by an old mine road. After a certain distance the private property signs appear with increasing regularity and as a result our initial recce became an unnerving affair. As we came upon the first of the inner security fences it seemed unwise to go further by car even though the gate was unlocked. We tucked the car just off the road behind some bushes and away from the video cameras, real or imagined, so that it would not attract attention. Out in the open we took deep breaths and surveyed the surveillance, which was beginning to feel serious if only because we were feeling the stress of having operated for weeks under the national state of emergency, in which the reward for foreign journalists caught doing their job was an assisted passage home. Then Lawrence the cameraman had a simple and inspired idea. He had noticed that the Luipaardsvlei security headquarters nestled among a circle of mine dumps and was protected more or less on every side by these man-made mountains of ancient mine sand. If we could get high enough up one of the dumps, he pointed out, we would be able to see into the heart of the operations centre. Relieved by this piece of lateral thinking, we stumbled our way through a veritable moonscape of golden slime and sure enough at the end of our journey, just as Lawrence had predicted, we could see the heart of the Gold Fields Security centre in all its glory.

On a first glance past the barricades of security fencing with their multitude of miniaturised razor blades set in coil, we saw lines of military vehicles filling and fuelling up. Away to the left were a clutch of Caspirs, armoured boats on wheels, sinister, surreal and specially designed by the State arms procurement agency Armscor to avoid mines in the bush. Then there were little groups of men marching with their dogs, which they released when they reached a certain point. The animals took their cue perfectly, transformed from passive patrol dogs, moved into attack mode and rushed off to savage the grotesque dummies used by Gold Fields to train the animals in the company's distinctive brand of last-resort personnel management. Beyond the dogs were huddles of men on a parade ground, some dressed in brown paramilitary uniforms with black combat boots and peaked caps; others, much more numerous, wore olive-green combat fatigues. Suddenly they became animated, formed into platoons and started drilling at breakneck speed, the heels of their boots answering to the barked orders of the drill sergeants with a crunching uniformity of sound and what seemed like the occasional spark. Overall, even from a distance, we gained the impression that Gold Fields Security meant business and if it had its way in the mines, then metaphorically the trains would certainly run on time.

On a second visit, we got an even better view of operational activities, at first through the powerful 50 to 1 zoom lens on Lawrence Jones's film camera, then later from closer still as another and entirely unexpected company of Gold Fields Security troopers marched right up to us from the rear and then doubled past our car in military formation, one two, one two, squad, by the right quick march. We were petrified as they came within feet of where we were sitting, our hearts momentarily on parade too. For Lawrence, a cheeky Mancunian with as much bottle as a fleet of milk floats, was quietly filming their progress. The tension was such that the gentle whirring of the film running through the gate on the camera sounded like a nuclear-powered car alarm; and since the window was open to increase the picture quality the noise was being publicly broadcast. If our recent experiences were anything to go by, the soldiers would surely notice. Our sense of fear was more developed than usual because we had just had a narrow shave at Gencor's Marievale Mine. There, two days before, we spent several unhappy hours in the company of mine-security officials and had fully expected to be thrown out of the country for taking some shots of a mine where a plan to harm a union activist had recently been uncovered. Thankfully our luck held first at Marievale and then again at Luipaardsvlei. The Gold Fields Security troopers marched right on past our hired car and into the camp, disappearing out of view just near a large corporate signpost, which confirmed among other things that Gold Fields Security had a sense of history. It announced in Latin that the company took its British origins and Baden-Powell's militaristic boy scout injunctions very seriously and was 'SEMPER PARATUS – Always Prepared'. The signpost was conveniently placed for Lawrence, who finished his shot with the paramilitaries neatly clearing frame against a British company's Latin motto.

At this sign from the gods, we retired for the night and looked forward with keen anticipation to our morning meeting with Peter, who had first told us about Gold Fields Security. We were feeling pleased with ourselves and wanted to tell him that we'd got some pictures of Gold Fields' finest in action. Sure enough, when we met the following day, he was delighted with our achievement. 'I'm very glad you got those pictures,' he said nonchalantly, reaching into his briefcase, 'because this is a very special kind of organisation you're dealing with, as these documents show.' At this point his serious face broke into a beaming, almost comic smile and he suddenly pulled a great sheaf of paperwork up from beneath the table and set it out in front of us for examination. The first documents in the pile revealed the serious anxieties of Gold Fields of South Africa's finance chief, B.R. van Rooyen, the executive director, Colin Fenton, and the company chairman, Robin Plumbridge, about the growth of black trade unions in the country. What worried them most was that Gold Fields Security employees, who were far from generously paid, might experience a conflict of loyalties and seek to join a black union. The company's preferred solution to this dilemma, the documents made clear, was to lobby forcefully at Cabinet level for an exemption in the new Labour Relations Act to deny these workers the new freedom to organise. But the government wouldn't play ball and the Gold Fields directorate were working hard to devise an alternative policy based on those old Gold Fields stand-bys of spying and intimidation to keep mine security free from the unwanted incursions of democracy.[1]

Besides the exchange of letters and position papers on this problem, Peter handed us two other sensitive background papers on the origins, structure and role of both Gold Fields Security and another organisation the State had fostered on the mines. This was the Mine Security Reserve (MSR for short), the shadowy and heavily armed élite force of ultimate resort set up on a white-only basis at every mine in the country. Both documents had the Gold Fields Security 'Always Prepared' emblem on the cover and were classified as 'Restricted'. In both cases the covers also carried the warning that 'The contents of this document are NOT to be communicated either directly or indirectly to the Press or to any person NOT authorised to receive such information.' If he had been caught copying these documents or handing them to a foreign journalist at a time of national emergency, Peter would have lost more than his job. In the over-heated atmosphere of the South

African security State he might well have been jailed for effecting such an unauthorised disclosure. But Peter made no mention of this. Like the Polish dissidents who cleared the way for Solidarity, he seemed to have decided that an unfree society could only be effectively challenged if some people started living freely.

We found an extraordinary array of information had been given to us in the documents by this courageous and unusual man. Perhaps most interesting of all was a secret background paper on the predecessor organisation for Gold Fields Security, the Mines Security Force. This began with a historical résumé which put Gold Fields at the centre of policing the migrant labour system from its inception. Gold Fields Security turned out to be a recent, privatised version of an old mining-house police force set up in 1902 after the Boer War, called the Mines Police Organisation. This had patrolled compounds, searched visitors, broken strikes and kept black unions out of the industry for many decades. In a series of changes in the late 1960s and early 1970s, the document explained, the force had been modernised, renamed the Mines Security Force and brought under the managerial control of a private company called Gold Fields Security. This operated on a cost-recovery rather than profit-seeking basis so that it became acceptable to the whole mining industry. The documents also showed that Gold Fields Security was a worrying fusion of those features found in any run-of-the-mill private security company, with the totalitarian methods found in the East German Stasi, the Chilean DINA secret police, or South Africa's own Bureau of State Security. There were routine tasks, of course – the prevention and detection of theft, the protection of company assets and the like. But there was also, the documents revealed, a highly partisan and political side to the operation. The service was 'designed to cater for control of vulnerable and vital areas, the screening of personnel, combatting labour unrest, combatting subversive activities . . . [and] Liaison at a local level with the South African Defence Force, the South African Police and Civil Defence.'[2]

The document also gave detailed information on the equipment of each Gold Fields Security unit at individual mines. These routinely included 'a mobile element in anti-riot vehicles, an assault team using riot dogs and a support team equipped with anti-riot equipment'.[3] The overall command structure of the force was to be kept in entirely white hands and, while each unit was responsible to the white manager of the individual mine where Gold Fields Security held the contract, there was also a central command and control facility to co-ordinate operations nationally. And this

131

was what was run out of the Luipaardsvlei compound which we had secretly filmed. By 1986, we established, the force had 6,000 men under its control on mines throughout South Africa, arresting, questioning and frequently beating and even shooting miners who got out of line or attempted to hold union meetings.

The documents also showed how Gold Fields Security played a central role in the operation of another, equally sinister force on every single mine, the Mine Security Reserve. The MSR is a secret network of trained and armed white people on the mines who were called into existence under the terms of the South African government's tough emergency legislation known as the National Key Points Act. This legislation, which designates hundreds of industrial installations throughout the country as areas of special national sensitivity, was part of the apocalyptic 'Total Onslaught' scenario which successive white minority governments developed to criminalise, discredit and destroy the African National Congress, the Pan African Congress, the South African Communist Party and other opposition groupings. And despite the many changes in South Africa in the past couple of years the force still exists.

The paranoid style of the Mines Security Force was evident in another extraordinary Gold Fields Security training document Peter leaked to us. The terrorists would, the document stated unequivocally, 'block mine shafts and start underground fires, disrupt the labour force, infiltrate hostels and cause unrest, indoctrinate and intimidate black employees . . . attack VIPs and abduct children'.[4] The ANC has never attacked mine shafts or villages, started fires or abducted children, and has traditionally had a tough policy commitment against terrorism of this kind. Nevertheless the document went on to make further claims about what black terrorists would supposedly do to the white mining community. The terrorists, the document stated, would operate by 'Intimidation, creating unrest in the residential area, hostel riot overflowing into the residential area; murder, rape, robbery and terrorism'.[5] The consequences of a well-connected British corporation officially sanctioning such a cocktail of racial and sexual phobias to discredit the black opposition can only be guessed at. But the likelihood is that such corporate paranoia worsened human relations on the mines and added to the dense undergrowth of violence in the mining culture of South Africa.

Ziliboy Daza was one of the victims of Gold Fields' special contribution to that culture of violence. It cost him his eye. Ziliboy, a fit and healthy young man of twenty-seven, was working as an underground miner at Gold Fields'

Venterspost mine in January 1986. One day early in the New Year the mine management allowed the South African army in to conduct a search of the compound, possibly in a bid to unsettle the workforce. In the course of the search a great deal of money was stolen from the miners' rooms, inflaming an already tense workforce and leading to an angry strike, which a number of Venterspost miners felt the company had deliberately provoked to flush out union activists and give them the sack. Before the day was out the mine management had called in Gold Fields Security with a view to driving the miners out of their hostel rooms, where they had gone to sit until their grievances were met and negotiations were under way. This was seen as an invasion of Gold Fields' private property and Gold Fields Security was sent in to force the men into the open and compel them to go back to work. In the end to break the strike Gold Fields Security used riot vehicles, tear gas, rubber bullets and sjambok whips. Many miners were injured, Ziliboy Daza among them. Ziliboy was not a rioter; he was just unlucky that he was in the wrong place at the wrong time. He was coming out of a washroom after a shower when Gold Fields Security struck. Although he was taking no part in any act of resistance to Gold Fields Security, a fact that Gold Fields seems to have accepted because at no subsequent stage did the company seek to dismiss him, he was shot in the face by a rubber bullet and badly wounded.

'I came out of the shower and heard shooting by the compound gate,' he told me. 'I looked over towards it and then suddenly there was this terrible pain in my face. I had been shot with a rubber bullet, I later found out. I took the headscarf I was wearing and pressed it over the bleeding area and went to my room. I asked someone there to get me water to wash the blood off my clothes, but I was still bleeding a lot and I walked over to the gate. Then I got into the ambulance and it took me to the hospital at the Libanon mine near by. There they put me to bed and there I stayed for a week. At the end of that I went to Mzilikazi Hospital for some more treatment but it never amounted to very much. After another fortnight I came back to the compound hospital and there they told me that all the nerves in my injured eye were dead and I should have it removed. I was very reluctant but my good eye started hurting and in the end I agreed to the course of action they recommended.' Ziliboy Daza received no compensation for the loss of his eye and no one from Gold Fields Security was questioned or disciplined to see if there might have been any irregularity. While Ziliboy was not sacked, with one eye missing he could no longer work underground, where he had earned on average 300 rand a month, enough to feed his wife and four children. With his health permanently impaired he was transferred to surface work at little more than half his previous earnings.[6]

Gold Fields Security was also frequently wheeled into action at the Gold Fields' East Driefontein mine, part of the giant Driefontein super-mine which is the single most profitable gold mine in the world producing gold at 100 dollars an ounce when the market price periodically reached 600 dollars, a profit of 500 dollars an ounce. In one such incident in February 1985 some 11,000 East Driefontein workers struck over the mine management's continuing refusal to negotiate about their grievances on over-charging in the compound stores, the sale of rotten food, dirty eating places and poor meals in the canteen, ill-treatment and assaults by white miners. Frustrated by months of delaying tactics by management, the miners on the night shift declined to go to work at 5.30 p.m. and instead staged a procession to the main gate, where they stayed all night, chanting and singing. At 9 a.m. the following morning the police and Gold Fields Security assembled outside, with armoured vehicles, guns, batons, dogs and tear gas. Percy Dyanase was an eye-witness to what happened next.

'There was a helicopter overhead buzzing around and around. Then the mine security threw leaflets over the wall saying this was an illegal strike and we must go to work or they would come amongst us. The strikers said that they would not negotiate with Gold Fields Security and must speak to the management, but the management refused to come. Instead the police and security men came closer, threatening to shoot us if we did not disperse. As they moved closer we stopped singing and then suddenly they opened fire with live bullets, rubber bullets and tear gas. There was chaos, people were running everywhere to avoid the shooting and the whipping from sjamboks. I was shot here on the left-hand side by one of the cans of tear gas and was put into one of the houses. Others ran away, hundreds of them up into the hills behind the mine to escape the ferocity of the attack.'[7] The attack left 145 injured; twenty-two men including the entire union committee were arrested, detained in prison and subsequently fined and banned from the Carletonville area. An additional 800 men were sacked and sent home to the labour reserves.

It was a series of events like those at East Driefontein which finally prompted a young white lawyer called Richard Spoor to put his job in jeopardy in March 1985. Gold Fields had sponsored his law studies at the University of Witwatersrand and after he had finished his degree he went to work for them as a labour relations lawyer. A tall, dignified man with the build of a Springbok prop forward and a strong sense of justice which soon led to dissident political opinions, Richard Spoor became increasingly troubled by aspects of the work he had to do. In particular he was shocked by the fact that he had to provide top management with a precise breakdown of the ethnic and 'tribal' mix of the labour force at all Gold Fields' mines so that senior management could fine-tune the labour supply through TEBA, the Chamber of Mines' recruiting monopoly. 'Every week one of Gold Fields' directors went through these figures very carefully and adjustments were constantly made,' Spoor said. 'It pretty soon became clear to me that the purpose was to ensure that the workforce was deliberately kept divided. Senior management took advantage of divisions and antagonisms among Africans of different origins and played different groups off against each other.'[8]

But it was an assignment to report on events at Gold Fields' Rooiberg tin mine which caused Richard Spoor to begin to question the integrity of senior Gold Fields' management. Five black miners had been killed during disturbances at Rooiberg after an outburst of protest in the compound. Again the company answered dissent according to its standard business practices – with the heavy hand of repression. Police and Gold Fields Security were sent in to quell the protest, which made matters worse. At the end of the affair 'order' was restored and five black miners were in the mortuary. When Spoor examined the background to these tragic events, he found that the cause of unrest at the mine was a poorly handled change in the method of wage payments and a failure to explain deductions that had been made from the men's wage packets.[9] In any workplace with free collective bargaining and union recognition, Spoor felt, there would have been consultation and agreed procedures for dealing with such problems, should they arise. Gold Fields refused to introduce any such structures. As he examined the repeated instances of violence on Gold Fields mines, Spoor couldn't help but note that the fateful decisions were always taken by white people who lived with their wives and families in decent housing subsidised and paid for by the mining companies. They were people without empathy or sympathy who knew nothing of the lonely, pressurised and manipulated lives of the men who were kept in the compounds and who thought of black people in a thoroughly racist and hostile way. He concluded that this was at the root of Gold Fields' recurrent problems and felt that he should help the black miners' union gain enough strength to transform the system that was everywhere in force in Gold Fields' compounds.

In an interview recorded in the back garden of his tiny house in the Johannesburg suburb of Melville, Richard Spoor recounted the story of how he, a head office corporate lawyer, had begun secretly to help a black union, and how though it cost him his job he had no regrets. 'I was dismissed by Gold Fields after they received information from the South African police security branch that I was actively assisting black trade unions,' Spoor said. 'Gold Fields' relationship with the security police was an intimate one. They advised me at the time of my dismissal that they had taken the trouble to get a security report about my activities when I was a university student. Then when the first suggestion came from the security police that I was involved with people building independent black unions they monitored my meetings with union people and told me that I had to leave.

'I took my job with Gold Fields through financial necessity. As a university student, I had a Gold Fields' scholarship to help me pay my fees and part of the agreement was that I would work for them after I completed my studies. I did not arrive at Gold Fields with the view that the company would necessarily satisfy the criteria I set for myself and the kind of organisation I would be happy to work for. But I was ill prepared for the shock I experienced when I began to visit the mines themselves and in the end I left with a very strong feeling that this was a dangerous and even obnoxious company, one that was absolutely ruthless in the way that it dealt with black people in its employment and with those whites who dared to show any initiative or threaten the set up in any way. In time I came to think that Gold Fields was an exploitative and aggressive company determined to secure their profit at any cost.'[10]

When Spoor first joined the company he was sent to one of the mines to attend an induction course, which is compulsory for all new head office employees. His first impression on arriving at the mine was one of neatness and organisation, of discipline and cleanliness. 'On the surface', he said, 'things looked very structured, very disciplined and seemed to run very smoothly. It was possible to be impressed with the neatness, the tidiness and so on. But for anyone with a degree of empathy it did not take long to appreciate the real horror under the veneer of order and decency.'

It was the presence of Gold Fields Security on the mines that first caused his anxieties to gell. 'It worried me from the beginning, Gold Fields Security, this very well organised, well disciplined and somewhat sinister security force that controls all access to the hostels. No strangers, no unidentified workers were allowed in. They were always monitoring things, secretly watching people, gathering every scrap of information they could find. And they were ever ready to make physical interventions.

'The next thing I noticed was the attitude of the whites working at the mine. It was quite clear that there was an absolute barrier between whites and blacks, a complete lack of social intercourse. The whites who have a lot of dealings with black people and who administer their lives in the hostels are the hostel managers. These people can often speak one or other of the African languages or at least have a crude smattering. But their relationship with the black miners is paternalistic and authoritarian in the extreme.'

Every morning on Gold Fields' mines, Spoor found, disciplinary meetings were called to punish mineworkers or compound residents who had infringed one or other of the many rules and regulations the company had devised to reinforce its power over people. 'It's clear that the individual miners are terrified of the whites because they have absolute power to dismiss them, either for one serious offence or even for an accumulation of petty offences. Dropping litter is a disciplinary offence, distributing union pamphlets without permission would be an offence. Having a stranger in the room is another. Using a white-only toilet would be another, or drinking out of a white-only tea cup. It would even be an offence to put a match head up into the shower head to affect the flow of water and obtain a more satisfactory shower. Such things are treated very seriously by Gold Fields and they add up. The first time the result might be an oral warning, then a written warning, then a second written warning, then a final warning and then summary dismissal. So if management was gunning for you it wouldn't take long to find three or four offences and give you the sack.'

As Richard Spoor's knowledge and experience of the company grew, he discerned the patterns of strict apartheid spreading throughout Gold Fields. The company was, he began to think, a perfect microcosm of South African society. All the wealth and power was concentrated in the hands of a monopolistic, white power structure. But their power was so autocratic, so remote and so completely lacking in legitimacy that in the end they could only run things by increasing dependence on violence and repression. In the townships, the violence was perpetrated by the army and the police; in Gold Fields' mines it was used in house by the Security Division.

'In no sense do black and white miners enjoy the same rights and privileges at Gold Fields,' he said. 'The black miners rise at three o'clock in the morning and are queueing up at the turnstiles to clock in and go below. The whites arrive at a much more convenient time. They go down long after the black miners and come back up before them. Blacks, the overwhelming majority of the workforce, have to stand in long, noisy queues and are literally packed into their cages. Whites have separate cages and only they ride in

137

them. Even if they are half empty, blacks have to wait for the cage to go all the way up the shaft and come all the way down again. Sometimes this can mean a wait of half an hour or sixty minutes. The white miner has his own piccanin, or personal assistant, a raw, new recruit who carries his food, water, equipment. He's a sort of batman who does no work other than as a personal servant. Yet the working miners have to subsidise his wages as well as the white man's when both do nothing for the good of production.

'Below ground the white miner strolls to the workplace where the black miners are waiting. They've set up the machinery and the white miners' role is simply to overlook and supervise. The whites not only have all real power in the mine, they have full control over their own social lives, a control that is flatly denied blacks. Whites have housing that is very, very cheap, a nominal rent for accommodation, water and electricity. They can live with their families wherever they come from. The infrastructure and social facilities are first class, good sporting and social clubs and all the excellent amenities that whites expect to enjoy in this country. Blacks by contrast live eighteen to a room, sometimes in bunks stacked three tiers high. They have no control over the food they eat, over the films they see or the entertainment that is provided. They are flatly denied normal access to the company of women and can only meet other men in circumstances in which they are spied on. Over the allocation of resources even for sport and recreation facilities, blacks have no control at all. Management decides where the money goes. They don't even have the right on Gold Fields' mines to receive visitors in their rooms and if they want to see their families they get an opportunity once a year to occupy for a few days the so-called married quarters built in tiny numbers just outside the compounds.

'I have no doubt that Gold Fields had the resources to cope with these problems. A mine like Kloof made one million rand every single day of the year in profit. If there had been any real will to accommodate the men as human beings, with their families, then the company could have made giant strides. On reflection I believe that the migrant labour system suited Gold Fields perfectly. This way they need only care about the individual miner who is working for them. They need not concern themselves about the miner's family or about his welfare after he has left the mine. I doubt very much whether even 5 per cent of the miners employed on Gold Fields mines ever reach retirement age. It's very arduous work they do, an enormous strain on a person's physical resources. I think a black miner has a working life of fifteen to twenty years. I don't think there are many who can last longer than that and when they are burned out they are

138

shipped back to the homelands and it is no longer the mining company's problem.

'Experience has taught me that Gold Fields does not respect the basic human rights of its employees. Just take the question of the right to speak freely and its corollary in any industrial situation, the right to organise in a union. There may be exceptions in other mining companies, but at Gold Fields unions are still pretty much regarded as subversive institutions. Many of the miners are simply frightened of the consequences if they join the union. Freedom of speech is severely restrained. It would be an offence to address a group of miners on the compound or off the compound, anywhere on mine property in fact. Unions have to arrange their meetings a long way in advance. They have to give two or three weeks' notice to management; they have to submit an agenda of the topics to be covered at meetings; they have to give management a list of the speakers and any person addressing the meeting who is not employed by the company. And the company also has a whole armoury of security personnel and national security legislation which they don't hesitate to enforce either themselves or by calling in the police from adjacent towns.'

What shocked Richard Spoor about Gold Fields more than anything else was that in spite of the organisation's strong British roots and connections, he saw no evidence of liberal influences or democratic convictions in the running of the company. 'I sometimes asked myself why this is. Gold Fields owns the richest mines; they make the biggest profits of all the gold-mining companies and coming from overseas you might have expected something better. There was enormous scope for the company to improve the conditions of the black workers on the mines. But instead of adopting such policies Gold Fields always tried to hamper and restrict the black unions, tried to concede as little as possible, as if they were determined to hang on to every penny of the huge profit they were making. I think in truth that the apartheid system and the migrant labour system suited them very well because they could operate in such a way as to preserve those excess, inflated profits they made so readily under this system.

'I'm saying that Gold Fields has been a company which has reaped enormous benefits from collaboration with that system. They were not passive beneficiaries. They had a very real relation with tens of thousands of workers. They were able through simple and straightforward actions like uniting black miners with their families, even on a temporary basis, through the building of large numbers of quarters where families could come and visit, to bring about massive improvements in the lives of a large number of black people in this country. They had the power and the financial leverage to persuade a large number of other business corporations and the mining industry in general to criticise apartheid and participate far more actively in the struggle against apartheid. What stopped them doing so? Pure self interest. They were happy with the way things were run. So happy that they obstructed change, prolonged the crisis and used their own troops physically to attack union-minded workers, people who tried to hold a meeting or get something done about a grievance. They called their company Gold Fields Security but it was no more than a private army whose very existence poisoned the industry and seems irretrievably to have corrupted the company.

'You can see its effect in the very statements of senior company officials,' Spoor went on. 'There was the remark by Robin Plumbridge in the wake of an incident at the company's Deelkraal gold mine when Gold Fields Security used tear gas and rubber bullets against striking miners in 1985.' Plumbridge, the man behind the worldwide marketing of Krugerrands and a board member of the British parent company Consolidated Gold Fields, was completely unapologetic about the company's repeated use of force at its Deelkraal gold mine. 'If you have got group violence, you have to use techniques involving tear gas and so on,' he told the *Guardian* in London. 'It doesn't give us any pleasure. But you get to a no-go stage where you have to act and fairly decisively.'[11]

Other senior Gold Fields' executives echoed these sentiments, Spoor recalled, often using formulations which embodied a completely brutalised view of the miners caught in the migrant labour system. One senior labour relations executive, Anton Lombard, responded to an outbreak of discontent on a mine with the remark that black miners 'were like savages dancing round a fire', a remark he later withdrew. Another senior official speaking off the record to a representative of the South African Council of Churches about the lack of black promotion prospects in the company, claimed that blacks 'could not compete intellectually'.[12] The hard line also involved Gold Fields, Spoor recalled, in the development and patenting of its own rubber bullet, another token of the British company's unique approach to industrial relations in South Africa.

Richard Spoor's analysis of Gold Fields as an organisation with a cruel streak embedded in its corporate culture seemed well supported by the evidence, particularly after the report of a worrying incident early in 1987. In February, in the week Gold Fields celebrated its centenary, an important article about the company's South African security organisation appeared in the independent Johannesburg paper, the *Weekly Mail*.[13] Written by Phillip van Niekerk, a resourceful and reliable reporter, the report stated that officers in Gold Fields Security had been involved in the torture of two black miners at Gencor's Stilfontein mine where Gold Fields provided 'security'. The miners who told their story to the *Weekly Mail* were 57-year-old Daliwonga Gxaleka and 55-year-old Phuzethu Mfaniswas. Interviewed separately, both miners told van Niekerk that a Gold Fields Security investigation into the theft of food from mine kitchens had culminated in their brutal torture. Mr Gxaleka explained that on 28 January 1987 he was taken for questioning by the Gold Fields Security mine police and told that if he did not tell the truth he would 'meet the tokoloshe' or evil spirit, a euphemism for an electrical generator. He was taken into bushes near the main Potcheftsroom Road. His hands were handcuffed between his legs. A large canvas bag was put over him and he felt something being taped to his body. 'I felt terrible pains all over my body,' he told van Niekerk. 'This continued for about ten minutes. All the time I was told to speak the truth.' He said the spasms of pain he experienced were so severe that at one stage he had asked a white security officer to shoot him.

The second man who gave details of his torture by Gold Fields Security was Phuzethu Mfaniswas; after his encounter at Stilfontein, he was spitting and urinating blood and had to be admitted to hospital. He was also taken into the bushes and a canvas bag put over his head. While he was being electrocuted, the Gold Fields Security officers abused him by squeezing his genitals viciously with their hands. Van Niekerk interviewed the men some days after the date of the alleged torture. He found that Mr Mfaniswas still had marks on his body where the electrodes had been attached. Despite the press publicity there was no proper investigation of the allegations either by Gold Fields Security or by an independent legal body. As a result the two former South African police officers who were the subject of these specific and well-supported allegations continued in the service of the company.

Nor were there any statements of anxiety or concern from group headquarters in London, where the directors were celebrating a hundred years of uninterrupted profitability with a centenary banquet, a special dividend for the shareholders and by publishing a special book, *Gold Fields – a Centenary Portrait* by Paul Johnson, the former editor of the left-wing weekly the *New Statesman*.[14] In his descriptions of his journey through South Africa, he does not record a single conversation with a migrant miner, there is no mention of the migrant labour system, no appreciation of the fundamental incursions into human rights it involves, no reference to the low wages, anti-union attitudes, poor food, bad housing, inadequate shower rooms, dirty toilets and damaged human relations which predominated in Gold Fields compounds. Instead Paul Johnson's book is full of references to the 'moral authority' and 'creativity' of Gold Fields. He compares business in general and Gold Fields in particular, the single most important business enterprise constructed by British civilisation in the course of its tragic engagement in South Africa, to a work of art. To any uncluttered eye, Johnson's 'independent impressionist portrait' of Gold Fields in South Africa was at best a poorly executed parody. In reality, few companies could have been further from the elevating and liberating values embodied in a work of art. In reality Gold Fields crushed the human personality and confined the spirit. In this it was in harmony with the State and the structure of apartheid, which had been designed with these goals in mind.

Besides policing the mining industry on behalf of the apartheid State and obstructing moves for reform inside the Chamber of Mines, Gold Fields supplied the architects of apartheid with intellectual justifications for migrant labour and gave succour to the minority regime throughout the 1960s, 1970s and 1980s. After Sharpeville, for example, Robert Annan, the Gold Fields chairman in London, stated:

> It is not easy for any government in South Africa to frame and carry out a policy aimed at higher standards for all its peoples, while preserving security for all. Recent events in other parts of Africa have shown only too clearly that too rapid political advancement of the native peoples can have disastrous results.
>
> With the present widely varied levels of education and civilisation it is inevitable that the State must for the time being differentiate in measures applied to its inhabitants.[15]

Sixteen years later in the wake of the Soweto revolt the chairman of Gold Fields South Africa, Adriaan Louw, returned to the theme in his statement for 1976: 'It is my conviction that implementation of the populist cry for majority rule on a unitary basis whether in Rhodesia, South-West Africa or the Republic [of South Africa] is no more likely to benefit the majority than it has in any "liberated country" where race relations and colour differences are decisive factors.'[16]

In the 1980s, as the minority government became embroiled in a deepening cycle of repression in the black townships, the intellectual

142

succour continued, with the company still engaging in unconditional defence of the migrant labour system its founder Cecil Rhodes had helped to devise a century before. The centrepiece of Gold Fields' justification of the system was a crude and self-serving vision of its mine compounds and business practices as somehow 'civilising' the ostensibly underdeveloped personalities and culture of 'the native'. It would be fair to say that the company continued to reproduce this argument for decades after the moral and political quicksands on which it had based its corporate fortunes were clearly identified.

In his novel *Cry the Beloved Country* Alan Paton underlined the questionable morality of developing great industries and amassing great fortunes on the basis of the poverty and exploitation of other human beings. Paton's comments were pointed directly at the mining houses.[17] His thinking was deeply influenced by events in the South African gold mines during the war, when tens of thousands of black miners pressed for better wages and conditions. Consolidated Gold Fields spearheaded the resistance inside the Chamber of Mines to any form of negotiation and the worst scenes of violence during the resulting strike in 1946 took place at the company's Sub Nigel mine, where miners were forced back to work at gunpoint and shots were fired into the crowd, causing a number of deaths in the ensuing panic.[18] Gold Fields persisted with its hard line when leaders of the African National Congress began to develop the case against migrant labour. In an article in 1955 Nelson Mandela wrote of the direct link between forced removals, migrant labour and the need to provision a vast market of cheap labour for the mining magnates and farm owners.[19] In his powerful book, *Let My People Go*, Chief Albert Luthuli, winner of the Nobel Peace Prize, forcefully argued that the imposition of the apartheid system had changed the idiom of slavery for ever.[20] In the southern United States, slave owners had owned plantations and slave workers. But in South Africa under apartheid, Luthuli warned, the minority took possession of the resources and people of a whole country and this new Leviathan would cause violence and heartbreak on an unprecedented scale. To British investors and mine owners these were lonely voices crying for justice in an increasingly profitable wilderness and Gold Fields' London directors chose to ignore them.

Gold Fields was also unmoved by the publication of two important books about the migrant labour system in 1972 by the South African writer Francis Wilson. *Labour in the South African Gold Mines* and *Migrant Labour in South Africa*[21] were the fruit of intensive research and anxious reflection by Wilson, an economist at the University of Cape Town. A free-thinking Christian with

143

strong democratic instincts, he came from an unusual family background. His parents were anthropologists with an unshakeable respect for African peoples and their culture.

'Because of my background I had always seen South Africa from a much wider perspective than is normal for a white South African,' Wilson explained to me. 'I grew up in the Eastern Cape and went to university in Cape Town but studied physical science. Then I realised more and more that if I was to be involved in the issues that would decide the fate of the country even in a small way I would have to go beyond the natural sciences and study economics.'[22] He began a journey of inquiry into migrant labour by studying the economics of discrimination in the United States. He soon discovered that American work on the subject was not particularly relevant to South Africa, and that in many ways any broad focus was inadequate. He began to seek a more appropriate prism through which to view his homeland and soon fastened on the mining industry.

'Like all South Africans I was interested in the mines. But it was notoriously difficult to get serious information on the industry and I thought that if I could unlock independent data on the country's most important industry I could make a real contribution towards understanding how the political economy of the country worked. My research became first a thesis for a doctorate and then a book, *Labour in the South African Gold Mines.*'

His first book was an appraisal of the migrant labour system. He had a gift for finding or coining interesting phrases to describe the web in which black miners were caught. He hit on the concept of 'oscillating migrancy' to describe the constant journeying between the two worlds of home in the sending countries and employment at the heart of South African industry. But his sense of justice gave the book a critical edge. As well as outlining the origins of the system, the book painstakingly identified its unfortunate human consequences, from infringing human rights, breaking up families, encouraging social dislocation, violence and crime to the wholesale impoverishment of the sending countries and the concentration of the vast bulk of the wealth produced in the hands of white businesses grouped at the centre. Wilson did a masterly job in filleting obscure official documents and retrieving disturbing nuggets of information few dreamed they would contain. From Chamber of Mines' accident reports he obtained details of mining deaths over the years, added up totals and ending with the horrifying figure of 19,000 men killed, 93 per cent of them black, in the country's gold mines in the three decades from 1936 to 1966. He reinforced his argument with quotes from George

Orwell's essay 'Down the Mine' and by publishing as an appendix the fierce poem 'In the Gold Mines' by the great African writer Wallet Vilakazi.

A second and in some ways more powerful book soon followed. Written as a report for the South African Council of Churches and its 'Study Project on Christianity in Apartheid Society', Wilson called it *Migrant Labour in South Africa*. The result of much dedicated wandering in parts of town and country that few whites ever bothered to visit or think about, this was a no-holds barred attack on the migrant labour system. Illustrated with photographs of the grim conditions endured by black contract labourers, the book successfully conveyed the sense of wounded rage black South Africans felt at what was being done to them. Furthermore, Wilson emphasised, the migrant labour system was still spreading. Vast new mines were being built on the basis of the single-sex compound. Old, abandoned mine compounds were even being brought back into use to house workers brought into the big cities to feed the needs of industries expanding rapidly in the midst of economic boom. Wilson dissected the arguments developed by apologists for the system and then itemised the objections to such a cruel system. In case anyone should miss the point, he stated explicitly, 'Anyone who believes that blacks are contented with the migrant labour system is living in a fool's paradise.'[23]

To concentrate public attention on the migrant labour system, Wilson and other white South Africans staged a 'Pilgrimage of Penitence' over the Christmas period in 1972. 'Involving a thirty-day separation of the "pilgrims" from their wives and children, this was a wonderful occasion,' Wilson recalled later. 'The journalists who came along thought we were heroes. They came for the first three or four days and those were very hard indeed for all of us. Then they went away thinking it was just the same right through to the end. But after the first few days things got very much better and we became fit and able to cope. We completed the walk to parliament buildings in Cape Town in high spirits and enjoyed being lionised for all the sacrifices the journalists imagined we had made! At one level the Pilgrimage of Penitence was an effective publicity stunt. But at another it was more than that. It was after all a direct public statement from a group of Christians on the wholesale immorality of the migrant labour system.'[24]

Wilson's critique of the migrant labour system was reinforced in Britain by the radical research group Counter Information Services, who produced a tough 'anti-report' on Consolidated Gold Fields.[25] Founded by Mike Armitage, a successful London stockbroker with a social conscience, CIS had the inspired idea of producing 'alternative' reports for some of Britain's biggest and most controversial corporations. The well-researched report on Consolidated Gold Fields also mounted a forceful attack on the migrant labour system, the racism endemic in the mining industry and the growing wage gap between blacks and whites. The sting in the tail of this report was the long list of Conservative, Labour and Liberal councils with investments in Gold Fields and the identification of a host of Church bodies – from the Poor Clergy Relief Corporation to the Society for Promoting Christian Knowledge – who took in dividends from the company's involvement in migrant labour. So did twenty-two named Conservative MPs, including the then Home Secretary Robert Carr, the Minister for Overseas Development, R.F. Wood, Enoch Powell and Nicholas Ridley. One Labour MP, Michael Meacher, also had shares in the company, which he soon sold.[26]

The spotlight was also directed at Gold Fields in 1973 by a British House of Commons sub-committee. After Adam Raphael's powerful series in the *Guardian* investigating the conditions and wages paid by Slater Walker, Pilkington, Courtaulds and other blue-chip British companies, the House of Commons took the unusual step of convening a sub-committee to look into the poor wages and conditions of black South African workers employed by British companies. Gold Fields submitted a special memorandum of evidence,[27] an unqualified defence of the migrant labour system which the company insisted had 'important social and political advantages'. The British company disassociated itself from any acceptance of poverty datum lines and minimum wages, saying that they trusted in market forces in the rural areas of Lesotho, Mozambique and South Africa to set wage levels.[28] When he came to give evidence before the committee, the Gold Fields chairman, J.D. McCall, spoke plainly.

'We have got to bear in mind that something like half of the black population of South Africa ... are today leading a tribal life, and the same sort of life which they have lived for hundreds and hundreds and hundreds of years.

'If we think that with our ideas we can turn that mentality, that approach, that way of life or that philosophy – call it what you like – to our way of thinking we may do far more damage than if we allow these tribal people to evolve in their own way and their own thinking.

'The African has only been in touch with the Europeans in South Africa for a very short space of time and the men I am talking about, the tribal Africans, have really only been in contact with the Europeans perhaps during this century. Let us not try and jump too far in seventy or eighty years what it has taken us, let us say, a thousand years.'[29]

The chairman of the committee described the evidence of the Gold Fields chairman as 'revealing'.[30] The House of Commons Select Committee probe led to the publication of an inconclusive report, which noted in passing that Gold Fields' mines were so profitable that the company could easily have increased the wages it paid to African miners.[31] The investigation also caused the Department of Trade and Industry to draw up a code of conduct for companies operating in South Africa. In line with the thinking developed in American business circles by the Reverend Leon Sullivan, a black director of General Motors, the DTI Code set out some minimum acceptable standards for big corporations operating in the troubled context of an apartheid society.[32] To implement the code an experienced and sympathetic labour attaché called Bill Vose was assigned to Pretoria. Vose was appalled at many of the things he found out about the way workers were treated by British firms in the Transvaal and soon began to focus a critical eye on what was going on in the mining industry, not least on the British-led mining house with nearly 60,000 black employees and the richest mines.[33]

Gold Fields resented such outside interference and became progressively more hostile to what the directors believed was unwarranted public intrusion in its private affairs. The extent of the company's shareholding in its South African arm, Gold Fields of South Africa, was soon trimmed back from just over 50 per cent to an equally powerful controlling interest just under the half-way mark.[34] This had the, for Gold Fields, pleasing effect of taking the company with the biggest presence of any British business in South Africa out of category A in the DTI reporting structure, which required full disclosure of information, and putting it into category B, which did not. Thereafter the company filed returns under the code of conduct which were so lacking in detail or substance as to be highly provocative. On one occasion the Gold Fields' return amounted to a short letter of a few sentences from the group executive responsible, D.E.S. Barton, enclosing a poorly photostatted copy of a paragraph from Gold Fields' South African company report to its shareholders.[35] This was a publicly available document already on file inside the British Department of Trade and Industry.

The House of Commons probe, however mild, had energised some parts of the slumbering British social fabric. British churches were becoming concerned about Britain's economic relations with apartheid and they realised that their own pension and investment funds often drew a substantial income from companies which supported the system they questioned. As if to underline the point, exiled black Zimbabweans friendly with Counter-Information Services' Basker Vashee began picketing Gold Fields' annual general meetings in support of disinvestment. The protesters soon struck a chord with the United Reform Church and the Roman Catholic diocese of Westminster. In July 1976, with memories of Soweto in their minds, the United Reform Church decided to send its treasurer, L. Palmer, and the secretary of its Church and Society Department, to see Gold Fields' deputy chairman, G.J. Mortimer. At the meeting Mr Mortimer spoke repeatedly about the excellence of the facilities on Gold Fields' mines. When the churchmen asked about the attitude of the company to apartheid, Mr Mortimer stated: 'The Board has no problem with apartheid because that is not something within our competence to comment on.'[36]

Next Mr Mortimer ventured on a strong defence of the South African bantustan or homelands policy of divide and rule. 'As far as the creation of the homelands is concerned, we see that as a device for giving to Africans political equality before they are ready for it . . . Given the desire of the Africans for political equality the whites have searched for another solution. We accept the homelands are too small but we do not agree that they contain only the worst land.'[37]

Next the United Reform Church leaders asked if it was a fair justification of the company's involvement in South Africa that it could slowly prompt 'gradual, beneficial change closer to our own idea of democratic capitalism'. The churchmen could scarcely believe their ears when the Gold Fields' executive answered, 'We are not so sure about "democratic capitalism".'[38]

In response to the refusal of Gold Fields' London directors to consider social and moral obligations, the United Reform Church finally decided to disinvest from Gold Fields. Looking back at the campaign, John Johansen-Berg, URC moderator at the time, told me that the most the church achieved with its lobbying of Gold Fields' board was an increase in the corporate public relations budgets. 'We got nowhere on the critical issues, effective unionisation, de-racialising the compounds, allowing Africans to live near their work and be with their families.

'Of all the companies we had dealings with,' he added shaking his head sorrowfully, 'I came to regard Cons Gold as the toughest nut to crack. This was the company in which there was the least likelihood of any response at any level. Some companies were anxious to show willing, to respond to criticism, to participate in dialogue. But not Gold Fields. There the directors and the shareholders were happy with their behaviour and regarded our criticisms as unwarranted interference. In my view their sole concern was the profit motive and at Gold Fields the profit was always kept high.'[39]

The Roman Catholic leader in Britain, Cardinal Heenan, also became preoccupied with the issue of church bodies holding shares in companies like Gold Fields. After the issue was emphasised yet again in a tough pamphlet from Christian Concern on South Africa, Heenan initiated his own discussions with Gold Fields' directors on their policies. He asked them where the company stood in relation to the ending of the migrant labour system, the formation of free trade unions for black workers and the ending of racially based wage structures. The discussions got nowhere and Cardinal Heenan died before he could take any further action. In July 1977 the Roman Catholic Diocese of Westminster finally moved on the issue and announced it was selling all its Gold Fields' shares because, after protracted discussions with the company about its policies, the diocese felt sure it was 'unlikely to make any further progress by this means'. The company, the statement noted, was 'unwilling to encourage the formation of unions of African mineworkers and. . . considers that migrant mineworkers have a high degree of choice'.[40]

In September 1977 the European Community adopted a code of conduct for businesses operating in South Africa.[41] The new European code was unequivocal in its insistence that foreign companies must initiate and foster change. In particular, companies had to ensure that blacks denied democratic involvement in society at large, should not be thwarted at work. The European code therefore insisted on forward-looking industrial relations practices. Workplaces should be completely desegregated, racist wage and benefit scales should be dismantled, no employees should be paid wages below poverty datum line levels and African workers should be given genuine encouragement to form trade unions of their own choosing. In a blunt paragraph dealing specifically with migrant labour, the code stated: 'The system of migrant labour is, in South Africa, an instrument of the policy of apartheid which has the effect of preventing the individual from seeking and obtaining a job of his choice.

'It also causes grave social and family problems,' and employers therefore 'have the social responsibility to contribute towards ensuring freedom of movement for black African workers and their families. In the meantime employers should make it their concern to alleviate as much as possible the effects of the existing system.' The code posed a few problems for Gold Fields and caused group executive Don Barton to write longer letters to the Department of Trade and Industry claiming that considerable progress was being made on the ground in South Africa.[42]

In fact, far from initiating and prompting change, Gold Fields was uncompromisingly ranged against it. The group steadfastly opposed the more progressive employers in the Chamber of Mines who favoured larger wage rises and the encouragement of black unions and collective bargaining as an alternative to the existing system. Merle Lipton highlighted the contradiction inherent in the British company's position in her important 1980 report on the mining industry, *Men of Two Worlds*.[43] She criticised all the mining houses for their abject failure to face up to the critical issues even as they were piling up the mountainous profits occasioned by the boom in the world gold price. Instead, she argued, they relied on 'meliorism', slow, cautious and inexpensive change, essentially cosmetic in nature, which stopped far short of fundamental reform. But Gold Fields she noted, didn't even believe in meliorism. In a bid to explain the British company's record of opposing reform, Lipton theorised that with its strong foreign connections Gold Fields took a shorter-term view, preferring to maximise profits now, and take them out of South Africa ahead of any change.[44] Twenty-four hours before publication of the Lipton report in Anglo American's house journal *Optima*, Gold Fields threatened legal action. Early copies of *Optima* containing the piece were rounded up by panic-stricken functionaries of the Chamber of Mines who pressurised Anglo to insert a disclaimer which questioned Lipton's professional integrity.[45] In her statement announcing successful settlement of her libel claim against Anglo, Lipton pointed out that Gold Fields was the only mining house in South Africa to refuse her access and information:

I have on balance supported 'constructive engagement' – the use of foreign investment to encourage basic change in apartheid labour policies. Hence I was particularly interested in this large and profitable, 47 per cent British-owned company which employs more black workers (over 62,000) than any other British company in South Africa.

It is regrettable that GFSA should have threatened to stop publication of my article, warned the South African press (already heavily circumscribed by political and libel laws) not to refer to sections of it and issued unfounded allegations and threats against me.[46]

While Gold Fields in South Africa was engaged in trying to suppress or spoil critical research about the migrant labour system, group head office in London produced an extraordinary pamphlet on the subject. In contrast to all the thinking behind the European Community code, this insisted that

'Migrant labour is essentially voluntary being economically motivated and apparently is not regarded as a social evil by those involved.' In a forced and inappropriate comparison, the pamphlet added, 'Tours of duty by naval and military personnel and the current increase in mobility among businessmen are akin to migrant labour.'[47]

After 1983, when the South African Chamber of Mines finally and belatedly agreed to allow a few crossing points in its century-old Berlin Wall against black trade unions, Gold Fields' character was tested once again. According to the theory of constructive engagement, Gold Fields should have been in the van of progress and reform. With its strong foreign ties and the powerful influence of the British board of directors, who frequently flew in and out of Johannesburg, the company should in theory have been keen to extend to its black South African miners the freedoms its staff in Britain, Australia and the United States enjoyed as basic rights. But to the man charged with leading the drive to unionise black miners, the only freedom Gold Fields seemed to care about was its freedom to make as much money as possible.

Cyril Ramaphosa dealt with Gold Fields through the difficult days of 1983, 1984 and 1985, when against terrible odds he and his colleagues were trying to build a union in an industry many black radicals were sceptical could ever be organised. He had initially hoped for some sign of tolerance from Gold Fields because of the company's British connections. He soon discovered that Gold Fields was a bitter opponent of the union and gave no quarter in its fight to preserve the *status quo* on the mines. In obvious defiance of the European code and the DTI code, Ramaphosa recalls, Gold Fields made it as hard as possible for NUM to recruit members, denying the union access to the hostels. In the 1984 wage round and again in 1985 Gold Fields, its profits soaring to unimagined heights, dragged its feet and paid lower increases than the rest of the Chamber. In both years disputes broke out as a result of this provocative policy. The disputes were harshly dealt with, thousands sacked and troops, police and Gold Fields Security used to enforce the company's will inside its grim compounds. In the course of an interview in London, Mr Ramaphosa set out his feelings about the British company.

'I think one needs to give a little credit to some of the mining companies, in that they have tried to move away from the overcrowded housing of black miners. They have tried to accommodate say four or five people in one room, but even that is the exception. The large majority of the companies still accommodate black miners up to twenty strong in small rooms six metres by eight. This is particularly the case with companies such as Gencor and Consolidated Gold Fields.

'In its company statements Gold Fields states that it does not accept the view that its operations in South Africa support apartheid or are detrimental to the well-being of black Africans. But I think that if Gold Fields were able to convince anybody that they paid their workers a living wage, that they don't exploit black workers, that they did everything in their power to get rid of the abhorrent migrant labour system and started accommodating the miners with their families in houses rather than in their existing hovels, I would have admitted that yes, maybe they could be right. But there is no such evidence, no evidence at all that they did anything other than pay starvation wages while at the same time paying huge taxes to the apartheid government and themselves taking huge profits out of the country.

'It would be fair to say that Gold Fields is actually the worst company that we have to deal with. There are other companies which in negotiations have a fairly reasonable approach to the union and are able to bargain in good faith. But not Gold Fields. The racism that one finds in Gold Fields is quite ridiculous. There is completely unfair treatment between white workers and black workers. Gold Fields has been declared an enemy company by our union. What they did was to repress workers who sought to join the union. The list of victimised workers runs into thousands and thousands from mines owned by Consolidated Gold Fields.'[48]

Paul Kennedy, a lawyer who was employed at Gold Fields' head office for some years before seeking a more humane environment in which to work, also came to believe that Britain's biggest corporate investor in South Africa had developed a damaged world view. To illustrate what he believed was a cruel authoritarianism embedded in Gold Fields' corporate culture, Kennedy focused on the company's response to health and safety issues, recalling an extraordinary head office discussion in 1983 between one of the company's senior labour relations advisers, Mr Mueller, and one of its top public relations officials, Helene Mendes.

Ms Mendes, he recalled, was concerned about the apparent lack of sympathy for dead and injured miners evident in corporate press releases about rockfalls and other mining accidents. As miners were often killed and injured in Gold Fields mines, the company equally frequently had to put out press releases explaining what had happened. As head of public relations, Ms Mendes felt that press releases about dead miners should, if only for reasons of taste, have some trace of compassion. But Gold Fields' press releases were issued according to a time-honoured formula. After a mine accident, the Gold Fields' way was to issue a release containing the briefest possible account of what had happened, mentioning no details of dead or injured black miners and invariably concluding with a standard sentence which stated simply, 'Production will not be affected.' It was as if this was the main point, Ms Mendes underlined. And, she added in a concerned tone, it was unforgivable that there was never any expression of regret for the loss of life and limb.

Mr Mueller argued strongly against change. The existing press releases were quite sufficient, he believed. 'Anyway,' he added, 'they don't see the Johannesburg *Star* in the backwoods of the Transkei.' This remark was greeted with laughter by some senior staff.[49] But in the end, after some considerable argument even Gold Fields' press releases were re-modelled. 'Gold Fields regrets to announce that four workers died and eighteen were injured in an underground pressure burst,' ran the reformed first sentence of a May 1985 release about a tragedy at Kloof mine. In this release from Gold Fields' new public affairs department headed by Ms Mendes, the critical investor information about production was tastefully transformed into an additional 'Note for Financial Editors' strategically repositioned as a footnote below the main text. Reassuring as ever, and in a sense every bit as prominent as before, it stated baldly, 'No loss of production is expected.'[50]

For Bafana Baningi such changes were skin deep. He was the first black university graduate to work at Gold Fields' head office. I met Bafana, a fit, articulate young man with an intense love of cars, shortly after he had quit Gold Fields' after two desperately unhappy years there.

'I left Gold Fields very disillusioned. I had arrived with such high hopes and yet within a few weeks of arriving I realised that even at head office they were simply unable to treat a black person as an equal. At the mines where I had to go in my job the situation was even more extraordinary. When we had a cup of tea, I was given a different and of course inferior kind of tea cup. The staff out there were obviously worried about drinking from the same cup as I. I just thought that I wasn't going to take this. So I refused the special cup and resolved that I was not going to go to different toilets. But I was one office worker on my own doing accounting work and only on the mine for a few days at most. A black miner who did what I did would have been fired on the spot for indiscipline and quite possibly assaulted before he was fired.

'The company chairman in South Africa Robin Plumbridge went on record in the mid-1980s that as far as head office was concerned discrimination was a thing of the past. But I know this to be untrue. I came in and instead of getting an accounting job I was given a secretarial one. Whites with inferior qualifications were picked for jobs over me. I applied for an assistant accountant's job, and a white man was selected. He couldn't cope and left. I applied again and was told the job had been scrapped. Actually it was given to a white woman, perfectly nice, but with less qualifications than myself.

'Perhaps the worst case I came across was the black librarian with twenty-seven years' service. The head librarian's job became vacant and he applied. But he was passed over in favour of a white woman. And she didn't even have matriculation. It was her colour that got the lady the job.' The discrimination at head office, overt and covert, made black people there deeply unhappy, Bafana stressed. 'Black people know they will be clerks until they die, unless a great change comes. Gold Fields is a thoroughly racist organisation. There's not a single black person with a company car, and no one with a higher position than a bookkeeper. On the mines what's needed is a completely fresh start.' There racism is endemic and deeply rooted. At head office, an urgent programme to increase the number of blacks in senior positions was needed. 'Unless and until the company initiated these changes as a minimum, there would be no serious progress,' he insisted. 'Yet we must move urgently towards a situation where whites begin to accept that racism and exploitation are ugly deformations of the human character, and serious obstacles to social progress.'[51]

Like virtually every other knowledgeable witness I met in the course of investigating Gold Fields, what pained Bafana most was that it was a British mining company which so flagrantly defied human rights and even, in his view, sought to profit from the vulnerability of the majority. 'How did this happen?' he asked repeatedly. I could never give him a satisfactory answer and in the end the best I could do was promise that one day I would try to set out the beginnings of an explanation.

8   The Gold Standard: the Legacy of a British Business in South Africa

In the ten years between the Soweto uprising and the declaration of the nationwide state of emergency in 1986, Gold Fields took profits of at least £575 million out of South Africa.[1] These outsize economic gains were made possible in part by the gyrations in the world price of gold. But there was another factor – the impact of apartheid. Apartheid concentrated political and economic power exclusively in the hands of a racial minority and made it impossible for Gold Fields' rightless migrant labourers to obtain any equitable distribution of the wealth which resulted from the golden harvest of the Rand. Inside Gold Fields as a business organisation a choice was made throughout the 1960s, 1970s and 1980s to neglect human rights and social responsibility in favour of the extraction from South Africa's finest gold mines of the biggest possible surplus. As Rudolph Agnew, Gold Fields' group chairman, put it in London in 1985: 'We are involved in a highly cyclical industry and we should take the strain during periods of recession and crisis by maintaining the owners' income at the highest practicable level.'[2] The highest practicable level meant exaggerated profits for the head offices and shareholders in Johannesburg and London, while on the mines themselves, ventilation was underfunded, engineering design was constrained, food was poor and facilities were unsatisfactory to say the least.

These exaggerated profits had another fortunate consequence for London. They funded the continuing growth of the Gold Fields' group inside South Africa without any need for investment from outside. Gold Fields' mines were simply so rich, so productive and so profitable that the British parent company gained a lion's share of the resulting wealth without any serious risk or effort on its part. It put in little or nothing by way of technical expertise or mining capital and it became a mechanism for siphoning the wealth created by poor, underdeveloped sending communities on land around Johannesburg first to the Chamber of Mines mint, then out through the golden veins of the international bullion market to the metropolises of London, Geneva, Paris and New York where the gold was sold.

Signs of the bonanza which was to develop in the 1980s could be detected in the London company's 1979 report, which spoke of 'the growing stream of dividends from South Africa'.[3] By 1980 South African gold mining was the greatest contributor to group profit. When Mrs Thatcher came to power, the Callaghan government's modest attempt to monitor the behaviour of British companies in South Africa was effectively undermined and the concerned labour attaché Bill Vose was sent home. (He was never replaced.)[4] The Gold Fields' group chairman Lord Erroll of Hale, a patrician and former member of Harold Macmillan's Conservative Cabinet (who was seldom to be seen without a cigarette either in his hand or mouth and sometimes with one in both), read the signals accurately, according to the London *Evening Standard*. 'A tough new breed of investor has replaced the timid types scared off by Pretoria's policies . . . says Lord Erroll of Hale, Consgold's chairman and he should know. He says South Africa is a damned good investment and one nobody should miss out on.'[5]

The year 1981, after the gold price started vibrating, was a revealing example of the process that was under way. Seven Gold Fields' mines turned in a profit of £995·6 million pounds, with tax payments of around £500 million to the apartheid state and most of the rest either left the country to boost dividends or finance the acquisition of mining companies in South Africa and abroad.[6] At the East and West Driefontein mines Gold Fields' earnings were so sizeable that it became imperative to recast the financial structure of the mine.[7] A. P. Cartwright, Paul Johnson's predecessor as Gold Fields' historian, long ago grasped the magnificent qualities of Driefontein as a mining property. He wrote that it 'might with some justification have been named the fountain of gold'. It was, he added, 'incomparably the richest mine the world had ever known' and produced 'more gold per year than all the mines of the USA'.[8] On the back of the soaring gold price, Gold Fields in London, encouraged by Mrs Thatcher's unequivocal support for Pretoria, boosted its holdings in the South African group company by 2 per cent and increased London's additional direct investments in the Kloof, Driefontein and Deelkraal mines, all of which were expanding rapidly.[9] During this period what London pressed for was financial return, which became a matter of ever greater concern as South Africa's internal crisis deepened and London's directors began to suspect that the political conditions which guaranteed such high profits would not last for ever. Throughout the balmy years of the 1980s, therefore, no funds were diverted from this generous outward flow of profits to tackle the migrant labour problem. Indeed Gold Fields' new mines extended the migrant labour system and involved the construction of still more grim, single-sex compounds.[10]

In Britain, the *Sunday Telegraph*, a newspaper which shared many of the philosophical positions of Gold Fields' directors, identified the extraordinarily generous nature of the gift apartheid was making to the rentiers in London. 'Cons Gold,' it reported on 29 June 1986, 'which intends its partly-owned local subsidiary GFSA to finance most of the massive investment in the new Kloof gold mine internally, is still in a position to draw half of any profits.'[11] The South African stockbrokers Martin & Co also pointed out the indulgent nature of the tax treaties negotiated by British business in return for its embrace of the apartheid regime. 'Dividend income from South Africa goes into Cons Gold tax free and does not even incur South African non-resident shareholders' tax.'[12]

As the movement for sanctions against Pretoria grew in strength, the Gold Fields' group chairman Rudolph Agnew lashed out against anti-apartheid campaigners and any suggestion of sanctions to promote change in southern Africa. 'I never thought I would see the day when we would be ruled from grubby offices in north London,' he told shareholders.[13] In essence Gold Fields in London enthusiastically defended the white South African regime so that it could carry on taking as much money out of the country as possible. The company's extensive contacts with the British Conservative Party proved helpful in this task. The company provided Mrs Thatcher with a senior industrial adviser, George Guise, who was on loan to 10 Downing Street.[14] Gold Fields was a major contributor to Conservative Party funds. The company's financial support also extended to the National Association for Freedom, Aims of Industry and the Institute for Policy Studies think tank.[15] Faced with growing pressure in Britain and the Commonwealth for some sign of practical opposition to apartheid, the Conservative Government declined to take any effective action and even provided Gold Fields with a piece of legislation making it illegal for British local authorities to boycott companies with links with South Africa in their purchasing and tendering programmes.[16] As a group with extensive business interests in the British construction and building materials industry, in addition to its South African mines, Gold Fields was specially vulnerable to local authority pressure and was only saved from widespread and effective boycott by the direct intervention of the British Prime Minister.

The flood of wealth which went from South Africa to London could and should have been used differently, according to Francis Wilson, by now the Professor of Economics at the University of Cape Town, who kept a watchful eye on the development of the migrant labour system throughout the 1980s. 'South Africa today is their legacy,' he said in a measured interview delivered after he had counted off the desperately needed hospitals, schools, housing, clean water and sanitation Gold Fields' £575 million appropriation could have funded. 'Gold has been responsible for both the wealth and the poverty in South Africa, a society with perhaps the greatest inequality in the world, where in some of the rural areas there is real grinding, starving poverty.' He added, 'It needn't have been like this. I think history is going to look back on this last decade or so of the mining industry and the mine managements and the company directors who made the decisions very harshly indeed. It was a once and for all opportunity when the price of gold started to rise dramatically, at a time when there was increasing consciousness and pressure by mineworkers themselves, not only about wages, but about living conditions generally.

'If they hadn't seen it before then, then certainly by that stage and no later, the mining houses should have seen the writing on the wall. They had the opportunity then, for the resources were available as never before, to restructure the whole way in which the mines had been developed over the past hundred years. I'm thinking particularly of the compounds. They had the opportunity to redress the sins of the past and try to structure the industry in such a way that people could live with their families. We failed, the mining industry failed, Gold Fields failed and this opportunity was largely squandered.'[17]

None of the mining companies spent serious money on fundamental reform, but Gold Fields, with the richest mines and the biggest profits, behaved worst of all. It obstructed reform, attacked the emergent black union and delighted in playing the laggard inside the Chamber of Mines when it came to any serious proposal to boost wages and narrow the huge gap between black and white pay rates. Merle Lipton was obviously on to something when, in her *Optima* article and her subsequent book *Capitalism and Apartheid*, she argued 'that the extent of foreign ownership made a critical difference and that an absentee company would want to take out more in the short term and worry less about the long term'.[18]

The net result of Gold Fields' dalliance with apartheid, besides the prolonging of an unjust and wasteful form of society, was, therefore, the disappearance overseas of hundreds of millions of pounds that might have helped to restructure the country. Today, with the money gone, the British end of the company taken over by the Hanson Trust and Gold Fields' South African mines run by an outpost of the Rembrandt business empire belonging to the Afrikaner millionaire Anton Rupert, the country is left with a tragic legacy of problems in its richest gold mines. Bafana Baningi's question remains: how did a great British company come to make such a bequest to the people of South Africa? And why did a blue-chip business become so myopic and morally blind? The beginnings of an answer lie, I believe, in the circumstances of Gold Fields' journey to the heart of the South African mining industry, in the personality and beliefs of the group's founder Cecil Rhodes and in the financial assumptions and associated attitudes and corporate habits of mind he and his co-directors bequeathed to the company.

In South Africa Gold Fields was not only a business organisation. It operated in a country colonised by conquest, where all land, all mining rights and all opportunity were the 'legal' monopoly of whites. Colonial relationships are unequal relationships of a very special kind, shading and complicating the usual problems of stratification and inequality in any society and adding substantially to the hidden injuries sustained by those excluded from wealth or power. Having looked carefully at the origins and development of this great company it seems clear to me that it was this colonialist component which was the decisive factor in cementing and sustaining such a rigid, authoritarian, profit-driven corporate culture in Britain's greatest and most lasting economic enterprise in southern Africa.[19]

The company founder, Cecil Rhodes, went to South Africa to seek his fortune and gain the protection of the climate in June 1870. A Hertfordshire vicar's son, he had had thoughts of being either a barrister or a vicar before emigrating.[20] He arrived in South Africa at a critical time in the country's transformation from an agricultural to an industrial society, and had a fine eye for an economic opportunity as well as an ingrained desire for wealth and power. In addition to these qualities, Rhodes had an unerring political instinct and a special ability for dressing narrow, selfish interests in the language of high ideals. He understood instinctively how the romance of empire could be used to power his corporate vehicles. 'The British flag', he once said, 'is the greatest asset of all time.'[21] He dreamed of a British empire in Africa which stretched from the Cape to Cairo, and saw himself as the modern equivalent of a Spanish conquistador pulling great continents into the slipstream of a dominant imperial power. He floated chartered imperial companies to embody those dreams and used them ruthlessly to deliver gener-ous profits to himself and his circle of friends and associates. He paid himself handsomely, always ensuring that he received huge finder's fees, preferential allotments of shares and, in the case of Gold Fields, a special director's share of all company profits, which he eventually cashed in for the then unprecedented salary of £300,000 a year.[22] And even before John D. Rockefeller Rhodes learned the trick of disguising private greed with a suitable veneer of charitable good works.

Rhodes also worked hard to obtain patronage for his business enterprises. His British South Africa Company, which was linked with Gold Fields, enjoyed the direct sponsorship of Queen Victoria in the form of a royal charter. To obtain the charter Rhodes dealt in the rich, the famous and the influential. Earl Grey; the Duke of Abercorn, a prominent member of the Conservative Party and close friend of the Prime Minister Lord Salisbury; the Duke of Fife, a prominent Liberal, banking partner in the firm of Sir Samuel Scott & Co and son-in-law of the Prince of Wales, all became directors of Rhodes's companies. Horace P. Farquhar, another close friend of the prince's and a treasurer of the Conservative Party, was on side. Lord Robert Cecil, son of Lord Salisbury, was offered and accepted the post of standing counsel. *The Times's* correspondent J. Scott Kelte was brought in for his literary endorsements. Sir Charles Dilke and Lord Knutsford were allotted shares. Rhodes kept tens of thousands of shares in the British South Africa Company, which were specially earmarked as gifts for influential people in Cape Town, London and other European capitals. The entire shareholding of the British South Africa Company was allotted without any public offering of any kind.[23]

Over his business associates and the shareholding public Rhodes exercised a near magical influence. Even the South African writer Olive Schreiner, later to become one of his sternest critics, was initially attracted by his air of mystery and found herself anxious to believe in his sincerity. But as she began to analyse his record of civic behaviour, she grew more detached and in the end concluded that Rhodes was one of the most unscrupulous characters that ever lived. 'Why do you surround yourself with such men?' she once asked him about some of his friends and associates. 'Those men! My friends?' he replied. 'They are not my friends, they are my tools and when I have finished with them I throw them away.'[24] Meeting him after he had voted for a Bill which allowed whites in the Cape to beat their servants, Schreiner declined to shake hands with Rhodes. Later she recorded, 'The perception of what his character really was in its inmost depths was one of the most terrible revelations of my life.' She felt that she could discern 'below the fascinating surface, the worms of falsehood and corruption creeping'.[25]

Falsehood and corruption were business methods which the architect of Britain's empire in Africa used repeatedly. Faced with the prospect of the Cape Parliament imposing a scheme of corporate taxation for the first time, Rhodes seems to have been involved in ballot rigging and ghost voting to defeat the measure.[26] In the light of Rob Turrell's careful researches, it seems fair to conclude that Rhodes was involved in trying to sabotage pumping equipment at Kimberley to enlarge his influence and his income.[27] But as his influence grew, Rhodes and his associates became involved in business dealings which had truly fateful consequences for relations with the indigenous peoples of southern Africa.

The patterns of this behaviour were most evident in two exercises of colonial rowdyism central to the development of Gold Fields as a company – first, the forcible annexation of Matabeleland (which led to the proclamation of a whole country called Rhodesia) and second, the Jameson Raid, the failed coup which aimed to seize the gold-bearing lands of the Transvaal. Both involved dishonesty, deliberate fraud and direct acts of physical violence and territorial aggression engineered by business organisations. The annexation of Matabeleland by Rhodes's chartered company was a dangerous and illegal affair. Lobengula, the king of the Matabele, was essentially duped into signing a concession which he had no power to give. To get him to do this Rhodes bribed him with arms, a fact that had to be carefully disguised from London for fear that it would cost the company its royal charter. As a result of his experiences at the hands of Rhodes's agents, Lobengula came to believe that the white men had 'come not only to dig the gold but to rob me of my people and country as well'. His instincts were sound. For Rhodes and his associates had concluded a highly provocative secret agreement to parcel out land, money and mining claims to induce people to join their 'expeditionary force' (a polite name for a raiding party). The secret agreement was in flat contradiction to the honeyed words of the company charter.

Defeated militarily but still unbowed, the Matabele king eventually surrendered his wealth. Explaining his decision, he stated, 'The white men will never cease following us whilst we have gold in our possession, for gold is what white men prize above all things'. In fact the raiders wanted land as well and before this disreputable campaign was at an end thousands of indigenous people were killed and millions of acres of their common lands enclosed by illegal force of arms.

Even though it had the imprimatur of royalty, there was no basis in English law for any of this behaviour. The law of England reserved all land obtained by conquest for the State, but the disinherited African peoples had no legal rights, no legal representation and few friends or defenders; and Rhodes and his business associates had no scruples.[28]

The whole unedifying process was dignified by the fashionable journalists of the day and the theft of a country turned into a 'triumph' for the British race. Indeed the destructive, colonising spirit of the times in Britain was so strong that Rhodes's reward was not disavowal but celebration and praise in huge quantities and from the highest level. In London a stream of influential visitors came to pay court to the conqueror at his hotel. The Prince of Wales, close to Rhodes's circle because of his need for ready money to feed his love of gambling and night life, graced the platform of a meeting specially summoned to celebrate the raid and welcome the founding of Britain's Rhodesian colony. In the course of the meeting, held at the Imperial Institute in London, Dr Jameson raised the science of self-advertisement to new heights. Soon afterwards Rhodes visited Queen Victoria at Windsor and was made a Privy Councillor.[29] Thereafter Rhodes was unstoppable and a new and equally fateful venture in colonial enlargement by violent and illegal means soon resulted – the Jameson Raid. In this squalid enterprise, the nemesis of those Victorian values which have recently returned to fashion in Britain, the disturbed Scottish doctor once again worked to the specific instructions of the imperial hero from Hertfordshire. Their raid set out to repeat the 'triumph' over the Matabele on the Afrikaner farmers of the Transvaal Republic, where the gold-bearing lands were so inestimably valuable that Rhodes schemed to annex them to the British crown. Working through a spurious campaign for representative government, Rhodes found a pretext for a rising and again used the techniques of colonial rowdyism to achieve his ends. On this occasion, his Gold Fields company was the vehicle for his conspiracy.

Gold Fields' facilities were used as supply lines for the distribution and storage of rifles, explosives and the other technologies of conquest. Once again Leander Starr Jameson tried to march in and steal the land. But the *coup d'état* was poorly co-ordinated and easily defeated by the Afrikaner president and his troops. In the aftermath of the raid, the extraordinary complicity of Gold Fields was brought out in court. A number of Gold Fields' directors were tried for treason for their involvement in the coup and some of them even sentenced to death for the critical parts they played.

Then later, in interesting circumstances, they were reprieved and set free in return for the payment of hefty fines.[30]

The ideology of racism played a central and even irreplaceable part in these developments. The metaphors of a 'higher form of civilisation' justified conquest, camouflaged corruption and seemed in some quarters to paralyse all capacity for scepticism. Gold Fields' founder, Rhodes himself, was deeply corrupted by racism. 'I prefer land to niggers,' he said on one occasion.[31] On another he expressed his hatred of 'the mission world' by revealingly and xenophobically categorising them as 'the negrophilists of Exeter Hall'.[32] And one of Rhodes's South African biographers, the poet William Plomer, has advanced the suggestion that Rhodes himself was implicated in racial atrocities when in August 1886 in the Enkeldoorn area of South Africa seventy Africans were massacred with his active involvement.[33] The conquistadorial attitude found eloquent expression in Rhodes's talk of 'space for the British race', a form of words whose core of meaning has become more obvious in its German equivalent *Lebensraum*. Sir Sydney Shippard, one of the key colonial officials Rhodes used to help steal Matabeleland (who later became legal adviser to Gold Fields), was also deeply corrupted by racial arrogance. During the raid he explained that he wanted to see 'the Matabele . . . cut down by our rifles and machine-guns like a cornfield by a reaping machine'. 'And I would not spare a single one if I could have my way,' he added.[34]

Later in Gold Fields' history the toxin of racism was to be harnessed to justify more routine forms of inhumanity than ethnocide. But conquistadorial attitudes left their mark on the company and ensured that throughout Gold Fields' one-hundred-year history an ugly, deformed and dominating ideology permeated the corporate culture. The company's American-born consulting engineer John Hays Hammond gave typical expression to it – and was greeted with laughter and applause – at the company meeting in London in 1899.

'With good government,' he stated, 'there should be an abundance of labour, and with an abundance of labour there will be no difficulty in cutting down wages because it is preposterous to pay a Kaffir the present wages. He would be quite as well satisfied – in fact he would work longer – if you gave him half the amount. [Laughter.] His wages are altogether disproportionate to his requirements. [Renewed laughter.]'[35]

After the Boer War, an unnecessary war once again fought for gold, Gold Fields led the way in introducing compounds to the Rand, and cutting wages and reducing feeding costs so that high profits could be made from low-grade gold mines. The company's mines became a byword for difficult conditions, poor food and racial authoritarianism. This unabashed racism remained in evidence right through to the present day – in Gold Fields' 1986 training manuals, where 'the Bantu' were crudely caricatured as inferior beings. The Gold Fields' world view pictured Africa not as a continent of intrinsic value where peoples' rights and cultures should be valued, but as a place to be subordinated and scrambled for. This philosophy found its way into all the standard operating assumptions of the company and its mining compounds. In the end, it was this complex of attitudes which predisposed a great British company first to help devise the migrant labour system and then to collaborate so enthusiastically with apartheid.

There was of course a strongly opportunistic side to this collaboration. Serious amounts of money could be made from it, and Gold Fields drew a particularly generous dividend from its business partnership with the South African state in an unusual form of society – a capitalism of racial domination or 'racial capitalism' as the new wave of South African historiographers have described it. At the heart of this racial capitalism was a cruel and inexcusable flaw, beautifully captured by the writer Adèle Lizard, who discerned the underlying realities of the gold standard that Britain and its empire had constructed in South Africa.

The mining companies

> had no scruples, no feelings, no sentiments, no illusions about justice. To them the black man represented no more than a strong body to be harnessed to the yoke of industry, to make its owners rich and to provide them with a comfortable source of income.
>
> They never realised, or never wanted to realise, that the native was a man. He was just a great lumbering beast of burden and must be treated as such. Cattle. That is how the mining industry saw the natives of Africa. Just black cattle to be driven and whipped; to make the wheels go round . . . no leniency should be shown to the native, for leniency, it was argued, was a sign of weakness.[36]

Gold Fields showed no human weakness and, correspondingly, no human strength. Looking back at the company's century-long engagement with the people and natural resources of South Africa, it is difficult to disagree with the conclusions of William Plomer, who reasoned that in the scramble for Africa something precious and essential to the human species was lost to colonising individuals and the organisations they built. Their character structure was, he argued, fatefully distorted by the process. He mourned the loss of gentleness, spontaneity, kindness and consideration.[37] Certainly Gold Fields' corporate culture had no place for any of these qualities. Fierce in its love of order, passionate in its search for cost effectiveness and high profits, fussy and authoritarian in the way it ran its camps and compounds, the company became poisoned in its heart. Cut off from the impulses of generosity, contemptuous of pluralism and democracy and implacably hostile to black trade unions, the tramlines of tradition ensured that Gold Fields refused even to begin the process of thinking out how it might live in a just way. In the end this flaw became apparent to tens of thousands of black miners caught inside its pit cages, mine crushes and colonial compounds. In their own way they began to ask an age-old question: what shall it profit a man if he should gain the whole world and lose his soul?[38]

9 Dust to Dust: Mining Companies and Environmental Catastrophe in the North Western Cape

In the words of Paul Brodeur, America's foremost writer on environmental pollution and industrial disease, statistics are human beings with the tears wiped off. Today Booi Visagie, James Serubele Ebang and Frank Molwaggae are statistics, single digits on South Africa's confidential register of terminal cancer caused by the negligence of the asbestos mining industry. But in 1981 when I first went to South Africa to investigate the health and safety record of the country's mining industry, the three men, aged thirty-five, forty-eight and fifty respectively, were still alive, fighting for breath and hoping the end would come easily. The likelihood is that they were denied this final wish. For death from mesothelioma, the cancer caused by asbestos dust, is long-drawn-out and painful beyond belief.[1]

All three men had worked for major South African mining companies – Booi Visagie for Anglo American's Cape Industries, Frank Molwaggae for Gencor's Griqualand Exploration and Finance and James Ebang for Everite-Eternit's Kuruman Cape Blue Asbestos, a company with strong Swiss and Belgian connections. In the course of a five-week-long journey through the North Western Cape Province, a relatively remote part of South Africa where the fertile farmlands of the country begin to give way to the sandy desert of the Kalahari, I traced the three men to run-down charity hospital wards where they had gone to die or found them in the shacks and shanties that black miners call home. I went to the North Western Cape via Johannesburg and Cape Town to see if the tragedy of asbestos, which had been played out in Britain and America with thousands of people killed by one of the most toxic substances known to man, had been repeated in the land where the asbestos had been mined.[2]

In the course of the journey my worst fears were exceeded a thousandfold. In the 1980s, more than a decade after blue asbestos had been banned in

Britain, I found houses built of the deadly blue fibre in South Africa. There were whole towns and villages through which lethal dust from mine dumps was frequently blown in the wind. Rivers and water supplies were polluted with it, lakes and lagoons blue like Caribbean seas with it, cows grazing on topsoil tinted with it, so that the fibres found their way into milk and meat. There were children playing in it, miners whose food was contaminated with it on a daily basis. Most inexcusable of all, there was hard evidence of a concerted attempt over many years to keep people in the dark about what the industry was doing so that the mining companies could carry on making profits from the continued exploitation of their mineral deposits. Even today, years after I made that journey through the asbestos mountains in the North Western Cape, the images of a land despoiled and of a people so cruelly diminished are still with me.[3]

A blue door to a tiny shack, a wasted man with impending death written across his face, and a partner called Emily fierce in her anger – that is how I remember the late James Ebang today, nine years after we filmed him and eight years after his inevitable death. 'My lungs seem to close up if I walk too fast or when I pick something up,' he told me in his deep voice, a last echo of the other, larger man he had been. 'I have lost a lot of weight, I wasn't like this, I was a big man,' he said. 'Yes, sir,' Emily cut in, 'this man wasn't like this before. He was a big, strong, healthy man, beautiful and attractive. He is very weak now compared to the time we got married. Now he is a skeleton, finished.

'I cannot go out to work because he gets sick often. At night he is feverish and cannot breathe. The company he worked for never put their feet here. If they had any conscience or feelings then they would have come. They have abandoned him. I feel sad and bitter. If he dies I won't be able to bury him properly because I do not have money. I will have to bury him in a sack.'[4]

James Ebang knew he was dying. Born in 1933, he was aged forty-eight when we spoke outside his little house. He had nine children, the last born four years before we were speaking, now in his teens and an orphan with few memories of his father. As James made ready to die, one of the things that most pained him was the fact that as a result of his illness he and his wife could no longer afford the fees to educate their four children of school age. From the condition of the house, the clothing of the children and the ragged appearance of both parents, it was clear that the Ebangs were living in conditions of acute poverty. Yet Mr Ebang was one of a tiny handful of black contract mine workers to have received any compensation payment

167

for dust diseases. Before 1977 they were given nothing and were sent back to the reserves or homelands by the mining companies and left to die of chest diseases, poverty and starvation. Mr Ebang's plight had been spotted by investigators from a local hospital, who were counting the depressing number of diseased and injured men left behind in the area by the North Western Cape's biggest industry besides agricultural production – asbestos mining. As a result his disease was certified as work related and he qualified for a pension. But the pension was affected by the differential calculus of apartheid and Mr Ebang received only forty-one rand a quarter, or roughly £2 a week, from the State. This meant that after he and his wife had bought a sack of mealie meal and some coffee there was no hope of money for school fees.

James Ebang, company number 8210 at Kuruman Cape Blue Asbestos, had spent sixty months undergound working as an asbestos miner before he was transferred into the mill at Whitebank near his shack. Classified as suffering from asbestosis in 1977 and then in August 1981 dealt another blow when doctors confirmed that he had mesothelioma, the incurable cancer of the lining of the lung for which asbestos is the only known cause, Mr Ebang served his time in the asbestos industry working for the South African component of the Everite-Eternit multinational. This is a well-funded and highly profitable business organisation, with Swiss and Belgian company registration and Spanish connections stretching all the way back to the Duke of Wellington's quartermaster and his descendant Juan Marsh, banker industrialist and multi-millionaire who once claimed it was his mission to clean up the asbestos industry.[5]

Mr Ebang saw no evidence of any such campaign. 'At KCB conditions were very very dusty. I worked in the packing room sewing the hessian bags shut after they were filled and at the weighing scales. I had absolutely no protection. Others I worked with died from chest diseases too – Adam, Oodboi and Assagai; another was Tenjas Kabele. Last month I was in hospital. They operated on me but they did not tell me very much. The children suffer, they do not have clothes, no soap for washing, no fresh blankets, no Sunday clothes to go to church. My wife keeps mending their clothes like an old woman when she is still young. When I worked we had enough money but now we have little or nothing.'

Having met the Ebang family, I wanted to see the factory that had laid James low. I drove to Whitebank, the Swiss-Belgian multinational's main mill in the Kuruman area. I was sure that conditions wouldn't be as bad any more. Things would have changed for the better and the inexcusable working conditions that had marked James Ebang's life would no longer obtain. And these had been sensationally bad at Whitebank. According to Dr Chris Wagner, the emigré South African asbestos researcher I had met at the Medical Research Council Laboratory near Cardiff before my trip, there had been a huge plume of dust over Whitebank in the 1960s. Local pilots used to navigate by it.[6] There was no great blue cloud overhead as I approached Whitebank by road, but some distance from the mill, possibly even a mile away, I noticed that the ground was tinted blue along the side of the road, where the curly blue fibres were trapped in grasses. The place was thick with dust; when I got out of the car I could stretch out and pick up clumps of fibre by the handful. As I drove closer to the plant I could see why. There were mountains of asbestos tailings stretching as far as the eye could see. Some of the mine roadways had clearly been surfaced with the fibre, a practice which was supposed to have stopped twenty years before; and there were huge quantities of dust at the entrance gate and in the parking lot. At the sorting plant I sneaked a look into the changing room, which was thick with dust. There were no lockers, only hooks for the miners to hang their clothes on and a broken-down asbestos cement seat for them to sit on. Whitebank was, in other words, so dirty that James Ebang could not have been the only asbestosis or mesothelioma victim.

I made repeated attempts to interview the directors of the Kuruman Cape Blue Asbestos Mines and their associates in the Everite and Eternit companies about the poor conditions at Whitebank. I wanted to ask them why they had milled fibres known to be dangerous to human health for twenty years after the risks were recognised, why they had deposited the deadly leftovers of their toxic trade in mountains of blue asbestos slag around the countryside. I wanted to ask them what if anything they were going to do to help James and Emily Ebang and the other sick and injured former employees they had abandoned. But senior company officials seemed reluctant to make themselves available, and were unwilling to discuss either the causes or the consequences of their actions. The best that they could do was provide an off-camera briefing with the Eternit health consultant, Fritz Baunach.[7] He told me at an initial meeting to discuss a possible interview that the campaign against blue asbestos had been inspired by German trade unionists 'as part of Willy Brandt's sinister international campaign to achieve workers' control throughout the western world'. Tall and powerfully built, he seemed uncharacteristically frightened by the idea of a television interview.

He showed no such reticence in other fields of activity, and had manfully worked to put himself in a highly influential position in the strange world of South African government-sponsored research into the health risks of asbestos. He sat on the advisory panel set up to review the work done by the National Centre for Occupational Health and the Pneumoconiosis Research Unit; and, although he had no scientific qualifications, he had the right to request alterations in the phrasing of scientific papers which had been put forward for publication and even to veto publication altogether.[8]

Beyond Whitebank lay another asbestos property, Wandrag, owned by Duiker Exploration, part of the British Lonrho group. The material Lonrho mined at Wandrag was so dangerous it had been effectively banned in Lonrho's home base for over a decade. I turned a corner as I drove up and another blue lagoon of toxic waste came into view, blinding me with the intensity of its colour. Lonrho's dirty blue lagoon, complete with dead bird floating on its surface, is where the dust recovered in its mill is pumped after it has been emptied from the sacks which trap it and then carefully mixed with water for ease of disposal. Once it reaches the lagoon the water, itself heavily polluted with asbestos, returns to the water table while the asbestos dries in the sun. As the winds and breezes move over the area, the fibres are taken up and spread over the surrounding countryside.[9]

The blue lagoon was as nothing compared to conditions in and around the mill itself. Outside one of the doors two men were working hard with wooden moulds, knocking out breeze blocks which they fashioned from a mixture of cement and blue asbestos fibre, a process as dangerous for their clients as it was for their own health. Their faces were gnarled by their many shifts in the intense sun, and, surrounded by asbestos dust, they were in obvious danger of contracting asbestosis, mesothelioma or one of the many other cancers with which asbestos is connected. When I tried to speak to them both men maintained a studied silence and carried on with their work as if I did not exist. Inside the mill the workers wore hard hats, but had no masks or air-fed respirators although the air was heavy with blue fibre. The conveyor belts were thick with it; there was dust all over the floor and the machinery, and along the pipes and electrical conduits – everywhere. I wondered at the double standards of a British company operating anywhere in defiance of British industrial safety laws fifty years after they were established in its mother country.[10]

As I left the mill block I looked into the smiling faces of two young black men who worked there. In them I saw people who in twenty years or less would follow in James Ebang's footsteps, grow prematurely aged and sick, short of breath, their fingernails clubbing, and their lungs filling up with fluid just as their homes would fill with sorrow in anticipation of their untimely and unnecessary deaths. A few days later I returned to Lonrho's blue asbestos mine with my colleagues Simon Berthon, David Woods and David Odd. We began to film the blue lagoon, the men making toxic breeze blocks out front, and we even scuttled into the main mill-room to snatch shots of the young men working covered in dust without even the most primitive forms of protection. Then suddenly a powerfully built man in Tuf boots, denim shirt and shorts and a blue hard hat appeared in front of David Odd and said, 'What the hell do you think you're doing here?' David replied in the only way he could – with a statement of the obvious. The man in the hard hat told us he was the mine manager and ordered us to follow him to his office. 'Here we go . . .' David whispered out of the side of his mouth. 'How do we talk our way out of this one?' David Woods asked calmly out of the side of his. 'We'll see,' said Simon. We were ushered into the boardroom, where the mine manager repeated his question and waited for an answer. Each of us gave him a bit of it, pious and embarrassingly sincere, like highly disciplined choirboys who knew by instinct how to add a pleasing descant to a predecessor's lines and embellish the phrasing. We referred in turn to our love of his country, our interest in his mine and our determination to make a travelogue called 'South African Journey', a title David Odd had scrawled on to a piece of camera-tape which he had stuck on to a can of exposed film so that if we were apprehended on mine properties our explanations would be supported by at least one piece of visual evidence.[11]

The manager, Mr Howard, was about the same age as we were. He was on home ground and he was tough, tired and cynical. The only time he became really agitated was when one of us mentioned that the cameraman had met Tiny Rowland, the boss of Lonrho. 'Frankly, I couldn't give a damn if one of you has met Tiny Rowland,' he cried. The exercise in name-dropping was a complete flyer and it might have backfired. But within sixty seconds it was clear that he was interested if not impressed. 'Which one of you met him?' he inquired curtly. 'He did, he did,' three of us said in eager unison, pointing at David Odd. David took a deep breath and launched into as fine a line in blarney as ever it has been my pleasure to witness. Yes, he explained, he had met Mr Rowland after filming in Rhodesia and he added by way of a makeweight that one of our other colleagues was a close friend of his. 'Almost like a son to him,' added David, trowelling it on, his natural

171

diffidence by now giving way to another side of his character, mischievous, expansive and debonair.

The mine manager came back strong and hard. 'It's very, very impolite to come in here uninvited and unannounced. I just don't like people who behave like this. It's rude and it's trespass on private property. The only reason you got away with it is that round here we don't have the usual mine security set-up – that's probably why we make a profit. If you'd have come and asked me, I'd have taken you round the place myself, shown you its good points and its bad points. And yes I know it's a shitty mill,' he added, continuing with his outburst. At this point the phone buzzed and the manager picked it up in exasperation at being interrupted. 'You can't get through,' he said angrily through his teeth into the mouthpiece, speaking it seemed to the mine switchboard operator, who had, we assumed, been trying the police. 'Can't get through, can't get through. That's always the story round here,' said Mr Howard in clipped tones of rage as he forced the receiver back across the handset. Instead of calling the police who could not be contacted and who in any case might not come, Mr Howard gave us another tongue-lashing, reminding us again of our rudeness. We apologised profusely and then he said, 'Go on, get out of here.' We were only too happy to oblige, falling into the Volkswagen minibus as if we had just finished a ten-year jail sentence. With David Woods stretching the machine to hitherto unimagined limits, we sped off the property. Later back in Britain I asked for an interview with Lonrho about the terrible conditions in the mine, but this was refused on the grounds that we had committed an act of trespass, law-breaking which the company could not condone. With no interview from Lonrho we showed the film of the company's plant to an old friend, Ted Rushworth, a former British factory inspector who had first inspected asbestos mills in the late 1940s. He was almost speechless when he saw the conditions which obtained in the plant and condemned them roundly once he had recovered from the shock.[12]

Our next port of call was the mission hospital St Michael's at Bathlaros, not far from the home of James and Emily Ebang. Recently reassigned to the Bophutatswana government, a nominally independent government of a nominally independent homeland broken into scattered pieces as part of Pretoria's perfection of the ancient policy of divide and rule, the little charity hospital tried to do its best for asbestos victims living locally. But as the nurse on duty, Sister Seamaco, pointed out, in a country without a health service for African people the charity hospitals functioned on very limited resources. As I explained a little of what had brought me to the area, it was clear that Sister Seamaco was hungry for knowledge about asbestos and disease. 'Is the relationship between asbestos and mesothelioma cancer an established one?' she asked anxiously. 'Long since,' I replied. 'At least in Britain and America, France and Germany, Italy and Spain, Australia and Canada.' The sister paused for a moment's reflection and then said worriedly, 'We have one man with us now in the isolation ward. His wound just won't heal.'

As we entered the bare little room, it did not seem as if there was anyone in the hospital bed, least of all a grown man. A malnourished child perhaps, but not a grown man. Quietly Sister Seamaco switched on a sidelight and now I could see that there was a patient in the bed, lying flat under a single white sheet without even a pillow to elevate his head. 'For the past fortnight he's not been able to stand a pillow. He just lies here all day, silent and still. He might toss and turn at night I suppose when no one is looking, but in the day time at least he just doesn't have the strength.' The patient's name was Frank, the sister explained, Frank Molwaggae, a fifty-year-old black man from Gatlosi, about thirty-five miles from Bathlaros on the road to Sishen.

It seemed unfair to disturb him any more that evening, so I arranged with Sister Seamaco to return the following day near the beginning of her shift. The next day the sister greeted me warmly and sat me down for a private talk. Once again she asked if the relationship between asbestos and cancer had been proven. I filled out my answer of the night before, stating that fifty years ago in Britain when the government was drawing up the first asbestos regulations there were people who even then were worried about asbestos causing cancer. 'And in 1947', I added, 'a famous medical inspector of factories by the name of Mereweather began to publish his research on the asbestos–cancer relationship, showing that people who got asbestosis and survived, had a much increased chance of getting cancer.[13] But', I added, remembering other even more relevant information, 'it was here in the North Western Cape twenty years ago that the key work on mesothelioma and asbestos was done, by South African doctors.' The sister was bemused. 'I've heard nothing about that,' she said. She explained that she had asked questions and made requests for written papers and information, but the doctors seemed to keep all knowledge to themselves. She had seen many people building houses with the blue fibres. 'The fibres make the cement go further, that's why they use it, and it's readily available all round here.' I explained that in Britain the material was considered so dangerous that it was banned and no one should work with it even in protective clothing, far less live with it in the walls of their houses. 'The doctors all know about people using it for bricks and cement, but they have never told anyone not to use it,' said Sister Seamaco. 'We don't see it as our job to tell people these things,' she added carefully, lifting her eyebrows to underline the point, which I took to be that doctors and nurses in South Africa are not supposed to rock the boat.

At this break in the conversation the sister suggested we see Mr Molwaggae, who this time was conscious and awake. In daylight, it was obvious that Frank hadn't long to live, probably only a few weeks at most. Like James Ebang, he had inhaled asbestos dust in the course of his job, working with the Gencor mining group. He had fallen sick at the beginning of the year and was on his deathbed by the end of it. He was in the isolation ward, he explained, because an incision in his chest to drain the huge quantities of fluid in his lungs had become infected and would not heal. His wound, he stated matter of factly, now gave off a terrible smell of sickness and decay. It was all he could do to stand it and, he explained, it wasn't fair to inflict it on other patients. Mr Molwaggae's wound had become infected, I surmised, because it was difficult for a sick man living in poverty without running water, a toilet or bathroom in his home to keep it clean. Later a doctor who knew about Frank's case suggested another possible cause – poor aseptic technique at the hospital, not surprising given that St Michael's had poor facilities; it had only three doctors and needed at least four more. Whatever the cause, Frank Molwaggae lay in bed each day and smelled his own impending death. Separated from his wife and without any children, he was completely alone and could scarcely even speak, each clause or sentence being preceded by a squeaking hiss of air taken in through the tiny hole in his chest, and much of it seemingly coming back out the same way. In the course of our brief conversation before pain brought it to a halt, he explained that he had had no compensation, or help of any kind, not even a visit from a representative of his employers GEFCO, the Griqualand Exploration and Finance Company, part of Gencor which Harry Oppenheimer had given over to Afrikaner business interests in the 1960s. 'I feel abandoned, quite abandoned,' Frank stressed, adding that a few beers might ease the pain, but since he had no pension or disability allowance, and no help of any kind from his employers, he had no money to buy them. I took his remark in the spirit in which it was intended, and returned with some tins of lager. Later I sent him some clothing and a little money from Johannesburg. With a bit of luck the parcel would have reached him before he died.

Having seen Whitebank mine and mill, the source of James Ebang's painful injuries, I thought I should take a look at the places where Frank Molwaggae had been compelled to work under a contract labour system which removed all choice about employment from individual miners, compelling them to go wherever they were sent by the Chamber of Mines recruiting organisation. The next day I drove beyond Kuruman into the surrounding countryside to see GEFCO's mines. I went first to Coretsi, west of Kuruman, where Frank Molwaggae had worked. Here the sorting plant was in full swing, with women hand-sorting the rock for fibre and working with no protection at all. Underneath the conveyor belts the dust had built up in sizeable quantities and it seemed clear that human health was not a serious priority in the way the operation was designed and conducted. Then the increasingly familiar blue expanse of a gigantic asbestos dump drew my attention and I got back into the car and drove higher up so that I could survey it. It was an astonishing sight, with a gleaming blue lagoon in the middle and a herd of cows drinking water from it.

Next I went to another GEFCO mine, Asbes, which was every bit as bad as Coretsi, with waste tips located so that winds and breezes would blow the dust into the compound where the migrant miners lived and then downwind to Cape Town and other places reached by the prevailing winds. At GEFCO's Bretby mine the African workers wore no protective clothes or equipment, and their only recreational facility was a crude football field, partly made of asbestos and dwarfed by another gigantic dump which rose above it like some ghostly modern, toxic equivalent of the pyramids. Here too the ground underfoot was thick with deadly blue asbestos fibre.

Next on the list were GEFCO's Bute, Heuningvlei and Pomfret properties, some way to the north into the Kalahari. We had been warned that Pomfret would be a different kettle of fish, not nearly so approachable as the other older mines, where security was lax. It was a big, modern mine and mill right out in the open countryside, with tight security. The same member of the Church of England who gave us the warning suggested a solution – travel with a priest or borrow a priest's collar. In the end we tried the latter. As we neared Pomfret, the passenger next to the driver donned a black artificial silk shirt-front topped with a magnificent dog collar as cracklingly stiff as it was sparkling white. This all-in-one masterpiece of ecclesiastical tailoring, was known in the trade as a 'one and a quarter inch thick Cardinal'. Manufactured by Wippell & Co. of Exeter, London and Manchester, it worked a treat. Instead of searching the van, and spying the cameras and film, the security men were busy crossing themselves and saying, 'God Bless you, father,' as we swept past.

Pomfret was modern looking by comparison with the other asbestos mines we had visited. Built by the British company Cape Asbestos, it was then sold to Barlow Rand and then on again to GEFCO after Cape lost its insurance cover in the American marketplace and Britain further tightened its restrictions against blue asbestos because of the cancer risk. Here at least the companies seemed to be using impermeable sacks as stipulated fifty years earlier in one of the many provisions of the 1931 British asbestos regulations. And there were signs of functioning dust-control equipment. But in a sense this was beside the point. The dust vents, the plastic sacks and the accompanying modern methods of heat-sealing them or using plastic closures were Johnny-come-lately frills on a fundamentally dangerous operation. Here too dust was everywhere, monster piles of tailings thick with the fibres, compounds next to dumps, and men exposed by the hundred. The natural environment was once again disturbed to reveal a toxic material that leading British scientists like Molly Newhouse, who had been counting Cape's mesotheliomas in the London borough of Barking since the 1950s, insisted should not be mined at all.[14] We took our shots, granted absolution to a few senior white employees in front of the office block and then left for our next destination.

We arrived at General Mining's opencast Bute Mine at about 2 p.m. on a glorious Sunday afternoon. While this meant the mine and the mill were not working and we could not see what sort of toxic plume came off the installation when it was in production, it also meant that we could talk freely to the workers and obtain access to the compound, which was a remarkable place. The miners lived without privacy or comfort, twelve and sometimes twenty to a room with grim, iron bedsteads, no sheets and no furniture. Instead of mattresses the company, part of one of the richest mining groups in the world, issued them with thin felt pads of roughly the same thickness and consistency as poor-quality carpet underlay. But this was not the most serious neglect of the miners' health and comfort that we found. The workers told us that GEFCO gave them no protection inside the mine and mill. They told us – and we easily confirmed this – that asbestos dust blew into their huts through the gaps between the walls and the roofs. They also told us that the asbestos dust got into their food. As we moved around Bute, we saw immense piles of tailings, blue as the sky above and obviously thick with fibre. Children played ten or fifteen yards away, goats were reared and pastured on land irretrievably polluted with the material; and it was abundantly clear that the standards of construction and housekeeping in Bute were so poor that when the wind was in the right direction, the cookhouse would be visited by ambient fibres picked up and floated on the breeze.

Heuningvlei, literally the hollow of the honey where water gathers, was even further into the Kalahari, roughly a 200-kilometre drive from Kuruman, through a stunning landscape rich in living creatures, plants and human beings who had, in the process of evolution, adapted themselves to an extraordinary environment. The asbestos dump slowly becomes visible, then the compound, all of it thick with a lavender carpet of dust which the owners had failed to clean up when the mill was finally shut down by the Health Department in 1978. Heuningvlei was a small, highly specialised operation which had for years belonged to the British company Turner & Newall. They seemed to have taken a policy decision to get out of blue asbestos some time in the late 1960s or early 1970s when the medical evidence moved from being merely incriminatory to being overwhelming. But they didn't just close down. Instead they sold the property to GEFCO, who, like Turner & Newall before them, carried on milling the stuff for all they were worth and polluting the surrounding environment to an extraordinary degree. The crudity of the engineering at Heuningvlei, and the attendant neglect of the natural environment and human consequences, are well evidenced in a letter dated 8 December 1958 from a firm of air-conditioning engineers in Lake View, Johannesburg, which we found among a clutch of correspondence dumped amidst several tons of loose asbestos waste. In the third paragraph was a description of some of the technical problems the company was having in collecting asbestos dust on its makeshift equipment, which the air-conditioning firm was offering to redesign. 'Your mill fans', the letter stated, 'are at present exhausting to atmosphere.' What this meant was that the poisonous dust inside the mill was being sucked up into an extraction fan after a fashion, but instead of this keeping the dust permanently out of the atmosphere it pushed it up through a vent and deposited it on the wind.

Even though Heuningvlei had closed down three years before, it was still 'exhausting to atmosphere'. Nowadays the asbestos fibre came from the tailings dump or from the abandoned machines inside the mill, which were thick with the toxic material. Both places were feet deep in the fibre and even on the calm day during which we made our visit to film the scene, the breeze was strong enough to transport dust visibly around the locality. For the hundreds of people who live in the area, Heuningvlei is a place of inordinate importance. Here in the Kalahari water is in very short supply. At Heuningvlei by some accident of nature, there is water and people come from many miles around to draw their supplies. In the local economy it is also important for another reason. It's a natural salt pan, attracting many more people, who work for hours to obtain salt supplies for domestic consumption. The local people have no knowledge of the health hazards of asbestos, and no idea what might happen to them later in life because they have played among Turner & Newall's dumps as children or panned salt contaminated with the deadly dust.

As if the threat to casual visitors was not enough, Heuningvlei was also being used during the week as accommodation for schoolchildren coming into the area for education. My colleague Simon established that the tepees or concrete rondavels, which Turner & Newall had constructed for the miners, were now being used to house school students. They came to Heuningvlei to be exposed to learning, but unknown to themselves they were also being exposed to toxic dust. After finishing the panning shots to illustrate the relationship of the waterhole and the salt pan to the asbestos dump, we sat down, talked for a while and shook our heads in sorrow. This was the beautiful Kalahari, a place of wonder that we had read about, famed for its rich inheritance of human and animal life, but in reality ravaged by the mining companies. What sort of civilisation was it that defecated in its own bed? What sort of companies were they that had specialised and detailed knowledge of the dangers of this dust and left it to blow around the desert lands and injure local people who knew nothing of the threat that faced them?

I was reminded of a statement by Lewis Mumford which I had read in a 1960s book called *Philosophies of the Earth – Conversations with Ecologists*: 'What we are demanding is a different kind of technology, one that is in a better relationship to life, not one that is concerned merely with increasing the Gross National Product . . . or providing enormous profits for those in control of the system.'

Mumford continued:

This isn't being anti-technology. It's being in favour of another kind of technology that can continue in existence indefinitely. It's only by putting into the system what you have taken out of it that you can have a system that is in equilibrium. Our lopsided technology is now in the process of breaking down and must eventually undermine its own existence.[15]

We drove away from Heuningvlei, the hollow of the honey where water

178

gathers and pollution has left its indelible mark, in total silence for an hour or more, a bad thing on a long drive. David Odd, normally a first-class driver, was deep in thought and was, we suddenly noticed, going at breakneck speed towards the solidly constructed road sign in the middle of the T junction where our dirt track intersected with the road back to Hotazel. Our shouts awoke him from the spell, and he turned aside just in time. Thereafter we went more or less straight back to Johannesburg, slept fitfully overnight, and the following morning presented ourselves at Gencor's headquarters in Hollard Street in Johannesburg's business district. There we asked for an interview with the directors in the hope of questioning them about their lack of regard for human beings, human rights and the natural environment.

Inside the Gencor head offices I asked two of the company's managers of asbestos production, L. K. Jooste and Colin Officer, if we could film an interview with one of them or with Wally Walters, who had run the company for many years. I stressed that I would be most interested to gain access to documentation which supported a statement by Mr Walters in one of GEFCO's annual reports that there was 'a welcome and mounting volume of worldwide scientific evidence disproving many of the allegations traditionally levelled against asbestos'.[16] The request for an interview was turned down and no details of the welcome and mounting evidence were forthcoming, which is not surprising since it does not exist. It was a pity about the interview though. There was an unkind part of me which would have enjoyed asking a representative of the company about the conditions on the company's properties we had visited – Bute, Heuningvlei, Bretby, Pomfret and Coretsi. I would have liked to have asked one of them, if perhaps somewhere from their group's millions of pounds' profit that year they might have found a few rands to buy Frank Molwaggae, dying as a result of the company's negligence, a few more beers, some fresh clothing, a radio or even a small television set to ease the pain during his last few weeks or months of life. And then, changing tack, I would have liked to have had the opportunity to remind them of their company's problematic record in Bermondsey, south London, where the House of Lords had ruled that Gencor's Abbey Lane premises were 'a slum factory', run in flagrant defiance of the law and calculated to do serious injury to both employees and the local community. In the course of this case some truly shocking details of the asbestos industry's conduct came to light.[17]

In its London plant Central Asbestos, General Mining's British milling and marketing arm, had a small sample mill in use in the 1960s exactly like the unguarded machines we saw at Heuningvlei. The mill in London had no safety attachments, no exhaust to lead away the dust, no hoods, no ventilation. For good measure the sample mill was secretly installed in a pit dug into the factory floor in Southwark. When factory inspectors came to call, evidence showed it was swiftly covered over with false floorboards topped with hessian sacks to disguise its existence. The lawyer representing the British workers injured by Gencor's business conduct in Bermondsey, Anthony Woolf, believed that the evidence of criminal conduct was easily sufficient to have the directors of the company charged with conspiracy to cause grievous bodily harm, but the Director of Public Prosecutions had never brought a case against a polluter in the history of his department. The crimes of the powerful were not part of his frame of reference and he demurred.[18]

GEFCO eventually shut up shop in Britain, moved back to South Africa, where there were no compulsory asbestos safety standards to flout, and carried on exposing thousands of its contract workers and the large local populations who lived in the vicinity of the group's blue asbestos mines to the deadly fall-out from its operations. If what happened in Britain before the trial in 1970 was conspiracy to cause grievous bodily harm, how do we characterise continuing violations on such a grand scale in the 1980s – ten years after being caught in Britain?

There remained one last asbestos mining company whose behaviour in the North Western Cape needed to be probed – Cape Industries, a British-registered part of Harry Oppenheimer's Anglo American empire which had been among the biggest asbestos producers from the beginning, and another company whose British factories had been shown to be so negligently run that they brought death, disease and injury to the communities around them. While Simon Berthon and I were busy following up the companies which had damaged Frank Molwaggae and James Ebang, a courageous South African doctor working with us had been looking around in Prieska, the main railhead in the area. In addition to his considerable expertise in those lung diseases caused by industrial pollution, Neil White had a special talent. He could persuade white South Africans living in a part of the country that was far from progressive to open up and talk. We'd travelled from Cape Town together across the lonely and beautiful expanse of the Karoo in a trusted old Volkswagen and then split up so that while we looked at Bathlaros, Kuruman and other places in the north of the asbestos country, he concentrated on Cape Industries' centre of operations in Prieska. Neil had been born in Rhodesia to a medical family of Scottish extraction and his father had been promoted to a senior hospital job in Natal. Neil developed his interest in the hazards of work at medical school and during a postgraduate research project into the 'brown lung' disease which workers in cotton mills contract if the environment in which they work is polluted, which it often is. Neil felt it was essential to check out the situation in Prieska very carefully. So when we reached the town he extracted his long frame from the car and set off on foot round the medical community. Prieska was the place where the 300-mile seam of asbestos-bearing deposits in the northern Cape was first commercially developed by Cape Industries. This was confirmed by a 1918 book on asbestos in South Africa published by the South African Ministry of Mines, which gave a wealth of geological and geographical detail about the spread of the deposits through the northern Cape and spoke of the material in the glowing and enthusiastic terms more often found in advertising copy than sober mining manuals. The material, the book noted, could be used 'in the manufacture of tents, motor-car hoods, sun-blinds, wagon-sails, tarpaulins, sun-helmets, saddle-girths, lawn-tennis nets, and many other purposes to which cotton, linen and hemp are put'. And that was not all. 'The special variety of crocidolite,' it continued, 'would perhaps find a use for hospital wool . . . as jackets for pneumonic patients.'[19]

Neil shattered immediately the fantasies of asbestos companies helping hospital patients with pneumonia. In Prieska and two outlying towns Neil had visited between Prieska and Kuruman – Danielskuil and Postmasburg by name – asbestos seemed to be sending large numbers of people to hospital with the lung disease known generically as pneumoconiosis. In Postmasburg Dr Eckstein was seeing on average six people with mesothelioma every year. Dr Smith at Danielskuil had diagnosed fourteen people as suffering from the disease since he arrived in the town two and a half years earlier. And in Prieska itself, Neil reported, he had found his way to 35-year-old Booi Visagie. Like Frank Molwaggae at Bathlaros, Mr Visagie had been taken into hospital for an operation to drain off fluid that had accumulated round his lungs. Neil had visited him in the ward and feared the worst. 'Mr Visagie told me that he thinks he's going to get better as soon as the water is taken off. But the respite will only be temporary, I'm afraid. He's been told that it was the mine dust from Koegas, where he worked, that made him sick. But you should see how terribly wasted he is, how very thin he's become and how laboured his breathing is even though he's just lying in bed. I'm pretty sure Mr Visagie doesn't have long to go.

'He has a wife and two children and he's just thirty-five years old,' Neil continued, 'but he's had no help or compensation of any kind from

181

Cape Asbestos, the British firm who employed him. He started work at Cape's Koegas mine at the age of fourteen and he'll be dead before the year is out.'

I wondered how many other miners from Koegas had died or would die from mesothelioma or have their lives ruined by asbestosis, an even more common form of choking and disabling lung disease, which kills in a marginally less painful way but over a more protracted period. I told Neil about my friend in Glasgow, John Todd, who tramped the streets for years visiting the dying in his union branch of insulation engineers. It was only his commitment and persistence, I explained, that had established once and for all that literally hundreds of men on Clydeside had died from the disease they called 'the bug'. And I told him about J. P. McKenna, the branch's diminutive full-time secretary, who spent a day or two almost every week attending funerals of deceased members.

'That's a terrible story,' Neil commented, 'but this is going to be worse, much worse. The contract labour system means that the sick men have left at the end of contract or been simply sent back to the homelands on some pretext and never re-engaged. The grinding poverty in the labour reserves has always ensured that more present themselves for jobs however bad the conditions. And so the cycle goes on. Since the contract labour system denies people the right to live with their families in a stable environment, far more people work in the asbestos industry in South Africa than elsewhere. They oscillate between home and work, employment and unemployment. Dust levels are also extremely high and there is massive environmental exposure. So the toll of death and injury is probably very much higher here. But at the same time it's conveniently hidden away and no one will be able to calculate the final death toll from Cape Asbestos.'

We decided that I should drive out to Koegas to see the place that had laid Mr Visagie low while Neil stayed on in Prieska to see the local doctor, André Pickard. 'He's been here a lot of years,' said Neil. 'He'll have a shrewd idea of the scale of the problem.' In the early hours of the morning we said goodbye again and I drove off to Koegas. The mine was between the road and the Orange River. It had recently closed, partly because of the action of London dockers who had banned the unloading of blue asbestos after one of their colleagues had contracted mesothelioma.[20] But the mine, brought into production after the Second World War in a joint venture with the American asbestos giant Johns Manville, was also near the end of its life. Production had therefore been concentrated at Pomfret, the much newer and more modern operation further north on the edge of the Kalahari.

Koegas might have been closed, but the place was filthy with blue asbestos. Much to my surprise, a group of men were still working high on the roof, taking apart the dust cones and collection system, and the piping that went with them. They were covered from top to toe in the deadly dust. I asked them if anyone had warned them about the dangers. 'Dangers – what dangers?' came the reply. 'No one said anything to us about dangers. We're just doing a job on contract.' I walked away towards the river and the huge pyramids of asbestos waste and tailings that had accumulated from years of mining and milling. Once again these were sky blue and open to the air. The tailings dumps were composed of the material left over once the milling process had been completed and the fluffy wool fibres were packed for export. The waste was always heavy with fibre and highly dangerous, particularly when left exposed to the air or, as it was here at Koegas, on the bank of a river from which many people took their water supply. As I looked around it became clear that someone else had been at least slightly concerned about the dangers of environmental pollution and the risks to anyone who lived near Koegas or who took in air polluted with dust from the mine. Someone had ordered the company to put up a warning sign, and the company had duly followed instructions. It said ominously, 'Asbestos-contaminated area – keep out.'

An interesting footnote to the history of the environmental movement could be written by probing ineffective product and hazard warning signs: in that study the one at Koegas would surely be one of the worst. The fact that the asbestos contamination was in the open air meant the sign was meaningless. You could be yards or even miles away from the fence and the sign, but the wind could lift the dust and bring it straight to you. I shook my head and got back in the car. I drove up to the office buildings, the best part of a mile away. A car was parked outside and it was clear that the company still maintained an office there. No one was about. I left a message saying I would call back again in an hour and went for a walk. I passed various offices, the detention block and the remnants of the compound where the migrant miners used to live and then I came upon the mine manager's old office. The door was open, swinging backwards and forwards and creaking in the wind. I thought I'd sneak a quick look in to see the clocking-in machines and the compound rules, if they were on display. These had long since gone, but piled across the floor, in line after line, were some other fascinating documents – Cape Asbestos Bantu Personal Details Records, as the British company, which worked so closely with the apartheid system called its personnel records. There were thousands

183

of these in neat, cream-coloured wallets just like the records department at a major hospital. They had once been in alphabetical or some other sort of order, but they had obviously been disturbed so the first one was for Fuzeni Nontondozola, a thirty-year-old Xhosa contracted in April 1975. Inside the wallet file was a card from the Medical Bureau of Occupational Diseases, the government department which was supposed to supervise the health of the miners. Of course this outfit did its job in accord with the savagely discriminatory provisions of the apartheid system, with lower payments, worse facilities and even poorer quality X-rays for the black miners who did most of the work. For this reason Fuzeni's little miniature X-ray was stapled to his card. Full-plate X-rays were reserved for white miners. Lying on the floor near Fuzeni's form was another worrying document. This was the return by Cape as the owner of a controlled mine showing the number of shifts every quarter worked in an especially dusty atmosphere. There were thousands of such shifts, which meant that Koegas's role as a propagator of death, disease and injury was truly spectacular, given that dangerous concentrations of dust anywhere in the vicinity of the mine were obviously being topped up by even more extreme doses delivered in confined spaces underground or in the workshops. I left Koegas with a Tom Paxton song about mining safety fixed in my mind.

> The rock slide may not get you, the fire may pass you by.
> When the gas explodes, it may not be your time to die.
> But every year gets harder, just to take a living breath.
> When the blacklung gets you, it's the kiss of death.

Paxton had written his song in the 1960s during a famous strike by American miners to obtain proper compensation for those crippled by pneumoconiosis. I wondered what he would have made of this situation, with tens of thousands of men exposed to a cocktail of toxicity, without a union to defend them, without a health service, without a vote, without lawyers, without access to telephones or even in many cases a proper postal address where they could receive documents and usually without an education to enable them to read them. Back in Prieska, in the bar of the main hotel in a town described in tourist brochures as 'pristine-clean, picturesque', I told Neil White what I'd seen. He nodded his head calmly and then fell silent, sipping his beer. 'What's wrong, Neil?' I asked after a couple of minutes. 'I've had a long talk with Dr Pickard's wife,' he replied. 'And I just can't get over it. The situation in this town is almost unbelievable.

'They've lived here for nearly forty years,' said Neil, 'and for a good many of them she's been the matron in the local hospital. The story itself goes like this. There was a mine and a mill here – the operation closed ten years ago. But Cape Asbestos just moved away, without doing any serious cleaning up. They left everything and the dust was everywhere. You could pick up tufts of it in the main street.

'Whenever the west wind blows, the dust comes over the town and into the streets, the public buildings and the houses. Many, many people, hundreds have died from asbestos cancers. The latest case was a thirty-six-year-old white man who died in Cape Town, a typical story of someone born in the town, exposed to the dust as a youngster who moved away and then some years later suddenly took sick and died of cancer. There are 12,000 people in Prieska, 2,000 whites and 10,000 blacks and coloureds. The feedback comes from the white community. She said, "People don't like to think of it too much. It's very debilitating. Someone came and measured dust levels in the attics of our houses. And they've been saying for years that they would concrete over the rubble and asbestos tips. But there's so much of it and little or nothing has been done."'

The following day Neil went to see Dr Pickard about the plight of the people of Prieska. Dr Pickard had graduated from the University of Cape Town medical school in 1938 and worked in Prieska since the early 1940s. He ran the TB clinic and had been a local National Party councillor. 'Personally I have seen over 900 cases of mesothelioma cancer in my years in this town,' he told Neil. 'And I have heard of many more cases in the surrounding area from other people. Currently there are eight people I know dying from the disease. Of eighty white miners who worked at the Prieska mine, seventy died of the disease. Whole families were wiped out by it such as the Stewarts and the van der Merwes. The pastor's wife recently died of it.

'The mine and mill was owned by Cape Blue Asbestos. It was very, very dirty and people complained so they tried using water to damp the dust down, but while this had some success it was never enough. The mill and the nearest dump were at the west end of the town and when the fierce west wind blew, large amounts of fibre came all over the houses. It collected under roofs, lay on floors and piled up on windowsills. In some places where Cape Blue Operations were located there was up to two feet of fibre left behind. They knocked down some buildings and moved useful machinery but they have still done nothing about the pollution round and about the mill. They have now sold out to Rand

Mines, a disgraceful thing to do, selling the mill and doing nothing to clean it up.'

Eleven years earlier I had met a Manchester lawyer called John Pickering in the course of a construction disaster investigation in Cumberland. He told me that he lived in a little Yorkshire village called Hebden Bridge where a company I didn't know milled a substance I'd never heard of. It was my introduction to asbestos and the asbestos disaster. In the course of subsequent work on Hebden Bridge we found out that Cape Asbestos had come to the village during the Second World War, particularly after its reputation at Barking in East London, where it had built a plant in the 1920s, made it difficult to attract labour. In Hebden Bridge, where there were laws against such activities, the company had operated exactly as it had done in South Africa. In Britain, we established, this had involved defiance of the 1931 asbestos safety regulations. Cape failed to extract dust, failed to use the appropriate type of sacks, to provide dust masks, to clean the plant with care and attention, and to treat the surrounding environment with a modicum of respect. Thanks to John Pickering, the local MP, Max Madden, and the injured local people who found their own voices to tell what had gone on, the behaviour of Cape Industries became the subject of newspaper articles, television programmes and even a parliamentary inquiry by the Ombudsman, who sought to find out why the Factory Inspectorate had failed for so long to protect people who worked in or lived near the plant. The result of the company's actions was that of the 2,200 people who had worked for the company in Yorkshire, 279 had by 1981 developed asbestosis.[21] There had been similar tragedies at the company's plants in the Lake District, in London and in Scotland. But here in Prieska, South Africa, there were no compulsory asbestos regulations for the company to worry about flouting; as a result the quantities of dust, the numbers of people exposed and the overall situation were much, much worse – which made Dr Pickard's figure of 900 mesotheliomas seem entirely possible.

None the less this was an amazing figure. In Johannesburg scientists at the National Centre for Occupational Health, and the Medical Bureau for Occupational Disease were sufficiently worried about the overall situation in South Africa to have opened a national mesothelioma register. But that register, its compiler, Dr Ian Webster, had told me no more than a week before, had only some 500 cases recorded on it and that was for the whole country.[22] Here we were in a little town where the community's leading doctor, a cautious and well-respected figure, was stating quite unequivocally that he had seen 900 cases in this immediate vicinity alone. This time Neil and I shook our heads in unison. This wasn't an industrial accident, or even a chapter of accidents. This was a public health disaster, an environmental catastrophe. Worse still, it wasn't over. Because of the negligence of the mining companies, hundreds and thousands of local people were still being exposed to the deadly lavender fibres. How many of them would subsequently die? How many more migrant miners, isolated back in the homelands or labour reserves, would yet succumb? And where did the Orange River or the prevailing wind take the dust from the mountainous tips? In that tunnel of time between the warnings of Rachel Carson and the catastrophes of Three Mile Island, Chernobyl and Bhopal which gave us our present-day keywords for industrial catastrophe, the only point of reference Neil and I could come up with was Minamata, the mercury-poisoning tragedy in Japan, where hundreds of children had been born deformed. But this wasn't one community being cut down by the toxic leftovers of the modern, science-based corporation. This was on an incomparably bigger scale, and threatened communities across the Kuruman Hills and Asbestos Mountains, all the way to Penge in the Transvaal.

Neil White and I were both anxious to question Cape Industries and their parent company, Anglo American, about their behaviour in continuing to mine and market a material they knew to be unsafe. We asked for an interview with Harry Oppenheimer, the leading figure in Anglo American and a man who is on record as supporting the free flow of information in society. He declined to appear. Next we tried John Kay-Green, director of public relations at Cape's London head offices. He told us that while the company's managing director Geoffrey Higham would probably not wish to give an interview, we should set out our question areas in the form of a telex. Cape duly received a lengthy telex, which began with a request for straightforward information such as the dates that the Koegas mine and Prieska mill closed. Then, in the fond hope that someone from the company would come forward to defend the corporate record, we outlined the areas of questioning we would want to pursue. These focused on the company's private state of knowledge about asbestos and cancer and its failure to warn customers or members of the public about the environmental risks associated with its products; in conclusion we indicated that we wanted to ask about the company's responsibilities to former employees and people living near the company's plants who were dying from asbestos-related disease. Twenty-four hours later we received a short telex by way of reply. The first sentence said, 'Thank you for your telex and the trouble taken in spelling out the scenario.' The second – and final – sentence stated,

'We can only reconfirm that our entire mining interests in South Africa including all attendant legal rights and obligations were sold ... we are therefore no longer in a position to comment upon the issues you raise.'[23]

At the time there seemed a poignant contrast between the penniless plight of Booi Visagie and the situation in Bloomington, Illinois, where an American jury, incensed at the evidence of Cape's persistent failure to warn its customers about the health hazards associated with the products they were buying, had just handed out a fifty-two million dollar award in punitive damages against the company to eighteen local asbestos victims.[24] The American lawyer who handled the case, the first of a growing number of American asbestos cases where a jury awarded punitive damages against asbestos companies for their 'wanton and wilful misconduct' in exposing people to hazards only too well known to the corporation, was an extremely resourceful litigator called Jim Walker.

'There were publications about cancer in the 1930s,' Walker told me. 'But for sure in the 1950s Cape knew both from their own experience and from the medical literature that asbestos caused cancer. In this situation there wasn't a probability, there was a certainty that a number of workers would contract asbestosis and die.' Walker was a farm boy who had grown up on the outskirts of Bloomington, a market town a hundred miles south of Chicago at the heart of some of America's richest farmland. He combined a strong sense of right and wrong with a considerable populist ability to translate the intricacies of corporate behaviour into the language of the common man and woman.

'What Cape did', he explained, 'is not dissimilar to the situation where someone fires a gun into a crowd of people. You may not know which of them will be killed but you know for certain that some of them will be killed. The asbestos companies produced two things in asbestos plants, asbestos products and diseased and dead asbestos workers.' We stitched Walker's powerful statement in just before the end of the film 'Dust to Dust' and cut straight to Booi Visagie, who was obviously dying. In concluding we underlined that Mr Visagie was one of the obligations Cape Industries had disposed of when they sold their South African asbestos mines two years earlier for £15 million.

10   Conduct Unbecoming: Mining Companies and the Suppression of Cancer Research in Southern Africa

We had hoped that Cape Industries would do something for the dying man who had started work at the Koegas mine at the age of fourteen and who was, as we interviewed him, preparing for a tragic and inordinately painful death due to corporate neglect. We were disappointed and Mr Visagie died without any help from the company and without any compensation for his shattered life. As we compared notes, Simon, Neil and I wondered how many others shared the plight of Booi Visagie, Frank Molwaggae and James Ebang. Were their deaths isolated incidents or part of a larger pattern of disease and injury slowly accumulating over decades in the isolated areas from where asbestos miners were drawn within South Africa's borders? And what of the sending areas outside the country like Botswana, Malawi and Mozambique, which for years had been sources for the supply of contract labour for the asbestos mines? How many workers there had contracted diseases and received no help or compensation?

At Bopelong Hospital in Mafeking I found Dr Jennifer Tallent, one of the few people in South Africa able to answer these questions. Dr Tallent was one of three researchers on a little publicised but important project to trace at least some of the people who had worked in the industry. Published under the title, 'Prevalence of Asbestosis, Pleural Changes and Malignant Neoplasms in Black ex-Miners and Female Cobbers', the research project had been set up in 1973 by the South African National Research Institute for Occupational Diseases. Overseen by Dr Ian Webster, a South African specialist on industrial health matters, the project was based at St Michael's at Bathlaros near Kuruman, where a doctor, nurse and driver had the job of tracking down former workers from the blue asbestos industry to check up on their health.[1]

By the time I met Dr Tallent she had moved away from Kuruman, though the research was continuing. I told her about my meeting with Frank Molwaggae. She did not respond to my opening comments and for a longer time than is usual in such situations it seemed as if our conversation would not move beyond social niceties. Then Dr Tallent suddenly spoke up, 'As for the survey, you would do much better with Professor Webster, but here goes.'

She explained that the original survey had started in 1974, finished in 1979, and the results were published in 1980 and 1981. The research team which she had headed had worked away for months before they settled on a precise method for doing the work. Then they had discovered sets of old Kuruman Cape Blue (Eternit) and GEFCO (General Mining) passbooks for black contract employees. 'This was a marvellous basis on which to proceed,' she said. 'The registers told us each person's date of birth, the district they originally registered in and the name of the local headman. With this as the basis for organising the follow-up of miners, and the project fieldwork in the capable hands of Cyprian Gabetse, the black driver, we had a wonderful success rate, 95 per cent, almost everyone.'

1962 was selected as a base year because the researchers wanted a twelve- to fourteen-year interval to have passed, over which to trace the development of any diseases. Although there was no reference to it in the project title or in Dr Tallent's summary, cancer, more particularly mesothelioma cancer, was what the survey was designed to pick up. I was to learn later that cancer was a word the South African asbestos industry strove to avoid.

'We finished up with a death rate of 0·5 per cent of the people employed,' said Dr Tallent. 'And we must set that comparatively small number against all those many people who benefit from the industry. If we took the industry away, many would suffer. And it's a very useful product giving much gainful employment which I think, on balance, is more important than a small minority who suffer.[2]

'By the way,' she continued, 'I just wanted to say how much I liked the older people's names. They had names like "Listen to me" and "Breakfast"; nowadays they'd be called things like Michael. As time goes by they're destroying the passbooks. Now, some people complain about the pass system, but from the point of view of finding people it's the best thing ever. Now we have nothing.

'I'm really sorry I had to leave. I wanted to do another similar study in the Transvaal but I couldn't. No one has ever looked for mesothelioma victims there and I'm sure we would find them. Still, some work is continuing, finding people who are resistant, you know, blood samples and immunology. But I suppose the overall situation is bad.

'Whole families are affected. Mrs Wayland, the shopkeeper in Crown Reserve died aged seventy of mesothelioma last year. Earlier her own father and her daughter died of it too. In one black family, where survival depended on hand cobbing or separating of asbestos, three people died. The surviving sister begged me to check her to ensure that she hadn't got it.'

Dr Tallent explained that before the survey work was done the companies had insisted there was little or no asbestos in the community at large. 'But we found a lot of environmental asbestos,' she said. 'In other words the situation was affecting people who didn't work in the mines or mills but just happened to live near them. It's bad really. And thanks to the survey, black asbestos workers got some compensation for the very first time. They got 1,300 rand a year, but there was nothing for environmental victims. You got nothing if you hadn't worked for the mines.

'The government Medical Bureau for Occupational Disease used to be in the Kuruman Cape company offices. I often wondered if that was appropriate. Now they've moved out. MBOD is for whites and coloureds only, by the way.'

Cyprian Gabetse was the key to obtaining the 95 per cent success rate in the sample. Locally born and raised, with a good, church education and firm views about justice and injustice which, given the situation in South Africa, he kept to himself most of the time, he had spent six years of his life scouring the area sixty miles round Kuruman in the first-ever attempt to find some of the people who had worked as contract labourers in the asbestos mines. Mr Gabetse was almost as proud of the big Ford he used to drive around from place to place as he was of his own extraordinary efforts. In his work he had to leave the tar roads, and drive for miles on sand and stone pathways to find the places where asbestos miners had either lived or might now be living. The Ford was the fifth vehicle he had used in the course of the survey, used that is until each was incapable of further maintenance or movement. Previously he had worn out two Datsuns and two Mazdas. 'The Mazdas were better than the Datsuns and the Ford was the best of all,' he told me. He ought to know, for he had driven every track and road in a vast area of the country stretching from Prieska in the south to Pomfret in the north.

Mr Gabetse did not incline to the view that only a tiny minority of those surveyed had health problems. Of 1,000 men he had traced who had contracts in the six years between 1957 and 1962, 290 had already developed asbestosis, he told us.[3] Inevitably a relatively high proportion of these men would later develop asbestos-induced cancers as well. In addition, he estimated that there had been as many as 1,000 deaths linked to asbestos in the area he had covered since the survey began. And privately he had grown increasingly worried about the conditions in which asbestos miners still had to work and live. 'The compounds are very badly polluted,' he said, 'and people who live near them are in danger.'

Two hundred and ninety men with asbestos from a traced population of 1,000 is a terrible figure, more suggestive of casualties in trench warfare in the Somme than of a modern enterprise. Indeed the figure seemed to suggest that as many as a third of the workforce might have had their lives ruined by the asbestos mining companies. This put the plight of James Ebang, Frank Molwaggae and Booi Visagie in a tragic context.

One of the places that particularly troubled Cyprian Gabetse in the course of his travels was the Penge asbestos mine in the Transvaal, a mine that Dr Tallent also felt should have been the subject of a major study. The mine had employed tens of thousands of contract workers in the course of its life as another major production centre for Cape Industries besides Prieska or Koegas. Penge took its name from the pleasant suburb in London, a city where the company had its international headquarters and marketing departments. Sadly there was nothing remotely pleasant about Penge in the Transvaal. The area lies at the heart of the amosite or brown asbestos deposits in southern Africa and Penge is a Cape Asbestos enclave and company town. Amosite, the name for the somewhat unusual fibres of asbestos mined there, is derived from the name of one of the company's South African business divisions – AMOSA, Asbestos Mines of South Africa. Simon Berthon and I spent a day taking pictures of the operation at the Penge mine with a growing sense of disbelief. The tailings dumps were like a vast moonscape: layer upon layer of the toxic sludge had been pumped up from mines and mill to dry in the sun and then be pulled into the atmosphere.

It was obvious even from a cursory inspection that at Penge Cape had risked the health of people who lived and worked in the area to an extraordinary degree. The British registered company's business methods at places like Penge had been challenged from time to time over many years, but obviously not forcefully enough to compel a fundamental rethink.[4] One South African doctor I tracked down in the United States had questioned the health situation at the mine in the late 1940s, when worries about the relationship between asbestos and cancer were finding their way into the annual reports of the then British Chief Inspector of Factories. Dr Gerrit Schepers had retired to one of Washington's comfortable suburbs. When I talked to him more than thirty years had elapsed since his visits to Penge, but his memories of what he had seen in the British-owned mine still pained him.

'One day I descended on an unscheduled mine in the eastern Transvaal. It was Penge. In the morning as we came down the valley there was a mist over the small mine town, a little morning mist. I didn't know until lunchtime that it was asbestos dust, but that is what it was. It was trapped in the area and had nowhere to go because of the lack of movement in the air currents at that hour of the day. It was like that most days and it meant that there was asbestos dust absolutely everywhere in the mornings. For example we were eating some toast one morning and I remarked to one of my colleagues, "Goodness me, this is gritty marmalade." And then the penny dropped – it was asbestos dust we had been chewing.

'We were X-raying the miners and I decided to inspect the inside of the mill, where all the dust was coming from. One of my technicians said, "Come over here and take a look at this." I went into a corner of the mill room and I saw a big, strong man with a sjambok whip. It was his job, it appeared, to hit a hessian sack on the ground below the end of a chute, with the sjambok, the big bull whip. I heard a little yelp coming from inside the bag.[5]

'When he stopped the whipping there were odd movements and sounds from inside the sack. I grew more and more agitated as I began to work out what was happening. I said, "What on earth is going on here?" I pushed aside the man with the whip and looked inside the sack. Inside was a little boy of ten or twelve. It was his job to get inside the bag and trample down the fluffy asbestos. He was cheaper than machinery or safe sacks. He was covered from top to toe in asbestos dust so I grabbed him and took him off to the X-ray machine. The X-ray showed he was already suffering from asbestosis.

'I was told that Cape employed a lot more children and I gave instructions to my technician that he was to round up all the children in the village with the little Cape Asbestos copper identification bands riveted round their wrists – identification tags, just like slaves, so they couldn't run off. A number of the other children had asbestosis too. The conditions were unbelievable.'

Dr Schepers confirmed that officials in the health and mining departments were already seriously worried about the relationship between asbestos and cancer by the time of his visit to Penge. But it was the news about overall working conditions that Schepers and others brought back to the government mining engineer which caused a crisis of conscience in at least one senior official in the Department of Mines, T. L. Gibbs. Mr Gibbs took it upon himself to get the asbestos mines scheduled and controlled, at least in theory, by government regulation. But he met with stubborn resistance from mining companies who used all their power behind the scenes to make life difficult for him. Gibbs went out in the field in 1951 and was so worried by the hazardous conditions he saw that he took the unprecedented step in South African mining history of confiscating the main electrical fuses at a number of mines and paralysing operations until some discussions and promises at least of a token clean-up were forthcoming.[6] But the industry was poised on the verge of its huge, post-war expansion and Mr Gibbs and his anxieties were soon sidelined in the rush to profit from the booming world market. The result at Penge was nothing short of catastrophic.

By the time we began investigating the problem in 1981, Cape Industries had lost its insurance cover for selling blue and brown asbestos in the American market. The company had tried to steer round this problem by setting up a chain of dummy companies to market the fibre in such a way that it could not be sued for damages and did not therefore need insurance. This involved setting up a front company in Lichtenstein, one of the world capitals of hot money and illicit business activity, called Associated Minerals, in which Cape secretly owned shares.[7] In the end the company became so worried about the extent of Anglo American's liabilities for deaths and injuries that they sold the mines, including Penge, to Barlow Rand, another company with strong connections to Harry Oppenheimer. The medical director of Rand Mines, the mining division of Barlow Rand, Dr R. D. W. Reid, fiercely attacked the 1981 Granada *World in Action* programme which set out the result of our investigations, saying it was a complete exaggeration and few of the miners were getting mesothelioma any more.[8] But in 1984, because of an industrial dispute, the conditions in one of the mines Dr Reid had been responsible for came under the scrutiny of Marianne Felix and two South African journalists, Phillip van Niekerk and Carolyn Dempster.[9]

In that year a bitter strike broke out on the Penge asbestos mine over pay and conditions. Van Niekerk and Dempster visited the area and again documented the scale of the tragedy. They discovered that while the company claimed only thirteen Penge workers contracted asbestosis in 1982 in its annual report, other documents at the mine recorded that the true figure was seventy-nine. A report by the Penge manager H. E.

Fouche showed that in the decade from 1973 to 1983, 780 workers at the mine contracted asbestosis. In a confidential report on dust figures at the mill the dust in the atmosphere had recently been measured as sixty-five times higher than the local level recommended by the South African mining authorities, and 260 times higher than the legal limit in Britain.[10] Van Niekerk and Dempster documented instances of children playing on one or other of the many asbestos dumps in the area and found a school where the playground was made of the fibre.

Most worrying in regard to the mining houses involved in South Africa's asbestos tragedy was the state of their knowledge. Because of their activities in Britain, Europe and the United States, where there were developed industrial safety laws, they knew that they were dealing with a uniquely hazardous product which could cause havoc if they were not very careful. Nevertheless, they carried on their business with disregard to the environmental and social consequences. Worse still when independent scientists drew attention to what was going on, they refused to face reality and worked hard to derail, distort and suppress scientific investigations which might damage their business interests. The net result of this was that vital information about the relationship between asbestos and cancer that might have saved thousands of lives throughout the industrialised world never saw the light of day.

I had found convincing proof of this inexcusable state of affairs among some yellowing reports I retrieved from Cape Industries' abandoned mine at Koegas and in the vaults at the Institute of Bio-Statistics in Johannesburg. The cover up began with the planned and co-ordinated response of the mining companies to the work of two men, Dr C. A. Sleggs and Dr Christopher Wagner. The story of how their pioneering work was at first taken up with a degree of enthusiasm and support by the asbestos industry and then, when it produced incontrovertible evidence of a causal link between company products and cancer, was remorselessly undermined, truncated and suppressed, is a shaming one.

Dr Sleggs was the first person to document the cancer link in South Africa, when he was working in Kimberley in the 1950s. I tracked him down in a retirement suburb down the coast from Cape Town. A self-effacing man with orthodox views about the alleged benefits of apartheid, Dr Sleggs seemed an unlikely combatant against the might of the mining companies. But he was clearly a redoubtable medical researcher and once he had made up his mind that what he was seeing in a growing number of his patients at the West End hospital in Kimberley was not, as others insisted, tuberculosis, he refused to give up.[11]

Dr Sleggs's worries about cancer in the northern Cape began with a Miss Joubert, a missionary who had been born at Paarl and visited Kuruman for one month a year. She had contracted a rare cancer of the lung and Dr Sleggs formed the view that it was a mesothelioma. Then he became worried about another case, a woman living in Kimberley who was the proprietor of the first dry cleaner's in the region. She too contracted this unusual cancer and soon died. Dr Sleggs began to connect these cases with environmental exposure to asbestos dust. He made slides of damaged tissue and sent them off to the South African Institute for Medical Research at Johannesburg. Repeatedly he was told that there was nothing to worry about and that his patients had been suffering from TB. Sleggs knew that this was wrong and persisted with his observations. In 1956 he began treating another apparent TB victim called Hensop Liebman. Once again the patient did not respond to the powerful new drugs which were eradicating tuberculosis in patient after patient. Dr Sleggs put Mr Liebman under close observation and did his best to help him as his disease progressed towards its inevitable conclusion. Fluid progressively filled both of Liebman's lungs until he died of heart failure. Dr Sleggs sent off a post-mortem report, and then in November 1956 wrote to the Director of the South African Institute for Medical Research, reiterating his view that Mr Liebman had died of mesothelioma not tuberculosis and underlining that he was worried that there was an increased incidence of cancers throughout the district.

Dr Sleggs's persistence paid off and eventually the death of Hensop Liebman was ascribed to mesothelioma cancer. In the course of his research Dr Sleggs had been finding that people with lung damage of this kind had either worked at some time in the Cape asbestos mines or had some environmental exposure to the dust, whether as children playing near a dump or as adults living near a mill or working in a dry cleaner's where asbestos miners brought their clothes for cleaning. With his diagnosis of Hensop Liebman now accepted, Sleggs's next move was to present his findings at the Feburary 1959 international conference on industrial lung diseases organised by the South African Council for Scientific and Industrial Research in Johannesburg.

Dr Sleggs's identification of mesotheliomas and his isolation of asbestos as the probable cause received important backing at the conference from Christopher Wagner, a scientist at the government Pneumoconiosis Research Unit. Dr Wagner's father had been involved in an early scientific survey of the industry as it developed in the Cape Province, and Christopher's doctoral research involved a pioneering survey of postwar conditions in the North Western Cape. As he travelled round the mines and mills of the South African asbestos industry, the younger Wagner found unbelievable conditions.[12] The roads on the huge mining properties were made from asbestos waste; there were great plumes of blue dust over the mills. The industry used unlined hessian sacks, which were cheaper and easier to fill than impermeable ones, although they had been supposedly outlawed by the British asbestos regulations in 1931. Every time the sacks were moved, loaded or unloaded, asbestos dust escaped from them. In some places asbestos was separated from the rock by hand by women, often with babies strapped to their backs. Immense dumps of milled asbestos waste, heavy with fibre, lay open to the wind. As much as 18 per cent of the raw fibre was being blown away on the wind. People who had lived in the area for short periods, or who had simply passed through, were developing cancers.[13] At the conference in 1959 Dr Wagner called urgently for a survey of the Sekhukuniland Reserve, from where many of the black contract workers recruited by the mines originated. In the last sentence of his paper, Wagner underlined the significance of his own and Dr Sleggs's work. 'The problem requiring most urgent investigation', he wrote, 'is the high incidence of mesotheliomas on the Cape asbestos fields, where a very serious hazard may exist.'[14]

In the wake of the conference the government sanctioned a wide-ranging Pneumoconiosis Research Unit investigation of the asbestos industry throughout the North Western Cape and at Penge in the eastern Transvaal. This was initially supported by the asbestos industry, which put up some money in return for a say in shaping research proposals and vetting any reports which might be published. The survey involved scientists, doctors and technicians travelling round the affected communities, visiting one household in four in places like Koegas, Prieska, Kuruman and Penge and measuring exhaustively the increased incidence of cancer. But as the survey got under way, South Africa was becoming an ever more paranoid and secretive country where the disenfranchised majority of the country had to be kept in check by growing use of state violence. In 1960 came the Sharpeville massacre. A senior team member with whom I discussed the asbestos research project more than twenty years later emphasised that this had a profound impact on the work they were doing. 'We were simply prevented from going into the Tswana reserve to study in detail the impact of the industry on men who had worked in the mines and mills. After

Sharpeville neither the government nor the mining companies wanted any
survey which might well lead to the discovery of hundreds of blacks dying
from industrial disease.'[15] This meant that the survey had to proceed very
cautiously. Nevertheless the first phase was complete by April 1962. Even
though no exhaustive survey of former contract workers was allowed, the
results were devastating. According to a confidential report dated 30 April
1962, the survey showed that 'even after the most critical reassessment of
the findings ... people who live or have lived in the areas of Prieska,
Koegas, Kuruman and Penge are in danger of contracting asbestosis even
though they have no industrial exposure to asbestos dust inhalation'.[16]

Worse still were the unpublished findings on cancer. The report noted:

an alarmingly high number of cases with mesothelioma of the pleura [the
lining of the lung] has been discovered among people who live or have
lived in the North Western Cape area, and there is evidence to suggest
that this condition is associated with an exposure to asbestos dust which,
again, need not be industrial.

Experiments at the Pneumoconiosis Research Unit over the last three
years suggest that crocidolite asbestos dust may be the carcinogenic
[cancer causing] factor ... These discoveries make it imperative for
both the Department of Mines and the industry to assess present dust
control and disposal methods and to take immediate steps to effectively
deal with this hazard.[17]

Dr Wagner's brother-in-law Dr (later Professor) Ian Webster was in
overall control of the survey and charged with the task of telling the asbestos
industry about the public-health time bomb in the northern Cape created
by mining activities. The report recorded the corporate response as follows:
'the industry was apprised of this fact by Dr I. Webster. Unfortunately this
knowledge appears to have excited various untoward reactions.' Not the least
of these was the immediate decision of the asbestos mining companies to
cut off funds for further research. They had initially paid 8,000 rand (about
£4,000 at the time) towards the research, but after this report there was to
be no more. Furthermore, according to the scientists involved, a campaign
was launched to denigrate them. They were accused of 'trying to destroy a
valuable export industry for self-aggrandisement'. They were told they were
meant to be looking into silicosis not cancer, and it was made abundantly
clear to them that they were no longer welcome on the company properties
they had to visit if they were to conduct further research.[18]

The report, which has still never been published, says that these 'unto-ward reactions' meant 'the cessation of all field work and accordingly the Mobile Unit [for X-rays] was recalled'. An investigation into mesothelioma and air pollution in Prieska was to continue but would now be called 'An Investigation into Possible Air Pollution by Asbestos Dust' with no direct reference to any possible relationship to the term mesothelioma. The asbestos companies, besides polluting the environment, were now polluting the science of the subject as well. Dismissing public health considerations and the fundamental human right to know what is going on in health and envionmental matters, among others, the companies were determined that nothing would stand in the way of long-standing investments and continuing profits.

The 1962 report also spelled out clearly why nothing was to be said:

> The unfortunate publicity that was given to the survey in the early days has resulted in certain mining groups feeling that reference to a form of cancer has attached a stigma to the area in which they operate, and that such stigma could adversely affect not only future recruitment of personnel for their mines, but even the economy of the industry as a whole.
>
> While emphasising that this unit realises its obligation to humanity, it is desired to point out that it will endeavour to continue what is regarded by us as necessary research as discreetly as possible and with due consideration of all policies which may be involved.

This discretion was soon put to the test. When scientists at the Pneumoconiosis Research Unit broached the matter of publishing their research, the asbestos industry was again consulted. The response of the mining companies, a number of them with companies incorporated in Britain, was that they would allow publication, but only if the cancer hazard was passed off throughout as tuberculosis![19]

The question of suppressing the research or allowing it to be published haunted the unit for two more years, with the director Louis Walters trying to salvage something from the mess. The best he could manage was a compromise. In a letter dated 23 June 1964, Walters explained,

> it was subsequently proposed by the Director of the unit that the survey as such be 'finalised' by the submission of the findings that had been made and a statistical analysis of these. Such a 'report' would not be published

199

or made available outside the unit, other than to sponsors and the various members of the working committees that had been concerned with the conduct of the survey. This proposal has now been carried out.

This meant that an important research project on asbestos and cancer, which highlighted the environmental hazards of the material not only for those who worked with it but for those who came into contact with it in casual ways, was suppressed. For years thereafter the companies who were party to the suppression denied that their products could in any way cause cancer among end users or members of the public. They funded the South African Asbestos Producers Association in South Africa and the Asbestos Information Centre in Britain to spread the party line and to defend their markets, investments and profits. Meanwhile other people paid for their decisions with their lives.

I found a copy of the suppressed report, and the covering letter which outlined the strategy for burying it, among a clutch of yellowing documents at the Institute of Bio-Statistics. I had been guided to it by two men, one involved in the original survey, another vainly trying to repeat work that had already been done twenty years earlier. Both men are respected South African doctors, of some courage and commitment but who none the less, even today, decline to be identified. The suppression of the 1962 survey is an ignominious chapter in the history of medical research in South Africa. It is impossible to calculate how many lives in South Africa, the major producing country, or in the many other countries around the world which have imported the product and with it the associated diseases, have been sacrificed so that South Africa's multinational asbestos mining and milling corporations, usually with strong British connections, could protect their profits. But if the information had been acted upon Booi Visagie, Frank Molwaggae and James Ebang might not have lost their lives and whole areas of the country would have been spared an enormity of pollution.

In South Africa, belatedly, a new generation of freer-thinking and less politically compliant researchers is at work investigating the afflicted areas and counting the human toll, which has continued to rise due to the companies' insistence on carrying on as if nothing had happened. In Prieska, a cohort study is under way at the time of writing to examine the death certificates of everyone born after 1936. Of sixty-two deaths traced so far in the earliest group, 13 per cent, one in eight, have been found to be certified as due to mesothelioma. In a random population, researchers would expect to find one death in a million from such an unusual cause.[20]

The new director of South Africa's National Centre for Occupational Health, Tony Davies, believes that this renewed survey work is very important. He is on record as saying that South Africa has the highest mesothelioma rate in the world and that he expects it to continue rising for some years to come as this avoidable disaster works itself out.

Not far from Penge, Dr Marianne Felix and a team funded by the HIVOS, a Dutch non-governmental organisation, have begun taking stock of the legacy that has been left behind in one of the smaller asbestos mining districts. Operating in an open, participatory way, and based in the 11,000-strong Mafefe community, they involved local people in assessing the scale of the problem and working out solutions, no mean achievement in a society where the majority have for so long been denied basic rights.[21] In the team's report on the first phase of the project, serious worries are identified. In the triangle between the Strydpoortberge, the Drakensbergs and the Olifants River the team found fourteen major tailings dumps, seven of them situated alongside roads which are used daily by local people. The remaining seven are frequently traversed by cattle, cattle herders and people searching for firewood. Nine of the dumps are in valleys whose streams or rivers are used for water supplies and have contaminated the supply. Spot water-sample readings show asbestos fibre content from 0·3 million to 5 million asbestos fibres per litre of water. Livestock lie on asbestos waste during the day and then at night when they return to the houses or kraals of the local people they take along the fluffy fibres on their fur.

The team also found that asbestos fibres used for road surfacing in the 1940s and 1950s frequently show up when the roads are graded, as they must be to keep them level. Many houses and public buildings are made of materials incorporating asbestos fibre. These include Moshate, the tribal office, the Mafefe post office, the bar lounge, the clinic, seven out of twelve schools and eight out of nineteen shops.[22] Dr Felix and her team have also been examining the health of people in the area. Of 800 adults so far examined, 30 per cent in the twenty to forty age group have identifiable pleural changes; 40 per cent have them in the forty to sixty age group and 62 per cent in the sixty to eighty age group. 'We haven't yet [May 1990] written up the air sampling tests,' she told me, 'but the medical examination of the 800 adults shows how serious the situation is. All these people we examined had significant asbestos exposure, certainly enough to increase the risk for mesothelioma.'[23]

Meantime a team from Potcheftsroom University is working to cover up the worst of the dumps. With a relatively small budget, they are doing their best to limit the damage to future generations by building retaining walls and concreting over the dumps. But the scale of the hazard is enormous and their progress is slow and highly selective, leaving dozens of dumps and sources of pollution untouched. The likelihood is, therefore, that the detritus of the South African asbestos mining and milling industry will continue to damage people and the environment for many years to come. This saga of warnings ignored has not reached its last act and may yet take hundreds more people to an early grave. As they have privately calculated the liabilities and their responsibilities for and involvement in criminal acts, corporations like Cape Industries (Anglo American), KCB (Eternit) and GEFCO (General Mining) have been quietly selling their asbestos-bearing properties and even in some cases trying to give them away to nominally independent black South African homelands. The idea is to put some space between profitable companies and the wrongs for which they might be held accountable in a post-apartheid society. As corporate manoeuvres continue, various spokesmen for the industry still repeat the ancient and dishonest lines about asbestos being safe. Unwittingly they contribute yet another fitting climax to what Paul Brodeur describes as 'a fifty year history of corporate malfeasance and inhumanity to man unparalleled in the annals of the private enterprise system'.[24]

11 Endless Washing Softens the Stone: the First Steps towards Freedom in the Mines

> I work for a political company which in conjunction with the mining houses seeks to obtain control of the souls as well as the bodies of their wage earning dependents.
>
> D. Ivon Jones[1]

From its beginnings on the Rand, the mining industry relied on a range of repressive measures to propel African peasants away from the land to become the muscle power of the mines. Charles Sydney Goldmann, a Fellow of the Royal Geographical Society and successful mining company promoter who published one of the first comprehensive financial surveys of mining on the Rand, explained the situation frankly: 'I may mention that the whole point of the law is to have a hold on the native whom we have brought down ... at considerable outlay to ourselves ...'[2]

George Albu, the founder of General Mining, an early chairman of the Association of Mines and later a member of the Chamber of Mines executive committee, expressed his business needs equally clearly. He told a Commission of Inquiry in 1897:

> The reduction of native wages is necessary for two reasons ... The one is to reduce our whole expenditure and the second has a very far-reaching effect upon the conditions which may prevail with regard to native labour in the future ...
>
> The native earns between fifty shillings and sixty shillings per month and he pays nothing for food or lodging. In fact he can save almost the whole amount he receives. If the native can save £20 a year, it is almost sufficient for him to go and live on the fat of the land.[3]

This was an inconvenient and unappetising prospect for mine owners like Mr Albu, as he explained in an exchange of views with one of the members of the Commission.

ALBU: I would make African labour compulsory . . . Why should a nigger be allowed to do nothing?
COMMISSIONER: If a man can live without work, how can you force him to work?
ALBU: Tax him then . . .
COMMISSIONER: Then you would not allow the Kaffir to hold land in the country, but he must work for the white man to enrich him?
ALBU: He must do his part of the work of helping his neighbours.[4]

In the early days the response of many black miners to the difficult conditions in which they worked was to break their contracts and desert in droves from the more unpleasant mines. As Sean Moroney has shown, the miners had an expressive private code for identifying these properties. The Dreifontein mine was '*Estokisini* – in the stocks'; New Midas was '*Mgewini* – a person of low morals'; Jupiter was '*Mjungwu* – a stabbing pain in the back', while Bantjes mine went by the name of '*Mafolish* – cattle food'.[5]

To pass laws and an oppressive Master and Servant Act, which made 'desertion' even from a dangerous mine a breach of contract and a criminal offence, were joined hut and poll taxes and a variety of other measures designed to oppress the black majority and encourage them to fuel the juggernaut of white mining and agriculture. The most iniquitous legislation was the Native Land Act, which stripped the indigenous peoples of their land rights, confined them to the most marginal or barren land and deprived them of human rights. Sol Plaatje, the founder of the African National Congress, described the pitiable conditions that resulted from the enactment of this law.[6] Peasant and tenant farmers and their families were forced off farms and left destitute. When their children died of hunger they were denied any rights of burial. Africans in British South Africa, he concluded, had fewer rights than wild animals and the insects of the field. 'The foxes', he said, quoting the New Testament, 'have holes and the birds of the fields have nests; but the Son of Man hath not where to lay his head.'[7]

Despite the ferocity of the assault on their way of life, African mineworkers still found ways to resist. As Charles van Onselen has shown in his unorthodox and moving *Social and Economic History of the Witwatersrand*, mineworkers denied freedom of self-expression and organisation used the compounds to build a chiliastic New Ninevite Army which operated secretly in many parts of the Rand.[8] Dunbar Moodie, another of South Africa's new historians, has argued that even those migrants who did not protest at conditions in the mines often engaged in a Faustian bargain with the mining companies, exchanging temporary submission to the corporate structure for the chance of earning cash wages which could sustain a peasant household in the rural areas.[9] Nevertheless, as Luli Callinicos shows in her powerful book *Gold and Workers*, protest including industrial protest was far from unknown. In 1913, three years after the abandonment of the 'experiment' in Chinese labour in favour of workers from Mozambique, the first concerted black strikes began to take place. Nine thousand African miners in four mines were involved in disputes that year, according to Callinicos. During these strikes a notice was pinned to the door of one compound explaining the strikers' grievances. These were poor pay and racial assaults by whites underground. During the dispute the army and the police were used to break the strikes and arrest the supposed ringleaders, the beginning of an enduring pattern; and in the end the strikers were forced back to work after three days. Then in 1918, faced with huge increases in the cost of living without any compensating increase in pay, black mineworkers began boycotting company stores; and in July that year, following widespread industrial discontent among municipal and electrical workers, black miners from Crown Mines, Robinson Deep and Ferreira Deep refused to go to work unless increases were paid. Again police were called and miners forced down the shafts at gunpoint.[10]

In February 1920 an even more widespread movement began in an East Rand Proprietary Mines compound, where, following widespread campaigning by various black groups, 25,000 men went on strike seeking higher pay and the release of two Zulu miners who had been jailed for their persistence in urging black miners to take collective action. The strike soon spread to twenty other mines along the Rand, and involved a total of 71,000 miners. According to the President of the Chamber of Mines, this 'was for the first time a native strike in the true sense of the word . . . an absolutely peaceful cessation of work'. Once again the police intervened to assist the Chamber of Mines and the strike was broken.[11]

In 1922 in a bid to boost profitability the Chamber of Mines moved to confront the racially exclusive sectional unions of the white labour aristocracy in the mines, provoking the famous Rand Revolt, with its slogan which presaged the emergence of full-blown apartheid a quarter of a century later: 'Workers of the world unite and fight for a white South Africa.' After the revolt had been put down, the mining companies set about reducing costs, introducing more black labour, restructuring production methods and widening the range of tasks done by blacks.[12] But as David Yudelman has shown, in the wake of the strike with a new ecology of power in place the mining companies set about ensuring a long-term sweetheart relationship with the white workers in the mines. Thereafter mining capitalists and white workers, the capos in the camps, jointly manipulated racial discrimination to their mutual advantage.[13] In Stanley Greenberg's phrase, they buried the hatchet – in the heads of the black miners.[14] No tenderness or toleration was ever extended to black union organisation, which remained outside the law, an intolerable subversion of the mining companies' right to a continuing flow of cheap black labour. And just in case other less critical forms of independent organisation should provide a seed-bed for democracy, blacks on the mines were denied churches, sporting clubs and virtually all voluntary organisations of their own, and of course fenced in and spied upon on a daily basis.[15]

In the 1930s, faced with a variety of radical efforts to organise black unions in a range of industries, the Chamber of Mines argued forcefully that attempts to organise black unions anywhere in South Africa should be resisted because organisation in any major South African industry would soon spill over into the mines.[16] The Chamber's uncompromising anti-black union position continued throughout the Second World War, which saw a rapid upsurge in South Africa's industrial development, considerable inflation and a huge rise in black aspirations for dignity and freedom, particularly among the younger and better educated. This mood of optimism soon spread into the mines, and was reflected in the political activity of members of the African National Congress and the South African Communist Party, which was virtually the only white group to defend black rights.[17]

At a Congress in Johannesburg in 1941 the new situation led to the formation of an African Mine Workers Union. From the beginning, according to Ruth First, the union highlighted the profound injustice of the compound system, offering to engage a group of architects to design township schemes with proper family homes on mining property.[18] Initiated, like its successor forty years later, mainly by mine clerks together with some surface workers, the union came into existence at a time of inflation, hunger and drought in the reserves and struck a deep chord in the compounds of the Rand which were visited by its officers, J. B. Marks and James Majoro.[19] But the hostility of the Chamber never gave the union the space or time to grow. Recruitment in the field was made more and more difficult, with members and organisers frequently arrested under a convenient wartime emergency order prohibiting meetings. Mine fences were made higher and more secure and perimeters and boundaries were extended and heavily reinforced to make unauthorised entry virtually impossible.[20] The two officers tried again and again to get the Gold Producers' Committee of the Chamber to meet the union; but in the words of the veteran South African labour leader Solly Sachs, the Gold Producers 'contemptuously refused'.[21] As a direct result of the Chamber's ruthlessness, tension on the mines grew. There was a noticeable increase in the number of spontaneous disputes. Sensing trouble, the government appointed a commission of inquiry under a High Court judge, Mr Justice Lansdown, to look into wages and conditions. The African Mine Workers Union marshalled its case in an effective memorandum outlining the grievous inadequacy of economic and social relations on the mines. The memorandum justified its claim for increased wages on the basis of the extraordinary profitability of the industry since South Africa came off the Gold Standard in 1932. The union asked for extra pay for overtime and Sunday work, which black Africans did without pay. The memorandum also stressed that no wage increases had been granted to blacks since 1914 and pointed out that black workers in other industries were infinitely better paid.[22]

The radical Johannesburg newspaper the *Guardian* published extracts from the memorandum and found itself sued by four mining companies. The companies persuaded the judge that their spotless reputations for humane treatment had been libelled and they were awarded damages of £750 each plus costs. One other complainant came unstuck – Captain Trigger, the unappetising boss of security for Gold Fields, who had insinuated a spy into the counsels of the union, a form of behaviour which, the judge said, left a bad taste in the mouth.[23] Trigger's manoeuvrings were a portent of what was to come. The Chamber declined to implement the Lansdown recommendations and still refused to talk to the black union, even though throughout this period it engaged in 'normal' collective bargaining with the white miners' union. The resulting sequence of events was burned into the consciousness of Cyril Ramaphosa and his closest associates, the people who would spearhead the drive to build a union in the 1980s. In the fate of the AMWU in 1946, they saw the rocks on to which many in the Chamber still hoped to draw them forty years on.

In those areas of the west Rand where the union was strongest, demonstrations and protest strikes took place in April 1946 and were soon crushed. Nevertheless, on 12 August 45,000 black miners came out on strike for a wage of ten shillings a day. The movement grew again on the next day but soon the government and the police moved to crush dissent. They arrested strike leaders and used violence to intimidate the strikers to return to work. In all, the strikes involved 75,000 workers and affected twenty-one out of forty-seven mines. One thousand miners were arrested; 1,248 were injured and nine were killed as a result of the intransigence of the Chamber, most of them at Gold Fields' highly profitable Sub Nigel property, where police fired into the crowd killing two, with six more dying in the ensuing panic.[24] James Phillips was only twenty-one when the crisis burst. With the arrest of J. B. Marks and James Majoro, the miners' leaders, he was drafted in to be a member of the strike committee. Chairman of a branch of the garment workers' union, Phillips nevertheless had considerable personal knowledge of the degrading conditions on the gold mines.

'I saw the conditions for myself and I can assure you that they were absolutely horrible,' he told me in an interview shortly before he died in 1989. 'My uncle was a hawker and I went with him regularly round the mining compounds as he peddled his wares. The food was poor, miners cooked in their rooms. The latrines, the washrooms were a terrible mess, and the wages very, very bad. When the strike broke out every mine was surrounded by the police and virtually the entire leadership arrested. As the reports of deaths and injuries came in we decided that we had better call it a day and summoned a meeting in Johannesburg with a view to calling the strike off. Miners from the Rand were trying to march to that meeting when they too were attacked by the police and at our meeting I was given five minutes to disperse the crowd or the police would fire into it, as they later did at Sharpeville. The government and the Chamber were two sides of the same coin and worked so closely together. In the end there were lengthy trials, jail sentences and repression all to protect the wealth of the mining companies.

'I left the country in 1954 and came to Britain. I became a singer and founded an African choir in one of the great churches of Bremen in Germany, where I taught white people to sing the wonderful music of Africa, including the freedom songs we had sung during the 1946 strike. For the rest of my life I wondered how it could be that the British government, which supposedly had the final say in South Africa, a Commonwealth country, could allow this complicity between the Chamber, a business monopoly and white South Africa's prime minister Jan Smuts to oppress my people. I never found the answer.'[25]

Behind the scenes the Chamber of Mines' president, Stowe McLean, a hardliner from the Gold Fields' stable, worked astutely to pass off the strike as nothing more than the work of an unrepresentative and sinister Communist conspiracy,[26] an analysis which was entirely misleading. Nevertheless it was taken up by Smuts, the South African premier, and even found its way into the British press, including the normally liberal *Manchester Guardian*. Initially the *Guardian* had been sympathetic to the mineworkers and had carried an article on them by Solly Sachs, who made no secret of his affiliations with the South African Communist Party. But a month later the *Guardian* carried an extraordinary piece called 'South African natives – a critical period'. In it the paper's South African correspondent wrote that the strike had been engineered by the Communist Party as 'part of a plan which, had it been successful, would have thrown the country into the utmost disorder and probably have produced race riots and death on a shocking scale'.[27] Marks and Majoro, the miners' leaders, were both members of the Communist Party, but there is no evidence for the fantasies about insurrection. Indeed the evidence indicates that employers were far less worried about the 'Red menace' than about the role of the Basotho migrant workers from Lesotho, the British protectorate surrounded by South Africa. The 1946 strike wave had been spearheaded, as a British High Commission report now available in the Public Records Office underlines, by Basotho workers at the Vereeniging steel works. Basothos on the gold mines had also been active supporters of the strike and three of the Africans killed had been from the British Protectorate. This led a number of employers to stop hiring Lesotho citizens, the report noted, because they were thought to be too prone to join unions.[28] At the British High Commission in Pretoria, one unnamed official was anxious to probe a little deeper. In a lengthy memorandum prepared for Viscount Addison, the British Secretary of State for the Dominions, the official stated that 'it would be foolish to dismiss the whole matter as an unfortunate result of agitation because ... the native mineworkers ... had good reason for discontent.

'Even after the £6 a year increase granted by the government, the African miner was still at least £4 short of pre-war levels,' he wrote. What's more, the miners were 'shockingly exploited by the owners of concession stores: and it was understandable that they should compare their wages of less than four pounds a month with the wages of twice and three times this figure being earned in unskilled or semi-skilled jobs above ground in other industries'. In a prescient comment about violence he added: 'through their failure to provide any satisfactory channel for negotiation between native workers and employers, the Government must bear some of the responsibility for the tragic consequences of the use of force to settle an industrial dispute'.[29]

Regrettably this and other such warnings from the margins were to go unheeded. For more than a quarter of a century, as the South African mining industry went through its greatest period of expansion, the human rights of the migrant miners continued to be ignored; whole new mining areas opened up, always on the basis of anonymous, single-sex compounds in which a certain kind of order, cruel, aggressive and colonising, did obtain. As the flow of wealth from these mines increased, few voices remained to speak for the migrant miners. There was the radical Anglican priest Michael Scott, who had spoken out at the time of the 1946 strike and who developed an unrivalled understanding of the evils of the contract labour system through his work in South-West Africa.[30] There was the work of Peter Abrahams in his finely wrought novels; and Nelson Mandela, who had worked briefly as a mine clerk, spoke out about the mining companies' dependence on labour reserves to provision their enterprises with cheap labour and suborned workers. Mandela soon found himself on trial for his life. One of his co-accused in the first of his major jousts with the South African State was the journalist and political activist Ruth First. In 1961 while in the dock during the famous treason trial, First, a writer with commanding investigative skills as well as a perceptive grasp of submerged issues, published an important essay entitled 'The Gold of Migrant Labour' in the magazine *Africa South in Exile*.[31] She noted the huge shortages of labour the mines were registering and their ever-more extravagant sorties into surrounding countries to find more black labourers to drill the stopes and haul the ore. She reported:

> 1,300 miles of special Witwatersrand Native Labour Association roads had been cut into Bechuanaland, motor barges ply the Zambesi and the rivers of Barotseland, the Eastern Caprivi Strip – running from South West Africa to Northern Rhodesia and dividing Bechuanaland from Angola – is preserved as a game reserve, but the WNLA obtained permission from the Union government to cut a private WNLA road through the strip on which no transport is allowed other than WNLA vehicles on WNLA permits.

She disclosed that South Africa, one of the oldest members of the International Labour Organisation, had ratified only eleven of the 111 International Labour Conventions passed since 1917. Significantly, she showed, South Africa had not ratified the 1930 convention on forced labour or its 1937 update, or endorsed its 1949 convention and recommendations for the protection of migrant workers. She attacked the mining companies' seemingly endless capacity for self-delusion. The gold mines' claims that the migrant labour system was a mechanism for 'civilising' native peoples she found particularly offensive.

She wrote,

> the mines have always possessed this marvellous facility for believing that their own self-interest coincides with the general good. For seventy-four years they have posed as South Africa's fairy godmothers. Men were to be recruited for the mines so that the 'civilising habit of labour' could be inculcated in them. Profits were a factor too, but not advertised as such.[32]

For nearly thirty years after the destruction of the African Mine Workers' Union, the elaborate white authority structures of the mining compounds were overpowering and unchallengeable. But with the growth of black consciousness, the collapse of Portuguese power in Africa and major changes in the recruitment patterns and educational background of migrant miners, by the 1970s younger miners were unwilling to put up with the everyday repression of the mines. Denied any channels they found legitimate or fair, miners began to vent their grievances and frustrations in explosive ways. Between 1972 and 1979 there were at least eighty-one riots or disturbances on South African mines.[33] These frequently had tragic consequences: at least 205 miners were killed and over a thousand seriously injured in eight years, in compound conflicts, or at the hands of mine police or the army, who were ostensibly restoring order.[34]

At first, in accord with the distorting lens of white racism, these incidents were passed off as ethnic conflicts, faction fighting between different national groupings. But as the miners began to find their own voices and some unusually independent thinkers in the South African churches and universities began to scrutinise the mining industry, such crude explanations were swept away and the South African mining industry began its hesitant journey towards the unthinkable – limited acceptance of black unionisation. The company which was initially most responsive to the riots was also the worst affected. This was Anglo American, the giant of South African mining, which proclaimed its adherence to liberal values in its fine publications but ran its mining compounds according to the standard principles of mining authoritarianism. On New Year's Day 1975 about 3,500 miners at the company's Free State Saaiplaas gold mine struck against an imposed new scheme to defer some of their pay and transfer it to family bank accounts in Lesotho. On 3 January Basotho miners at the company's Western Deep Levels mine also struck for the day, returning to work only after a Lesotho government representative was flown in to address them and explain the scheme face to face.[35] On 5 January at Vaal Reefs, the biggest mine in the country, the deferred pay scheme was again the catalyst for serious discontent. At one point in the afternoon some miners broke into a bar at Vaal Reefs South. The police were called in, serious violence ensued and by the time unrest subsided on 15 January ten miners were dead and thirty-four seriously injured.[36] In any country where respect for human rights was established there would have been a thorough public inquiry into the situation and proper inquests. This was not standard practice for black miners in South Africa. There were token inquests, but since the widows and relatives were far distant and too poor to engage lawyers, and there was no union to help them, the inquest process was at best unsatisfactory.

Nevertheless, to his credit Dennis Etheredge, the chairman of the Anglo American gold division, initiated a serious study of disturbances. Etheredge, one of Anglo's top executives, had become deeply worried about the yawning gap between public relations statements and the reality of the compounds and feared there would be many repetitions of these events if the company was not careful. He had learned to value serious research as a young man, writing a doctoral thesis on the early history of the Chamber of Mines, and quickly moved to set up a working party to investigate the underlying situation.[37] Etheredge realised there had been a profound change in the reaction to the compounds by the younger miners and that their behaviour was naturally influenced by events in their own home countries, Lesotho of course, but also Mozambique, Malawi, Zimbabwe and South Africa itself. Mine reports and documents were quickly pulled together; members of a hastily constituted working party visited four mines – Free State Saaiplaas, President Brand, Vaal Reefs and Western Deep Levels – with a black company official, M. S. Ntshangase, interviewing miners directly involved in the disturbances. A diary of events in each of the many hostels was built up and analysis focused on identifying initiating groups, usually younger miners and members of dance and football teams who picketed the mine cages and moved around the hostels urging support for the strike.[38] At Vaal Reefs the findings including worrying evidence of South African Police and Security Branch involvement in the troubles, with mine management being approached to let a paid agent who had for years avoided prosecution because of his police connections, into the compound. It was alleged that this man helped armed men to enter the mine from outside and blew a whistle to initiate one of the attacks by some Basotho miners on Xhosas at Vaal Reefs.[39]

The most disturbing part of the report related to the underlying causes of the 'riots'. In tackling this issue, the authors did not, as is the way in many corporate investigations, shrink from unpleasant truths, but tried to set out clearly how Anglo American management had implemented the policy changes of the Lesotho government without any significant attempt to inform, consult with or be influenced by the wishes and feelings of the miners themselves. With hostels often allocated on ethnic or factional lines and with only a top-down, undemocratic and largely discredited information flow through *indunas* and *isibondas* or tribal prefects, the results of poorly managed change were many unnecessary and unavoidable deaths. The report also grappled with the mechanisms whereby an informal black leadership emerged in the mines to formulate demands, calm and discipline the miners as a collective and seek solutions. This of course is the tap-root of trade unionism and free collective bargaining and from this moment on a few centimetres of critical space began to grow inside the closed system of the mining industry.[40]

'A . . . significant point', the report stated, 'is the emphasis workers seem to have placed on electing spokesmen with status in the workplace, rather than tribal or traditional status . . . Where spokesmen were elected they appear to have played an extremely positive role. Management spoke in positive terms of these men.' The report also noted that little difficulty seemed to have been experienced in the mechanics of choosing either small or large delegations, that the spokesmen were impressive and articulate, that they grasped their representative role very well and that it would be a pity if the worker representatives who emerged during these disturbances were simply to disappear into the labour force.[41]

The report saved its most difficult observations for its concluding pages:

> There is a need to point to a deeper reality. Mine management generally remarked on the suddenness and unexpectedness of these disturbances . . . The proximate and very real cause this time was deferred pay. Last year there was a clash over women in the Thabong village. It is impossible to predict what sort of issues may lead to a recurrence in the future.

What has created or heightened this predisposition towards violence?
... a heightened sense of assertiveness amongst blacks coming from
independent Black countries; a heightened sense of self-consciousness
among South African blacks on the mines who cannot be completely
[shut] out from the general rise in the consciousness and self-awareness
of blacks; the normlessness of migrant labour culture where so many
of the social sanctions which prohibit violent behaviour are absent. Has
migrancy created a form of delinquency in the rural areas? The increased
skill and responsibility levels of black miners are causing frustration
with regard to the old systems of work and hostel administration and
regulation.[42]

The report stopped short of recommending unionisation; instead there
was talk of briefing groups and a better information flow. Anglo's human
face was also severely compromised by the addition of short paragraphs
recommending a more 'secure' or manipulative design of hostel accommodation and better training and equipment of the Mine Security Departments.
    The apartheid government was also alarmed by the outbursts of discon-
tent and violence on the mines. Its economic and political grip depended
on the continuing production of gold, and in March 1975 it set up a
Commission of Inquiry to investigate the underlying causes of the riots
and to recommend steps to prevent any recurrence. Chaired by L. L. A.
McKay, the five-member commission included a direct representative
of the South African armed forces, Major-General C. P. Pretorius. The
committee's report, officially secret, was a curious mixture.[43] It contained
a strong element provided by Dr van Warmelo, an off-the-shelf 'Bantu
expert' as ethnocentric as the original architects of apartheid themselves,
who succeeded in persuading the commission to take seriously the nostrum
that 'the southern Bantu tribes are particularly inclined to become violent'.
Then, in marked contrast and probably as a result of evidence from Dennis
Etheredge, there was a measure of recognition of the degrading social
structures created by the mining companies, the migrant labour system
and their single-sex compounds.
    'The unusual and unnatural circumstances in which migrant labourers
find themselves in the compounds and hostels', the report noted, 'definitely
contribute to a feeling of uncertainty and insecurity, boredom and frustration
which may in turn lead to their [the miners'] resorting to violence on the
spur of the moment.'[44] When it came to recommending change, however,
the committee had few insights and absolutely no compassion. Instead the

214

report concerned itself exclusively with how compounds could be more effectively designed and patrolled by the South African police, army and mine security.

Circulated a few months before the Soweto revolt of school pupils was put down with unrestrained violence, the report provides an important insight into the schizoid, security mind of the minority government in the 1970s, as it worked to prepare a few 'presentational' or 'cosmetic' reforms for international consumption while privately strengthening the forces of the state. In the mines in 1975 this involved fitting out hostels 'as attractively as possible but with the minimum of barricades or the use of material which can be converted into weapons'. Security video-taping was to be introduced to identify ring leaders and strikers. Mine security personnel were to be better armed and equipped with tear gas. There should be regular and effective search parties for weapons, and then, as sops, 'more gardening, more singing and more religion'. There should also be a few more shops for black miners to go to but, the commission added in a revealing document summarising its recommendations, 'the mining industry is not anxious to institute fun palaces for its black employees'.[45]

Dennis Etheredge and other free-thinking colleagues in Anglo's Orange Free State mines had stressed in the last paragraph of their 1975 report that there was 'a need for a continuing . . . and much more penetrating investigation of the feelings and perceptions of black mineworkers'.[46] Etheredge was now privately obtaining guidance and advice from personnel managers respectful of the insights available in modern social theory. In particular he and his colleagues had become aware of the fact that, in the words of the American economist Kenneth Boulding, 'almost all organisational structures tend to produce false images in the supposed decision maker', and that the larger and more authoritarian the organisation, 'the better the chance that its top decision makers will be operating in purely imaginary worlds'.[47] Etheredge and his colleagues concluded that what was needed was 'a study which provides a full and accurate profile of the black miner in both statistical and attitudinal and perception terms. The advisability of involving someone outside the Corporation in the design and execution of this study should be considered.'[48] By the time the study was complete, Anglo American management was to be in possession of an abundance of worrying evidence that South African mines and compounds far from resembling fun palaces were in fact cruel habitations, human warehouses grievously damaging the migrant workers unfortunate enough to live in them.

After a tough controversy inside Anglo's gold division and the main board, Etheredge won his fight to involve an outsider. The man chosen for the highly sensitive assignment was Dunbar Moodie, Professor of Sociology at Johannesburg's Witwatersrand University. Moodie had just completed a lengthy study of the role of Afrikaner religion in the rise of Afrikanerdom. With a somewhat shy outward manner which disguised an extraordinary empathy for human beings, particularly the disadvantaged, Moodie, was a devout Anglican. He had been deeply influenced both by the insights of Christian theology and the sensitive social theory of the Italian thinker Antonio Gramsci.[49] At first he was troubled by the prospect of working directly for South Africa's richest company and tried to pass the assignment on to a friend, the historian Charles van Onselen. But in the end he decided that he should take on the job and transformed his doubts into a positive set of guarantees that he would be allowed complete freedom of publication for his work and a veto against politically motivated editing. With this agreed he began directing the ten-week intensive study of black miners at Anglo's Welkom mine in the Orange Free State. Working in tandem with the Agency for Industrial Mission, a group of radical Christians who had initiated some remarkable studies of the industry by theological students in their vacations, Moodie selected and trained a team of four black field officers. Each was involved in designing the study of the Welkom Number One Shaft and Compound. After their period of living and working in the mine compounds they were interviewed at length by group industrial relations officers and the interviews were transcribed. Moodie then wrote up a first version of his Anglo report, which was edited but not on this occasion censored by the Anglo American Industrial Relations Department.[50] In May 1977 Anglo American released selected extracts of the report at a press conference in Johannesburg. Desmond Quigley in *The Times* in London described the report as 'a chronicle of degradation, humiliation, corruption and near-institutionalised homosexuality suffered by black African miners'.[51] The report did not identify the Anglo mine, which I have established was Welkom, today part of Anglo's troubled Western Holdings mine. Anglo's anxiety over the name of the mine being disclosed is only too understandable, given the shaming congeries of misery and exploitation the report disclosed.

Moodie's survey of Welkom probed the best hidden and most secret corners of the social structure of the giant mine. He and his theological students followed the miners from their homelands to the TEBA recruitment centre at Welkom, noting how shamelessly they were abused by the

216

staff, who pushed and shoved them as they queued for medical examinations in which there was no respect for privacy and individuality. The corruption and brutality of mine staff were captured in unforgettable paragraphs. The subtle dialectic of human beings reacting to an unnatural and oppressive environment is superbly documented in what is a heart-rending if little-known classic of modern sociological research. The bitter fruits of escapist drinking and drug taking are set out. The exploitative forms of sexual release occasioned by the all-male atmosphere of the mine are explored with sympathy and understanding for both prostitutes and their clients, for the thousands of men who have recourse to the most elemental forms of prostitution in near-by townships where women are so poor that prostitution can be their only source of income. There was understanding too for those miners who in the circumstances go up the slope with other men not out of free choice but because any interaction with women is denied them.[52] The immunity of the *isibondas*, the tribal prefects in the mines, from prosecution even for the cruellest acts of male rape, is recorded,[53] as are the appalling conditions of lavatories, kitchens and beerhalls. Throughout the report Moodie and his team manage to keep their focus on the most important aspect of the social structures of the mines or indeed any social structures – how human beings trapped inside institutions feel about them and how in fundamental and unforgivable ways they are irretrievably damaged by them.[54]

It is unusual for the British media to concern itself with mining conditions anywhere in the world except perhaps for a day or two in the wake of a newsworthy disaster. But on this occasion Desmond Quigley's summary of the Moodie report in *The Times* began to resonate, at least on BBC Radio. Brian Widlake, then presenter of the *World at One*, described it to his audience as 'a horrifying report on conditions' and for a day or two something approaching controversy reigned in the South African and British media about the conditions of the hundreds of thousands of migrant miners. Reached at his home in London Harry Oppenheimer, the billionaire owner of Anglo, admitted to the *Citizen* that the catalogue of misery set out in *The Times* was 'fundamentally true'. But, he added, *The Times* had treated it in a sensational manner. 'I am surprised *The Times* has chosen this time to publish these facts,' he said. 'I have known about them for some time.'[55]

If for once Anglo was unusually long on disclosure, it was short on remedies. It proposed no serious programme to tackle the root problem, the migrant labour system, and end the single-sex compounds, replacing them with proper family housing. 'In many respects mines have to be run like army camps for safety reasons,' Dennis Etheredge told the *Financial Times*. Anglo, he added lamely, had already allocated twenty million rand to house more migrant miners. 'Building will commence soon, but housing for all migrants and their families would prove too costly.'[56] Privately, in tandem with its consideration of the Moodie Report, Anglo had costed out a proper programme of reform. Its studies showed that it would cost 10,000 rand including water and electricity for each unit of family housing. To house 10 per cent of the company's migrant gold miners would cost 130 million rand, about four months' net profits for the corporation. To house them all would cost 1·3 billion, about four years' profits. By contrast Anglo estimated that the cost of providing single accommodation for black migrants even in the refitted compounds was a mere 2,000 rand, one-fifth of the cost of a family house.[57] So in the wake of the Moodie Report with its disclosures of racism, brutality and human degradation on an unparalleled scale, financial decisions led to the continuation of the compound system. A limited sum was made available by South Africa's most progressive mining company for a little more black family housing. This was no more than a token gesture in the face of some of the gravest injustices in the corporate world, and all the more worrying since it must have been obvious to everyone concerned that fundamental reform was long overdue. But, true to habit, Anglo retreated to the narrow and blinding definition of 'costs' which since it excludes social and human costs has bedevilled the development of civilisation since the Industrial Revolution. Once again, to use Randall Packard's apposite phrase, fiscal road blocks were put down in the way of the advancement of the human beings trapped by the migrant labour system, that particularly repugnant feature of apartheid. Hiding behind government regulations and the posturing of the white miners' union and looking straight at the financial bottom line, Anglo's main board opted to continue apartheid on the mines and threw away a vital opportunity for reform.

As for Dennis Etheredge, he concluded he could push no further for the end of the compounds. But if Anglo declined to initiate fundamental change, his advisers reasoned, then conflict would continue and intensify. In such a situation a safety valve was imperative. Without some form of works councils or even union rights for blacks, they warned, the South African mining industry would combust and the compounds, for so long the all-powerful instruments of colonialism, become centres for explosive and unpredictable protest and even, given the hot-house atmosphere, for outbreaks of insurrectionary violence.

Questioned by the magazine *South African Mining* about union rights after the release of the Moodie Report, Etheredge stated, 'We don't consider it our business to bring trade unions into existence. Nowhere in the world does management do that. It must rise spontaneously from the men. But if the men came to us with a good sound constitution, and they appear to have the support of a great number of workers of course we would start talking to them.'[58] The turmoil of the mine compounds between 1973 and 1977 had at last opened doors to a future in which black miners could build something for themselves. The Chamber of Mines' century-long united front against black unions had begun to crack and in time would begin to be moved aside.

At first the opinions of Etheredge, and his liberal colleagues in the Orange Free State and at head office were thought to be dangerous even for Anglo American. But Anglo was soon to pay a heavy price for its failure to do more than engage in cosmetic reforms. Another internal Anglo report written without outside involvement had heavily underlined how intractable the problems were. This report dated March 1976 examined a range of options for ameliorating the monotony of the compounds at Anglo's Western Holdings mine through an expanded range of leisure activities.[59] The options canvassed included more adult education, more mine dancing and football teams, training in shoe making and tailoring, the introduction of television and a broader range of films in the mine cinema than the traditional diet of carefully censored, all-white westerns imported from America. But as the report of the group discussions held with black miners during the investigation made plain, what most worried the miners was their separation from their families. They viewed other measures as palliatives which failed to deal with the real problem. In the discussions they expressed their views in powerful and poetic ways.

'We live like animals in the compounds without our wives,' said one member of the discussion group at Western Holdings. 'We cannot begin to be in a mood for such things as sporting activities while our whole way of life is painful,' said another. One supervisor put the point even more strongly when he said, 'The life we lead here is worse than slavery or the life of a beast of burden – at least a beast of burden is harnessed side by side with its mate; and perhaps a slave is chained together with his wife.' The report concluded, 'The groups blamed the migratory labour system which made them live away from their families for most of the problems which are experienced on the mines.'[60]

Early in 1979 the intractable problems of compound life exploded into violence and discontent once again, this time in a particularly embarrassing way for the meliorists of Anglo American. Early in April 1979, Anglo American was getting ready for an important day in the corporate calendar – the official opening of its new gold mine, Elandsrand. The mine was the subject of much publicity. It had been specially designed by the AAC central architects' department to take into account the group's new thinking on industrial relations and the design-for-security comments of the 1975 McKay Commission. Elandsrand boasted computer controls for workers clocking on and going through the mine crush to travel to work. Its single men's quarters were supposed to be excellent. At Elandsrand Anglo had also introduced a new hostel management system and set up a black employees council which, under the influence of the new thinking in the wake of the Moodie Report, was supposed to provide a free flow of information between workers and management and even 'a forum for the expression of dissent and the negotiation of solutions'.[61] Yet just two days before the Anglo American chairman and the President of the Deutsche Bank from West Germany were to officiate at a grand ceremony in which these numerous but essentially cosmetic changes would be the subject of much self-congratulation, groups of miners denied solutions to their problems went on the rampage and seriously damaged whole sections of the new mine. When violence broke out on 8 and 9 April, Anglo, despite its affirmations of liberalism, refused all access to the press, called in the police, discharged workers and issued statements that, despite a lengthy meeting, its managers had been unable to get the miners even to explain what their grievances were.[62]

The public relations posture that the disturbances were mindless violence was maintained until the South African police had 'restored order', until many of the miners concerned had left the mine for good and the somewhat compromised opening ceremony was out of the way. Then Anglo invited the Chamber of Mines' Human Resources Laboratory to analyse the situation and establish the causes of the conflict. The lab sent in an investigating team co-ordinated by Peter de Vries and Kent McNamara, who worked with four experienced black interviewers to identify what had gone wrong. Their lengthy report on the underlying realities of the new, 'model' mine was another shaming document.[63] The talk of a 'humane', 'mould-breaking', 'high-tech' mine disguised a complex and often brutal underlying reality, with the recurrence of many old problems and the emergence of many new ones caused either by the process of change or its mismanagement. And, far from the workers concerned being unable to explain their grievances, they readily listed dozens of them.[64]

They were not being adequately paid for overtime. The new complex administrators were not dealing with their problems over bonus payments. These were compounded by computer errors which marked people absent when they were at work and at work when they were absent. People were wrongly sacked as a result of these errors, which were never rectified. Workers transferred from another mine near by, Western Deep Levels, complained about the poor pay and inferior living conditions. There were severe food shortages, particularly of meat, in the hostel canteens. The dining hall was dirty. Because of poor organisation, fresh food was being wasted on a huge scale in one part of the kitchen while in another leftovers from the previous day were being reheated for consumption the next. The food in general was of poor quality, particularly the porridge and the soup. Cooking utensils were dirty. There were 'foreign bodies in some of the meals'. There were shortages of mugs because dishwashers broke down. There were constant shortages of toilet paper; rooms were overcrowded; the building programme was six months behind schedule and people were having to sleep in very difficult conditions with their rest frequently interrupted by the arrival or departure of workers on other shifts. Most of these problems had been identified and reported up the line through the traditional *isibonda* system long before the dispute broke out. Food-related problems, the report showed, had been brought to the attention of management, even further up the line, on ninety-six occasions between November 1978 and April 1979 without redress. Management, presumably, were either too busy or just plain out of touch.[65]

Worried by the accumulating crisis, one hostel manager underlined these points and made more of his own in a three-page memorandum which he sent to the mine personnel manager long before the outbreak of violence. The manager (whose memorandum was annexed to the Chamber of Mines' report) itemised forty serious specific grievances.[66] In addition to reiterating anxiety over those grievances identified by the *isibondas*, the hostel manager added that discipline in the hostel was too strict; people were being discharged too readily; people were being assaulted by room prefects and complex administrators; private belongings were 'getting lost' in the changing rooms; there was not enough milk and sugar for tea and coffee; blacks complained of extensive violence underground by whites and the manager even had evidence of whites taking sticks underground; whites were insisting on preferential access to the hoists at the end of shifts; underground workers were working seven days a week and had no rest days; clock cards were disappearing and workers being falsely shown absent as a result; there

221

were insufficient warnings when underground blasting was due to take place and safety committees were still operating on a racially exclusive basis and excluding black team leaders.[67]

Many further shaming details of the racism, brutality, and management double standards, giving whites immunity from punishment even in cases where they committed unprovoked assaults on blacks, were contained in the Chamber of Mines' report, but the authors lacked the vision, independence or courage of Dunbar Moodie and failed to publish their data in accordance with the wider public responsibilities of social scientists. Nevertheless the wealth of detailed information showed the essentially cosmetic nature of the changes being made to the migrant labour system and the continuing failure even of Anglo, undoubtedly South Africa's most progressive mining employer, to face the truth. Despite investment of time and money in new facilities and structures, it was impossible for the hierarchical management of these gigantic institutions to deliver on their promises. Like the large Victorian mental hospitals which had come under fire from concerned relatives, doctors, nurses and social workers in Britain and America, these 'total institutions', 'labour batteries', the description of Francis Wilson, were fundamentally flawed. They were degrading and inhuman in essence; and so large and all-encompassing that they were unsteerable and out of control. The migrant labour-compound system itself was the problem, it was abundantly clear, not this or that detail of its operation on this or that mine. Like the USSR in the 1980s, the South African mining industry needed change, openness and democracy. The tragedy was that even in Anglo American, South Africa's biggest, richest and undoubtedly most 'liberal' mining company, there was no willingness to spend the money necessary for fundamental reform, even though the entire board of directors and all thoughtful people in the bureaucracy of the company knew that it was essential. Many unnecessary deaths of both black and white South Africans were to result from this failure.

Why did Anglo fail? First and foremost because at different levels in the corporation there was a want of commitment and imagination. On the mines there was lethargy or downright hostility to any real change. Many members of the racist mine bureaucracy feared that change could curtail their power or even cost them their jobs. Even at the top the company seems, despite the valiant efforts of Etheredge and his allies, to have lost its way. In 1979 Harry Oppenheimer's successor as chairman of Anglo, Gavin Relly, stated unequivocally in a speech to Assocom (the South African Associated Chambers of Commerce), that on gold mines, 'Migrant labour is here to stay ... and should be accepted as a permanent feature of our economic and social order.'[68] This was no more than a repetition of what Dennis Etheredge had reluctantly stated in 1977 after the Moodie Report. But what was indefensible in 1977 was, after Elandsrand, inexcusable. After Elandsrand the newly ameliorated contract labour system was shown to be just as dangerous, and destructive of human dignity and lives. Relly's blunt insistence that migrant labour was to continue as 'a permanent feature of our economic and social order' was for many thoughtful blacks the last straw. Thereafter, though Anglo behaved a good deal more responsibly than other mining houses, it was a compromised force as a propagator of change. Relly's statement was made with the full backing and support of the Oppenheimer family. A deeply conservative man, Relly had been appointed Anglo chairman in the knowledge that he was 'safe' and did not favour fundamental reform. At the time the Anglo liberals had hoped that a more radical, free-thinking chairman would be appointed. But the Oppenheimer votes went behind Relly and in Anglo it was the dynastic Oppenheimer votes that counted.[69]

Another of Anglo's dreams died at Elandsrand. This was the black employees' council, a type of works council modelled on those adopted by many British and American employers in response to the wave of radicalism generated by the First World War. At Elandsrand there was to be one 'complex council' for each hostel block, or 'complex' as they had been renamed by the wordsmiths in Anglo's industrial relations department. Each complex council was to elect representatives to a central black employees' council for the mine as a whole, which was to meet every two months.[70] But because the mine personnel manager was overstretched and Anglo head office would not sanction the appointment of an extra industrial relations officer at Elandsrand, the minutes of the meetings were produced very late and the two-monthly cycle had already fallen away by early 1979, months before the official opening ceremony had even been performed. Worse still, by the mine management's own admission, the black employees' council had no teeth at all. As the report noted:

The major problem with these councils in the opinion of the laboratory, and of White management interviewed on the mine, was that they had no formal powers.

In the final analysis, management's decision-making powers overrode all, and any change, concession or improvement brought about through the councils was due to management's good will ... In the case of a disagreement between workers and management there was no provision for recourse to an extra-mine body for settlement or arbitration. In such a case, management's view held, the workers had to give way.[71]

After the Elandsrand explosion, the faction inside Anglo who favoured immediate progress towards trade union recognition on the mines was enormously strengthened. They began to argue more and more successfully behind the closed doors of modern corporatism that the development of unions was vital. Without unions, they insisted, catastrophe was looming.[72] Inside the Chamber of Mines itself they had some limited support. The old guard had recently been replaced and labour relations matters had been given an apparatus of their own. For years labour had been a subdivision of low standing within the Chamber's technical department, but in 1977 a new department was set up and a labour relations supremo, Johann Liebenberg, appointed. The son of a white trade union leader, Liebenberg worked hard to move the Chamber at least some way from its authoritarian past. It took him two years to get the Chamber to draw up guidelines for union recognition and when these were finally drafted they remained so severe and restrictive that someone in the Chamber leaked them to the press to break the log jam. There were two further rounds of compound riots and social explosions in 1981 and 1982 before the Chamber finally granted any meaningful recognition and then the real struggle to build a lasting black trade union presence on the mines began, with companies like Gold Fields and Gencor trying to obstruct any progress. Various groupings declared an interest in getting recognition and before long it became clear that the Council of Unions of South Africa affiliate, the National Union of Mineworkers, would establish a powerful presence on many mines and become the fastest growing union in the country. A new day was dawning and a new cry was beginning to be heard throughout the beloved country – 'Viva, NUM, viva!' After nearly a century of exploitation endless washing had not only softened the stone it had begun to break.

12   Conspiracy of Hope: the Rise of NUM

In his official, centenary history of the Chamber of Mines of South Africa, John Lang speaks of the emergence in the 1980s of a new consensus in the ranks of South Africa's mining companies. The companies put their past behind them, Lang insists, opting instead for an open, enlightened approach.[1] Outside Johannesburg, away from head offices and public relations departments on the mines themselves, enlightenment and openness were – and still are – hard to find, as Mlungisi Nelani was to discover. Mlungisi, or 'Solomon' as unenlightened senior mine officials named him to avoid the inconvenience of addressing an African by his own name, first came to work for Gencor at its Marievale gold mine in 1982. In 1985, some time after the dawn of John Lang's new enlightenment, Mlungisi found that his efforts to promote reform in one of the company's most backward compounds led to a plot to have him intimidated, beaten and possibly even killed.

A capable, well-educated young man, Mlungisi was perturbed by the conditions he found at the mine on his arrival.[2] The hostel room where he was billeted slept twenty-two men on two-storey concrete bunks, with a two-inch-thick polyurethane foam bedroll as their only mattress. Newcomers didn't even get this meagre provision until they had been seen by the mine doctor, but since this could take anything up to four days, they would have to sleep for three nights on bare concrete or gather together a do-it-yourself mattress of newspapers, old clothes and rags. Even after the thin, foam bedroll arrived there were no sheets. Besides the lack of privacy, wardrobes and clean, convenient washing facilities, Mlungisi was struck by the poor hygiene. Bins full of old, decaying food were left outside the entrance for up to two weeks, sending flies and foul smells everywhere. The problem was compounded because miners were always using the stove in the dormitories to cook their own meals and supplement the poor food provided in the compound. All air vents and windows were set high near the ceiling for 'security' reasons, so the cooking meant that doors could never be shut except in winter.

Concerned at the poor conditions, Mlungisi, a clerical worker in the mine office, became active in the National Union of Mineworkers and was eventually recognised as the chief steward at the Marievale mine, one of the older properties on the reef and therefore with some of the worst mining and compound conditions. Taking advantage of what he imagined to be the new spirit of enlightenment in the mining industry, Mlungisi first resolved that something should be done about the atrocious food in the canteen, particularly the mealie-meal porridge, which was a staple diet on the mine. The mealie pap was so badly cooked, he observed, that, unless a person was used to it, it had an unusual effect. When you swallowed it, instead of bringing nourishment, it caused serious stomach aches and on occasion something worse. With a view to getting things put right, NUM pressed for Mlungisi to be transferred from his clerical job at Marievale so he could supervise the work in the compound kitchen. Initially the company agreed and Mlungisi was able, for a time, to make some change to the quality of the canteen food.

Not everyone in the kitchen was wholeheartedly enthusiastic about Mlungisi's arrival or his endeavours to bring change. The kitchens in South African mines are often subject to rackets whereby food is misappropriated and sold off. Before long Mlungisi established that just such a racket seemed to be operating at Marievale. The best supplies were not being used for the miners; they were being disposed of. Working to stamp out these routine misappropriations, he introduced meat and rice three times a week and ensured that the food was cooked somewhat more caringly. But the sudden imposition of higher standards in the kitchen upset people at various levels in the compound staff. To prepare decent food some people were having to work harder than before and the opportunity to engage in profitable fiddles had come to an end.

Suddenly, after a couple of months in the kitchens, Mlungisi was moved back to his old job and food standards declined again. Whether it was true or not, he was told that Gencor head office thought the extra effort and expenditure he had put in was 'wasteful'. As chief steward of the new black miners' union, Mlungisi Nelani had no shortage of other issues that needed to be taken up. He began to process complaints relating to conditions underground. NUM members at the mine were particularly bitter about whites who flouted safety regulations and urged black colleagues to take unnecessary risks. They also resented the lengthy wait black miners had to endure while getting to and from their work due to the racial basis on which mine work and transport was organised. This particularly annoyed black miners because they received no pay for waiting time.

Quiet and likeable, Mlungisi communicated his faith in the union to his fellow members in an articulate and intelligent manner. He had a gift for imparting confidence to people whose humanity had been crushed for many years. Instead of bringing him distinction and respect, his qualities made him a marked and dangerous man as far as the mine's management was concerned and a number of senior company officials soon ventured on an unorthodox scheme to discourage Mlungisi from continuing with his endeavours. The best way to do this, they resolved, was to 'fuck him up'.

Mlungisi found out in an interesting and unusual way about the plan to lean on him. He had taken leave just before the 1985 national pay round, a series of negotiations which occasioned great tension at Marievale and other Gencor mines because of the company's hard-line stand against paying increases in line with other mining houses. This led to a strike, during which many Marievale miners were dismissed from their jobs even though they were involved in a legal dispute. Concerned about the situation, Mlungisi returned from leave and resumed his duties as union representative. The first indication that he might be threatened came when he discovered that a group of black trusties known to be close to mine management had tried to trace him to a girlfriend's house in a near-by black township. From time to time Mlungisi stayed there to escape the rigours of compound life and to enjoy some female company. It surprised and worried him that strangers should be looking for him there. Then a few days later, as he left the mine, a car pulled up beside him as he walked towards the main gate. Though he did not know a single person in the car, the driver and his fellow travellers were worryingly insistent that Mlungisi should accept a lift with them. He declined. Later his anxiety turned to fear when a mine clerk called Zwalake approached him with extraordinary information.

Zwalake explained that he had been called to a meeting with the assistant hostel manager, Johannes Spamer, the man responsible for the part of the compound in which Mlungisi lived. Zwalake told him that the mine manager, Mr Jacobs, a white supervisor, Mr Owen, and two black men Isaac and Pyinga, known to be management trusties with a reputation for strong-arm methods, were also present at the meeting. Spamer told those assembled that he had a problem – an individual he called Solomon and they knew as Mlungisi Nelani. Isaac and Pyinga should, Spamer continued, 'do a job' on Solomon.

As he learned of his likely fate, Mlungisi became alarmed. He would not be the first or the last NUM member to be shot dead on or near a gold mine. Having thought the situation through, he decided to contact NUM head office. He told his story to a union official, who put him on to Clive Thompson, at the Johannesburg civil rights law firm Cheadle, Thompson. After interviewing Mlungisi and taking a witness statement from Zwalake, Thompson asked Zwalake to arrange a second meeting with Johannes Spamer at which Zwalake would talk the company official through the plan with a concealed tape recorder strapped to his body. Zwalake, an unusually courageous man, agreed to this. He arranged the second meeting and obtained a devastating tape recording, which Clive Thompson used to obtain a Supreme Court injunction against Marievale mine restraining the Gencor company from in any way harming NUM officials.

The tape of this meeting starts with a lengthy exchange between Zwalake and Spamer over the likelihood of sacked workers winning reinstatement at the mine. Then Zwalake changes tack, asking Spamer what it is they are supposed to do according to his plan for Solomon. The transcript of the tape continues:

SPAMER: That plan to do what? To fuck him up?

ZWALAKE: Mmmm.

SPAMER: You must go on with it. If you can work out something to fuck him up, fuck him up . . .

ZWALAKE: Mmmm.

SPAMER: I want people to fuck him up too . . . I don't want to promise you anything, but I'll give you something if you fuck him properly. But you must fuck him good and solid. Fuck him up in such a way that he cannot walk again, something like that. But you must make no mistake. The quicker the better. If I can just hear . . . the stories that Solomon was fucked up . . . Fuck him up good and solid.

ZWALAKE: Yes . . .

SPAMER: Fuck him up with a kierie, man [a hefty wooden stave]. Fuck him up with a kierie. Do you want to do it alone? . . . I'll give you the trick if you can catch him somewhere. First you blicks him [stun him] with a kierie, OK? And then you fuck him. And then what you do – those tendons here, you cut it off with a sharp knife. You know I worked in the prison service before and I know my ... [inaudible]. You know those tendons here, if you cut it off with a knife here ... you won't walk for fucking nine months. Just cut it off here. Or maybe you cut it off there and you take the ear, you cut it off and then the ear, you bring it with you ... we put it in the boiler there. That's all you do ... he won't come back.[3]

Mlungisi Nelani is just one of hundreds even thousands of NUM organisers, shaft stewards, union officials and rank and file members who have been threatened, beaten, bullied, sacked, bussed back to the countryside or otherwise degraded in the course of building an independent black union since 1982. By then it is true the ineluctable build up of pressure in the compounds had forced something of a change of heart, first among the Anglo group, then inside Rand Mines and finally from 1979 to 1982 even inside that bastion of authoritarianism, the Chamber of Mines. But it would be a superficial observer who tried to describe the turbulent, complex and many-sided process of change as the simple march of 'enlightenment' and 'openness' from on high. And in so far as there was a smile of benevolence from some sections of the Chamber, behind the smile was always one knife, if not more. As a result, time and time again after the opening came in 1982, the black miners had to go to or even beyond the brink to get even the most minimal changes. Keeping the pressure on for real change caused hundreds of crises, led to tens of thousands of sackings and the loss of dozens of lives. Cyril Ramaphosa, the committed young lawyer drafted in by the Council of Unions of South Africa in 1982 to initiate the organising drive in the nation's greatest industry, captured the reality in a 1985 speech to the South African Institute of Race Relations:

When the National Union of Mineworkers was formed an experienced unionist said to me 'organising workers in South Africa is the art of the possible'. But organising workers in the mining industry is the art of the impossible ... impossible because it has been the art of trying to make a fundamental change in a system by using structures and instruments that were designed to perpetuate that system ... the art of making a revolution with modern tools that were invented to prevent a revolution. Because of the nature of the mining industry which is conservative or ultra-conservative by any definition, the black miner has been condemned to seek radical ends within a framework which was designed to prevent radical ends.

229

In order to understand the full flavour of this system one must see the industry against the larger canvas of a country which has permitted one nation to systematically oppress a whole people as a matter of public policy. It is within this larger context that the mining industry, its ancient industrial relations practices, its mindlessness, its violence, must be situated.[4]

The birth of NUM in 1982 was the result of two complementary initiatives which intersected in an interesting and productive way. From below, a group of mine clerks working for TEBA, the Chamber of Mines employment agency, had finally reached the point where they could take no more. Influenced by their employers' impressive if somewhat sinister use of organisation to provision South Africa's many mines not only with an ample but a finely tuned and carefully divided supply of labour, they began lobbying the Council of Unions of South Africa (CUSA) to help them unionise. Simultaneously inside CUSA, the general secretary Phirowshaw Camay and Cyril Ramaphosa found themselves wondering whether the time might not finally be right for the unthinkable to happen. In the light of events in the compounds in 1981 and 1982, they thought it might at last be possible to propagate the idea of an independent black union inside the country's bastion of authoritarian industrialism.[5]

The CUSA discussions had been prompted by a wave of spontaneous strikes, in 1981 and 1982. The 1981 disturbances involved 13,000 miners at three gold mines, East Rand Proprietary, Blyvooruitzicht and President Steyn. The causes were arbitrarily imposed and poorly managed changes in the miners' death benefit scheme, a cause of concern because there were so many deaths and injuries in the deep gold mines. The changes were so poorly implemented that many miners thought they were having their wages cut rather than their death benefits – and the contributions they had to pay – increased. (Seven miners died as a result of the mishandling of the changes and the resulting explosions of unmediated conflict.) Then in the middle of 1982 in the course of the year's pay round, 30,000 workers at gold mines belonging to Gencor and Gold Fields, the two companies who paid the lowest increases, went on strike.[6] This was a momentous development and was cited in the August 1982 Council of Unions of South Africa conference resolution which decided that steps should be taken to form a National Union of Mineworkers. (In these 1982 disputes ten more miners died, again as a result of the explosion of discontent and the companies' ready use of repression.)

. The situation at the Johannesburg TEBA offices developed more or less simultaneously, and the small group of friends who initiated a series of secret meetings to discuss what they should do about the intolerable conditions in their workplace were to play a critical role in the growth and development of NUM, providing the union with its first members and its first paid organisers. The TEBA offices in Eloff Street are a combination of human auction rooms and a sheep pen for migrant miners. This is where migrants from all over the subcontinent are brought if they are destined for the gold mines along the Rand east and west of Johannesburg, the biggest consumers of labour in the country. At Eloff Street they are sorted, weighed, measured, examined in cruel and humiliating ways and then assigned for 'onward shipment' to the mines.[7] But TEBA had a big staff and not all of them were sympathetic to the accepted ways of the white power structure. Increasingly the younger clerks were better educated. Moulded by the fierce national pride of Lesotho, or fired by the post-Soweto determination of younger and better-educated South African blacks, many of them were appalled at the way black miners were treated, and, just as important, were unable to accept the degrading treatment meted out to them by senior white TEBA officials.

In the summer of 1990 in Maseru, capital of Lesotho, I tracked down one of the young men who in 1982 sat down in secret with some friends at TEBA to see if there might be a different way. An open, generous man with an inexhaustible supply of energy and optimism, Putseletso Limpho Salae, Salae for short, is today banned from South Africa and its mines. He was one of thousands of Basothos sent back to their homeland after the 1987 dispute between NUM and the Chamber. Before he left, however, Salae was among the handful of people who first broached the idea of a union in the mines, and then set out to give it physical form by spreading out along the Rand, reaching into the big mines and persuading often highly sceptical and poorly paid black mineworkers to part with some of their cash to build a union.

Sitting in his office, where on behalf of NUM today he helps run the Basotho Mineworkers' Labour Co-op, to provide work and hope to some of the 17,000 Basotho sacked by Chamber companies in the course of the 1987 national strike, Salae was understandably proud in answering my questions about the early days of NUM. At first he just beamed and shook his head from side to side; and then with a tiny gesture of the eyes he indicated that he still looked on those as extraordinary days. 'They were tough and hard and exciting. We often thought we would all be killed. At the beginning it

231

was a bit like trying to break into prison; then once you were inside, you had to be on the alert all the time to stay out of sight of the mine security.'

Salae's journey towards the idea of a union began, I think it is fair to say, in 1976 shortly after the Soweto revolt.

One of his bosses at TEBA's Johannesburg office at the time was a troubled man who seemed to take a special pleasure in humiliating his black employees.[8] A few days after Soweto, Salae recalls, this man jumped up on a desk in front of his staff to lay down the law and deliver a special message. 'Anyone who comes into this office with any black power', he cried out, his voice reaching an anguished crescendo, 'will face these two barrels of white power.' As he spoke he pulled a pistol from each side of his body and held them aloft. 'It was a chilling moment,' recalled Salae.

'Conditions at TEBA were unbelievable,' he went on. 'You know people with fifteen years service and an unblemished record were sacked on the spot for being five minutes late. Black people were not allowed to answer the telephone. People were fired for talking or joking. The management style was one of harassment and abuse. It was so terrible I have only just learned to talk about it with a degree of calmness, thanks to the passage of time.'

Salae and a couple of trusted friends spent more and more of their breaks considering what they should do about the situation. As clerks they were literate men. They read avidly and one of them picked up some information about the possibility that CUSA might be trying to start a miners' union. They talked about the possibility themselves and started lobbying CUSA to go ahead, but nobody knew quite what to do. Meanwhile conditions at TEBA continued to deteriorate. One Sunday after a long and anxious discussion among themselves Salae and some of his friends met a young progressively minded Catholic priest. He was appalled at their stories of what went on at TEBA and, without knowing it, he stiffened their resolve and helped prepare the group for their leap into the unknown. They met together again and drafted a leaflet, which said simply that TEBA employees should not have to accept bad conditions, injustice and abuse. TEBA staff should, the leaflet urged, join CUSA. 'There was no name of any specific union, just a call to join CUSA which, we explained, would help with benefits and look after you if you got dismissed.

'Lewis Mangwanese put the pamphlets round while people were sleeping. The plan was to test the reaction by having a quiet meeting. We had the meeting and there was tremendous feeling. The workers from the Transkei seemed to be the firmest. Many of them had worked in factories in and around Cape Town where unions were powerful and they knew exactly what to do. But before long T E B A management was on our trail and in September three of us were dismissed. But by this time we were in touch with Cyril Ramaphosa, who had been chosen by C U S A to head up the attempt to organise the industry. N U M needed members. Thanks to T E B A we became some of its earliest members and, after we were sacked, its first organisers.

'The first mines we tried organising work were Libanon and Elandsrand. We chose them because they were near the city and we could, if things got hot, escape back into Soweto. Five of us went to these mines with leaflets, arriving at the time when workers would be around the main gate in serious numbers. We were very fearful of arrests and worried about getting a beating so we sort of threw our leaflets at people and quickly faded away to escape arrest. We didn't get very far. People were sceptical, wondering who we were, wondering what would happen to them if they joined. Based on what was happening, Cyril decided to change tack. He negotiated an access agreement first with Anglo American, then with the Chamber of Mines. That changed the situation greatly and allowed us to enter some compounds legally. I suppose we had high hopes when we returned to Elandsrand. But even with permission it was very hard going indeed. We'd spend eight or ten hours at a time in the compound, trying to talk to anyone who would talk to us. But in a day we'd be lucky if we got one or two members. We were a little disheartened and I began to think that the key to developing the union was working out which were the places where our own network of contacts would help us. I felt sure this would be better than arriving at these places and starting from nothing. The continued questioning among the miners, the suggestion that we were just some sort of insurance or benefit society trying to take some of their money away from them confirmed us in this and I began to talk to Cyril about going out to Vaal Reefs.

'There at Vaal Reefs, the biggest mine in the country, I had many contacts among the Basotho. The network I felt I could rely on was formed of members of the Basotholand Congress Party, the opposition party banned in Lesotho and illegal in South Africa. Banned or not I could still identify and talk to their circle in the location and connect with friends and friends of friends in the mine. Because of the restrictions that were placed on me this became very important. I had to concentrate on one shaft only and I had to sign in at 9 a.m. and out at 4.30 p.m. The police presence was considerable and I was ordered to sit in the office much of the time. This

233

is not necessarily the best way to recruit miners. The mine manager told me that this was all for my own good. "The Xhosas", he insisted, "might kill you otherwise." Anyhow through the BCP, the tide began to turn and we built it up to the point where we were soon getting a hundred members a week and running out of forms. I phoned Cyril for some more and told him what was going on. He was amazed and delighted.

'We had our first NUM national Congress at the Roman Catholic Church in Jouberton Location and thanks to the efforts of all my friends and of the other main organiser at Vaal Reefs, Jeffrey Magida, we had sixteen busloads of miners go from Vaal Reefs to the Congress. This amazed the mine management. They had thought our organising efforts were confined to one shaft but in fact we had people come from virtually every section of the huge complex.'9

The news of CUSA's decision to initiate a union of black miners spread along the Rand in a variety of ways, by word of mouth, via the circulation of photostats of newspaper reports and through the activity of the union's earliest partisans and organisers. At the giant Western Deep Levels mine, the news had a profound impact on another Basotho, James Motlatsi, who was to become the first president of the new union. Built with the physique of a black American footballer or Olympic track star, Motlatsi had been born at Mohale's Hoek in Lesotho and, when he left school in 1970, travelled a familiar road, becoming part of his country's export statistics by working at Welkom in the South African mines. He left Welkom in 1973 because supervisors there were demanding payments or bribes in return for granting promotions to better paying jobs. Signing on at Western Deep Levels, he worked first as a winch driver then as a team leader in the underground mine stopes. Hearing that CUSA had appointed Cyril Ramaphosa to oversee the development of the union, Motlatsi phoned CUSA's offices; introduced himself to Ramaphosa and offered to work with him. During the run up to the first national congress, Motlatsi and Ramaphosa became very close, and a partnership formed.

Ramaphosa was an inspired choice to initiate the union. With an unshakable commitment to black action, Ramaphosa's years of training as a lawyer and his experiences as a young political activist helped him greatly in avoiding the many pitfalls that were to be placed in the way of the union's development. Born in Venda in the northern part of South Africa, his grandfather had worked in the diamond mines. He cut his oppositional teeth as a student at Turfloop University. For his involvement in a public rally in support of Mozambique's national right to determine its own future,

234

Ramaphosa was put in detention. He stayed in prison for eleven months, and during four of them was interrogated every day. Deeply affected by the Black Consciousness movement initiated by Steve Biko, he was detained again for six months shortly before the Soweto uprising. After this he finished his studies as a lawyer, and while in the end he decided that practising as a lawyer was not the most effective way he could contribute to the process of uplifting and enabling the mass of rightless South Africans, his legal knowledge and political experience undoubtedly helped him develop into a first-class strategic thinker who honed aspirations into strategic goals and then, with a discerning appreciation of the forces ranged against the union, came up with a measured calculation of how far in each set of circumstances it was possible to go.[10]

In the autumn of 1982 eight gold mines were put at the top of NUM's target list – Western Holdings, Free State Saaiplaas, Western Deep Levels, Elandsrand, Kloof, Libanon, Blyvooruitzicht and Venterspost, employing 150,000 workers. With targeted recruiting in each place, the next step was to lay the basis for an inaugural national conference. During November 1982 a planning committee of three shaft stewards from each of the mines and two other key organising centres met to draft a constitution for the first conference. This was held on 4 December 1982 in Jouberton, Klerksdorp. About 1,800 people attended, electing a secretary, Cyril Ramaphosa, a president, James Motlatsi, a treasurer, adopting a rule book and creating a national executive. The union decided not to register under government industrial relations legislation and called on the Chamber of Mines to adopt a challenging programme to break down the institutionalised racism of the mining industry. NUM was on its way.

The union's first office was in Lekton House in Wanderers Street, Johannesburg. Here in cramped premises above the Industrial Aid Society and other self-help groups aiming to help the wounded workers of the Rand, NUM, soon to be the biggest union in Africa, began to grow. The offices closely reflected the industry the union had set out to challenge and transform. Sparingly furnished, in something of a contrast to the colonial palaces of the mining houses and the Chamber of Mines, there were 20 officials in a suite of rooms no bigger than a Victorian cottage or workman's dwelling. There was a battered telephone switchboard and a telex which seemed to ring and chatter simultaneously without interruption day and night seven days a week, bringing news of problems from every corner of the Rand and beyond. The staff showed endless patience in these difficult conditions which, in times of crisis – and there were many of

235

those – made it virtually impossible to think, fill in forms or do the simplest arithmetical calculation, never mind audit a set of accounts. In such difficult circumstances, an intense commonality of purpose, a deep longing for freedom and an excited sense of history provided the fuel to keep them going. NUM was the love of their lifetime, worthy of any sacrifice, and it was this that steered them through the punishing routines of the early days, the endless rounds of meetings and discussions, the seemingly limitless organisational tasks. South Africa's system of racial capitalism had been cast in the furnace of the mining industry and NUM staff exuded an irrepressible sense of confidence that they were involved in a mission to reverse apartheid's wounding and disabling effects once and for all.

Lekton House soon became the operational centre of a great crusade. In atmosphere it was somewhere between the emergency ward of a great hospital offering remedies to those who had been denied them for generations and an open university where black miners had the opportunity to build their own structures of democracy under black leadership and control. CUSA was committed to black leadership of the unions and NUM was determined to deliver this in an industry where after a century of discrimination, racism and apartheid had put down powerful roots. From the beginning, NUM was an all-consuming, demanding and remarkable exercise in free-form improvisation conducted at breakneck speed, with Ramaphosa, Motlatsi, the organisers and working miners drafting rules, delineating structures, designing forms, isolating problems, canvassing solutions, and securing the base of the union by getting more and more people to join. From dawn to dusk the tiny offices were crammed with people, Basothos in their beautiful blankets, Zulus with their beaded wristbands, Xhosas with their sonorous language, a marvellous assortment of humanity bonded together by common involvement in mining and a deep longing to be free. They displayed their new-found sense of unity and purpose determinedly: as they stepped inside the door of the offices they took off their bright, yellow miners' hard hats as a mark of respect; on leaving they were scarcely out of the lift or down the stairs when on went the helmets, symbols that submission had given way to pride, and an announcement, if one was necessary, to the golden city of Johannesburg, that the miners were on the march.

Out at Vaal Reefs, Putseletso Salae and his colleagues, Wilfred Saloyi, Jeffrey Magida and Mubyiselo Mthotsha, were still hard at work, trying to capitalise on their successful initial organising efforts at the 40,000-strong mine. But despite the considerable support for NUM's right of access at Anglo's head office, things were becoming difficult on the ground.

People in all societies resent change. For good reasons and bad they want to hang on to old ways of living and find methods to slow down, obstruct or challenge change. The more authoritarian the institution or society, the worse the obstruction becomes. And for obvious reasons. Change, particularly democratising change, threatens material interests, whole officialdoms whose prestige and daily bread comes from dispensing the old ways.

'Vaal Reefs mine was very, very rough,' recalled Salae. 'Intimidation by the local police was a daily event. I quite remember them coming to the house where I was staying, again and again and again. Policemen would call in to tell us to stop our union work, our "trouble-making" as they would often call it. Sometimes they would offer me employment, saying, "Why not work for our side? We can give you money and a house." I was visited by *impimpis*, or thugs, and seriously threatened. Things improved a bit when we got our first union car. It was a battered old Volkswagen Beetle, not even roadworthy. I bought it from a white man at the courthouse near by. He was up in court and had just been fined seven hundred and fifty rand and was going round saying he would have to sell his car to raise some money. I offered him one hundred and fifty rand for it without a thought that he would accept. But he accepted my offer without hesitation.

'I had no licence until a helpful white welfare officer at Vaal Reefs taught me to drive. But the police were soon on to the car. Someone had suggested to them that the car was not roadworthy so they made a road block five metres away from where I was staying. After that I sold the car and had to start walking. Without a car of course it was very easy for the police to identify and catch me, or indeed for anyone else who didn't like what we were doing. The next trick was to arrest us for trespass. We had no passes or permits allowing us to stay in Jouberton, the location near the mine. We were asleep on the floor of a friend's house one night when the knock came and we were hauled away. We were charged with failing to have a valid lodgers' permit, kept in jail for a day or two, then fined fifteen rand each.'[11]

At the national level, the Chamber of Mines was also trying to pull a few strokes on Cyril Ramaphosa and James Motlatsi, even though the ink was scarcely dry on the June 1983 recognition agreement which gave the union some freedom to organise. In a historic first the union's leaders were invited in by the Chamber to negotiate national wages and conditions. The meeting took place only a few days after the conclusion of the recognition agreement; but the immediate desire of the Chamber negotiators was to

237

bounce Cyril Ramaphosa and his colleagues by forcing them to settle at a figure predetermined by the Chamber. If the union did not accept what the Chamber was offering within a week, the union leaders were told, the Chamber would implement the proffered rises unilaterally and put them straight into miners' pay packets. NUM's leaders were caught in a dilemma. They needed a continuing relationship with the Chamber to enable the union to grow and develop some critical mass. On the other hand they deeply resented the 'take-it-or-leave-it' attitude of the Chamber. Ramaphosa and his colleagues tried to disguise the weakness of their position. They accepted the Chamber's 'offer' and then tried to distance themselves from the mine-owners by putting the package out to a ballot of the members. The members rejected the offer and NUM then tried to get the Chamber to reopen talks. The Chamber of Mines once again found it easier to break with its authoritarian past in theory rather than in practice and declined. The leaders of the emergent union were left in a difficult position.[12] Before long, however, Cyril Ramaphosa and his union colleagues devised a counter strategy.

There was one particular point in the nexus of gold production where the mining companies were uniquely vulnerable. This was the Rand Refinery on the East Rand, where every morning the rough gold from the mines' smelting operations went by armoured truck to be turned into the pure bullion beloved of bankers, jewellers and the criminal fraternity. Jointly owned by the gold mining companies, through the Chamber of Mines itself, this was the single most profitable metal foundry on earth. But inside conditions were very poor, with an abundance of noxious gases ever present in the atmosphere and a host of attendant chest complaints among the men who shaped, hammered, melted and poured the chunky bars of yellow gold. NUM struck back at the Chamber for its bad faith in the national wages round by declaring a dispute at the refinery and, while unable to win all its demands, won some concessions and recovered its dignity.

There was another example of bad faith in the early days. In July 1983 in the middle of the wage negotiations, NUM sent a letter to the Chamber stating that it would take action, including legal action, against any blacklisting of dismissed workers, either by the Chamber or individual mines.[13] A Chamber of Mines spokesman dismissed the union's claims, indicating that the Chamber did not blacklist people or ban them from mines for specific periods. This came as a surprise to Cyril Ramaphosa, whose union contacts in the industry had provided him with a docket from TEBA concerning Gencor's Buffelsfontein mine. The form had a line in which each worker's so-called 'Desirability Code' was to be entered. In the case that had been brought to Ramaphosa's attention, the card showed that the miner in question was never to be employed at Buffelsfontein again or taken on at any other mine in the Gencor group. The prohibition was marked as lasting 'indefinitely', which on further investigation turned out to be the worst on a precisely tabulated if top-secret sliding scale of arbitrary punishments, which started with a three-month temporary ban, and then increased to sixty months or life.[14]

This kind of arbitrary and secret behaviour was unacceptable in principle, Ramaphosa insisted, and was wide open to abuse. In this case, he pointed out, the worker concerned had committed no offence. In July 1982 at a time of tension in the mine following a strike, he had indicated his desire to leave the hostel and go home to escape any confrontation. When he took another contract T E B A told him there was work at Buffelsfontein but that he could not go there. Ramaphosa turned the evidence over to the *Rand Daily Mail* who approached the Chamber for an explanation of the inconsistency in its position. Faced with the evidence, the Chamber quickly reversed gear, abandoned a 7 July 1983 statement that the charge of blacklisting was 'not true' and confirmed that there had indeed been a blacklist. A spokesman assured the *Rand Daily Mail* such practices had come to an end 'a few weeks ago'.[15]

In September 1983, before it was even a year old, the fledgling N U M faced its gravest crisis yet. Sixty-eight miners were killed in a methane explosion at a coal-mine in Natal called Hlobane. In March 1983 Ramaphosa had gone on a six-week trip to Europe and America to build relations with mining unions abroad. Besides raising money, he was examining the structures of foreign miners' unions with a view to creating the strongest possible architecture for N U M in South Africa. He was particularly impressed with the British miners' unique combination of powerful regional unions inside a nationwide organisation. On his travels Ramaphosa had made many contacts that were to prove invaluable in the crisis that now confronted him. At Hlobane, for the first time since the Coalbrook disaster in 1960, the union won the right to represent some of the dead black miners, and to be party to the joint inquest-inquiry which would be held under the Mines and Works Act. The union called on Clive Thompson and his colleague Paul Benjamin, both from the law firm Cheadle, Thompson, to work on the disaster team. A retired mining engineer Jack Curtis, a man with strong views on the industry's flawed safety record, also added his considerable knowledge; and through the

239

British and American miners' unions, NUM found top-class independent technical advice in both Britain and America. (The host of inadequacies, illegalities, and mining malpractices they identified in the conduct of the mining operations at Hlobane is described in Chapter 13.)

More than any other issue, safety is the one that unified underground black miners. Their exclusion from any control over engineering conditions and working practices underground inflicted enormous tension on the miners below ground. In the way they handled the aftermath of Hlobane, NUM's leadership spoke to miners' deepest anxieties. The union drafted a miners' bill of rights that stressed respect for the living as well as the dead. This put the emphasis positively on the human rights of those who worked in the industry: their right to a safe environment, their right to freedom of information about working conditions and safety problems, their right to the best equipment and machine design and participation in shaping their working lives.[16] In addition the union organised its first-ever stoppage, calling for a nation-wide memorial stayaway for half an hour in memory of the dead. With this formulation all but the hardest hearted of the mining companies had to show a mark of respect. According to NUM as many as 30,000 miners participated in the union's memorial for Kinross.

As 1983 gave way to 1984, NUM was moving out of its founding phase and beginning to accumulate critical mass. It had built up an impressive membership of 55,000 by its second annual conference at the Philip Smith Community Hall at Thabong, the black township outside the white mining town of Welkom. Appropriately enough at this conference the entire front of the hall was taken up by a cohort of injured miners in wheelchairs who had joined the union at the Ernest Oppenheimer Memorial Hospital near by. NUM started the new year with three important new recognition agreements for the nurses at the Rand Mutual Hospital and the Western Deep Levels Hospital and the ground staff at the Chamber of Mines' sports ground. By the time of its special conference at Klerksdorp in June in preparation for the 1984 national pay round, the union had perhaps as many as 70,000 members. Six hundred delegates and 3,000 observers attended. NUM's strategy was to seek increases of around 30 per cent with a view to closing the awesome wage gap with white miners and meeting the growing aspirations of the black membership who wanted change speedily. In the event the Chamber offered only 10 per cent and held firm. The result was a testing battle which, while it did not produce significant economic gains, appeared to strengthen the loyalties of rank and file members. In the end the dispute was settled when the Chamber marginally increased its offer. But the settlement came at the eleventh hour and did not give NUM the chance to explain the agreement to its members everywhere along the Rand. As a result in some places strikes went ahead and twelve more South African miners died in the conflict and repression that ensued.[17]

Early in 1985 the union was again experiencing difficulties at Vaal Reefs, where from this time onwards the tragedy of South Africa's mines would periodically be played out. In March 1985 the black miners started boycotting the mine liquor outlets and concession stores, charging that they were being exploited. NUM was busy on a number of other fronts; while negotiating for recognition at one shaft, it was trying to get accreditation of its shaft stewards at the two other shafts where it had already struck a deal. But it had also become the focus for the underlying grievances felt by the black miners and their union representatives. Some of them were very upset because local management had taken office access rights away from NUM officials, claiming that rules regarding office use had been broken on a number of occasions. Even more provocatively a 10 per cent supplementary local pay increase had been granted to white mine officials, ostensibly to make their salary scales 'competitive' with surrounding mines. NUM stewards understandably felt the same increases should be paid to their members. Although the draconian Master and Servants Act had been repealed, white officials at Vaal Reefs still had their 'piccanins' (personal servants), who carried their satchels, ran errands for them underground and provided them with papers and comics. The 'piccanins'' wages are paid for out of the mine budget for black labour, but the white miners' piccanin or 'batman' contributes nothing to production, a fact bitterly resented by black miners and team leaders.[18]

As Cyril Ramaphosa was later to explain to a meeting of the South African Institute for Race Relations: 'Shaft stewards at Vaal Reefs thought there was something wrong with this practice and approached one of the miners and asked him why he had a piccanin. The miner was dumbfounded and could not respond except to say, "This is how the system works." An instruction was given to piccanins to refuse to carry satchels as it was not part of their jobs to carry another man's food, comics and newspapers . . . There was general panic among the white miners who could not believe this was happening. Some resigned and went to other mines. Management panicked and used this resistance as one of the reasons for dismissing 14,000.'[19]

The sacking of 14,000 men at Vaal Reefs was another decisive turning point in NUM's history, with weeks passing before any reinstatements were secured. On reflection it seems clear that Vaal Reefs' management had been allowing the situation in the mine to slip closer to the edge of crisis for some months. There was a refusal to change or modernise and as a result there were countless disputes all over the mine. In some parts black miners were declining to work full shifts because they had been denied pay increases given to whites. Others were refusing to do blasting jobs which were theoretically the responsibility of whites. But although they pocketed the wages, they did not do the job, assigning it to their African colleagues. Black miners were also determined to try to end to the practice of whites coming down to the working faces last and leaving first. One way and another grievance interlocked with grievance and the mine management inflamed the situation by insisting on protecting mining's system of racial injustice. Soon Vaal Reefs, a grim, gargantuan place even before the disputes, became unsteerable, out of control like Elandsrand in 1979. Management was conducted by ultimatum. A supposedly progressive company committed to the development of free collective bargaining threatened black miners who would not 'work normally' with immediate dismissal. No matter that the definition of 'normal work' involved carrying white miners' satchels, accepting an unfair pay system and doing blasting work for which another was paid.

Another aspect of the complex situation centred on alcohol. As Dunbar Moodie has shown in his important essay 'Alcohol and Resistance on the South African Mines', the March 1985 alcohol boycott at Vaal Reefs had unintended and unfortunate consequences. Despite a unanimous vote at a union meeting to launch the boycott, serious divisions soon showed inside the black workforce. The first day the boycott worked well, but on the second day a group of heavily dependent drinkers, in this case mostly Xhosa-speaking Mpondos, marched into the store with white sheets over their heads and arms in their hands. They sat down to drink and by closing time the bar was as busy as ever. The boycott was over. A fortnight later the union voted overwhelmingly for another boycott. With enthusiasm running so high, the shaft stewards failed to allow a day for the heavy drinkers to lay in alternative supplies. Moodie reported:

White-sheeted men bearing arms broke the boycott again. Once again the new militants underestimated the importance of alcohol in the old miners' culture and the effectiveness of local management and mine security support for the conservatives.

242

Mine police had twice condoned the serving of liquor to men carrying weapons. In retaliation, someone threw a petrol bomb into the liquor outlet. For several days thereafter the strike breakers roamed the compound . . . allegedly in full view of management and accompanied by mine police, seeking to attack any union shaft steward. They succeeded in seriously wounding one and killing two others. The shaft stewards had seriously disrupted their drinking, they said, and management had given permission to root out these union leaders.[20]

In December 1985 a major scandal broke in the mining industry. Mining companies, even enlightened ones like Anglo, finally had to admit that some of their mines were fitted with industrial systems for stunning workers with nerve gases. In the wake of the 1975 McKay report into security on the mines, a number of companies had dug up roads and adapted buildings so that disabling gas could be pumped through special ducts into certain parts of the compounds. The man who brought the matter out into the open was Malcolm Fraser, former Prime Minister of Australia. A deeply conservative man, Fraser was none the less appalled when, over dinner in New York, he heard a Witwatersrand University lecturer describe a gassing system which had been installed at an Anglo American gold mine.[21] Fraser made his disclosure just before he visited South Africa as a member of the Commonwealth Eminent Persons Group (then trying to secure the release of the ANC leaders and develop a process of negotiation whereby apartheid could be dismantled). At first Anglo American public relations executives tried to deny that any such equipment existed. They described the allegations as 'malicious rumour and conjecture'.[22] But later Peter Gush, the chairman of Anglo's Western Deep Levels, confirmed that such a system was installed at his mine; it delivered disabling gas to liquor stores, hostel kitchens and the hostel administration offices in case these were attacked by migrant workers, he explained. The system was hurriedly removed following Mr Fraser's remarks.

Gencor then admitted to the South African business magazine, the *Financial Mail*, that it had a similar system at one of its mines near Klerksdorp, which the company declined to name. In short order Anglovaal, another mining house, admitted that it had gas canisters in place in liquor outlets and dining rooms in three hostels at its Lorraine gold mine in the Orange Free State and at four hostels in its Hartebeestfontein mine near Klerksdorp.[23] The explanation offered by the mining houses was that the systems had been installed in the wake of the 1975 McKay commission which recommended tougher security to combat outbursts of discontent. Three mining houses, Rand Mines, Johannesburg Consolidated Investments and Gold Fields, stated that they did not use such systems. But they had other only slightly less controversial instruments of South African industrial relations in their mine arsenals, including armoured riot-control vehicles, specially designed rubber bullets, teams of savage dogs and large quantities of live ammunition. Throughout the period of NUM's growth these techniques were frequently used by two companies in particular, Gold Fields and Gencor, the businesses which fought harder than any others inside the Chamber of Mines, not only to slow down change but to obstruct it and if possible prevent it. NUM declared both companies 'enemy companies'. The behaviour of the two mighty corporations caused thousands of their employees to lose their jobs and some of them to lose their lives.

In 1985 the union's leaders had devoted a great deal of time to developing NUM's regional structures, talking to, encouraging and training the layers of enablers and initiators who could spread the union's influence and consolidate its base. The leadership wanted to give the union enough leverage to make serious changes to the unjust structures of the past during the 1986 negotiating round with the Chamber of Mines. But making fundamental change in a society is seldom a linear process and NUM's leaders had to find time to promote their members' interests in other ways. They started to develop a Southern African Federation of Mineworkers which would enable miners in Zambia, Zimbabwe and Namibia as well as South Africa to pursue common strategies and goals in negotiation with the multinational mining companies.

In December 1985 NUM's leaders played a leading part in founding a new nationwide federation of trade unions in South Africa itself. The Congress of South African Trade Unions (COSATU) was launched at the beginning of December 1985 and Elijah Barayi, NUM's vice-president, a former personnel assistant at Rand Mines' Blyvooruitzicht gold mine, became its first president. With the arrival of COSATU and the growth of the United Democratic Front black South Africa looked poised to win major victories, but the promising landscape was soon blighted once again.

The situation inside the apartheid government was becoming more and more tense with pressure accumulating for a tough crackdown. The regime was losing control in the black townships and becoming increasingly isolated internationally; shaming pictures of state-sponsored violence were being bounced around the global television village. This crisis of control was evident inside the mining industry, where the unresolved grievances, the unassuaged hunger for the substance not the appearance of change had heightened tension once again. Senior Anglo executives became worried about developments and thought a joint study with NUM might relieve the accumulating pressure. This time the study focused on the resurgence of violent inter-group conflict on five mines, President Brand, President Steyn and Western Holdings in the Orange Free State, and Vaal Reefs and Western Deep Levels in the Transvaal. Directed by a steering committee of two Anglo executives, and two NUM officials, this project again involved outside academics, Professor Jim Leatt from Cape Town and Paulus Zulu from the University of Natal. In all the mines except Western Holdings there had recently been inter-group rivalry between Xhosas and Basothos, which had led to injury and death. Even when both groups were union members these conflicts still developed. The Xhosas from the Transkei tended to be more combative, ready to take direct action and to be highly critical of the Basothos, who at this time tended to be a little more cautious, possibly because of the situation in their own country and a need to protect their jobs.

The report was thorough enough, written with a perception of the real situation in the compounds and undoubted sympathy for the miners caught in the system. Nevertheless it had a tired, even bureaucratic tone, as if the authors felt there was a stalemate in the situation and a continuing unwillingness by the company to examine radical alternatives. Published in May 1986, one of its most worrying features was its disclosure that many of the degrading and humiliating practices which had been so roundly condemned by the Moodie report in 1977, and which Anglo management insisted at the time were being or had been phased out, were still commonplace, nearly ten years later.

The joint Anglo–NUM report noted tersely:

Despite many previous recommendations raised by various researchers who interviewed mineworkers, acclimatisation measures are still used, these being applicable to blacks only. This is resented, being an overtly racist practice . . .

Cap lamps are issued to whites first, with the result that blacks who do most of the work are given the weaker lamps, facilitating a higher risk of accidents. Mass nakedness, an issue confronted by reports in the 1970s, apparently still exists. Workers at Welkom [focused on by the Moodie report] complained of being paraded naked at the TEBA recruiting

245

office, dusted with a soap containing caustic soda, and sprayed. This was particularly resented.

Another outdated concept still being practised is that of the piccanin system, whereby a worker transports the shift boss, miners and mine captain, their tools and food around the mine. Workers also resent white miners eating underground when they cannot. Hoisting is another source of contention, whites entering last and leaving first. Although whites can take any cage to the surface, black workers cannot, so that a partially empty cage may proceed upwards without them.[24]

The fact was that neither the government nor Anglo had a programme for restructuring the mining industry; and for a variety of reasons neither had the desire to grasp the nettle of white racial domination in the mines or take steps to end it. With the compound system unreformed and white power still in place above and below ground on Anglo's mines there was little room for optimism.

In its conclusions the 1986 Anglo–NUM report made quite clear that the prime source of enduring tension in the mines was the deformed social structure, which was given physical expression by the evils of the migrant labour system:

Workers raised many issues of concern about the compound system, both about the system itself and around its everyday functioning. In particular the workers referred to the artificial environment of the hostels, commenting on the lack of women and family life, which they viewed as leading to a situation of social normlessness. This, they added, led to wild behaviour with decreased respect for individual rights and privacy and the rise of a violent, mine-based culture. Proof of this is found in the non-participation of workers living with their families in mine villages, such workers abstaining from inter-group violence.

What much of the above indirectly suggests is that workers either consciously or not, attribute many of their problems to the existence of the migratory labour system. In particular the seeming endemic corruption leads to much frustration and bitterness, both in the amounts that have to be paid to get promotion, as well as the lack of advancement of those who are either out of favour or unwilling to pay. This is directly related to the power structure on the mines.[25]

The section of the 1986 report dealing with Vaal Reefs was particularly worrying. White miners in the Emergency Protection Unit, the local force of last resort set up under the terms of white South Africa's obsessional counter-insurgency planning of the 1970s, 'carry out their duties with a vindictive ruthlessness and even know which blocks to attack and which to leave out, settling work-associated problems by attacks on the compounds'. And 'Kimberley', the police spy named in the 1975 McKay commission report, was still operating around Klerksdorp a decade later and now apparently had access to mine explosives, a situation which made union members at Vaal Reefs ever more suspicious about collusion between parts of management and gangster elements.

Finally, the report noted that Anglo American's 'enlightened policies' were more evident at head office than in the operating companies on the mines. Clive Thompson, the union's lawyer through these stormy years, felt that this was not wholly accidental. He had come to believe that the mining companies were, like the government itself, in two minds about real reform and were still mainly interested in using the union to achieve cosmetic change, deploying its structures and influence to reintegrate a deeply alienated workforce into the existing system. He summarised the situation in a short paper: 'The overall approach of employers to the unionisation of mineworkers has closely mirrored the government response to demands on the political centre. It has sought to incorporate the new forces into marginally modified structures in such a way that the pre-existing power base remains intact.' The civil strife of the last eighteen months was ample testimony to the failure of the government's plans and he warned that the strategy of the mining industry was similarly doomed.

'In 1986 it is no longer possible to maintain mining operations based on a repressive labour system. The unionised workforce cannot and will not allow the situation to endure.' Employer reliance on the grosser features of the apartheid order only served to deepen the division. 'A restructuring of the industry . . . will involve much effort and imagination, and even more cost. It is however a pre-condition for industrial peace.'[26]

Neither the mining companies nor the apartheid state were ready for lasting radical change in the industry or in the increasingly troubled land of which it was such a prominent part. They failed to tackle the capos in the camps, constantly protecting the white miners from the march of democracy. By 1986 the government of P. W. Botha was backtracking on its own lukewarm commitment to cosmetic change. In June P. W. Botha launched a tough state of national emergency, banned many opposition organisations, censored the press, threw foreign television cameramen out of the country and sent his troops into the townships to restore apartheid. None of the mining houses protested in a particularly meaningful way, and according to Anthony Sampson, most businessmen were essentially in agreement with this new turn of the screw.[27]

In June 1986, as the crackdown came, a British miner gained an unrivalled insight into the working of the four-year-old union and the optimistic mood about the future which then obtained, at least among rank-and-file members in mines where the social tensions were not too grave and organisation was expanding. Steve Brunt, a coal-face worker and part-time rescue man from Arkwright Colliery in Derbyshire, arrived in South Africa to a warm welcome from NUM officials and working miners alike. Brunt could scarcely believe the size of the problems black miners faced in South Africa, as he acquainted himself with conditions of work two miles below ground deep into the earth's core and the huge attendant safety problems this and South Africa's damaged system of human relations created. On his return to Britain he published an important report on the black union's growth, internal structure and aspirations, which contained an exhaustive breakdown of its membership and a list of the mines where NUM had recognition agreements or was close to obtaining them. Brunt noted that NUM had 155,315 paying members with a further 167,546 signed up, no mean achievement in less than five years.[28]

As he made his way from Yeoville, the pleasant little Johannesburg suburb where he was staying, 12 June 1986 seemed another routine day in Johannesburg to him, but on his arrival at NUM offices, he found the building crawling with policemen and soldiers. 'I was astounded to find armed police guarding the entrance to the building,' he recorded in his diary. 'The police and security forces had been in the building since 5 a.m. and were searching the building – for what only they knew. It also became clear that the security forces were active all over Johannesburg and many leading trade unionists were being arrested and detained.'[29]

In the midst of this national emergency, with the union's vice-president Elijah Barayi detained like thousands of others without trial, NUM had to face a national pay round, deal with the increasing number of problems of individual mines and compounds and, on the morning after white Johannesburg celebrated the industry's and the city's centenary, had to wrestle with another unexpected problem – the hideous aftermath of Kinross, the worst mining disaster in a hundred years. I spent many days in and around the union's offices at this time. Watching the young staff organise legal advice, print leaflets and identify the names of the 177

248

dead to go with the company numbers which was all that the owners Gencor could initially provide, seeing them trying to find out what had gone wrong and sensing the deep anger and inadequacy that everyone felt but had to control, was a humbling experience.

Despite the pressure, the union carried on with its normal work as best it could. Among the tasks performed on auto-pilot were the preparation of that year's wage claim and the press launch of N U M's major publication on safety, presciently titled *A Thousand Ways to Die*. In this well-crafted report, which went through the printers only a day or two before the tragedy, the union not only identified the host of safety problems facing the mining industry, but expressed its feeling that the battle for safety was being won. And then came catastrophe, with 177 dead from a simple, avoidable and unforgivable cause, the use of deadly polyurethane foam, banned in mines of other countries, below ground in a gold mine. Faced with this situation the people at N U M, whose hopes and aspirations had been crushed, carried on, their faith in the union, their belief in justice transporting them through the anger and pain.

For the best part of a year after Kinross I saw nothing of N U M. I returned in the summer of 1987. By this time the union had moved from Lekton House. To audible sighs of relief from the staff, it had moved into C O S A T U House, a modest enough building in the centre of Johannesburg but one in which N U M had two whole floors. This gave the staff space enough to study the Mines and Works Act or analyse a flawed set of bonus calculations at least a yard and a paper-thin partition away from the ceaseless meetings and discussions with branch officials and shaft stewards which were constantly going on all around them. Unhappily, as I found when I turned up outside the fine building, the new offices at C O S A T U House hadn't lasted long. Someone had put a bomb in the building and blown most of its six or so storeys into the basement. That someone was technically expert, well equipped and clearly had a lot of good intelligence. Guided in all probability by proper architect's drawings, the bomber had gone straight for a central supporting column; had a knowledge of when the offices were unprotected and probably, according to expert reports obtained by the union, even possessed a set of keys. A number of N U M officials speculated that the bombing might well have been done by off-duty policemen or somebody working for the State. At any rate as a result of the bomb attack N U M was forced to relocate to Rissik Street, where Kinross, methane explosions, pit-cage deaths, the developing problem of AIDS and compound disturbances notwithstanding, the union carried on working for a new beginning in the tortured world of South African mining.[30]

Later, in September 1987, NUM faced another difficult test when, in support of its national pay claim, it staged its first-ever national strike. Lasting three tense weeks, the dispute centred mainly on mines belonging to Anglo American; and, while it showed that the union could engage in effective industrial action, it also showed that relations between South Africa's premier mining house and NUM were deteriorating fast. Anglo's labour relations boss Bobby Godsell, one of the passionate reformers of the early days, still called himself a liberal. But a decade later he was insisting it was 'a big mistake to think that giving people room to organise means we give up our ability aggressively, assertively and effectively to promote our vital interests'.[31] Anglo had come under fire from other mining houses and from the more conservative members of its own hierarchy for being too kind to NUM, but it seemed to seize on the 1987 strike as an opportunity to demonstrate that its deposits of liberalism, like Namibia's diamonds, had been severely depleted. Anglo responded to the strike by sacking 30,000 workers. These mass dismissals caused the union to end the dispute in order to protect its organisation but left Cyril Ramaphosa an angry man. 'The strike', he told the *Financial Times*, 'proved there was no such thing as a liberal bourgeoisie.'[32]

'It was', he added, 'difficult to imagine co-operation with those who have derived wealth and power from worker exploitation and forged a bloody alliance with the state.' In a subsequent report on Anglo's treatment of the union during and after the strike entitled 'Horses and Hippos', Ramaphosa and his deputy Marcel Golding described Anglo's tactics as 'a reassertion of management prerogatives and control over the workforce, no matter what the cost'.[33] The report summarised the union's study of the state of its organisation after the dispute. It had been grievously set back, with local Anglo management withdrawing recognition, victimising union representatives and withholding office facilities at many mines. For some time before the strike, it seems, the more orthodox and conservative Anglo executives had become increasingly worried about the 'crisis of authority' in their gold mines and had entertained authoritarian solutions. They had backed unionisation as a safety valve but the pressure was, if anything, increasing as the failure to deliver serious reform caused new problems on every side. Top Anglo executives were troubled yet again by the situation at Vaal Reefs, where in a nine-week period from 24 October 1986 to 5 January 1987 a total of thirty-three miners had died in a variety of fights and conflicts.[34] This meant life at the surface of the mine was even more threatened than underground. In any normal society a major public inquiry would have been launched into the underlying causes of such a crisis and its attendant deaths. But in South Africa's troubled terrain, Vaal Reefs was never probed in this way and the union and its members, the management and its staff grew further and further apart. The joint Anglo–N U M study 'Reaping the Whirlwind' a year earlier had caught something of the drift of events at Vaal Reefs in the paragraphs it devoted to the gigantic mine. But nothing was done and South Africa's biggest mine continued to move to the edge of disaster and beyond. In a sense the mine had become symbolic of the fate of an entire nation locked in a deepening cycle of violence.

Anglo executives were also deeply troubled by events at President Steyn gold mine, where twenty-seven people died in a similar period of time. And even at Western Holdings they had lost their way. Until then Western Holdings had been seen as a model mine and, because it had experienced no violence since 1974, it was chosen as the 'control' for the March 1986 investigations. But in June 1987 there were eight deaths on the mine in just one day. As a group of 150 workers protested against being sacked, six black miners were shot dead by mine security; and in what some contended was an act of vengeance, two white men were killed on the mine. Lucky Nomnganga, the secretary of the union's shaft stewards committee, was one of seventeen migrant miners charged with murder after these tragic events. One of them, Ernest Gongela, never stood trial – he was found hanged in mysterious circumstances in his prison cell. Of those who came to court seven were found not guilty and everyone but Mr Nomnganga was sentenced to jail sentences of from three to ten years. Under the South African law of common purpose, and although there was no evidence that he had killed or even hit anyone, Nomnganga was sentenced to death. 'It is very sad today that I am being sentenced for something I did not do with my own hands,' he told the court. 'I have no one's blood on my hands, that is all.'[35]

As Valford 'Lucky' Nomnganga passed his time on death row, N U M launched a campaign to defend the union and secure reprieves for a total of four union officers, including Mr Nomnganga, who found themselves under sentence of death. At a rally, the president, James Motlatsi, accused the mining houses, in collusion with the State, of attacking the union and seeking to reduce its effectiveness and challenge its ability to function. 'Miners', he reminded his audience, 'do not carry rifles and tear gas. The only weapon they have is unity.' The campaign was eventually successful, the union continued to grow and the miners on death row were reprieved not least because, as the union pointed out, dual standards operated in the mines. Black union members were convicted of murder when there was not a scrap of evidence against them. By contrast, when black union members were killed at Western Holdings, no one was ever arrested or charged.[36] Faced with the mounting cycle of violence, NUM and Anglo tried to reach agreement on a code of conduct to regulate human behaviour on the mines, each side producing impressive drafts which emphasised their common interest in peaceful negotiation rather than violent conflict as a way of settling differences. But normal, peaceful collective bargaining was an impossibility under apartheid. Its perverse regulations were the cause of endless disputes and a constant souce of anger about the systematic injustice, discrimination and inequality black miners experienced above and below ground.

At Carletonville, Gold Fields' white-only town on the West Wits line, city officials tried to restore apartheid and re-erect Whites Only signs in the local parks in 1989. NUM resisted with protests and sit-ins reminiscent of Martin Luther King, the Student Non-violent Co-ordinating Committee and the Freedom Rides of the United States in the 1960s. At Carletonville NUM won the day relatively peacefully. But at Rustenberg Platinum, the process of challenging and transcending institutionalised apartheid ended once again in death. Rustenberg, a Johannesburg Consolidated Investments subsidiary, part of the Anglo American complex of companies, continued to operate on a strict apartheid basis into 1989. According to the NUM, black workers were not allowed to sit in chairs reserved for whites. There were segregated changing rooms and eating facilities, and separate toilets, the ones for blacks having no doors. None of the supervisors was black and only blacks were searched on arrival at work. Whites by contrast were allowed to enter without question, even those carrying guns and ammunition.

NUM launched a defiance campaign against these injustices, giving full support to its members who wanted to challenge the rules. On Saturday evening, 2 September, in the purification plant Jeffrey Njuza, one of the union's shaft stewards, took a drink from a cup that had previously been 'reserved' for whites. Later a white supervisor, Ockert Vermeulen, walked up to him and shot him dead.[37] Mr Vermeulen subsequently committed suicide. The union held a memorial service for Jeffrey Njuza, sent money and condolences to his wife and child and published a pamphlet showing how astonishingly widespread such practices still were in the mining industry and how loath the mining houses like J C I were to do anything to challenge them.

After Jeffrey Njuza's death the failure to change continued, now even less excusable than before. In October 1989 NUM responded to the drinks parties and celebratory dinners organised by the Chamber of Mines to celebrate the centenary of its foundation by staging a march. Because of the nationwide state of emergency, the union had to go to court to get permission for the march to go ahead. The polite, after-dinner speeches were matched by placards stating that the Chamber's century was 'One hundred years of exploitation', and the streets of central Johannesburg echoed with the miners' cry that NUM would overcome.

A great social movement operates like the ocean tides. For years powerful waves lap against the bottom of a cliff and nothing seems to be happening. Then suddenly the cliff falls in. Just before the end of 1989, that's more or less what happened in South Africa. First Walter Sisulu, the ANC leader, himself a former mine worker, and five other leading black opposition figures were released from prison. Soon Nelson Mandela, NUM's honorary president, was to follow Sisulu and the others to freedom and all of a sudden after years of impasse, the prospect of real change in South Africa and a new dispensation in the mining industry became a practical possibility.

In just eight years, against seemingly impossible odds, the black miners of South Africa had built their own union. A creative fusion of workplace organisation with a movement for civil rights and human dignity, the NUM was poised for its greatest challenge yet – the transformation of an industry which for a hundred years had symbolised colonial oppression and the exploitation of man by man. In 1990, in their defiance campaigns, the miners of South Africa made it clear that they would not give up before they had levelled the walls of the compounds, transformed the degraded working practices and human relations of racial capitalism and built new cities of dignity and hope.

After the euphoria at Mr Mandela's release subsided, no one believed that the walk to freedom would be easy, not least because the pace of progress was kept so slow by a government still determined to protect many of the privileges of the minority, particularly their economic privileges. Soon enough violence of precisely the kind that had brought tragedy to Vaal Reefs and President Steyn mines burst out in other migrant labour hostels along the Rand. Once again sectional differences exploded or were exacerbated into carnage and death amidst worrying accusations, again like Vaal Reefs, that there had been institutional and official complicity

253

in provoking troubles. But through it all working miners kept their eyes on the prize of a new society and a new way of living. In a letter that arrived recently from a trusted friend in the Orange Free State, I was reminded of just how far there is to go. The writer, whose name I withhold to protect his employment, a working miner from Lesotho, had been instrumental in building the union in another company. He had been victimised for his pains and then moved into the ambit of J C I and Anglo American in search of a future for himself and his family. He wrote to me from Blue Village at H. J. Joel Gold Mining Co. Ltd at Virginia in the Orange Free State:

This is to let you know that I am doing well in South Africa and so are the members of my family back in Lesotho. I hope that you'll be very much amazed when you get the letter after such a very long period of no contact. I'd just like to tell you about the way things are going here.

I'm sorry that I'm not able to see you or have a mouth to mouth talk with you. But I still hope that one day we shall meet again, Laurie, my friend.

The name of the mine is H. J. Joel. Unfortunately I don't know what the letter H is for but the rest is for Jim Joel, an honour for one of the founders of Johannesburg Consolidated Investment, the group that owns the mine.

First-hand oppression and professional exploitation are the main subjects of H. J. Joel Mine and as compared to other mines within the same group in other parts of South Africa, it is unique. Situated between the towns of Virginia and Theunissen, it was officially opened in December 1988. The security is so tight and it is fenced all around with a security fence. It has only one main gate for entry and exit into the mine premises.

The hostel is, of its kind, so beautifully constructed and double-fenced all around with gates that are computerised so that a non-worker of J C I has no chance of gaining entry. As for us if we lose our card we have the same problem. The kitchen is outside the hostel, a distance of about half a kilometre away from some places. There is a gate to go through when you are going to have meals, bad enough at any time, worse when it is raining.

The rumour has it that the reason the mine has so many gates and such tight security is to be able to curb any kind of industrial action. Please, just imagine how this mine is concerning unions. The very mention of the word can cause you to be dismissed. The management of the mine are mostly from Randfontein Estates and Western Areas and they are known by most black employees who have worked at those mines for their hatred of blacks and for the union.

Many black work seekers outside the mine area were arrested. On their arrival at Theunissen Magistrates Court they were charged for trespass and most were convicted.

As there are people looking for jobs daily, frequent arrests were the order of the day. In some instances security dogs were let loose to chase work seekers away, backed up by security personnel, mostly blacks, on horseback to chase and assault the poor black people. White work seekers were of course treated differently. Two officials were finally transferred. But even after they had gone, in the hostel we were woken from our sleep as early as 1.30 a.m. and instructed to open our lockers for searching. These are not fairy tales, but the real thing. Viva NUM Viva.

Rereading my friend's letter as I put it into my computer, various cameos of South African mining life that I was privileged to see came back to me. In the strongest memory of all, I was transported back to the lonely road out from the Kinross Mine where I went in 1986 to investigate the causes of the country's worst gold mining disaster. It made me think again of the strength and selflessness of the people I met, at once both ordinary and extraordinary, who had built their own union in the face of such terrible, seemingly impossible odds. I recalled again how in the wake of those 177 unnecessary deaths, the mine management seemed to have abrogated all responsibility, leaving the emerging union to be the only cloth that wiped away tears and soaked up grief.

13   Caution to the Wind: the Kinross Mining Disaster and the Evasion of Corporate Responsibility in South Africa

Ralph Waldo Emerson said of dinner guests: 'The more they talked of honour, the more I counted the spoons.' In the autumn of 1986, Gencor shareholders needed to start counting the spoons. After the worst disaster for a hundred years, Gencor's annual report carried a lengthy article on the subject of South African mining companies and the company's unflinching commitment to safety. But with 177 so recently dead in a Gencor mine, the author was forced to concede that, despite all the many achievements of the past, new efforts were needed. To this end, he announced, the company had decided to set up a special, multi-disciplinary task force of nine people which would conduct a wide-ranging safety review on a mine by mine basis.[1]

However, no mention of the team's efforts was made in the 1987 annual report and none of the details of the investigations carried out on Gencor mines has ever been made available either to shareholders, the company's employees or members of the public.[2] In the year following the Kinross disaster there are two reports which would be interesting to read, the safety reviews of Gencor's Ermelo coal-mine and of its St Helena gold mine, both of which were the scene of mining tragedies in 1987. In April 1987, less than six months after Kinross, thirty-four workers were killed at the company's Ermelo coal-mine as a result of an explosion caused by the accumulation of methane gas. Then on 31 August 1987, at the group's St Helena gold mine, another sixty-three men lost their lives when, disturbed by an explosion, a pit cage broke free of its moorings and plunged more than a mile to the bottom of the shaft below, inflicting hideous injuries and in the end killing every man aboard.[3]

In 1987 therefore, while preparing the new edition of the annual report and accounts, the public relations executives at Gencor's head office had what is known in the trade as a presentational problem. But they worked manfully to overcome this and and in a terse paragraph entitled 'Safety', the new report stated: 'Most mines in the group were again successful in the field of safety achievements. Unfortunately an explosion took place on 31 August 1987 at St Helena Number 10 Shaft where 63 workers lost their lives.'

Then in an additional sentence, the wordsmiths at corporate headquarters moved into overdrive: 'Excluding the Kinross (1986) and St Helena (1987) disasters, fatalities decreased by 12 per cent in 1987.'[4]

Gencor's safety record was so problematic, however, that even the *Daily Telegraph* in London, a newspaper not usually known for probing working conditions in South Africa, could see the pattern of neglect that connected avoidable deaths at Kinross with those at St Helena. The paper stated in an editorial: 'the government and the mining companies have little regard for the safety of those who dig out South Africa's immense underground wealth.' Because of Kinross, it went on, 'the finger of criticism pointed at Gencor in particular'.[5]

Within days of the Kinross disaster, advisers and officials of the National Union of Mineworkers had identified a long list of critical safety defects at the mine, ranging from unsafe welding bottles, dangerous electricity supplies, the lack of fire extinguishers and self rescuers through to poor emergency planning.[6] But in all the intense discussions that took place the main anxiety was the presence of the polyurethane foam which caught fire and the circumstances in which such a dangerous and obviously toxic product had been introduced below ground. Naturally many people began to ask whether the material was used in similar circumstances in other mining countries overseas. The beginning of an answer was to be found thousands of miles away in Scotland, in a series of events at Michael Colliery in Fife, not far from the original Kinross.

Michael is an old pit situated on the north shore of the Firth of Forth half-way between Kirkcaldy and Leven, and more or less exactly across the water from Scotland's capital city, Edinburgh. Opened in 1892, the mine still employed 2,000 in 1967 when tragedy struck. On 9 September fire broke out with tragic consequences. This was because after an earlier, minor fire, polyurethane foam had been installed below ground supposedly as a fire-retardant. Instead of helping to contain the new fire, the foam made it much worse. In minutes the foam, some of which had been covered with a flame-retardant coating, was all blazing with great ferocity. No sooner had it ignited, than it equally quickly converted into thick black smoke containing among other things carbon monoxide and cyanide. A cocktail of toxic fumes spread through various sections of the pit, killing nine miners before it finished its journey.

In accordance with an obvious need to learn the lessons of disaster in one mine to avoid its repetition in another, the British Ministry of Power ordered a public inquiry. This began within two months of the tragedy, sitting at the town hall in Kirkcaldy over five days. Presided over by H. S. Stephenson, Britain's chief inspector of mines, the inquiry heard eighty-three witnesses, with the right of examination and cross-examination given to all parties. Six months later an exhaustive official report was completed and presented to parliament. The report did not mince its words about the dangers of foam, recommending forcefully that it should never be used underground or put on any surface installations which were near air-intakes in case these might, during a fire, carry smoke and fumes underground. Anticipating the recommendations of the report before it was published, the National Coal Board issued a directive formally banning polyurethane foam.[7]

The exhaustive report also contained details of a set of experiments with foam performed at the premier mine-safety institution in Britain, the Safety in Mines Research Establishment at Buxton in Derbyshire. These experiments demonstrated conclusively the extraordinary combustibility of the foam and showed how deadly were the consequences when it caught fire underground. Fuller details of the experiments were published in a batch of scientific papers made available throughout the mining world, including South Africa, where the Chamber of Mines Research Department received them, filed them and summarised the first of them in a circular, dated 21 October 1969, which was sent to all members, including Gencor.[8] In Britain these early reports were followed up by publication of more damning evidence and the release of horrifying film footage of what happened in an experimental mine roadway when polyurethane caught fire.[9] As a result of all this activity, the memory of the sudden intensity of foam fires and the clouds of toxic smoke that were given off burned into the memory of mining engineers and safety representatives around the world.

These were the first warnings to be ignored by Gencor's gold mining division. Then came another, even more forceful, if one was needed – a mine fire in the United States. It took place on 2 May 1972 at the Sunshine Mine in Idaho, reputedly the largest single producer of silver in the United States and a key property in the mining empire of the then billionaire Hunt brothers. At the time of the fire 172 men were working underground; ninety-one of them were killed by the dense black smoke that spread through the workings. The official US Bureau of Mines' report on the disaster found that the fire increased in intensity, spread more rapidly and produced more toxic gases than is usual for underground fires.[10] The peculiar characteristics of the fire directed attention to a particular stretch of the outgoing airway in the mine, which had been constructed of marine plywood and lined with rigid polyurethane foam. When it caught fire, a toxic cocktail spread through the mine once again. The Sunshine Mine tragedy was also widely reported in the world's mining press. It too was logged and catalogued at the Chamber of Mines Safety Division in Johannesburg and further literature circulated among member companies. Back in Britain yet another round of well-publicised experiments at the Safety in Mines Research Establishment in Buxton, Derbyshire, got under way. In these, researchers showed once again the deadly dangers of using these foams underground. Because of the American mining company's failure to take note of the earlier tragedy in Britain, lawyers for the widows and orphans obtained punitive damages totalling six million dollars for the relatives.[11] Once again this was a warning that Gencor ignored.

There were other warnings in South Africa itself. According to the Chamber of Mines there were two serious fires at Buffelsfontein (a Gencor mine) and Vaal Reefs (an Anglo American mine) involving foam. But perhaps the clearest warning of all is to be found in a report by scientists working for Gencor's own coal-mines. This advice, circulated to all the company's coal-mines, stated simply: 'Polyurethane is liable to be a fire hazard . . . As a result it has been banned in collieries.'[12]

All these warnings pre-date Gencor's inferno at Kinross, which was caused, a company spokesman admitted unguardedly, by a shortsighted business decision taken in 1980. Then the company, for reasons of expediency, ease and speed, to try to stop small falls of rock on to the main tramming line for the haulage of gold in the mine, lined the tunnel with deadly polyurethane foam.[13] When it made this negligent and irresponsible decision, the company had other technological routes and choices available to it, including cement guniting. But these, Gencor's technical adviser Con Fauconnier admitted at a press conference, had been rejected because they took longer and involved the use of heavy machinery in the haulage-way.[14] The sub-text of Mr Fauconnier's remarks is worthy of consideration. For it is economic rather than technical. To block the main haulage-way would have halted the flow of ore through the mine. If ore can't be brought to the surface, then it can't be rough smelted and delivered on a daily basis to the Chamber of Mines Mint to catch the gold price of the day. In other words, it was the drive for gold which set the parameters for and underscored the Gencor management's decision to Elastoplast round a problem instead of solving it responsibly.

Herbert Eisner is the mine safety expert who advised the National Union of Mineworkers after the Kinross tragedy. A calm, fair-minded and instinctively cautious man who had only recently retired as Director of the Explosion and Flame Laboratory of the British Safety in Mines Research Establishment, he could not understand how Gencor could be using this material at any time after the Michael Colliery disaster report was published and the material banned in Britain in 1968. 'The two tragedies, first at Michael and then at the Sunshine Mine, were both very widely publicised,' he told me. 'The subject came up at almost all mining conferences. There was no lack of publicity. So it's very difficult to understand how this could happen. It's inexcusable really.'[15]

Since the disaster Gencor has placed great emphasis on the fact that it installed what it thought was fire-retardant foam in the Kinross tunnel. This argument is part of a company strategy to minimise its own responsibilities and shift them on to the small contracting companies who installed the foam. They of course bear some of the responsibility for introducing life-threatening materials into the hazardous environment of a deep mine with thousands of employees working more than a mile below ground. But Gencor's overall group responsibilities are not in any way diminished by their contributory negligence. If, as the corporation claims, it is one of the biggest and most successful mining houses in southern Africa, then out of respect for the human rights of all its employees it has a fundamental duty to acknowledge its mistakes and let people inside and outside the company learn from them. It is part of the continuing tragedy of Kinross that the company has not been prepared to do this and is still, even today, trying to minimise rather than face up to its responsibilities for the worst disaster in South Africa's troubled history of gold mining.

A major mine disaster is a moment for audit and scrutiny. After the living are recovered and the dead are buried, the time comes for reasoning and for reckoning. The normal procedure is to hold a full, public inquiry, with witnesses giving evidence on oath and with complete freedom of access to mine plans and company documents. This procedure is designed to restore public confidence as well as to procure the widest possible informational base about the real causes of tragedy. From this evidence a judge or inspector works to distil a definitive account of what happened and a full report is published so that everyone has the opportunity to absorb and act upon its lessons. In his book on British mining safety *The Hardest Work under Heaven*, Michael Pollard shows the central role of public inquiries in bringing about change in an industry which in nineteenth-century Britain killed 1,000 men a year, a death rate roughly equivalent to the one in South African mining today.[16] Prior to these inquiries there was, reports Pollard, little concern in Britain about this shocking and readily avoidable state of affairs. This began to change when the miners and those few doctors, scientists, politicians and lawyers sympathetic to their cause, began to campaign forcefully for redress. At public inquiry after public inquiry the miners built their case, showing that mining companies ignored, defied or evaded safety requirements and that strong government intervention was necessary to bring down the numbers of deaths and injuries.

In the past South Africa has relied on proper public inquiries to establish the facts and learn the lessons. In July 1888 a fire broke out underground at the giant De Beers' mine in Kimberley. In a disaster comparable to Kinross a century later, both in its causes and the extent of its tragic consequences, 205 miners were killed.[17] As Rob Turrell shows in his book *Capital and Labour on the Kimberley Diamond Fields*, black miners trapped undergound prepared themselves for inevitable death by singing. One Zulu known only as John repeatedly risked his life by returning into the suffocating smoke to rescue three white miners. Asked why he went back and back again, he replied, 'It is nothing if I die, but if the whites die it is a big thing.'[18] In their investigations the De Beers' directors exonerated the mine manager. But a proper commission of inquiry, which had full access to confidential business information and company documents, reached very different conclusions. The commission found that there were no fire extinguishers at the mine, that there was a serious lack of adequate ladderways, and that since the mine's escape shaft was closed at the time of the accident, mining operations should have been suspended.[19] Similarly, after the Coalbrook disaster in 1960 killed 435 men a major inquiry was set up, a probe into the underbelly of South Africa's mining safety system as thorough as it was controversial.

With Kinross, the accusations of negligence were so serious and the consequences of tragedy so extensive that there was every reason to believe an exhaustive investigation would again be set in train. After all, only through such an inquiry could the range of factors – commercial, technological, social and political – that precipitate disaster be dealt with in a probing and critical way. Such inquiries accord with all responsible visions of the conduct of science, technology and economic life; and through them the tragedies of that past can be transformed into the safety laboratories of the future. Without them, on the other hand, the public interest in knowing the truth is hopelessly compromised.

Despite the fact that it was the worst tragedy in a hundred years of gold mining in South Africa, no such probe has ever been undertaken into the sequence of events at Kinross. As a result, Matseko Lejalla and the other widows of the reserves have never had a proper explanation of how their husbands came to die. They are not the only ones denied this information. Because there was no free flow of information, thousands of people who still work for Gencor are denied their right to know. Yet on a daily basis thousands of them take serious risks in mines still operated by the company. The right to know of engineers and miners in other South African mining houses has also been denied. The world mining community, who in theory could learn from others' mistakes, has also been kept in the dark.

Yet the early indications after Kinross were that both Gencor and the South African government appeared to want to learn the lessons of tragedy. Gencor's directors spoke of 'being humbled', of it being time for the company 'to think again and start again in the field of safety'.[20] The South African government Minister of Mineral Energy at the time of the disaster, Danie Steyn, promised that 'a thorough judicial inquiry' would be carried out.[21] In retrospect, the first indication that a proper investigation might not be on everyone's agenda came soon after the tragedy. Dr Eisner was chosen as the black mining union's expert adviser. In line with the invitation from the then South African state President P. W. Botha, that 'responsible representatives of foreign governments and mining industries' should visit South Africa and 'ascertain for themselves what our safety standards and mechanisms are',[22] Dr Eisner flew to South Africa. Before he could reach the mine, a senior Gencor official cancelled permission for him to visit it. The Gencor official did this in the full knowledge that access to inspect the scene of a disaster is essential to any real understanding of what went wrong. Despite this, Gencor chose to deny Eisner access, trying for days to pretend that they had never officially received NUM's request for entry when it had been both received and granted. This turn of events infuriated the NUM general secretary, Cyril Ramaphosa, who accused Gencor of hiding information and getting rid of evidence. The union's forthright stand prompted another about-face at Gencor head office and permission for Dr Eisner and three other NUM officials and advisers to go below ground at Kinross was finally granted. But the row wasted a lot of time and the visit eventually took place two full weeks after the tragedy. By then repairs had begun, the scene had been sanitised and the inspection proved of little forensic use.

The visit was further soured by another extraordinary decision taken by Gencor's head office. Without telling the union, Gencor invited some sixty representatives of mining companies, the Chamber of Mines and even officials of other unions which had no members at the mine to turn up at the same time. Thus what should have been a calm, businesslike and unpressured survey of the scene of a major disaster turned into an open day which, far from facilitating the thorough inquiries Dr Eisner and his colleagues had in mind, meant they had little time or space to do the job properly. Nevertheless Cyril Ramaphosa and other senior officials of the black miners' union remained optimistic about a proper inquiry being convened. One hundred and seventy-seven men had been killed as a result of demonstrable negligence on the part of Gencor; the overall death rates in South African mines were alarmingly high; and in the wake of the Granada film 'Death is Part of the Process' about Kinross, controversy was growing about whether the industry's International Mine Safety Rating System was a proper safety system at all. But as time passed without any announcement of the terms or composition of a commission of inquiry, the union's leaders began to get worried. Gencor, they reasoned, certainly didn't want an inquiry – its entire safety record and corporate culture would come under the microscope if one went ahead. Perhaps the union's leaders began to speculate, the Chamber of Mines and the government shared the company's anxieties and even had others besides. Nevertheless the union persisted with its efforts. Then it became apparent that the government mining engineer and the South African Cabinet were dragging their feet; and finally the inquiry was formally postponed pending the announcement of a trial of one white miner and six relatively junior managers of Gencor's Kinross Mining company for criminal negligence.

Superficially this looked like a robust and purposeful way of dealing with the aftermath of the tragedy. But NUM's officers and their legal advisers feared that it put the cart of prosecution before the horse of investigation and effectively pre-empted the constitution of a proper, wide-ranging inquiry. With the benefit of hindsight it now seems that their fears were well justified. The Kinross disaster took place on 17 September 1986. In any open society, where 177 miners had been killed in such controversial circumstances, a tribunal of inquiry would have been constituted within a week and would have begun its work within a month. But Kinross took place in the heart of an industry that is South Africa's single biggest export earner and inside a company with the closest possible links to the Afrikaner establishment which has run the country for forty years. No public inquiry was called and instead the first opportunity for any public scrutiny of the causes of disaster came almost a year after the tragedy in the course of a regional court hearing at Witbank.

The hearing proceeded at a snail's pace with defence counsel putting up a series of successful technical defences against a lacklustre prosecution. Six months later, after a lengthy adjournment, the magistrate dismissed all charges of culpable homicide and found only one person guilty of anything. This was the white miner, Mr Viviers, who was convicted on two minor counts of breaches of the Mines and Works Act. He was fined fifty rand on each count, a total of 100 rand or about £40 sterling, less than 25p a life. NUM general secretary Cyril Ramaphosa launched a withering attack on the verdict and said the black union would send the white miner a cheque for 100 rand to pay his fine since his actions were not the real cause of the disaster. In an angry statement sent out by telex to all regional offices and issued to the press, the NUM general secretary underlined that the finding was 'offensive to our members' sense of fairness and justice' and would be viewed 'as a gross miscarriage of justice'.

> The fire . . . which claimed the life of 177 workers is, according to the court, not Kinross management's responsibility. The implication is that the fire was an act of God, like an earthquake or flood, which could not be prevented. The simple facts are as follows. The fire was caused by applying polyurethane foam to underground walls of the mine. This foam is outlawed in mines in Britain and North America and has been so for many years. Senior management of Gencor and Kinross were well aware of the documented dangers of this foam.[23]

Ramaphosa's anger had been fired by clear evidence laid before the court that Gencor executives were specifically warned about the dangers of the foam not only before it was installed at Kinross but again afterwards. Henry Rose, a Gencor group ventilation engineer, told the Witbank court that he had visited the mine in 1981 and found the foam in use. He had advised both local management and Carl Netscher, the group's chief consulting engineer at head office, that it was 'extremely dangerous'. He had further underlined his anxieties by direct reference not only to the disasters in Scotland and the United States but to a hitherto unknown set of tests done in Zambia within the Gencor group itself.[24]

Under cross-examination Mr Rose stated that he had raised the problem at a specially summoned meeting for ventilation engineers from all group gold mines. Further he had even issued a verbal instruction that the foam be removed from the mine. His intention was to follow through with a specific, written instruction from Carl Netscher at group head office. The written confirmation of the instruction had been agreed, but was never sent out. Defence lawyers for Gencor worked hard to counter with technicalities this damaging testimony from one of the company's own staff. Mr Rose didn't have the authority to issue such a verbal instruction, they told the court; and Kinross Mines was a separate company from Gencor and was, so to speak, protected from the burdens both of knowledge and culpability by the arcane details of corporate structure and limited liability.[25]

For months after the court case Cyril Ramaphosa repeatedly stated that he could not understand how the only punishment for the death of 177 miners could be a fine of forty pounds. 'It was and is extraordinary', he told me, 'that the company responsible was not criticised or censured or brought to book in any way.' Repeatedly he expressed the thought that if 173 of the dead miners had been whites rather than blacks, South Africa would never have heard the end of it. But with the court case out of the way, the NUM general secretary and his lawyers at least felt optimistic that there would now be a proper official inquiry into the country's worst gold mining disaster. Initially such hopes seemed entirely reasonable, and the black union leaders were happy when the South African government mining engineer, G. P. Badenhorst, belatedly announced, long after the disaster had faded from the public mind, that a public inquiry would go ahead as soon as possible.

The inquiry finally opened in Evander, the white mining town near the Kinross mine, on 28 June 1988, the best part of two years after the tragedy, when memories had faded and the heat had gone from the situation. None the less on the opening day the union's hopes for justice were high. Then at the very beginning of the proceedings, the man in charge, assistant government mining engineer Heindrik Leibenberg, made a surprise announcement. NUM's lawyers, he told the court, would only be allowed to cross-examine a witness if the union could show that its members at Kinross would be implicated or in some way blamed by that witness.[26] As NUM's members were all innocent victims of the fire and the real questions of substance related to Gencor's business decisions and state of knowledge of the risks, NUM was effectively gagged by this procedural ruling. Months of preparatory work assiduously done by its team of lawyers and technical advisers were invalidated at a stroke.

As a result of this ruling, the inquiry degenerated into a farce. The 'public inquiry' was over in just three hours, without a single useful addition to the body of public knowledge and no proper inquiry report. At one minute for each dead man, it was viewed by the union as a provocation every bit as tasteless as the 25p a life fine imposed by the Witbank court. The gagging order and the resultant incredible speed with which the inquiry was accomplished had another important effect. NUM's lawyers and senior officials were unable to develop any of their arguments about the overall context in which the disaster had taken place. Under this heading they had intended to bring to the fore a battery of convincing arguments about the systemic weaknesses, inadequacies and flaws inherent in the safety regime in South African mines. The union was fighting hard against job reservation and was determined to show it was iniquitous to have a situation in the industry where one highly paid group of white men, often on bonus rates, made all decisions relating to the safety of the majority, without any opportunity for meaningful consultation. In addition the union's lawyers had been probing into 'precursor incidents', anticipations and warning signs for Kinross inside South Africa itself, and the apparently inexplicable failure of the Chamber of Mines and the Government Mining Inspectorate to act upon them.

Paul Benjamin of the union's lawyers Cheadle, Thompson & Haysom had been researching the background to the fire and finally obtained the highly controversial minutes of a cursory but explosive inquiry into a polyurethane foam fire which killed ten miners at Anglo American's giant Vaal Reefs mine in October 1983. In every respect the Vaal Reefs tragedy is a precursor of the inferno at Kinross. The same kind of supposedly fire-retardant foam was in place for the same or similar reasons. The same use of welding and cutting tools with a naked flame set fire to the foam. The foam ignited with the same speed and was soon sending toxic fumes around the surrounding area. Johannes Vellema, the production manager who went to survey the wreckage, human and otherwise, soon grasped the issues. In a damning report he clearly set out the many dangers of using this material underground. He re-emphasised what the British research of 1968 had shown about the deadly dangers of foam. In particular he warned that from his experience it was vital to assume that all claims for fire-retardant qualities were completely false unless cast-iron proof to the contrary was provided.[27]

Paul Benjamin believes that the Vaal Reefs episode shows that three years before Kinross the government mining inspectors were in possession of hard information that a deadly material was still being used in South African mines. They knew the risks if the material was left in place and they knew the probable consequences if anything went wrong. Why, he began to wonder, did they not act upon this knowledge? Why did they not follow the example of the National Coal Board in Britain and ban the material from the industry? 'I believe this report shows a depth of knowledge that could have saved lives,' he told me, 'but nothing was done. There was no directive to ban the material from the inspectorate. This is a terrible form of negligence and draws a government department into the frame of responsibility alongside Gencor. At Kinross 177 human beings paid for this negligence with their lives. The company failed them and the Government Mining Engineer's department did so too. I'd like to know how and why this happened. The system failed. Mines were left to go their own way and do their own thing. This just isn't good enough.'[28]

Armed with such information, NUM's general secretary Cyril Ramaphosa and his legal advisers would have turned a proper public inquiry into a powerful indictment of the industry and the way it was being run. This was the greatest fear of the government, the Chamber and the Inspectorate of Mines; and was well founded. At an earlier inquiry into the disaster at Hlobane, which involved a mine developed and run for many years by Gencor, the new union, its legal advisers and experts had put on a commanding performance in respect of the thoroughness and vigour with which they had pursued the industry's inadequate safety record and held it up for public scrutiny.

Three years before Kinross, when the union was only a year old, disaster struck the coal-mine of Hlobane, which Gencor had developed near Vryheid in northern Natal. Opened to supply coking coal to the State-owned steel company Iscor, the name Hlobane is etched deep in the memory of South African miners both black and white. In 1943 a methane gas explosion had killed fifty-seven men.[29] In September 1983 when methane exploded again, the death toll reached sixty-eight. This second disaster came just after Gencor had run down its operations at Hlobane, laid off a third of the workforce, given the government notice of closure and then formally transferred ownership of the mine to Iscor, the state-owned steel company, in return for cash. But the poor mining equipment and working practices that Gencor initiated and Iscor had done nothing to modify, led to a relatively small methane explosion spreading through whole sections of the mine, killing sixty-eight workers, some of them up to 430 metres away from the immediate incident.[30]

Just as circumstances at Kinross turned a small incident into a major catastrophe, so too at Hlobane. In what was a notoriously dangerous and gassy mine with an earlier disaster to remind management of the dangers, half of the twenty-nine machines found in the stricken section of the mine had no flame-proofing, an obvious requirement below ground in conditions where the tiniest spark can initiate catastrophe. Testing procedures for methane at the mine were severely deficient, relying on outdated flame safety lamps. Properly run mines rely on methanometers to do the job because they are safer and more accurate, particularly when detecting the presence of gas in small quantities. Worse still, when the explosion came, conditions in the mine maximised instead of minimised its potential for development. Ventilation was poor and there was a lot of coal dust, which should have been watered down but was instead left airborne. This boosted the explosion and spread it, as did a defective cloth used to control the Hlobane ventilation system. It was combustible when it should have been fireproof and as a result failed to limit the spread but sending it through the mine instead of calming and containing it.[31]

The NUM rose to the occasion. For the first time in twenty-three years dead black miners and their families had their own representatives at an inquest-inquiry in South Africa.[32] As a result the normally staid inquiry, which was usually no more than a poorly attended formality, was transformed and NUM began to make itself into an effective watchdog for safety in the mining industry. Two international experts were flown in to help with the case, Robert van Dolah, the former research director of the US government Bureau of Mining Research in Pittsburgh, and Dr Eisner (who would later also visit Kinross). Together these experts, the union's leaders and their legal advisers asked many awkward questions and turned the inquiry into a exposition of the many weaknesses of the safety regime in Hlobane colliery and the South African mining industry of which it was a part.

Mr van Dolah showed how many lives could have been saved if the mine had been equipped with self-rescuing equipment. (Three years later at Kinross they still weren't in place.) NUM lawyers also showed that a white miner had detected the presence of methane in the Hlobane mine a week before the accident and even recorded it in his log book. This was the first warning that methane was present in the mine for some time. But his immediate superiors decided to ignore the reading and falsify the log book by deleting the entry. The purported explanation for this extraordinary behaviour, the lawyers established, was that mine management believed the white miner was lying and only mentioned methane in order to excuse poor coal production in his gang.[33]

Perhaps the most disturbing evidence came from the mine's chief ventilation officer, Peter Shand. He told the court that legally prescribed amounts of air essential to disperse any possible methane gas did not reach the working faces on any regular basis. Furthermore, in his eleven years as a Chamber of Mines ventilation officer, he had never once come across a single coal-mine in Natal that was able to provide the correct amounts of air to the working faces all the time. The mining safety regulations were in other words being flouted on a daily basis.[34]

What was particularly worrying about this statement was that Natal coal-mines had been recognised as prone to methane from the beginning of the century and the mechanisms of control had been clearly established and widely advertised for many years. As the 1910 report of the Union of South Africa Department of Mines stated: 'It was considered that the condition and character of the collieries of Natal, owing to their fiery nature and to the problems presented by the gas and dust explosions which have taken place in the past with such disastrous results, require special and careful treatment.'[35] A special commission of inquiry was even set up to investigate conditions, establish proper working practices and set standards. Yet as Hlobane showed, the lessons South African mining had learned from bitter experience seemed to have gone by the board, in the deregulated environment of the 1980s, with tragic and unacceptable results.

Despite the impressive performance of the union during the Hlobane inquiry, the court was lenient with the two companies responsible. Gencor, which had developed the mine and was responsible for many of the illegalities, escaped without criticism. The company owned the mine until just ten weeks before the disaster and bore a prime responsibility for the failure to flame-proof the machinery which caused the explosion. No such indulgence was shown to the dead white miner. The court found that the white miner should have tested for methane on the day of the accident. But he failed to do so and was killed. The magistrate also found the Vryheid Railway and Coal Company, bought from Gencor ten weeks before the disaster, criminally liable for the sixty-eight deaths. But he ruled (in apparent defiance of the facts which showed at least twenty-one systematic and continuing instances of safety regulations flouted by both Iscor and Gencor) that the main negligence was that of the dead white miner. As a result the subsequent prosecution of the company was a token affair resulting in a fine of 400 rand (6 rand or £2 a life).[36]

The derisory fine infuriated NUM secretary Cyril Ramaphosa, who underlined that fines of such a size would never provide a meaningful deterrent to a sloppy or corner-cutting mine management. 'They will continue disregarding safety because they know they will only have to pay a four-hundred rand fine,' he stated. 'And as far as we are concerned four hundred rand does not compensate for the lives of sixty-eight people. That doesn't seem to be a reasonable punishment.'[37] Despite the low level of the fine, the union's forceful and dignified behaviour at the inquiry brought it close to centre stage in South Africa's massive mining industry. Prior to the inquiry it had 40,000 members, an impressive figure organised in the face of much hostility from most of the mining houses. But the extent of the negligence involved at Hlobane and the extraordinary publicity brought the union much public sympathy and had a decisive impact inside the mine compounds themselves. As a result the union gained tens of thousands of members.

In a powerful speech concerning the Hlobane tragedy Mr Ramaphosa had given government and mining companies alike a powerful reminder of how pivotal the issue of mining safety would now be in South African history: 'We must warn the government that unless a commission of inquiry is instituted immediately to look into safety on the mines, there will be very little industrial peace on the mines. The black miner is rising and he is going to take heed of the unsafe environment he is forced to work in. Our safety record is the most appalling in the world,' he said, adding that NUM would leave no stone unturned in its fight for safety on the mines.[38]

After the even more disastrous events at Gencor's Kinross mine in which the negligence was if anything even more extensive, the last thing the government and the Chamber of Mines wanted was a public forum where the conduct and management of the industry would be put on trial. Two further disasters at Gencor mines in the course of 1987 reinforced this strategic consideration. On 9 April 1987, just six months after Kinross, thirty-four mine workers died as a result of yet another methane explosion at the company's Ermelo coal-mine. The changes below ground which turn buried trees into coal also create pockets of gas or methane; and wherever coal is mined methane will be found too. With sound engineering, good ventilation and flame-proof machinery designed to avoid sources of ignition, most major mining countries have controlled this hazard. But at

Ermelo something else seems to have been seriously wrong. This was the third methane explosion at the mine within five years. In 1982 eleven workers died in a similar explosion. In October 1984 six miners died from carbon-monoxide poisoning created by an explosion of methane.[39] Commenting on the mine's problems, NUM safety adviser Jean Leger stated, 'There can be few modern collieries in the world which have such a poor safety record as Ermelo.'[40]

Four months after Ermelo yet another Gencor company, the gold mine St Helena, was also visited by disaster. Yet another methane explosion took place, this time in an intermediate pump station in a newly sunk shaft in the mine. The force of the explosion caused steel work to collapse, breaking supports for the pit cage or lift, which hurtled to the bottom of the shaft a mile away in a free fall. Some fifty people were in it at the time. Between the runaway cage and the explosion the death toll that day came to sixty-three. Gencor didn't inform the National Union of Mineworkers about what had happened.[41] The union found out from the radio but was unable to put its knowledge or experience to good use because the company forbade union officials to visit St Helena. Cyril Ramaphosa protested at this latest indignity and recalled the eleven deaths at the mine as recently as 1982, again from a methane explosion.

With a growing crisis in Gencor's mines, a public inquiry was imperative, but the powers that be in South Africa's mining industry – the Minister of Minerals and Energy and the Chamber of Mines of South Africa – were in a position to prevent N U M from developing its case. If there was no proper inquiry there could be no proper investigation and the mining companies could once again rely on their public relations departments with their well-crafted statements of deep and continuing concern to forestall serious scrutiny or reform. Gencor, above all others, stood to gain from this strategy. As the owners of all three mines hit by the worst disasters of 1986 and 1987, Gencor would have found it virtually impossible to survive such a critical examination. Deep in an internal crisis caused by over-expansion, loss of purpose and control, Gencor had been described by one heavyweight business commentator as a 'headless chicken' even before Kinross.[42] The company has always had friends in high places in the white political establishment. The executive chairman Derek Keys, for example, moved in government circles and in May 1992 was appointed Minister of Finance and Trade and Industry in the cabinet of F.W. De Klerk.[43] The company had been specially tailored to bring the Afrikaner business and political establishment into the mining industry and to avoid the threat of nationalisation, which was their declared policy when they came to power in 1948.

In 1965 Harry Oppenheimer oversaw the assignment of the company to the Afrikaner banking and life assurance interests grouped in a company called Federale Volksbeleggings, and helped them to create Federale Mynbou.[44] Then, in 1979 the Federale Mynbou/General Mining group became a more powerful force in South African mining when it took over the Union Corporation, a company with a host of profitable mining properties. It was thought that the technical competence of the Union Corporation would sit well alongside the growing financial and business power of General Mining. But the expected synergy never materialised and by 1982 Gencor was in the throes of a profound and protracted organisational crisis. There was a fierce boardroom feud, which was followed shortly by what the newspaper the *Johannesburg Star* described as 'a massive fraud probe' into some aspects of group operations.[45] Nevertheless, the company continued to expand, buying an ill-assorted collection of industrial enterprises which it once again failed to integrate, and which lost a lot of money. The group also engaged in costly and unwise foreign exchange dealings. These put considerable extra pressures on Gencor's core precious metals business,[46] which had to lay the golden eggs to stem the mounting flow of losses elsewhere. By Christmas 1985 management consultants Arthur D. Little had to be brought in to sort out the paralysis at the uppermost levels of the company and in the critical weeks and months before the Kinross disaster, the main thrust of executive effort was focused entirely on devising new management structures rather than running the company in an open or creative, humane or efficient way.[47]

These and other details of Gencor's flawed corporate culture would have become subject to public scrutiny in the course of any protracted public inquiry into Kinross, an unappetising prospect for the owners and the Chamber of Mines. Two other factors underscored Gencor's exceptional vulnerability at this time. First, as two South African investigators have shown, the company's overall safety record was worrying to the point of being indefensible; and second, the company had a major skeleton in the cupboard over its extraordinarily cavalier attitude to safety and environmentally induced disease in its asbestos mining division.

Prompted by a hunch that Gencor's problems might be symptomatic of the industry as a whole, two young South African scientists, Anthony Zwi in London and Jean Leger in Johannesburg, decided to study all major

272

disasters in South Africa's recent mining history. They pulled in press cuttings and government reports of all 'major incidents', defined as they are in Britain as those disasters which killed six people or more. Using modern computers to help them store and analyse data, they grouped the long list of tragedies by the types of mines involved, the causes of the incident and the extent of the deaths and injuries. Another column denoted which company owned each mine hit by tragedy and calculated the differential death rates for the period from 1970 to 1988 group by group.[48] The results of the survey are particularly disturbing for Gencor. In the eighteen-year period under review 464 people were killed in twenty-two major incidents in the Gencor group. The Anglo American Group, the biggest single employer of labour, also had twenty-two incidents. But while Anglo's cumulative death toll in incidents killing six or more was a shocking 250 this is still a substantially lower figure than Gencor's.

Zwi and Leger next calculated the average number of deaths per disaster for each mining house with a view to ranking the companies in order of danger. The results were as follows:

Company	Fatalities	Nos of Incidents	Fatalities per Disaster[49]
Gencor	464	22	21·1
Anglo	250	22	11·4
Rand Mines	173	18	9·6
Gold Fields	153	13	11·8
JCI	61	9	6·8
Anglovaal	55	4	13·8

'Accident research like this is only a guide to the underlying reality,' Anthony Zwi told me, 'but I find these figures worrying. The mining industry as a whole seems to perform badly in South Africa particularly when we compare the numbers of disasters and the number of deaths to what happens in other major mining countries like Britain. But Gencor is way out in front on all the indices.'[50]

The details of Gencor's pollution of the environment in the 1960s, 1970s and 1980s in the course of its extensive mining of asbestos in the north-western Cape is set out in Chapters 9 and 10. But this aspect of the corporation's safety record would also have become part of the focus of any serious inquiry into health and safety in the South African mines after Kinross. The company, it is worth remembering, threw caution to the wind with asbestos every bit as much as with methane and polyurethane, simultaneously issuing public denials that there were any cancer hazards associated with mining the fibre and privately co-operating with other mining companies to ensure that damning evidence of those hazards was never published but was instead suppressed.[51]

In the summer of 1990 the National Union of Mineworkers was still persisting with its valiant efforts to defend its members' right to have proper public inquiries into mining disasters. Unwilling to accept defeat, the union applied to the Rand Supreme Court in November 1989 for an order declaring that the gagging device employed by the government mining engineer to turn the Kinross inquiry into a farce was unfair and unlawful. Judgment was initially reserved; but in the end Mr Justice Goldstein sided with the union. In the summer of 1990, nearly four years after Kinross, he ruled that the union should have had the right to question witnesses freely and to probe the company's record at the mine.[52]

This is a small inroad into the inflexibility and inhumanity of the mining industry; and while it offers some hope for the future, it will not undo the failure to probe Kinross and the company which caused it to happen. One perceptive observer of the South African mining scene has argued that the best description of the South African mining houses is that they are in organisational terms 'machine bureaucracies', hard, militaristic, authoritarian capsules of power which have operated for years on principles wholly inimical to those of democracy, human dignity and a free flow of information. When I think back on the many facets of the Gencor organisation that I have encountered in the last decade, it seems to me that Gencor is the most troubled, repressed and problematic mining organisation in the whole of South Africa. It was part of the declared policy of its chief executive, Derek Keys, who was installed in the wake of the Arthur D. Little report into Gencor's manifold organisational failures and who came to power just before Kinross to do something to modify this dangerous and authoritarian legacy. This is a very difficult task. For as the Russian poet Yevgeny Yevtushenko has pointed out about the problems of reconstruction in his own, equally afflicted, land: 'It is impossible to have a perestroika, without a perestroika of the memory.'

By 'perestroika of the memory', Yevtushenko means an honest reckoning with unpleasant and difficult truths. In Gencor's case, until there is some form of open, public inquiry and a serious official report into what went wrong at its Kinross mine in September 1986 during the centenary of the discovery of gold on the Rand, there will have been no break with the past, no honest basis of accounting and no serious indication that in future the tens of thousands of members of the company who work in its mines and live in its compounds will be able to live in a better way. Until then it will be safe to say, deploying the baseball phrase favoured by American industrial accident lawyers to describe what to them has become a familiar process in corporate life, the truth about Kinross has simply been 'deep sixed' – buried by political and organisational manoeuvre.

14 Death is Part of the Process: Frank Bird and the Illusion of Safety in South African Mines

In December 1981 the liberal South African newspaper the *Rand Daily Mail* stated unequivocally: 'SA gold mine safety – the world's best'.[1] The report came as something of a surprise to those people in the mining industry who could add up a column of figures. In that year 853 miners were killed in gold mining alone, one for every ton of the precious metal the country produced. The evidence brought forward to support the best-in-the-world claim was less than exhaustive. A South African Chamber of Mines spokesman merely stated that 'South Africa is the most advanced country in the world in terms of the safety measures on its mines . . . It is the best without a doubt.'[2]

The *Rand Daily Mail* was, until its closure in controversial circumstances, helpful to the white minority government in 1985, controlled by one of South Africa's premier mining houses, J C I, part of the Anglo empire. In the early 1980s until some younger, more sceptical reporters came on the scene,[3] the paper seemed to have unreserved confidence in the growing public relations output from the Chamber of Mines' offices in Hollard Street. In another *Rand Daily Mail* article published shortly after the first, an independent consultant called Tom Grant added his enthusiasm for the mining industry's accident record and safety arrangements. 'In South Africa', he assured the paper's readers, 'every possible precaution is taken to prevent accidents . . . South Africa has a perfect safety system . . . the fatality and injury rates compare very favourably with the best records in the world.'[4]

This message found its way into a number of books. For example, Tim Green, one of Britain's best-known observers of the international mining scene, stated in his book *The New World of Gold*:

At some mines people are schooled to say, 'Mina sindile' ('I am safe') as a standard form of greeting instead of 'Hello.' This passion for safety has paid off. Despite the fact that the mines are more labour intensive and are operating at much greater depths than mines elsewhere, their performance is often the best in the world. Five South African gold mines have been the only ones to achieve the maximum five stars of an international safety award rating scheme which includes mines in Australia, Canada and the United States.[5]

Mr Green made no attempt to look for underlying death and injury rates on the five award-winning South African mines or to evaluate the so-called International Mine Safety Rating System. Had he done so his conclusions might have been somewhat different. My own evaluation began with the first mine in the world to win five stars under the system, Anglo American's President Brand mine in the Orange Free State. This event brought a flurry of publicity from the public relations department in Anglo American's handsome old building in Main Street, Johannesburg. The public relations wordsmiths inside head office obviously felt little need for modesty on 2 August 1983 as they drafted the press release announcing that the exceptionally deep President Brand gold mine had triumphed in a worldwide competition.

'President Brand gold mine near Welkom has become the first mine in the world to gain the maximum five-star rating under the International Mine Safety Rating Programme for five consecutive years,' stated the release. 'The manager of the Anglo American-administered mine, Mr Jan Rossouw, this afternoon received the award from the President of the Chamber of Mines, Mr Colin Fenton.'[6]

Mr Fenton's speech to the award ceremony went further. 'No other mine in South Africa or in any other country in the world can match this record,' he said. There were, however, some facts about President Brand that Mr Fenton omitted to mention. In 1983, twenty miners were killed in the mine, with 408 others receiving disabling injuries. In 1982 the death toll at the mine was twenty-one; in 1981 twenty-four died; in 1980 twenty more. In 1984, the year after Mr Fenton claimed that no other mine anywhere in the world could match its magnificent safety record, thirty-six miners died at President Brand, a death rate of one miner every ten days.[7]

Another early winner of the award was Gold Fields' West Driefontein mine, the most profitable gold mine in the world. It was at West Drie that I first saw the huge blue and white billboards that are erected outside the mine so that each and every visitor as well as every employee would know that it had five stars for safety. Inside the mine office was a similar announcement and an imposing certificate, which said it had won the five-star award in September 1982. The certificate, I later noticed, was displayed with pride in company reports and reproduced in Paul Johnson's centenary history of Gold Fields. It came as something of a surprise therefore when I looked up the records of the government mining engineer and discovered that at the award-winning mine sixteen people had died that year. In 1983 the number killed was twenty-seven. Furthermore at the time of my visit Driefontein was still the subject of a major dispute between the owners and the National Union of Mineworkers over the company's insistence on its right under the racist provisions of the Mines and Works Act to have white workers order – on pain of instant dismissal if they did not comply – black workers to continue working in a place they had come to believe was unsafe. I talked to some of the Driefontein miners about their problems. They told me about being beaten underground, about a constant push for the production of gold, about people losing arms and legs, and a host of other matters which suggested that the mine was far from reaching the standards the award implied. Lastly I asked them about the Mine Safety Rating Scheme itself. They said that it had little or no impact on their working lives and was a paper exercise done by the management without their knowledge or involvement. I checked Frank E. Bird's International Mine Safety Rating System,[8] and sure enough it had no provision for such matters as employee participation, workmen's inspectors, free flow of information or the right of people taking risks to be consulted.

In a café near the mine in Carletonville I began to wonder what the South African tourist board would have to say about a hotel or restaurant which had five stars where someone died every fortnight, and literally thousands were injured. The scheme, with its billboards and stars, certificates and self-praise, seemed little more than a public relations exercise designed to make a highly dangerous industry look safe. I began to voice my growing sense of confusion and anxiety about Frank Bird and his international mine safety rating scheme to a number of South Africans concerned about industrial safety, among them Dr Anthony Zwi. Dr Zwi told me of some figures he had noted during a talk he had attended about the safety policy of the mine given by its chief loss control officer. At West Drie apparently there were two deaths a month, twenty reportable injuries, sixty-six disabling injuries and 400 minor injuries. The dressing stations on the mine which treated cuts and minor injuries dealt with 40,000 visits a month. By now confusion had given way to downright scepticism.[9]

With Jean Leger, one of the safety advisers to the National Union of

Mineworkers and a member of the Sociology of Work Programme at Witwatersrand University, I began to cast the net a little wider. 'How many stars did Hlobane have at the time of the 1983 disaster?' I asked. 'Four stars,' answered Jean. 'And Kinross?' 'Four stars at the time of the 177 deaths. Five stars the year before,' answered Jean. Faced with the disconcerting suggestion that the International Mine Safety Rating System was to say the least misleading, we redoubled our efforts to scour mining records and scout mines. Wherever we went there were huge blue and white hoardings or billboards announcing each mine's stars in the International Mine Safety Rating System. Almost all the boards featured four or five stars, always at 'Advanced Level'. I decided to ask Dr Eisner for his views on the International Mine Safety Rating System. 'Funny you should ask about that,' he said. 'I've just been working on the system. After the Kinross disaster I repeated an exercise I first did after Hlobane. The results of both sets of calculations are very interesting.'[10]

In his own quiet way, Herbert Eisner is the harshest of all the many critics of South Africa's International Mine Safety Rating System. I met him at his home in Buxton in the English Peak District in 1985 in the period between the Hlobane mine disaster in 1983 and the Kinross tragedy in 1986. The first observation he had to make about the South African Chamber of Mines and its International Safety Rating System was that it was not international.

'The British Health and Safety Executive has a computerised database on health and safety at work with some 54,000 references,' he stated. 'When I first heard about this scheme I organised a search of this database and I could find no mention of it whatsoever. Next I got in touch with a range of mine safety experts from the United States, from Germany and the various other European Community countries and asked them if they had heard of the scheme. But they had never heard of it, at least not until it was mentioned in an unfavourable light at the Hlobane Inquiry in 1983. Until then none of the experts in mining safety had heard a word about it.

'I then found just one single reference to the man whose name I had been given as the scheme's architect, an American called Frank Bird. I tried an American colleague but he couldn't find a single mine in America that was part of this International System, and I couldn't find a single one in Europe.'[11]

Dr Eisner's next worry arose out of the Hlobane tragedy. He had travelled to South Africa to give expert advice for the National Union of Mineworkers and had been in court throughout the hearing, during which it emerged that Hlobane had been graded as a four-star mine shortly before disaster struck in 1983. This high score didn't seem to Dr Eisner to accord with the many breaches of safety regulations and good mining practice at the mine which were itemised in court. Dr Eisner wrote to the Chamber of Mines about this seeming contradiction. The Chamber representative wrote back, agreeing that the system had certain imperfections which meant that the International Mine Safety Rating Scheme audit would not have picked up Hlobane's flaws. For a qualified and committed safety engineer like Herbert Eisner this is a serious obstacle rather than an imperfection. 'Hlobane was way below standard,' he told me. 'The failure to test for methane, the lack of flameproofing of machinery, the defective brattice cloth in the ventilation system, all these things should have been picked up by any serious safety audit.

'In the wake of Hlobane, I was sent a photocopy of the International Mine Safety Rating System handbook and I went through it item by item. It was only then that I began to realise that this was a very major paper exercise asking question after question in theory and involving precious few real checks on the ground. Indeed it was so voluminous that in order for a mine manager or section head to work through it, he'd have almost to fudge things in order to get to the end. There was also an aspect of the scheme where one of the Chamber of Mines people came and audited the mine with the manager. But again it was about words rather than realities and the Chamber of Mines auditor was almost entirely dependent on the manager's word. This is what made me realise that the scheme is inconsistent. It looks very good on paper but it breaks down in life. That's how Hlobane, a poorly run and dangerous mine, got one of the highest ratings for safety, four stars.'

Dr Eisner was also worried about the extraordinary number of South African mines which seemed, like Hlobane, to end up with the highest star rating. During his years as a scientist, he had come to distrust the idea that all mines were alike and uniform in their excellence. There was even a scientific metaphor to disprove this misleading assumption, called a bell-shaped curve. This is a statistical concept representing what Dr Eisner and other safety experts believe is one of the dominant realities of modern industrial life – that few mines in a country like Britain or Germany will be either very, very good or very, very bad. Instead most of them will bunch towards the middle with a few at each of the two extremes. Statisticians call this the pattern of normal distribution and represent it in a line drawing of a bell. At the beginning of his examination of South African mines in the International Mine Safety Rating System it was a bell-shaped curve or something close to it that Dr Eisner expected to find. But his scepticism turned to surprise when he plotted out the reality on a piece of graph paper. Instead of a bell, he had an Everest of industrial safety where virtually all the climbers who entered the competition seemed almost immediately to scale the highest peaks. The results he plotted were 21 five-star mines, 10 four-star, 10 three-star, 11 two-star and only one 1-star mine.[12]

Three years later when Dr Eisner next plotted the curve, this time after the Kinross tragedy, the results were even more unusual. Now there were no one-star mines whatsoever and just 5 two-star mines. The rest were all bunched at three to five stars. Now there were 10 three-star, 24 four-star and a thumping 29 five-star mines in the scheme.

'Years of training have predisposed me to expect a few excellent and a few lousy mines and in between a bell shape. But in this exercise there was not even one single one-star mine. By contrast there were 29 supposedly at the pinnacle of excellence,' said Dr Eisner. 'That's preposterous,' I said. Dr Eisner shook his head sadly.[13]

In his history of the mining company Randfontein Estates, published in 1986, Anthony Hocking tells the revealing story of how the mine awarded itself a Chamber of Mines safety rating for three million fatality-free shifts, even though in the last week of the qualifying period a miner was killed on the mine. On 13 August 1980, Hocking reports, Randfontein Estates was within sight of three million fatality-free shifts. Management had calculated that the mine needed only 22,000 more shifts or two more working days for victory. Excitement on the mine was running high and people were looking forward to the champagne celebration at the shaft head when suddenly there was a fatal accident. It looked, wrote Hocking, 'as if the achievement for which the whole company had been working had been snatched away at the eleventh hour'.

But, the author reports, management had a novel solution to the problem. Determined to give themselves the award, they moved the goalposts. 'Randfontein representatives scoured time-sheets for shifts somehow omitted from the official tally,' Hocking writes without a hint of scepticism. 'A recount was arranged and to everyone's relief it emerged that Randfontein had worked three million fatality-free shifts after all.'[14]

From Atlanta, Georgia, Hocking reported, the founder of the International Mine Safety Rating System, Frank Bird, added his weight to the celebration of this achievement. 'Wish I could personally convey the heartiest congratulations your management team deserves for the splendid attainment that has captured the interest of your mining colleagues everywhere. The achievement stands as an example to the mining people throughout the world.'[15]

Having cut away the pretensions of the South African Chamber of Mines International Safety Rating System to be international, and demonstrated that in these competitions there only seemed to be winners, Dr Eisner next turned his scrutiny on South Africa's accident statistics. Certain formulations of these were used by the Chamber of Mines to claim that the rates of death and injury on South African mines were falling dramatically, and, pleasingly, doing so very much in line with the progressive adoption since 1978 of the International Mine Safety Rating System. Before long Dr Eisner had found the statistics were as flawed as the scheme whose effectiveness they were supposed to demonstrate.

'Death and injury statistics have to be calculated very cautiously and very carefully if they are to have accurate meanings. Otherwise you will have statistical errors and distortions that are dangerously misleading,' Dr Eisner told me. 'I regret to say that on looking closely at the Chamber of Mines' formulations in South Africa I have found a good many problems and a good many misleading statements.

'To make comparisons and obtain accurate statistics you need to ensure that all mines are reporting on a standardised basis, rooting their statistics in the injuries sustained by the groups of workers who take the risks. It's only too easy to dilute the accident rate by dividing the number of accidents not by underground workers and the number of shifts they work, but by the total numbers employed in a mining complex. And in South Africa, where there are hundreds even thousands working in mine offices, in the administration or the compounds, the prospects for dilution are very high. There are also serious variations in what different countries consider to be an accident. In South African industry in general an accident becomes reportable if the injured worker has been off work for three days or more. On the South African mines the figure is fourteen days or more.

'The South African statistics seemed to show the injury rate falling beautifully over recent years, particularly since this Safety Rating System came into effect. In the ten-year period from 1974 to 1983, the government and Chamber statisticians claim to detect a much sharper fall in the accident rate since 1977 when the scheme came in. But a closer examination shows that they were falling long before this. The accident rate can fall for a host of reasons. It can fall because there is better medical treatment which gets people back to work sooner, ensuring that their accidents while they take place do not have to be reported. Then again changes in the amounts and ways people are paid can have an effect. If people are paid more and absenteeism is heavily penalised people will tend to get back to work sooner. Indeed there could in theory be any number of economic reasons which caused lower accident rates. If food prices suddenly became high, then poor people will stay away from work for less time and this behaviour could again be reflected in a drop in the rate of reported accidents.'

With all these worries about the comparability of injury rates, Dr Eisner decided to concentrate on deaths. Initially it looked as if, while South African fatality rates were higher than in Britain or other European Community countries, they were not much higher. But when he looked more closely at the situation, more worrying trends began to emerge. 'Most fatalities in mining happen to people working underground,' explained Dr Eisner. 'So if you divide the number of deaths not by the number of underground workers but by the total numbers employed, you will get a highly distorted picture. And that's what has been going on in South African coal-mines. I found that huge numbers of people who never did an underground shift were being included in their calculations. In Britain the ratio of surface workers to underground workers is 40/60. But in South Africa there are twice as many surface workers as people working underground. In the huge SASOL colliery and oil from coal plant I found that they were dividing the number of deaths and injuries by the total staff, including all the office workers. What's more I found that if I recalculated the figures making an allowance for this, then the death rates were rising rather than falling.

'The fairest comparison perhaps is coal-mining in both Britain and South Africa. In Britain the mines are deeper and conditions more arduous. South African coal-mines should therefore do better than British ones. But the statistics show they don't. Their fatality rates over a six-year period were six times as high as the UK and 1·7 times as high as American coal-mines. Fatality rates were not going down. When I looked at gold mines I found the injury rate was declining but not in the dramatic way they claimed. As for the death rate this was in fact pretty constant over time and wasn't declining in the way they claimed.

'The fact is that their statistics were a minefield and elementary blunders were being made. At first they challenged my data, but later they were good enough to admit that things were wrong and accept that in future they should be using a much more rigorous, accurate and honest basis for their statistics.'[16]

Once again I discussed the International Mine Safety Rating System with Jean Leger, the NUM safety adviser. 'You're right to be worried,' he said. 'There's something fundamentally wrong with an industry that kills six hundred miners every year, one for every ton of gold, which then tells you that it's the safest mining industry in the world. Can you imagine what an outcry there would be in Britain if six hundred people were being killed every year in one industry? Frankly I find this whole scheme offensive. It seems to me that its main function is to obscure what is really happening in the South African mines. It helps to disguise a host of really fundamental safety problems, noise problems, dust problems, foot and hand injuries, broken backs, rockfalls, heat stress and a great many deaths and injuries.'[17]

We decided that it would be an interesting exercise to draw up a list of the award-winning gold mines, but with one additional piece of information brought into the picture – the number of miners killed in each of Frank E. Bird's five-star mines over the preceding five years.

Working from Chamber of Mines figures, Jean, a qualified engineer, started putting the information into his computer. For five-star gold mines the death list came out as follows:[18]

Mines with five stars	Number of miners killed
Deelkraal	62
Kloof	123
West Rand Consolidated	52
President Brand	121
Venterspost	50
Rand Estates	84
Grootvlei	38
Western Areas	108
Hartebeestefontein	106
Free State Geduld	120
Western Holdings	75
President Steyn	91
Winkelhaak	37
Bracken	14
Leslie	14

Next we used the Chamber of Mines' figures for deaths and injuries matched to numbers of employees and shifts worked to construct a league table ranking South African gold mines in order of danger to human beings.

The resulting print out was as complex as a set of mine plans. But there is room here for those gold mines which came out as the most dangerous in the country. They are as follows: Western Deep Levels North, ERPM, Deelkraal, Elandsrand, Kloof and Stilfontein.

Five of the six deadliest mines in South Africa, it became apparent from this exercise, had either four or five stars under the Frank Bird/South African Chamber of Mines 'International' Safety Rating System. Second in this list is East Rand Proprietary Mines, but taking account of the smaller numbers employed there, ERPM probably outranks Western Deep Levels as the single most dangerous mine in the country. Yet under Mr Bird's scheme this mine had been promoted from four to five stars of alleged excellence.

ERPM is one of the most famous names on the Rand, a mining property that has been in almost continuous production since the discovery of gold in 1886. In the early part of the twentieth century it became the victim of a historic fraud as senior managers falsified the gold production figures and cheated the company's funds of tens of thousands of pounds' profit for themselves. This resulted in a major inquiry and a thorough company reconstruction.[19] In the 1950s ERPM became what was indisputably the deepest gold mine in the world with many levels being worked at 13,000 feet below ground following the golden reef. The risks grew with the extraordinary depth and, while the mine became one of the first to install hydraulic supports, the death toll went on rising. Inside the closed world of South African gold mining, ERPM's deep-seated problems were well known, with knowledge of the risk being kept only from those who had to bear the consequences, the working miners themselves.

The secret report of the South African government's McKay Commission into the 1973 disturbances among black miners on the Rand, describes ERPM as 'a difficult, hot and unpopular mine'.[20] It was common knowledge in the industry that few local blacks wanted to have anything to do with ERPM even though it was very close to the big city of Soweto/Johannesburg. As a result the mine became dependent on fine tuning or manipulating the supply of labour through the Chamber of Mines TEBA bureau so that enough innocent or inexperienced Malawians or Mozambiquans went there who would put up with the conditions for at least one contract.

One other factor affected conditions at the mine – ERPM was a loss maker. Under-invested in by Rand Mines, conditions underground deteriorated seriously. With them went morale and standards of good housekeeping and soon ERPM was a mine on the slide. But the South African government does not close loss-making gold mines. Instead by a shrewd mixture of tax breaks and subsidies it encourages the leaseholders, in this case Rand Mines, to keep the mine going, producing poor grades of ore while gold prices are high and preserving its best prospects for when prices are lower. This complex regime of government subsidy keeps the industry on an even keel and has the hidden political attraction for the government of keeping white mining towns like Boksburg, which is almost wholly dependent on ERPM, from becoming too adversely affected by market forces. The system is based on the accurate assumption that by keeping mines open for their longest possible life the State will recoup far more in extra taxes than it spends on subsidies. But ERPM was one of the weakest of the mines and had according to press reports in the *Financial Times* been on the verge of closure in the mid-1970s 'as a result of cost pressures which were exacerbated by the mine's age and depth'.[21]

In a series of conversations with a manager at ERPM after a disaster which killed seventeen at the mine in 1985, it became clear to me that while the subsidies kept Boksburg on its feet, the situation underground was going from bad to worse. 'Every time the more concerned members of the mine management argued for spending and change,' the ERPM shift boss told me, 'the argument came straight back that the mine couldn't afford these things.'

The great age of the mine meant that the underground layout was very antiquated indeed. The shaft design was poor and the mine was subject to a lot of breakdowns. For years therefore when major modifications were needed the mine simply wasn't allowed to embark upon them and instead had to patch things up. There was also a worrying knock-on effect for line management. They were supposed to maintain adequate supplies of stores, safety equipment and spare parts. But, as one shift boss explained, at ERPM money was in such short supply that deliveries fell behind.

'At the beginning of the month you were always trying to catch up. But this in turn meant that you spent your entire month's budget near the beginning of the month just to cover the backlog and this in turn meant that planning was no longer smooth. This was very bad for the mine as a whole. And because of the shortages at ERPM people started looking for ways around the system, including pilfering, depleting the stores and hiding a few pairs of safety gloves so that they had a supply even if it was at someone else's expense. Underground it meant that when a winch guard went we had no replacements. Now in a coal-mine in Britain a whole section of a mine must close down if there are no winch guards. In South Africa it's just that one winch which mustn't operate, or at least that's the theory. What happened at ERPM was that people felt production must keep running so they just went ahead without a winch guard.

'The other thing that happened at ERPM was that mine management lost their way. Management became demoralised; far too many people were acting mine manager or acting shift boss rather than being trained, equipped and paid for the job. This whole problem expressed itself very seriously in the most dangerous parts of the mine. In a couple of areas where I worked there had been a great number of accidents and quite a number of people being killed. What happened is that senior management and white miners started trying to avoid these areas or if they went into them, they went in – and out – very quickly. There were some fine people who were genuinely concerned. But I remember being with one underground manager in one of these problematic levels and I had to leave to go and get something. He really screamed at me and told me not to leave him there. Now this kind of thing has a powerful knock-on effect. What does a shift boss do if he knows the top management or the mine captain just isn't going to come into his area? He starts worrying about the situation and before long he's keeping out of the way too. Morale collapses, production drops, safety standards are relaxed, estimators don't want to go into certain areas and chose to estimate from a distance. That's what I saw at ERPM with my own eyes.'[22]

On the morning of 27 November 1985 there was a particularly serious tragedy at ERPM. The accumulated stresses in the rocks at K Shaft stope number 79, 3,000 metres underground, caused a sudden movement and 'pressure burst' in the area. The bottom of the underground roadway moved up and the top moved down to meet it. The space which had been wide enough to crawl through suddenly compacted to as little as ten centimetres and thirteen men inside the stope were crushed to death. As news of the tragedy spread through the mine, it became clear that more men were missing, even though they were some way away from the scene of the pressure burst. The death toll reached seventeen black miners, thirteen killed in the burst and four more laid low by falls of rock in another roadway near-by. The numbers involved meant that the Johannesburg press became interested and for once some space was given to the beginnings of a serious journalistic investigation. This showed that in 1985 deaths at the mine were very high, running at one a week on average over the year.[23]

Three days after the disaster, Sheryl Raine, a journalist on the Johannesburg *Star*, ran a story showing that Rand Mines had only released press statements covering thirty-seven of the forty-eight deaths at the mine since December 1984 and had withheld all information relating to eleven deaths in the year. In another accident earlier in the month, added Ms Raine, the company had only admitted that six people had been killed six days after the incident, and then only when news of the deaths was leaked to the press.

Rand Mines is part of the Barlow Rand group, an organisation which prides itself on its progressive management policies, as expressed in a corporate mission statement approved by the board. This states that the company upholds 'sound and fair employment practices, respect for the dignity of the individual ... and the maintenance of open lines of communication'. Challenged about the obvious double standards after the seventeen deaths in November 1985, Rand Mines' deputy chairman, J.R. Forbes, underlined that the company did not believe it had an obligation to disclose all deaths. Nevertheless, he claimed, everything was done to maintain high safety standards; and, he added, the mine was concerned about the death toll.[24]

The company had good reason to be concerned. ERPM has a truly extraordinary capacity to kill people who work for it. In 1981 thirty-nine were killed; forty died in 1982; twenty-four in 1983 and thirty-five in 1984. ERPM has been taking the lives of three miners a month for many years. Such levels of death should have alerted the government mining engineers and the mining inspectors that there was something fundamentally wrong at the mine. But no official action was taken. Instead, through the auspices of the Chamber of Mines, Frank Bird's scheme was employed, and, according to his patents and designs, a 'safety' audit was set up. It was so flawed that South Africa's single most dangerous mine came through with flying colours, graded in successive years with first four, then later five stars for 'excellence'.

I was sitting in the Swiss Ranch restaurant near Secunda on the evening of the Kinross miners' memorial with two colleagues from Granada TV, Phil Taylor and Lawrence Jones. We were numbed by the day's events and the usual flow of conversation was slow to come.

My attention was drawn to extensive preparations for what looked like a banquet at the next table. Three tables were being joined together. They were covered with linen and flowers were placed at suitable intervals down the centre. The cutlery and glass were laid with that careful attention to detail that betokens the arrival of important customers. About an hour went by and then the waiters and the *maître d'hôtel* stood to attention and in swept the party. They were the usual well-dressed corporate types who frequent such restaurants throughout the world, the men kitted out in shining mohair suits with sharply creased trousers and elegantly knotted ties even at ten o'clock at night. Their partners too were polished and well dressed. Only one of the men was unaccompanied by a partner. He was an unusual-looking man, powerful like a heavyweight boxer, but with his bigness foreshortened and compacted.

If it hadn't been for the mention of safety boots and the attractive American accent, I might have paid the party no more attention. But some sixth sense made me wonder if this was a rare moment of serendipity, whether the unaccompanied man might be Frank E. Bird of the International Mine Safety Rating System. I listened to snatches of their conversation with renewed attention as the American got into full flow, sometimes even repeating himself for the benefit of people at the other end of his table:

'Back in America people ask me why South African gold mines don't provide black miners with steel toe-capped boots. Why, they ask, do whites get free protective footwear, whereas blacks get rubber boots which they have to pay for? I say that I preach the gospel of total loss control and that's about all I can say. But at SASOL you have steel-toed boots. I just can't understand why the gold mines don't provide them too.'

He kept returning to the subject, probably because, having come from Secunda where the memorial meeting for the dead miners had taken place, the party were talking about Kinross. For the next ninety minutes, while they consumed their dinner, Phil, Lawrence and I sat in silence, shamelessly listening in to their conversation.

When, finally, Mr Bird and his party got up to leave I took a last gulp of Dutch courage and moved to buttonhole him. I explained that I couldn't help but overhear his remarks about safety and as a British television reporter covering the Kinross disaster I'd like to talk to him at greater length about the matter. He asked me if I knew who he was. I said I had guessed and then asked him where he was staying. By a further coincidence he was at the Holiday Inn in Secunda, as we were too. I asked to see him again to discuss Kinross and the International Mine Safety Rating System, and was agreeably surprised when he agreed to meet me over breakfast.

Mr Bird's greatest skill is his ability to talk. He talks in great rivers of words, which in turn fuse into a veritable rip-tide of language that makes Billy Graham seem like a man struggling to overcome a speech impediment. As our breakfast conversation continued it became clear that he really was a gifted evangelist, with a sure instinct for slogans, clichés and keywords, and the true missionary's zeal for talking both about himself and his pet subject – loss control – almost without end. 'I worked my way through college, you know. I was at the Lukens Steel Company on the shop floor, paying my way through school and bringing up my family. I said to myself, "Management must have a hole in its head doing things this way." Next I got involved with the Insurance Company of North America and I persuaded them to set up a safety academy. I first came to South Africa ten or so years ago. I had taught six South African mine managers on a safety course in Georgia and after that I went to South Africa to help the Chamber of Mines.

'Now you mustn't underestimate achievements here. These are world experts on heat and ventilation and it's truly been a great achievement to take migrant workers with no knowledge and give them an induction into modern ways. It's a fantastic achievement.' I reminded Mr Bird that South Africa was this very week mourning its worst-ever gold mining disaster in which 177 people had been killed at a mine using materials that had been banned in Britain for eighteen years and in his own country for more than ten.

'I told the Chamber of Mines in a report before this disaster, that some things were wrong and would have to change,' he replied. I asked him what these were, but he didn't want to discuss them since they were delicate and confidential matters and he was anxious not to lose his influence behind the scenes with the Chamber. He was, he declared, very worried indeed about what he had said at the Swiss Ranch Restaurant regarding the failure to provide black workers with safety boots being quoted or alluded to in any way. 'I'll lose my influence with the Chamber of Mines if I'm seen to have stabbed them in the back,' he explained anxiously. I tried to push Mr Bird a little further on Kinross, saying there was surely a problem there; the mine was very badly run, there were all sorts of elementary and highly dangerous malpractices being condoned and yet the mine had four or five stars for excellence under his own scheme.

'I told the Chamber of Mines before the disaster that I no longer wanted to be paid by them,' volunteered Mr Bird. 'I wanted to be seen not to be biased. I gave up a lot of money, Laurie. I don't know what your salary is, but I gave up two to three times what I pay for one of my people. What am I doing here in South Africa now? A one-day course for SASOL [the oil from coal plant]; some work for Middleburg Steel; probably some shopping next week, two public talks; probably seeing the head of safety at the Chamber of Mines and the top man at Barlow Rand. I'd like to think some more about the request for an interview. I'll think about it. But I must protect my relationship with the Chamber of Mines. I want to carry on being able to influence them to do good.'[25]

As arranged, I phoned Mr Bird that evening and asked if he had made up his mind about giving an interview on film in which the growing burden of criticism of his International Mine Safety Rating System could be put to him in a firm but friendly way. 'I'd like to sleep on that, Laurie. I'd like to sleep on that.' I rang again the following morning and was told, 'I'm afraid I have some bad news. People here feel I shouldn't do the interview. You know I'm bound to be called to give my view on the Kinross disaster at some time or another and they feel that it would be inappropriate for me to do this on British television before I've spoken to the people here who run the safety system in the mines.' I pressed Mr Bird a little further, saying that television viewers were very sophisticated people and might think that refusal of an interview meant that Mr Bird had something to hide. And, I asked, could we discuss this face to face, again over breakfast in the hotel?

Mr Bird was courteous enough to agree to have breakfast. Over coffee I asked him what allowances his Mine Safety Rating System made for the peculiarities of mining in a country dominated by apartheid. I explained that all the working black miners I had talked to were either critical or very critical about safety arrangements in the industry. They said that time and again they were asked to work in what they felt were unsafe places and many people were killed and injured as a result, sacrificed in the drive to win gold. 'That's not at all the impression that I get from talking to middle and upper management,' said Mr Bird. 'The thing that I came to recognise is that it is very difficult for outsiders like ourselves to understand the difficulties that a management group has when it has a workforce, 85 per cent of them illiterate, with many different languages, many cultural barriers between cultural groups.'

Next I attempted to put Dr Eisner's criticisms that Bird's was an unwieldy system of paper audits which, while it might be well intentioned, had no serious provision for closely examining processes and working conditions underground. Hlobane and Kinross made this argument very powerful, I added, given that both were chronically unsafe, badly run mines, yet had excellent ratings of four stars for safety under Mr Bird's scheme. At this point Mr Bird explained that he did not go on mine visits, he just designed the system and he bore no responsibility for what was missed and what was found. I countered, saying that for Mr Bird's critics this was the ultimate condemnation of the scheme. It was flawed, it failed and no one was responsible. Mr Bird disputed this line of reasoning, saying that he couldn't discuss specifics. I pressed him again for an interview on film. 'Well, my feelings haven't changed this morning as a matter of fact.' I repeated that it would seem to some viewers that it was unusual for the man behind South Africa's international safety scheme to be so near the scene of a major mine disaster in a mine his scheme rated so highly and yet decline to give an interview. But again Mr Bird's answer was no.

Next I attempted to pin Mr Bird down on the precise nature of the International Safety Rating Scheme. I asked him for specific details of which mines and companies in Europe, the United States and Australia were in the scheme and about the scheme's internal structures and executive board. There was no recall, no detail, no disclosure. I asked him why people said that the scheme and the International Loss Control Institute were based in Atlanta, Georgia, a city everybody had heard of, when in fact it was in a sleepy place called Loganville which no one had heard of. Again no satisfactory answer was forthcoming.

Finally I asked Mr Bird to confirm that prior to his involvement with the Chamber of Mines he had no mining experience. This he confirmed. I then put to Mr Bird just one more time the critics' view that the scheme was a cosmetic exercise so deeply flawed that on two highly dangerous mines, Hlobane and Kinross, it had not only failed to correct negligent and dangerous practices, it had failed even to identify them. With a combined death toll of 245, surely these disasters indicated that the International Mine Safety Rating System, in South Africa at least, was a lick of paint on a rotting door. At this point Mr Bird, a true believer faced with an agnostic, had to leave, to return to S A S O L, South Africa's oil from coal plant, to deliver another speech and collect another fee.

15 Blood on the Tracks: the History of Danger and the Danger of History in South African Mining

Near Johannesburg and little more than a couple of miles from the centre of Egoli, on land owned by the South African Chamber of Mines, is Gold Reef City, an industrial Disneyland where the mining, refining, moulding and pouring of gold is demonstrated, mostly to white visitors like myself. Here the traveller or the Johannesburger can catch the lift down a simulated mine shaft, view a well-appointed turn-of-the-century mine manager's house and watch the Zulu dancing in the Hippodrome. The culmination of this appointment with the past is the ceremonial pouring of a bar of molten gold in a specially constructed auditorium. The audience watches in silent wonderment as the liquid gold runs down the stepped elegance of a cascade pour to solidify in the bottom platform into a bar every bit as impressive as any ever stored in Fort Knox, the Kremlin, the Bank of England or the South African mint. After the gold has cooled the finished bullion is turned out on to a piece of black velvet and the price of the day for an ingot of this size is pronounced, to be greeted, unfailingly, with a gasp of amazement.

Gold Reef City is a project of the South African Chamber of Mines in which all the buildings, pavilions and shops have been donated or paid for by one of the big mining houses or by African Explosive and Chemical Industries, suppliers of dynamite to the Rand. In their care visitors are well fed, well entertained and misled by the combination of architectural pastiche, attractive restaurants, bars and cafeterias, plus diverting rides for the children, elegant souvenir shops and a marching band.

A moment's reflection on the realities of mining in South Africa today should be enough for even the most trusting mind to grasp that this is ersatz history, a hyper-reality conjured and created by an efficient department of misinformation. Tourists come not to worry but to wonder, and Gold Reef City does a fine job of taking South Africa's equivalent of William Blake's dark, satanic mills and transforming them into a video-effect of a 'fun palace'. Naturally, the conditions of the tens of thousands of black men who built the South African mines receive no mention, neither in words or pictures nor architectural form. The sponsors have seen to that – statistics, reminders, indeed all painful thoughts have been banished. So there are no replicas of the grim compounds in which mineworkers have been housed for decades. No impression of conditions underground is provided; nor is any suggestion that as well as the bewitching, beguiling lustre of gold, sorrow and anger should be placed on the historical record. Yet far from this motorised white and black minstrel show, away from the pleasing images of a past strip-mined and then carefully reconstituted into hype-as-reality, beyond the Bantustan casinos, and off the tar roads into the hills one can soon encounter the victims, the 'Tshipa' or lost ones of the mines who haunt the memory and break the heart.

They can be seen on the 'circle' at the central roundabout in Maseru, sleeping out at night, hungry and emaciated, dreaming of a job that will never come and unable to return to their villages because of the low state to which they have sunk. By five in the afternoon, they are feigning enthusiasm and singing for their supper at a Christian mission where old rules apply and hymns must be sung before anyone's hunger is assuaged.[1] But away from the towns, into the hills of Lesotho, in those remote parts of Mozambique, Ciskei and the Transkei where there is grinding poverty and tourists understandably never go, the lost ones are even easier to spot, their ill-fitting wooden legs or crude, prosthetic hands giving them away. These are the wounded images of reality which have been papered over by the Chamber and its public relations advisers who designed Gold Reef City. As I left the well-appointed car park on my last visit to the Rand's top tourist attraction, I decided to write to Ferdinand Vermeulen, the former South African Army Colonel, and one-time Bureau of State Security contact man for oil-trading operations in Thailand who oversaw the development of the museum, to explain my reservations. I don't know if he got my letter but if he did it seems to have been singularly ineffective. According to friends who have visited Gold Reef City in the recent past, nothing much has changed and the counterfeit memories are still pouring out of the kaleidoscope and being given away.

In 1982 after nearly three decades of service at one of Gold Fields' most venerable and persistently profitable mines called Venterspost, Tsibelo Mohape had an accident in an underground rockfall. Soon after he lost his leg, he received a letter from Gold Fields. It was a copy of the company's standard communication to all those migrant miners who had become surplus to requirements because of injury, and began, 'The black, company number . . . shall be repatriated to his home country.' Tsibelo was soon despatched, with a battered suitcase, across the border and forgotten. I found him high in the hills of Lesotho, somewhere in the hinterland of the university town of Roma, where he lived in a poverty-stricken village. A willowy little man who could have weighed no more than seven stone even before Venterspost took his leg, Tsibelo had a kind, intelligent face and restlessly communicative hands which gestured warmly to us through one of the gaily coloured blankets the Basotho have made into southern Africa's answer to the plaid of Scotland. A man who despite his circumstances seemed entirely free of self pity, he even hurled himself along the road on his wooden leg in a vain bid to chase a horse which had bolted at the sight of strangers with cameras and equipment and a priest with a dog collar as a guide. He spoke without bitterness of his own tragedy, a gloriously coloured Basotho equivalent of a balaclava on his head, triangulated at the top as if for a pixie and tied beneath his chin with plaited and beaded string.

'By the time I had my accident I had become the foreman or team leader. I knew I was working in a dangerous place – I had no choice. All of a sudden there was a little shower of pebbles. I decided to move, to go somewhere safer – but then a big rock came down and trapped my leg. I cried out and thankfully people answered my calls and came quickly. They pulled me out with picks and levers under the rock and because my leg was so badly crushed, put me on a stretcher. It took quite some time to get me to the surface and into an ambulance. The last thing I remember after arriving at the hospital was the doctor saying to me that my leg was dead and that since there was nothing he could do to repair the damage, the best thing was to amputate. The next thing I remember was waking in the ward to find my leg had gone.

'I have been unable to get work since the accident and for that matter I doubt if I will ever work again. The stump is very sensitive and I need to be in a comfortable place most of the time. When it is too hot I have to take the bandages off and when it's cold I have to put them on again. It seems like nothing but actually it is a constant and time-consuming routine. In any case jobs are hard enough for able-bodied men to find in Lesotho. For people like me there are no jobs – it is just impossible.

'I am experiencing serious financial difficulties right now as you can see for yourself. I have no shoes and have to go barefoot. My children are in the same position. Until the accident I did my best for them, keeping them at school. My youngest girl was at boarding school, but the accident brought this to an end. This causes me some heartache and pain for I do not know what the future holds for my family.

'My employers, the Gold Fields' group, did nothing to help me by way of rehabilitation or the provision of light work and the only communication I get from head office is the small pension paid once a month on the basis of which I and my family eke out our lives and more or less survive.'[2]

The possibility of accidents or injuries like Tsibelo Mohape's is perhaps the single most deeply rooted fear in the minds of South Africa's mineworkers. According to reliable estimates, he is one of perhaps one million human beings who have suffered a serious, disabling injury in the course of the twentieth-century development and expansion of the mining industry in this, the richest spot on earth. The death statistics are equally troubling.

So far this century perhaps 80,000 miners have died in accidents in the country's mines, 95 per cent of them black. At the current rate of death, 800 men a year, another 7,000 will expire with the century. Besides accidents, the final roll call of twentieth-century mining industrialism in South Africa includes another class of unnecessary tragedies – miners who died prematurely from avoidable diseases of the lungs like pneumoconiosis, asbestosis or emphysema. To these must be added the tens of thousands of miners who caught tuberculosis in the hot and difficult conditions of the mines, and were deported back to their homelands to die soon after. Given the scale of mining in South Africa, the unfortunate conditions which have obtained for so long and the size and vulnerability of the labour force, it is probably reasonable to assume that the roll call in these categories amounts to at least another 88,000 men. This is the bottom line – the production of South Africa's precious underground commodities will have in all probability cost 175,000 lives by the end of the twentieth century.[3]

It is always difficult to reckon with such statistics and it may help to think of these numbers of people in terms of a substantial book like the New Testament in which every word in the volume is a headstone for an unmarked grave, a memento of an individual life which ended in tragic circumstances and avoidable pain. Before the emergence of a black mineworkers' union in 1982 there was little or no public discourse in South Africa about safety in the mining industry. Instead with five-star safety rating schemes and creative use of statistics, the Chamber of Mines had complete hegemony in mining matters, saying all was well. There was no one to challenge their claims to be world leaders in the field of safety.

For a while in the wake of the Kinross disaster they were cautious with such claims. More recently, however, the claims have begun to reappear. In October 1990, for example, the Chamber of Mines contradicted an NUM statement that the industry had a callous disregard for the safety of its employees.

'In fact,' the Chamber of Mines stated in a press release, 'producing our gold and coal as safely as possible is the industry's primary concern and with few exceptions fatality and injury rates have shown a consistently declining trend in recent years.'[4]

As far as compensation for injuries was concerned, the statement added, the South African mining industry was a world leader. A scheme had been in operation long before it was legally required in South Africa or Britain.

This statement is a worrying falsification both of the industry's current record and of its dangerous past. *The Economist* seemed nearer to the truth in 1983 in an editorial titled 'Unsafe But not Sorry' in which it sharply criticised the 'appalling safety record' of the South African gold mines. 'The overall fatality rate has barely fallen in the last two decades,' the paper stated.[5] As for the Chamber of Mines' pretensions to have acted ahead of the law in the development of compensation schemes, this bears little relation to the truth, as South Africa's new historians have been at pains to point out. Since 1978 the University of the Witwatersrand has been running a series of history workshops as part of an attempt to reassess the past. One of the outstanding products of the workshop has been Luli Callinicos's two-volume *People's History of South Africa*. The first volume deals with the early history of the gold mines from the discovery of the metal on the Rand until 1924.

Among the earliest hazards of mining noted by Callinicos was the difficulty of getting to the mines, with hungry people covering vast distances, arriving exhausted, and in many cases dying before they could find work. Those who made it to the mines encountered new risks, with poor living and working conditions taking their toll of human life without hint of compassion or compensation.[6] The record of the pioneer compound, De Beers' Consolidated Mines in Kimberley, attests to the frequency of fatalities. In the early days, industry leaders and other doctors covered up a smallpox epidemic to help the mining companies. As a result there were hundreds of unnecessary deaths.[7] Below ground, as William Worger demonstrates, conditions were so bad that in 1886 a local representative of the British Standard Bank wrote to head office to complain about the 'reckless disregard for human life'.[8] A comparison of death rates between Kimberley and Britain showed that diamond miners were twelve times more likely to die than miners in the United Kingdom, who had begun to benefit from government regulation of the industry.[9]

The Tswana chief, Sekgoma, spoke out fiercely against conditions in the gold mines of the Rand. Early in 1903, reported the *Mafeking Mail*, the chief explained that he 'sent a batch of labourers to the Rand . . . at £3 a month, all found, for three months on surface work. On arrival there they were forced into a contract of six months, against their wishes, at 45 shillings.

'The death rate there was something appalling,' Sekgoma added. 'Dead bodies were hurled into an open cart and thrown into a large trench.'[10]

The Chamber's suggestion that the industry acted with decency or despatch to protect and compensate injured workers is a public relations posture without basis in historical fact. Progress came slowly to the industry and was the result of trade union pressure and government intervention. By 1893 President Kruger of the Transvaal had appointed his first Inspector of Mines, the Liverpool-born mining engineer Edgar Rathbone, a partner in the firm of Bewick Moreing and manager of the Salisbury Gold Mining Company. Rathbone assisted in drawing up the early mining regulations, his primary aim according to the *South African Dictionary of National Biography* being 'to reduce the accident rate, which he considered to be the worst in the world'.[11] In 1907 the Earl of Selborne appointed a commission on health in the mines. It reported in 1910 that an alarming number of black miners were dying of pneumonia in the compounds, and that large numbers of white miners were dying of respiratory diseases.[12]

This was confirmed in 1913 during a strike by white mineworkers, who pointed out that fourteen of the eighteen members of their 1907 strike committee had died of miners' silicosis in the intervening six years. Tom Mathews, the union leader who did so much to marshal the miners' case against the mine-owners on the health issue in 1913, was dead within two years, again of silicosis. In 1913, speaking of the mine-owners' failure to take measures to reduce dust levels underground, he stated pointedly, 'We consider that our health is more important than your dividends.'[13]

In this period parts of South Africa's mining industry came under the scrutiny of an outspoken inspector of mines for Boksburg called Fergusson: 'the death of a Native', he stated bluntly, 'is not looked upon by miners here as a very serious affair.

'It is well known to the directors that hundreds of men lose their lives annually through carelessness on the part of the miners and apathy on the part of the officials, and yet, speaking generally, they appear to make no personal effort in attempting to have matters improved in this direction.

'It is difficult to understand this anomalous attitude,' he continued, 'the explanation may lie in the fact that, as the old adage has it, "dead men tell no tales".'[14]

In 1913 the Australian writer Ambrose Pratt published the results of his investigations into conditions on the Rand. In the wake of the Selborne Commission he focused on the true death rates of the mining industry. The 1910 Selborne Commission Report, he underlined, 'makes it fairly clear that the death rate for white underground workers on the Rand must be from about 25 to 30 per thousand per annum, which is nearly four times the normal death rate of men of their age'. 'The Rock drillers of the Rand,' he continued, 'work from seven to nine years and their average age at death is thirty-five . . . The death rate from all causes in the British army during the Boer War was . . . substantially lower than amongst the white miners.'[15]

As for the death rate among black miners, Pratt reached even more worrying conclusions. Again looking at statistics quoted in the 1910 report, Pratt fixed the general death rate 'for all natives' at 75 per 1,000 per year with 'tropical natives' dying at a rate of 175 per 1,000 per year. But, he added, these figures only included people who expired on mine properties and took no account of those discharged through sickness or injury who subsequently died either on the road home or after arrival at their kraals from pneumonia, tuberculosis and silicosis or from serious accidents. Once these were estimated and put into the account, Pratt concluded that it was fair to say, 'The mines "polish off" tropical natives with remorseless expedition, practically decimating them every year.' Some mines, he added, had death rates 'for all natives' in excess of 100 per 1,000 workers per year. Others of a precisely similar character had a rate more than twelve times better, which proved that mining on the Rand was not inherently unhealthy. 'The high death rate is due', Pratt wrote, 'to some of the mines working in a manner that disgraces humanity . . . The system is one of thinly disguised, blood-smeared slavery . . . The foundations of it are the blacks, who toil for a pittance and perish like locusts.'[16]

Quoting E.J. Moynihan, a man whom he describes as an 'expert mining statist', Pratt stated that he was glad that he possessed no mining shares, because

Every £1,200 paid in dividends on these fields, in the five years ending with 1909, has meant the known and avoidable loss of a human life, without counting serious accidents and at least twenty illnesses known to the doctors.

299

If all the criminals in the Fort had been loose for five years, they would have done less harm to the community than this mining industry did in that time in this gold-stricken place where blood is spilt like water, human lives thrown away like dirt, where lungs are turned to stone below ground and above ground hearts [are] turned to flint.[17]

Conditions in some sections of the industry began to improve following government regulations and the formation of a Chamber of Mines Accident Prevention Committee in 1913. But the Chamber of Mines' membership was far from united in pursuit of responsible standards and many mining companies and individual mines dragged their feet. Even in those companies where there was some evidence of reform, the doctors and safety engineers charged with developing new routines were often put under heavy pressure. As Randall Packard has shown, the huge size of the labour force on the Rand, together with the appalling conditions of work and life, ensured that the mines would play a central role in the early development of tuberculosis in South Africa.[18]

Packard shows that doctors might have been aware of the problems caused by the intense heat, defective diet and poor living conditions on the Rand. But as Dr Brock, a government medical officer, explained to one commission of inquiry, he was supposed to examine 900 mine recruits in one day, with pressure to get through the examinations in three and a half hours. This was the equivalent of one 'examination' every fifteen seconds.

With the First World War, the era of total worker neglect came to an end. But mining companies still skimped on accommodation, resisted generous space allowances, claiming that black workers liked to huddle together, and flatly opposed the idea of allowing workers to live with their families in proper houses. Yet this was the solution favoured by the Chamber of Mines' special adviser William C. Gorgas, who had solved similar problems during the construction of the Panama Canal. Only if people were allowed to live together with their families, away from all the infections of the compound, he argued, would death rates come down. His argument was persuasive but he was ignored.[19]

There was change, but slow and belated, usually in the form of half-measures grudgingly adopted. Some commentators mistook the slightest cosmetic change for something more substantial. Writing in the 1930s Adèle Lizard stated:

The bad old days of indifference varying upon inhumanity which marked

300

the end of the last century and the beginning of this century have disappeared forever.

He [the migrant worker] is a long way from home but it does not matter so much now, for he is protected and cared for by an industry which has, with the passing of years, found a heart as well as a brain.[20]

These were comforting phrases, but they flew in the face of reality. Accident rates were unforgivably high. Miners who caught TB or scurvy, another disease of mine life, were deported back to their kraals without care or attention. There they acted as vectors of disease which moved out into their communities and cut down whole families. And while Adèle Lizard believed the mining companies had discovered their hearts, most of them remained preoccupied with their balance sheets, declining even to introduce water-borne sanitation systems. Prior to 1938 only four mines on the Rand had them, the rest relying on a degrading and unhygienic system of slopping out.[21]

Randall Packard detects a consistent pattern in the behaviour of the mining companies and white political parties and concludes that the 'South African authorities methodically removed the health problems of blacks from the purview of white society'. The persistent refusal of the white population to underwrite proper conditions of housing, education and nourishment for the majority was a conscious choice by leading elements in white society. They did not care for the black majority and used the resources of the country to look after themselves. The Chamber of Mines was at the centre of this process, which Packard graphically describes as the erection of fiscal roadblocks against virtually all serious attempts to improve social conditions for the majority.[22]

The Chamber of Mines continued with its parsimonious policies during and after the Second World War, resisting the attempts of black miners to build their own union, refusing to negotiate and toughening already stern regimes inside the compounds with new measures to improve 'security' against dissent. In the postwar years, the industry was to experience an enormous boom and make extraordinary profits. But on the critical question of safety and health, the central organising principle of the Chamber of Mines was still to do the absolute minimum and obstruct the radical reform which it was becoming increasingly obvious would have to come one day.

The pressing need for reform was underscored twice in the first three months of 1960. First there was a mining disaster few have heard about; then came events in a town that became world famous: that town, Sharpeville,

STUDDED WITH DIAMONDS

left an indelible mark on South Africa's political history and its troubled relations with the outside world. On 21 March sixty-eight unarmed people were killed by South African police, who fired into a crowd protesting against the pass laws. In one afternoon the South African government and police spelled out the inner meaning of the social structure they were putting into place in one of the most beautiful countries in the world. On the other side of Vereeniging away from Sharpeville and towards Sasolburg, lies the location of the other tragedy, which happened two months earlier. At Coalbrook, some twelve miles away from Sharpeville, vast areas of a coal-mine belonging to Clydesdale Collieries, a company with strong British connections, collapsed on 21 January. Four hundred and thirty-five miners were trapped underground and never seen again. A month after the disaster the company hadn't managed to produce a comprehensive list of the dead men. Just as Sharpeville illuminated the social structure of apartheid, so Coalbrook put the spotlight on the shoddy working practices and degraded human relations of the country's greatest industry.[23]

The numbing size of the disaster, the worst in all South Africa's history, sent shock waves throughout the country. The mining industry was seized with panic. The British Prime Minister Harold Macmillan was in South Africa, accompanied by a huge phalanx of the world's press. The white miners' union was in full cry over the failure of the safety system in the country's key industry and the Chamber of Mines decided to mount a high-profile rescue effort even though it was pretty clear that hope was gone. Amid great publicity, special drills were brought in, first from Iscor, the state-owned steel company, then from the gold mines at Kinross and Welkom and then finally from the United States. The government's anxiety over its flawed record on industrial safety was such that it was anxious to do anything in its power to give an appearance of activity. When a cranky diviner claimed he could identify the location of some of the trapped miners with his mystic powers, the Minister of Mines backed his appeal for a hole to be drilled. Support was only withdrawn when someone pointed out that the area the diviner had identified lay well outside any of the ground ever worked by the mine, which meant it was unlikely to contain anyone, alive or dead.[24]

Despite heroic efforts on the part of many individuals who worked day and night, the rescue effort was deeply flawed. The original drill to cut into the areas where the men were thought to be was far too slow. The positioning of the bore-hole was also handicapped by the fact that the staff of South Africa's geological survey weren't called on to help unscramble

302

the mine plans. In any case these were in such a grievously defective state that the rescue attempt became little more than a token effort, conducted without public acknowledgement that methane gas had spread through the mine. On 5 February, after fifteen days of declining hopes, misleading pronouncements by government officials and huge crowds of voyeuristic white tourists visiting Coalbrook with cars and picnic hampers, the Prime Minister, Dr Hendrik Verwoerd, told parliament that hope had gone. The directors of Clydesdale Collieries had, he reported, informed him with grave regret that there was no further hope for the 435 men underground. It was, said Dr Verwoerd, time for South Africa 'to . . . subject itself to the Will of the Almighty'. Mine disasters, like apartheid laws, were apparently the result of divine intervention rather than corporate neglect.[25]

The White Mine Workers' Union, acting for once like an organisation with serious obligations to all those who worked underground, took a different view. The union had been engaged in a long struggle against unsafe conditions in the newest and deepest gold mines in the Orange Free State and had repeatedly come up against the failures of the government mining inspectors to do their jobs properly. The union's leading officials inclined to the view that, in some cases at least, the indulgence shown to the mining houses was obtained by the payment of bribes. Then in December 1959, two months before the Coalbrook disaster, there was an explosion at a gold mine in the Welkom area which killed twenty-four miners. Faced with this latest loss of life, the white miners' union threatened strike action if there was no proper inquiry. The union also demanded that an inspector who was known for his independent spirit be put in charge of the inquiry. The inquiry had just begun sitting with the inspector in charge when the Coalbrook collapse took place.[26]

Faced with Coalbrook, a disaster of the greatest magnitude, the white miners' union again moved with speed, pressing three demands on the government of the day. First, the union insisted on the immediate dismissal of the government mining engineer. Second, they pressed for an *ad hoc* committee of experts to be appointed to investigate conditions in all mines where working miners had complaints about safety. And, third, they demanded that a full judicial commission of inquiry should be appointed to investigate government regulation of safety in South African mines. To press its point the union repeated its warning that it would no longer tolerate feeble supervision, ineffective regulation and the deliberate avoidance of proper public inquiries. If there was no break with the past there would be strikes in coal-mines at first but spreading to gold and other commodities if absolutely necessary. With growing evidence of serious negligence at Coalbrook, on the part of the Mines Inspectorate as well as the Coalbrook management, the government capitulated. The government mining engineer was sacked.[27]

In addition, an *ad hoc* committee was set up and a judicial commission of inquiry instituted under the chairmanship of Judge Jacobus Marais. The members of the commission were appointed on 1 April 1960 and held their first meeting at the Palace of Justice in Pretoria on 11 April. Then the commission started moving around the country looking at problems in the field and for five days a month from August to November heard evidence in public and under oath. Despite this promising start, the commission's work was not allowed to proceed to a proper conclusion. For its part the government was determined to calm the excited situation and worked hard to reintegrate the leaders of the white miners' union. The Chamber of Mines followed suit and made every effort to restructure the industry in such a way as to recover the loyalty of the white union.[28] The moment of danger in which there were meaningful contacts between white miners and black unionists involved with the South African Congress of Trade Unions passed and SACTU was soon outlawed in a wave of repression in the 1960s of which Sharpeville was only the beginning.

Throughout the rest of the decade the mines continued their heady expansion on a strict apartheid basis, with the white miner now an even more cosseted member of the management team, his extensive 'rights' to command, manipulate and even violently enforce his will on his black colleagues written in tablets of stone. He could even take his 'piccanin' home with him and use him as a 'garden boy' with the permission of the mines.

It was three years after the Coalbrook disaster that the Marais Commission's first interim report saw the light of day. The interim report covered only one of the commission's five terms of reference. It focused exclusively on the failure of the government mining engineer and the Inspectorate of Mines to enforce safe working conditions in the country's premier industry. Nevertheless, it was a devastating indictment of complacency, disorganisation and maladministration in these key government departments. Among the long list of failures catalogued were: 'lack of discipline; insufficiently frequent and insufficiently thorough routine inspections of mines; the almost total absence of mine plans for emergency purposes; wholly inadequate dust sampling; inadequacy of staff in almost all ranks; lack of leadership from the higher to the lower ranks . . . with many signs of suspicion and disloyalty

... factors [which] all played a part in bringing about the almost complete failure of the Division to meet the crisis precipitated by the Coalbrook disaster'.[29]

Judge Marais and his colleagues were to draft further reports dealing with the causes of the Coalbrook disaster and the broader problem of safety in the South African mining industry at large. Today, thirty years later, these reports have still not been published. Until the reports are finally published, the truth about Coalbrook and safety in the gold mines of South Africa will continue to be kept from the public.

At Coalbrook, as at Kinross, the stupidity and discrimination of the apartheid system added to the toll of unhappiness. A government disaster fund was opened; but it paid out on the usual differential calculus, generously to whites and parsimoniously to blacks. As a result, while the widows of the white miners got pensions for life of from £30 to £75 a month depending on how many children they had, African widows received a pitiful once-and-for-all lump sum of £180. This crude racial discrimination was duplicated at fund-raising concerts organised by the ostensibly liberal newspaper the *Rand Daily Mail*. Blacks could appear on stage at the benefit, but they were not allowed to sit in the audience. The memorial services for the dead miners were also organised on an apartheid basis – one at the mine for blacks only, one elsewhere for whites.[30]

In his important contemporary article on Coalbrook and mine safety in the magazine *Africa South*, Dr H.J. Simons underlined the fact that mining disasters were not acts of God: 'An accident is not a fortuitous, unavoidable event. It is broadly the result of defective adaptation to or control of the environment and could have been averted by the adoption of adequate care or technical and material safeguards.'[31]

The Marais commission appeared to follow this line of thinking in its deliberations. But because the government and the Chamber of Mines wanted to lower the profile on the tragic details of their failure to provide a safe working environment, its four further reports never saw the light of day. Another critical recommendation of the Marais commission has also been ignored. The commission noted that the drive to sink deeper mines in the Orange Free State was causing safety problems. As mines went deeper, so the stresses in the rocks accumulated and the likelihood of rockfalls and roof collapses increased. If the mining companies were to live up to their responsibilities they should investigate these problems systematically with a specialised research institute. This was not set up. Instead the mining companies headed straight for the lower depths without serious thought for the men who would bear the consequences. With the pace of development in the Free State increasing and a high rate of accidents in development of the new mines, Dr Simons, a law professor at the University of Cape Town until he was detained in 1960, noted there was now 'an accident death rate . . . similar to the incidence on the Witwatersrand fifty years ago'.[32] It is these deep mines which today have the most worrying accident rates, estimated by Jean Leger and May Hermanus of NUM as being so severe that for the men working in their deepest and most vulnerable areas there is a one in ten chance of being killed in the course of their mining careers.

With the impetus for reform buried in blood above ground at Sharpeville and the pressure for safety sidetracked by the neutering of the Marais commission, the scene was set for an intensification of the cruelty and double standards of the mining industry. Improved health-care systems were introduced for the white miners, the capos in the camps. But for the hundreds of thousands of black miners who did most of the work, the inadequacy of provision became even more pronounced. For their chest X-rays white miners were given full-plate radiological examinations. Black miners by contrast had miniature X-rays which, while they might be sufficient to detect the presence of tuberculosis, were next to useless when it came to picking up the early warning signs of silicosis or asbestosis. White miners who took fewer risks were supplied with free footwear with reinforced steel toe-caps. Black miners, who were more likely to have rocks drop on their feet, got rubber boots and in most cases had to pay for them. Injured white miners were given first-class medical care in white-only hospitals. Injured blacks by contrast were processed in the mining equivalents of charity wards.[33]

Even in the slightly more progressive companies there were fundamental ethical problems and medical limitations. Dr Michael Barry was a mine medical officer from 1949 to 1977 when he left 'with a cold, smouldering anger because I'd had enough'. Dr Barry worked at the Sir Ernest Oppenheimer Memorial Hospital, supposedly an Anglo showpiece for black miners. 'I saw a lot of preventable injuries there. But when I tried to raise the causes of them with my colleagues, they weren't interested. They were preoccupied with putting people together again, not stopping the things which injured them in the first place.'

Dr Barry tried to get some change on heatstroke, on better protective clothing, better lighting down the mines, a reduction of the black to white death ratio which, adjusted for numbers, he put at two to one. He also noted that skin infections were much worse among blacks, largely because they were denied equal laundry facilities and therefore washed and changed less frequently. Barry qualified as a mines rescue brigadesman so he could get to accident victims as quickly as possible. 'Men were dying between the face and the mine hospital. I would say let's get down there alongside them. But this was not popular with my colleagues.'[34]

Magnificent new clinics like the Medical Bureau of Occupational Diseases were built for certain miners in Johannesburg. Outside the clinic a fine statue depicts three men, one white miner and two black ones. While black miners could stand behind a white one in a statue, they were not allowed to follow him into the high-tech clinic because it was run on a strict apartheid basis. The differential calculus of apartheid extended to arrangements for post-mortems and funerals, but the extraordinary crudity of the process can perhaps be most clearly discerned in the compensation arrangements for black and white miners. In 1967 the mining companies and the State were paying out benefits of £5 million in compensation for lung diseases caused by the mines. Two-thirds of the total went to whites, who made up less than a tenth of the labour force. When white miners were crippled with pneumoconiosis they received £615 a year, a far from generous payment but none the less one on which it was possible to stay alive. Blacks crippled or dying from silicosis, tuberculosis, asbestosis or the mesothelioma cancers of the asbestos mines, qualified for no such regular relief. Until 1977 their only 'right' was a one-off payment of £228. This paltry sum, which many migrant miners dying of lung diseases and unaware of their rights failed to claim, was, in the view of some observers, a more or less direct invitation to the mining companies to use and abuse people. They could hire them and then discard them when they were sick, returning them to the labour reserves and replacing them with another tranche of expendable mine 'boys' recruited through the Witwatersrand Native Labour Association, the forerunner of TEBA.

In 1977, as the mines began to switch recruiting away from miners from sending areas outside South Africa and to look for a more stabilised labour force, there was a partial restructuring of this extraordinary system. Blacks now received regular payments rather than a once and for all pittance, but the ready reckoner of apartheid still applied. Injured or crippled black miners still were not – and still are not – entitled to the same benefits as whites. Instead the system became based on wage rates rather than racial classification. Since the wage gap is still huge between white and black miners, major inequalities persisted. As a result a white miner with a second-degree compensatable disease was, in 1986, entitled to a 33,207 rand lump-sum payment, whether dead or alive. A black man by contrast received 2,462 rand if the disease was picked up while he was still alive and just 1,641 rand, 33 cents after death. This is one-twentieth of the amount paid to whites.

For the first time after 1977, the mining companies began trying to help the growing number of paraplegics created by the mines. Before 1977 these injured black miners (who had lost one or both legs or had their spines crushed in rockfalls) were dumped in the labour reserves and denied any assistance other than the pitiable lump-sum payment of a few hundred pounds. After 1977 they began to get some sort of pension. In the more progressive companies like Anglo they might also be given light work or some kind of retraining. In companies like Gold Fields the sense of responsibility was not so developed: injured miners were given a free wheelchair and no help with re-employment. In an important research project, the Witwatersrand University sociologist Shelley Arckles dissected the many flaws in the new system, which while unquestionably superior to what went before, still left crippled miners bewildered, friendless and poor. In a series of interviews with crippled miners in Lesotho she showed that pensions were still inadequate and failed to cater for the special needs of disabled people – for equipment, travel and nourishing food. There were also, she documented, many serious problems in being confined to a wheelchair in a mountainous region where there were no proper roads or pavements.[35]

It seems clear that the South African mining companies are some distance from being world leaders in any aspect of mining safety, health, rehabilitation or compensation. It is also important to note that while on some fronts a modest amount of progress was belatedly being made, on others decisions were being taken which weakened South Africa's mining safety laws and deregulated the business environment of the country's greatest industry. This is the background to Kinross and the spate of other disasters in the 1980s. With the importation of Frank Bird and his safety scheme in the mid-1970s the Chamber of Mines tilted the balance decisively against government regulation of safety and opted for a particularly soft form of self-regulation, where mine safety was supposed to be achieved by paper audits conducted by inhouse auditors. Parallel with this move, the analytical framework for appraising the causation of accidents began to shift. In a 1981 survey Chamber of Mines' researchers reached the conclusion that 18,649 accidents out of the 18,997 industry totals were due to 'danger inherent in the work or to misadventure'. In the eyes of Britain's mining safety expert,

Dr Herbert Eisner, this is a ludicrous attitude to accidents. 'Dangers can't be inherent to work. There are choices and options all the time,' he told me. 'To ascribe 98·17 per cent of all accidents to causes which are essentially beyond control is to give up.' Parallel with the process of blaming the situation or the victim, Dr Eisner was becoming worried about another development. Government mining inspectors seemed to be in short supply as well as underpaid and demoralised.

South Africa, Eisner calculated, had about 800,000 miners in 1985 working in 893 units. The total number of inspectors to enforce the law was ninety-eight. Once allowances were made for the different scale of the industry, this was somewhere between a half and a third of the number in Britain, where traditionally factory and mine inspectors have been far from numerous. Yet South Africa's mines are among the deepest, hottest and most complex in the world.[36] South African mine inspectors were also, incidentally, expected to cover all the massive surface plants and operations, whereas in Britain such installations were the responsibility of the Factory Inspectorate. According to Jean Leger, one of the safety advisers to the black mineworkers' union, the government mining engineer's office is also seriously underfunded and unable to pay market rates to inspectors. The shortage is accentuated by the pressure of statutory work and particularly, since there are so many fatal accidents, the pressure to conduct fatal accident inquiries. As a result of this complex of pressures, the inspectors do less and less forensic or preventative work and the mines are left increasingly deregulated.

'Deregulation is without a doubt the key to what has been happening on the health and safety front here for some years,' says Leger. 'The tragedy is that the government and the state have bought the arguments of people like Frank Bird. They believe that mining companies can regulate themselves. This is a major departure from previous attitudes and beliefs, which, however poorly they were enforced, assumed that there were fundamental conflicts of interest.

'The Marais commission, for example, assumed that anyone digging below the surface of the earth was engaged in a dangerous act, and that there would always be a conflict between the pressure for production and the pressure for safety. It was the role of the State to mediate this conflict. But the Chamber of Mines has been pushing hard against this view of the world. In 1987 the government mining engineer and the Department of Mineral and Energy Affairs accepted the argument that there was no conflict. So mining inspectors are kept in short supply while the mining companies appoint loss control officers, whom they employ, to do the paper audits under the Mine Safety Rating System. Even where there is new legislation, like on noise, the government mining engineers and the inspectors have been unable to do anything about enforcing standards. This is a tragic state of affairs because the drills are so noisy and tens of thousands of people are going deaf as a result.'[37]

Faced with an almost nightmarish array of safety problems, the black miners' union has fought for the right of its members to elect safety representatives as the first way of breaching the battery of racist legislation that has held black miners in check for so long. Archie Luhlabo was one of the earliest black safety representatives, following an agreement at the Finsch diamond mine where he worked.

'The overwhelming majority of people who work underground in South Africa are black. Most of the time in my experience the white miner isn't even there while the black miners and team leaders are doing the work. Black safety officers have the same experience and practical knowledge as the working miners and speak the same language. If I see a place underground that's not safe, then it is my obvious duty to stop the job until it is made right. Gold mines are deeper and more dangerous than diamond mines and in the gold mines the push for production is enormous. The white miners who are supposedly responsible for safety are all earning huge sums on bonus. They push us into dangerous places to get production for the company and higher pay for themselves. That's why the gold-mining companies have resisted elected safety officers. That's why they hold back on allowing black miners to be scheduled persons with a right to take decisions about safety. But in the end we will get what we need because a safe working environment is a human right.'[38]

The miners of South Africa are understandably preoccupied with human rights; and gave expression to this concern by drawing up a safety bill of rights. In addition to the right to elect safety stewards or representatives, the bill underlines that miners should have the right to refuse dangerous work, the right to summon inspectors and accompany them on inspections, the right of access to all information about health, safety and the environment, and the right to high-quality training. Miners should also, the document concludes, have a right to a meaningful say in the running of the mines and the planning of the industry's future. As the union's former general secretary, Cyril Ramaphosa, explains, 'Our democratic rights have been bought with pain and paid for in blood. In the new South Africa that is busy being born, who shall deny us them?'[39]

16   Resources for a Journey of Hope

With South African society in transition, the mining houses are playing a cautious, waiting game, scanning the new environment, constructing scenarios, identifying options and trying to second-guess how much change the twin pressures of democracy and the black miners' union will in the end force upon them. Change is long overdue. For a century or more the generous harvests of the South African landscape, natural as well as commercial, have been allocated according to a unique and inflexible set of standing orders. The best of everything, of crops above ground and minerals below it, of water and power supply, of economic and business opportunity, of social provision from culture through medicine to recreational and sporting facilities, has all been reserved for whites only. The consequences of this entailment of all resources on racial lines cut through communities and consciences, and built Berlin walls in every township in the land. As a result South Africa today has the widest measured gap between rich and poor in the world. Ninety-five per cent of business undertakings, 87 per cent of the land and 85 per cent of wealth all are in white hands.[1]

In area after area property has been improperly obtained by direct and deliberate expropriation from black communities, families and individuals, involving a process of state-sanctioned sequestration on a scale well beyond the Highland clearances and one which has distinct echoes of the Kristallnacht in Germany in the 1930s.

In a country like South Africa, where there has been so much systematised injustice for so long, there is a certain bleak, unconscious humour in the talk of 'free markets' and 'free enterprise' now current. Nevertheless, as South African businesses reposition themselves for the period of turbulence and change which is now developing, it is behind the ritual incantation of these concepts that the giant mining companies hope to shelter. Crying business

311

freedom and the imperatives of markets, some of the most compromised corporations in the world hope to sanctify the dishonourable takings and forged till receipts of a hundred years of slavery.

The journalist Allister Sparks has likened South Africa to a giant Monopoly board at which the vast majority of the population has been forbidden to sit down until all the land has been occupied and all the properties have been bought.[2] The six great mining houses, Anglo American/De Beers, Anglovaal, Gencor, Gold Fields, Johannesburg Consolidated Investments and Rand Mines, are by far the most powerful players at the Monopoly board and leave neither seats nor elbow room for very many other players. After a hundred years of white domination, they own great swathes of the economy. Their financial, industrial and land holdings are immense, and their influence on the political economy of South Africa is decisive.

According to the independent publisher and researcher Robin McGregor, one group alone, Anglo/De Beers, controls the bank and runs the casino almost on its own.[3] The group controls companies worth more than 50 per cent of the total aggregated value of all the many businesses quoted on the Johannesburg stock exchange, he estimates. De Beers' chairman Julian Ogilvie Thompson prefers a lower figure and states that the extent of Anglo's vast corporate hacienda is 'only' 30 per cent of the total. Even this is an astonishing figure, unparalleled anywhere else in the world.[4] Research by a future government of South Africa will doubtless resolve the statistical dispute. Wherever the truth lies between 30 and 50 per cent, it seems fair to say that Anglo/De Beers floats upon the South African economy more or less as if the *Titanic* was parked in Johannesburg's Wemmer Pan or London's Serpentine.

The group's extraordinary power begins with its dominance over the worldwide trade in diamonds and spreads outwards to encompass all but one of the other five leading mining houses which group together in the South African Chamber of Mines. Anglo unquestionably controls Johannesburg Consolidated Investments, decisively influences Rand Mines and has significant minority shareholdings in the Gencor Group and in Gold Fields of South Africa. Of the big six mining houses only one organisation, Anglovaal, stands in any meaningful sense free of its writ; and even in this case there are important joint ventures and business links.

Taken together, the great South African mining companies form a maze of interlocking directorships, mutual agreements, restrictive arrangements, and monopolistic and monopsonistic business practices. Harnessing the ample supply of profits provided by a hundred years of racial capitalism,

312

these corporations, together with the big insurance companies, have been able to enclose not only the peaks, but the foothills and grassy uplands of most economic activity in the country. The Anglo/De Beers' group alone has interests in newspapers, brewing, paper-making, steel-making, car manufacturing and distribution, farming, chemicals, hotels, property and banking.[5]

The idea that Anglo operates or participates in anything remotely resembling a free and equitable market is not something accepted by *The Economist*:

The Anglo empire has grown to its present size not because it is more efficient than its world-wide competitors but because it is a master at running cartels and dominating markets. Any mistakes it has made have been papered over with profits from diamonds and from its dominance of the South African economy.

This secretive giant has shown little taste for competing in free markets. That explains why it has failed to become a global company despite its size and clout and why it now finds itself trapped within the gilded cage of South Africa.[6]

The burden of evidence suggests that the South African economy in general, and mining in particular, mimics the tense, inbred world of white political monopoly which has run the country for so long. Since their origins under British colonial power, the mining houses have had scant regard for human rights; and since the arrival in power of the Nationalists in 1948, the companies have collaborated closely with the apartheid State, voluntarily choosing to become entwined in its policies and brutalities and augmenting these with many cruelties of their own.

Today their mines and mining compounds are, as the evidence shows, dangerous places in which to live or work. Their business practices are dense, convoluted and often motivated more by a desire to camouflage realities and continue old ways than by any demonstrable pursuit of competitive efficiency. There is little meaningful accountability to shareholders, less to employees or society at large. Their engineering record is flawed and the real potential of mines often handicapped by short-term financial pursuits and the needs of an authoritarian culture concerned with the reproduction of hierarchical power rather than any free and fulfilling flow of goods, services or information.

The mining houses act as merchant banks as well as operational industrial companies and if the slovenly, corporate incompetence of Gencor, which caused Kinross, is anything to go by, they do not always excel at either task. Swollen, unfocused bundles of economic bounty, they have been arrogant in their disregard for the rights and dignities of human beings. It is therefore no surprise that their record for honouring the natural environment is so poor. And in the end just about everything they do is weighed down by the past and by the gargantuan size of their bureaucratic and compound operations which are, as the evidence suggests, out of control.

In present circumstances their public relations departments finger the rosaries of self-advertised 'responsibility' on a daily basis. Privately, and in their hearts, the real leaders of South African mining know that their behaviour during the apartheid years has cost them the last remnants of legitimacy. As Gordon Waddell put it to a JCI board meeting before retiring in frustration: 'Which of you wishes this company to be remembered as the IG Farben of South Africa?'[7]

With this collapse of morale in the world of South African mining, there is unlimited scope for well-considered radical change. In every mine in the country there is an oppressive compound which needs to be rethought and replaced by new towns, where people can live with their families as enfranchised citizens of a free country. In each mine a range of working practices will have to be put in place which extinguishes racism and colonial authoritarianism and replaces these disfigurements with a rights-based culture of optimism, co-operation and mutual regard. A major public inquiry seems essential if underground safety is ever to be assured. Without one it is difficult to see how a just system of compensation is to be achieved for the many victims of malpractice who lost family members or parts of their own bodies without proper compensation in the past.

In the broader business and industrial culture, an ethic of national purpose and social accountability will have to be germinated, replacing the short-term calculus of exploitative deal-making and easy profit. An exhaustive survey of the contrived, complex and secretive structures by which the mining companies have been conducting aspects of their businesses is also probably a precondition for any genuine progress. How otherwise will the huge resources and accumulated profits of the past be traced, identified and understood, let alone brought rationally into play in the reconstruction of a nation?

At this turning point it is important to remember that in addition to huge reservoirs of imprisoned human potential, South Africa remains especially rich in natural and mineral resources. For obvious social and environmental reasons it becomes vital in the new South Africa to organise their balanced,

314

orderly and benign development. This too will probably require a decisive break with the greed-driven methods which have characterised the last hundred years.

In years to come it will be the privilege as well as the responsibility of South Africa's newly enfranchised citizens to harness these resources and to devise the organisational structures which convert their country from a house of bondage into a home of freedom. The black miners' union, that estimable conspiracy of hope which it was my privilege to witness during its most heroic period, remains highly sceptical that, unprompted and unpressed, the mining houses are capable of serious reform. The union points to the continuing failure to make funds available to end the migrant labour system, with all its recurrent violence; and the union's leaders underline that without social change the political handcuffs will have been removed but the powerful leg-irons, which have hobbled an entire people economically for generations, will still remain in place. Accordingly NUM favours radical measures including public accountability and ownership in mining to ensure that safe working and living conditions emerge and future profits and surpluses are used to benefit the community as a whole.

Years ago Anthony Barker found words to express the agony he had witnessed while working as a doctor in those rural areas from which the mines drew their 'supplies' of 'labour'. He wrote:

> Economic or even social analysis of migratory labour will fail to reveal the full picture of its cost. To learn this you must listen to the lonely wife, the anxious mother, the insecure child. It is at the family level that most pain is felt and we cannot forget that the African cultural heritage enshrines a broader, more noble concept of family than that of the West . .
>
> Migratory labour destroys this, by taking away for long months together, the father, the brother, the lover, the friend. Each must go and no-one fools themselves that these men can live decent lives in a sexual vacuum . . .[8]

Some may be tempted to the view that the situation is not so bad nowadays. My own impression travelling through South Africa's 'homelands' in the 1980s, and looking at Lesotho in the early 1990s, is that a thin veneer of modernity disguises an immensity of pain. Agricultural society has virtually collapsed. There is increasingly widespread unemployment as the mines shed labour in an attempt to cut costs now that the majority of miners are free at last to bargain about their wages and conditions. The fragmentation of families and communities continues inexorably with spectacular levels of hunger, homelessness, alcoholism and want.

In an exhaustive study for the Carnegie Inquiry into Poverty and Development, Mamphela Ramphele and Francis Wilson underscore the scale of the tragedy, portraying a troubled southern Africa in unforgettable images and shocking statistics. Ramphele and Wilson also write eloquently of the processes whereby people at the top of the social pyramid are cut off from the lived experience of the majority, and how as a result of isolation, short-term self-interest, and a cordoned heart, they are 'made not to know'.[9] Sadly the evidence suggests that South Africa's six great mining houses are trapped in a parallel process of psychic numbing. They are still very reluctant to face the realities of the world they have made and appear, even at this late stage, to be unwilling to calculate and make available the economic and social resources needed to repair the damage.

Stripping away the fabricated 'good-will umbrellas' under which they increasingly shelter their activities and which they pay for directly out of the inflated profits of the apartheid years, the independent observer cannot but recall that the mining companies, with their legions of shareholders and dividend takers in Britain and Europe, have broken many human bonds and infringed human rights and dignities on an unrivalled scale. Their survival now depends on atonement, on what if anything they do by way of reparation.

As the poet and migrant worker Alfred Temba Qabula writes, this is a time when human costs have to be counted and debts have to be paid:

> the wheel is turning
> darkness-ending
> daytime-beginning
> the light has come
> Come freedom
> truth is unchanging
> its colours are stark . . .
>
> Return
> What is not yours
> The rightful owners are demanding it back.[10]

Notes

Introduction: Another Blanket

1 *Another Blanket* (Agency for Industrial Mission, Horison, Transvaal, 1976).
2 P. De Vries, *Should Mine Hostels Provide Offal for Hostel Meals?* (Chamber of Mines, Johannesburg, undated).
3 Verbatim transcript of State President's speech, Johannesburg, 1986.

1 The Life and Death of Tebalo Lejalla

1 Interviews with Matseko Lejalla, Tsime haHlasoa, Lesotho, July 1990.
2 Interview with Nmangaweze Lejalla, Tsime haHlasoa, Lesotho, July 1990.
3 Interview with Ntlebere Francis Thabisi, Tsime haHlasoa, Lesotho, July 1990.
4 Interview with Rakali Khitsane, Maseru, July 1990.
5 For the early history of Union Corporation see John Lang, *Bullion Johannesburg: Men, Mines and the Challenge of Conflict* (John Ball, Johannesburg, 1986), p. 75. Up-to-date information drawn from Gencor merger documents and company reports. Gencor is the result of the 1980 merger between Union Corporation and General Mining.
6 For the early history of Kinross see 'At Kinross Safety and Productivity Go Hand in Hand', *South African Mining World* (March 1985), pp. 46–53.
7 Fion De Vletter, 'Migrant Labour on the South African Gold Mines: An Investigation into Black Worker Conditions and Attitudes', draft report for the International Labour Organisation, Swaziland, 10 November 1977. See especially pp. 23, 24, 28, 29, 41.
8 Interviews with Kisisi Mathumbi at Secunda, September 1986.
9 Transcript of press conference at Gencor head offices, Johannesburg, September 1986. Recorded by VNS for Granada Television.

10 Ibid.

11 Interviews with NUM members, Secunda, September and October 1986.

12 Transcript of 'Death is Part of the Process', *World in Action*, Granada Television, Manchester, October 1986.

13 *Star*, Johannesburg (17 October 1986).

14 Ibid.

15 Ibid. (16 October 1986).

16 Report by Dr J.B.C. Botha, State pathologist of Namibia, retained as adviser to the National Union of Mineworkers. Report released by the union's lawyers Cheadle, Thompson & Haysom, 16 October 1986.

17 *Star* (17 October 1986).

18 Transcript of speech recorded by Granada Television, October 1986.

The author gratefully acknowledges the help of the Transformation Resource Centre in Maseru, an interdenominational library and information project of the Lesotho Council of Churches, in the preparation of this chapter. The translator was Lineo Nketu and the author also had especially generous assistance from Phiri Lelingoana.

2 De Beers and Human Rights in Namibia

1 Colin Newbury, *The Diamond Ring: Business, Politics and Precious Stones in South Africa, 1867–1947* (Clarendon Press, Oxford, 1989), p. 11.

2 Robert Vicat Turrell, *Capital and Labour on the Kimberley Diamond Fields, 1871–1890* (Cambridge University Press, 1987), p. 85.

3 Figures from ibid., p. 11.

4 Flora Shaw, quoted in Geoffrey Wheatcroft, *The Randlords – the Men Who Made South Africa* (Weidenfeld & Nicolson, London, 1985), p. 109.

5 Newbury, *Diamond Ring*, p. 126.

6 Michael Rosenthal, *The Character Factory – Baden-Powell and the Origins of the Boy Scout Movement* (Collins, London, 1986), p. 2.

7 *Daily Independent* (12 October 1880). Lead article quoted by Robert Vicat Turrell, 'Kimberley: Labour and Compounds, 1871–1888', in Shula Marks and Stanley Trapido (ed.), *Industrialisation and Social Change in South Africa* (Longman, Harlow, 1982), p. 57.

8 Confidential typewritten minutes of Diamond Producers' Conference, Cape Town, 19 February and 25 March 1930. Photocopies in author's possession.

9 Ibid., p. 34.

10 Ibid., p. 26.

11 Ibid., p. 29.

12 Ibid., p. 60.
13 For the origins of the Namibian gemstones see Eric Lloyd Williams, 'Diamond Harvest of the Namib Surf – the Story of CDM', reprinted from *Optima*, vol. 26, no. 2 (Johannesburg and London, 1978). *Optima* is the shareholders' magazine of Anglo American and De Beers; J. Bone and J.K. Gillett, 'The Recovery of Diamonds at CDM' (unpublished, 9 May 1950), photocopy in author's possession; and C.G. Stocken, 'The Diamond Deposits of the Sperrgebiet' (unpublished, Oranjemund, 1960), photocopy in author's possession.
14 For the early history of the diamond trade in German colonial times see Olga Levinson, *Diamonds in the Desert – the Story of August Stauch and His Times* (Tafelberg, Cape Town, 1983). See also W.P. de Kock, 'Diamonds in South-West Africa' (bound ts, Windhoek, Office of the Mines Department, 11 May 1936). This seminal work was prepared to enable the South African Secretary for South-West Africa to grasp the issues of mining governance and law. De Kock was a geologist and inspector of mines of great thoroughness. A photocopy of the work is in the author's possession and an original in the National Archives, Windhoek.
15 Thirion Report, *Eighth Interim Report of the Commission of Inquiry into Alleged Irregularities and Mis-application of Property in Representative Authorities and the Central Authority of South-West Africa* (Government Printing Office, Windhoek, undated), p. 54.
16 See de Kock, 'Diamonds in South-West Africa', pp. 37–56.
17 Newbury, *Diamond Ring*, p. 243.
18 Consolidated Diamond Mines of South-West Africa, accident report, 18 July 1924, photocopy in author's possession.
19 Undated police report to CDM Security, photocopy in author's possession.
20 CDM Compound Rules, undated, photocopy in author's possession.
21 League of Nations Mandate, quoted in Freda Troup, *In Face of Fear: Michael Scott's Challenge to South Africa* (Faber & Faber, London, 1950), p. 58.
22 Interviews with Gordon Brown, London, Cape Town and Windhoek, May–June 1987.
23 Memorandum on Ovambo meeting from Chief Security Superintendent, CDM, Oranjemund. The memo, dated 28 February 1972, reported on the Ovambo meeting at Oluno on 10 January.
24 Ibid., p. 2, 'Contract system is the form of slavery'.
25 Correspondence between CDM and Anglo American Corporation of South Africa (ANMERCOSA) January and February 1972 reports an immediate

drop of 200 in workers employed and a drive for increased productivity, photocopies in author's possession.

26 Letter from G.Y. Nisbet, CDM General Manager, to the Commissioner General, Oshakati, 26 January 1972, p. 3, photocopy in author's possession.

27 Architectural Department, Anglo American Corporation of South Africa, memorandum, 16 May 1972, 'Ovambo Hostels. Proposed Improvements to Existing Facilities'.

28 Confidential report, October 1972, 'Justifications – Improvements to Ovambo Hostels', October 1972, p. 1.

29 Ibid., pp. 2–7.

30 Anglo American Corporation of South Africa, letter from R.A. Mudd to J.L. Mackenzie, 29 August 1974.

31 P.J.R. Leyden of Anglo American, confidential final comments on draft 'Position Charter', 30 December 1974, photocopy in author's possession.

32 Confidential notes of management team dealing with the dispute, undated photocopy in author's possession, and CDM Monthly Report, March 1979.

33 Confidential notes of management team, undated.

34 Confidential telex from J.O. Richards of CDM to T. Lee-Jones of Anglo American, Johannesburg and V.P. Barrell of De Beers' Services, Windhoek, 28 November 1979.

35 Interview with Gordon Brown, Windhoek, June 1987.

36 Interview with Gordon Brown, Windhoek, 1990.

37 Confidential letter from Dr J.L.C. Whitcombe, medical consultant, Anglo American Corporation of South Africa, to the general manager of CDM, 9 September 1976; the letter was copied to P.J.R. Leyden and T. Lee-Jones of De Beers and Anglo in Johannesburg.

3 How to Steal a Country

1 Thirion Report, *Eighth Interim Report of the Commission of Inquiry into Alleged Irregularities and Mis-application of Property in Representative Authorities and the Central Authority of South-West Africa* (Government Printing Office, Windhoek, undated), p. 54.

2 Minutes of the Diamond Board of South-West Africa, various dates, 1926 to date, photocopies in author's possession.

3 Edward J. Epstein, *The Rise and Fall of Diamonds – the Shattering of a Brilliant Illusion* (Simon & Schuster, New York, 1987), p. 44 et seq.

4 Confidential letter to Anglo American head office in Johannesburg from G.Y. Nisbet, 9 May 1972.

5 Confidential memorandum from senior security officer, Kolmanskop, to chief security superintendent, 13 April 1972.
6 Confidential memorandum from general manager, CDM, to the chairman of the Diamond Board of South-West Africa, 12 November 1976.
7 Confidential memorandum by J.S.T. Fletcher, CDM's chief of security, June 1979.
8 Confidential report by Melvin Foster, 'The Prospecting and Development of Deposits Occurring Outside the Current Mining Security Area at CDM: a Mining Strategy', 2 April 1981.
9 See Thirion Report, pp. 167–200.
10 Interview with Mr Justice Thirion by John Coates, Pietermaritzburg, Natal, June 1987. In this interview Mr Justice Thirion declined to discuss anything but biographical details relating to himself.
11 My thanks to David Wilson for the translation from Afrikaans of the Thirion Report section on Alves.
12 Interviews with Gordon Brown, Cape Town, Windhoek, Manchester and London, 1986, 1987, 1989.
13 CDM life of mine review 1981, quoted in Thirion Report, p. 271.
14 Interviews with Eric Lang, Windhoek, London and Swakopmund, 1987, 1989, 1990.
15 Interview with Gordon Brown.
16 Interview with Eric Lang.
17 Ibid.
18 Ibid.
19 Ibid.
20 Interview with Gerhardt Visser, Windhoek, 1990. In this interview Mr Visser agreed to discuss only biographical details and personal views.
21 Ibid.
22 On the failure of State officials, see Thirion Report, p. 253.
23 Interview with Martin Marriot, the London-based diamond adviser who helped the government of Botswana set up their system of controls.
24 Telephone interview with Martin Grote, 1987. See also his submission to the Thirion Commission, unpublished photostat in author's possession.
25 *Cape Times*, 6 July 1984.
26 Ibid.
27 Interview with Gordon Brown, Windhoek, 1990.
28 Interview with Gordon Brown, Windhoek, 1987.
29 Gordon Brown, interviews and research papers.
30 T.L. Pretorius, 'Consolidated Diamond Mines of South-West Africa

– a Proposed Mining Lay-out', foreword by the mine manager, D. Borchers, p. 1.

31 Ibid., p. 3.
32 CDM Operations Research Manager, strictly confidential memorandum titled 'Life of Mine Strategic Planning', 31 January 1980, p. 1.
33 Thirion Report, p. 167 et seq.
34 Ibid., p. 255.

4 De Beers between Private Deeds and Public Relations

1 Transcript 'The Case of the Disappearing Diamonds', *World in Action*, p. 1, 28 September 1987.
2 Ibid.
3 De Beers' Consolidated Mines Limited and CDM (Pty) Limited, quarter page advertisement headed 'Granada TV Programme "World in Action"', *Guardian* (1 October 1987).
4 White Paper, *National Mineral Policy of South-West Africa/Namibia* (Windhoek, 1987). This document does not appear to have been properly printed. Obtainable from the Department of Civic Affairs and Manpower, the space on the cover relating to price was never filled in and the main distributor of the document appears to have been the CDM/De Beers' public relations office.
5 Information document concerning the *Eighth Interim Report of the Thirion Commission* (Windhoek, 1987), p. 68. This document was 'laid on the table' of the unelected national assembly of the time, thereby avoiding debate.
6 Telex number 1720/DEM to General Manager CDM Oranjemund from MacIver, Anglo American Company of South Africa, Johannesburg, photostat copy in author's possession.
7 Telex CDM 800, 10 September 1970, from CDM to Anglo American Corporation of South Africa, Johannesburg, pp. 2, 3.
8 Confidential letter titled 'Maximising Profits' from D.E. MacIver, Anglo American Corporation of South Africa, 2 October 1970.
9 Ibid.
10 Strictly confidential reply to MacIver from Theo Pretorius, CDM general manager, 31 December 1970, second paragraph.
11 Pretorius's reply, 31 December 1970.
12 Report dated 13 February 1971 by T.L. Pretorius, 'The Effect of Various Mining Policies at CDM'; the typewritten report was catch-lined 'Overmining'.
13 W.P. de Kock, 'Diamonds in South-West Africa' (bound ts, Windhoek Office of the Mines Department, 11 May 1936), p. 44.

14 Confidential production study, CDM, 20 June 1977, accompanying memorandum 103/77.
15 Ibid., p. 10.
16 Ibid., pp. 11, 12, 19, 20, 21, 24, 26, 29.
17 Interview with Gordon Brown, Windhoek, June 1987.
18 Anglo American Corporation of South Africa, Diamond Division, minutes of 13 January 1978 meeting of general managers held at the Premier mine, p. 11.
19 CDM general manager's review for the period January–March 1980, p. 3, sent to the Diamond Services Division (West) of the Anglo American Corporation of South Africa.
20 Interview with Gordon Brown, Windhoek, 1990.

5   The Tsumeb Take-away

1 Biographical details on the late John Muadfangejo are drawn from his work, which was intensely autobiographical, and from interviews with his family and friends in Namibia and his friends in London conducted by the author for a Channel Four *Rear Window* programme, 'My Name Is Loneliness: the Art of John Muadfangejo', May 1991. At the time of writing a Catalogue Raisonné by Orde Levinson was due to be published by Struik of Cape Town.
2 A selection of Ben Ulenga's poems is published in *Seeds* (Mibagus, Windhoek, 1988).
3 The details on Tsumeb are drawn from G. Sohnge, *Tsumeb – a Historical Sketch* (Committee of the South-West Africa Scientific Society, Windhoek, 1967); and from Robert H. Ramsey, *Men and Mines of Newmont – a Fifty-Year History* (Octagon Books/Farrar, Straus & Giroux, New York, 1973).
4 Ramsey, *Men and Mines*, p. 126.
5 Ibid.
6 Ibid., p. 134.
7 Sohnge, *Tsumeb*, p. 10.
8 Details taken from letters and memorabilia on display at the Tsumeb Museum, Tsumeb.
9 Letter from Christopher Jones to the Otavi Exploring Syndicate on display in the Tsumeb Museum.
10 Ibid.
11 Sohnge, *Tsumeb*, p. 17.
12 Memorabilia on display in the Tsumeb Museum.
13 Sohnge, *Tsumeb*, p. 40.
14 Ibid., pp. 41, 49.
15 Ibid., p. 52.

16 Ibid., p. 65.
17 Ramsey, *Men and Mines*, p. 33.
18 Ibid., p. 143.
19 Interview in Tsumeb, 1990.
20 Ibid.
21 See Ramsey, *Men and Mines*, pp. 142, 143.
22 Interview, Tsumeb, 1990.
23 Ibid.
24 Ibid.
25 Ibid.
26 Ibid.
27 Dr Kristian Vetlesen, 'Report of a Pre-Study on Occupational Health and Safety in TCL Mine and Smelter in Tsumeb, Namibia' (Norwegian Confederation of Trade Unions, International Department, 24 September 1989), p. 4.
28 Ibid.
29 Ibid.
30 Ibid., p. 5.
31 See for example Patrick Kinnersly, *The Hazards of Work, How to Fight Them* (Pluto Press, London, 1973), pp. 156–62, and Daniel M. Berman, *Death on the Job – Occupational Health and Safety Struggles in the United States* (Monthly Review Press, New York, 1978), p. 134.
32 Vetlesen, 'Report', p. 9.
33 Ibid., p. 11.
34 Ibid.
35 Ibid., p. 12.
36 Ibid., p. 14.
37 Ibid.
38 See Windhoek *Observer* (2 December 1989) for a background feature on the first anniversary of the tragedy.
39 Sohnge, *Tsumeb*, pp. 59, 88.
40 Details of the accident are drawn from the files of the Legal Assistance Service, Windhoek, which represented the dead miners' families for the Mine Workers' Union of Namibia.
41 Ibid.
42 Ibid.
43 Interview with Ben Ulenga, then general secretary of the Mine Workers' Union of Namibia, Windhoek, December 1989.
44 Information from Legal Assistance Service files.
45 Ibid.

46 Ibid.
47 Ibid.
48 Gail Hovey, *Namibia's Stolen Wealth* (The Africa Fund, New York, 1982). Summary published in Windhoek *Observer* (8 January 1983), pp. 20, 21.
49 Ibid.
50 Thirion Report, *Eighth Interim Report of the Commission of Inquiry into Alleged Irregularities and Mis-application of Property in Representative Authorities and the Central Authority of South-West Africa* (Government Printing Office, Windhoek, undated), p. 148.
51 Ibid., pp. 95, 96.
52 Ramsey, *Men and Mines*, p. 33.

6 Britannia's Fatal Shore: Consolidated Gold Fields Limited, a British Company, and Apartheid

1 *Financial Mail*, Johannesburg (3 October 1975).
2 The interviews with Gold Fields' employees on which Chapters 6, 7 and 8 are based were done in three stages in 1986, 1987 and 1990. In 1986 I made a *World in Action* programme, 'The Midas Touch', on Gold Fields' record in South Africa, which was transmitted on 24 November. This involved many weeks of work with Gold Fields' employees in South Africa and Lesotho. In 1987 I did another set of interviews in South Africa. And in 1990 I spent time in Lesotho with a number of former NUM members in Gold Fields' mines who had been sacked and then deported for their trade union activities.
3 *The Times* (5 February 1968).
4 *Sunday Star* (14 September 1986), p. 7.
5 Information drawn from confidential minutes of mine managers' meetings in the Gold Fields' group, 1984. See in particular details on inadequate ventilation given in the 2 March 1984 discussion. For further details on the development of Kloof, see Roy Macnab's South African version of the centenary history, *Gold Their Touchstone* (Jonathan Ball, Johannesburg, 1987), p. 224. This book is markedly more accurate, more revealing and more honest than the British version of the centenary history written by Paul Johnson.
6 For profitability figures for Kloof see *Financial Mail* (3 October 1975).
7 See A.P. Cartwright, *Gold Paved the Way – the Story of the Gold Fields Group of Companies* (Macmillan, London, 1967), p. 235.
8 The footage shot inside the Kloof compound was shown in 'The Midas Touch'.

9 Lord Erroll of Hale speaking at a Cons Gold shareholders meeting in London, 1980.
10 Details of the Theko Theko case are drawn from court records, press reports and interviews with David Theko Theko and his lawyer Paul Benjamin in Johannesburg in 1986. The case against Kloof Gold Mining is number NH 13/2/753. The judgment was reported in *Financial Mail* (17 January 1986) and *Employment Law*, vol. 2, no. 4 (1986), pp. 56, 57.
11 All quotes from author's interview with David Theko Theko, Johannesburg, 1986.
12 The pictures of Gold Fields' toilets at Venterspost were shown in 'The Midas Touch'.
13 Repeated attempts were made by me and my colleague Steve Bolton to question Gold Fields about these conditions both in Johannesburg and London. On all occasions the company refused access and company officials declined to be interviewed.
14 Gold Fields' Industrial Relations Manual, dated 14 April 1983, section 1g 'Closed Shop'.
15 Gold Fields' Confidential Industrial Relations Report no. 2, December 1984, p. 1.
16 Ibid., pp. 9, 12.
17 Extracts from this video were shown in 'The Midas Touch'.
18 Details of head office conditions given in several interviews with 'Paul', Johannesburg, 1986.
19 All details and quotations drawn from the 2 April 1984 minutes of the Gold Fields' quarterly Mine Managers' meeting.
20 Gold Fields' Doornfontein mine – background briefing paper given to invited visitors, undated and pages unnumbered, photostat copy in author's possession.
21 Gold Fields' Doornfontein Gold Mining Company confidential document, 7 May 1986, p. 3.
22 Interviews at Doornfontein mine, 1986.
23 Confidential minutes of a meeting at the Chief Compound Managers' office with representatives of the National Union of Mineworkers, 11 April 1986, p. 2.
24 All quotes from Gold Fields' training documents. The induction module prepared by Group Training Centre has an extraordinary sub-module on 'Blacks – Cultural Background', which is replete with racist statements including those quoted. Another document also in the author's possession and from which quotes are also drawn is titled 'Learner Officials' Training

Centre – 50 Things to Do with Bantu Workers', and is even more outlandish.

7 Defence of the Realm: British Business and the Security of the White South African State

1 The Gold Fields' executive B.R. Van Rooyen wrote an anxious note on the proposed unionisation of security workers for Gold Fields' chairman Robin Plumbridge on 26 October 1982. On 15 December Colin Fenton, Gold Fields' executive director for gold mining, wrote in confidence to the director general in the government's Manpower Department, expressing his worries. The company's lobbying tactics are set out in these letters and in a note from H. Nijland in the Gold Fields' Legal Division. Photocopies of these documents are in the author's possession.
2 Restricted Gold Fields' document, 'Mines Security Force', revised edition, January 1982, pp. 3, 4, 5, 6.
3 Ibid., p. 3.
4 Restricted Gold Fields Mine Security Reserve document, 3 January 1979, p. 2.
5 Ibid., p. 2.
6 Ziliboy Daza, interviewed for Granada's *World in Action*, November 1986. The details of his case were carefully investigated by both Steve Bolton and myself and even Gold Fields seemed to accept that Mr Daza had done nothing to provoke any attack on himself.
7 Interview with Percy Dyanase, Johannesburg, October 1986. Events at Driefontein are also extensively covered by Marcel Golding, 'Mass Struggles on the Mines', *South African Labour Bulletin*, vol. 10, no. 6 (May 1985).
8 Interview with Richard Spoor, Johannesburg, 1986.
9 Ibid.
10 Televised interview with Richard Spoor in 'The Midas Touch', *World in Action*, November 1986. All subsequent quotations from Richard Spoor are taken from the transcript of this interview or from the author's notes of the various off-camera interviews conducted prior to this interview.
11 Robin Plumbridge, chairman of Gold Fields of South Africa and a member of the London board of the parent company Consolidated Gold Fields, quoted in the *Guardian* (17 September 1985).
12 Quoted in the *Observer* (9 August 1987).
13 Phillip van Niekerk, 'Startling Tales of Torture on Mine', front page lead article in the *Weekly Mail*, vol. 3, no. 6 (13 February 1987).
14 Paul Johnson, *Gold Fields – a Centenary Portrait* (Weidenfeld & Nicolson, London, 1987). See in particular pp. 8–11.

15 Robert Annan's statement to the annual general meeting, reported in *The Times* (16 December 1960).
16 Gold Fields of South Africa, annual report, 1976.
17 Alan Paton, *Cry the Beloved Country* (Penguin, London, 1958). See in particular p. 126 for forthright statements about the mining industry.
18 The background to wartime discontent and the 1946 strike is outlined in various books. See John Lang's official history of the Chamber of Mines, *Bullion Johannesburg – Men, Mines and the Challenge of Conflict* (Jonathan Ball, Johannesburg, 1986), p. 383; Jack and Ray Simons, *Class and Colour in South Africa, 1850–1950* (International Defence and Aid Fund, London, 1983), has fuller information, pp. 554–78; Ken Luckhardt and Brenda Wall also cover the period in *Organise or Starve – the History of the South African Congress of Trade Unions* (Lawrence & Wishart, London, 1980), pp. 65–72; Dunbar Moodie's seminal article, 'The Black Miners' Strike of 1946', has details on events at Sub Nigel, p. 47.
19 Nelson Mandela, writing in *Liberation* (1953). Quoted in Mary Benson, *Nelson Mandela* (Penguin, Harmondsworth, 1986), p. 60.
20 Albert Luthuli's autobiography *Let My People Go* was first published in 1962. See in particular the important chapter 'Whose is South Africa?' (Fontana edn, London, 1963), pp. 78–86. In this Luthuli underlined that the forms of slavery changed with the times.
21 Francis Wilson, *Labour in the South African Gold Mines, 1911–1969* (Cambridge University Press, 1972), *Migrant Labour in South Africa* (South African Council of Churches and SPRO-CAS, Johannesburg, 1972).
22 Interview with Francis Wilson, London, 1989.
23 *Migrant Labour*, Preface, second page. The introductory pages of the book are unnumbered.
24 Interview with Francis Wilson, London, 1989.
25 CIS Anti-Report, 'Consolidated Gold Fields' (Counter-Information Services, London, 1972).
26 Ibid., pp. 31–3.
27 Memorandum submitted by Consolidated Gold Fields in minutes of evidence taken before the House of Commons Expenditure Committee (Trade and Industry Sub-Committee), 22 May 1973.
28 Ibid., section 6, wages policy.
29 Minutes of evidence, House of Commons Expenditure Committee, 22 May 1973, examination of witness, J.D. McCall, chairman, Consolidated Gold Fields, para 570.
30 Ibid., para 571.

NOTES

31 *Fifth Report of the House of Commons Expenditure Committee* (HMSO, London, 1974), p. 69.

32 *Department of Trade and Industry Code of Conduct for Companies Operating in South Africa*, Cmnd 7233 (HMSO, London, May 1978). The code was subsequently modified and adapted by the European Community.

33 Interviews with British civil servants who worked with Vose, London and Johannesburg, 1986.

34 See Consolidated Gold Fields annual reports, 1980 and 1981 and correspondence with the Department of Trade and Industry, 11 October 1979.

35 Letter and photostat sent by D.E.S. Barton, Consolidated Gold Fields Group Operations executive, to the Department of Trade and Industry, 30 September 1980.

36 United Reform Church, Office of the General Secretary and Clerk of the General Assembly, confidential minutes of the meeting with Consolidated Gold Fields, 13 July 1976, p. 2.

37 Ibid.

38 Ibid., and background briefing from URC officials about the meeting.

39 Interview with John Johansen-Berg, London, 1984.

40 Roman Catholic Diocese of Westminster, press secretary's briefing document and press release on disinvestment, 14 July 1977.

41 *European Economic Community Code of Conduct for Companies with Interests in South Africa*, Cmnd 9860 (HMSO, London, July 1986).

42 Barton, letter to the DTI, 30 September 1980.

43 Merle Lipton, *Men of Two Worlds – Migrant Labour in South Africa*, report commissioned by the Anglo American Corporation of South Africa and published in a special double issue of the Anglo journal, *Optima*, vol. 29, nos 2 and 3 (Johannesburg, November 1980).

44 Ibid., p. 133.

45 *Optima – Statement by the Publishers* (Johannesburg, 28 November 1980).

46 Statement issued on behalf of Merle Lipton by Michael Rubinstein of Rubinstein, Callingham, Solicitors, London, 16 January 1981, p. 2. For a fuller exposition of Lipton's important work, see *Capitalism and Apartheid* (Temple Smith & Gower, Aldershot, 1985).

47 Consolidated Gold Fields' brochure on the migrant labour system, London, 1981.

48 Interview with Cyril Ramaphosa, London, 1986.

49 Interviews with Gold Fields of South Africa head office staff, Johannesburg, 1986.

50 All quotes from Gold Fields of South Africa/Kloof Gold Mining Co. press release, Johannesburg, May 1985.

329

51 Interview with Bafana Baningi, Johannesburg, 1986.

8 The Gold Standard: the Legacy of a British Business in South Africa

1 The sum of £575 million was computed by Steve Bolton for Granada's *World in Action* on the basis of a careful analysis of company reports and reviews of Gold Fields by stockbrokers in London and Johannesburg.

   The Spring 1986 report from Counter-Information Services, *Consolidated Gold Fields – Partners in Apartheid* (CIS, London, 1986), shows how the generous tax regime Britain afforded to businesses operating in South Africa meant that little tax was paid on these huge profits. See p. 21.
2 Statement to the annual general meeting of Consolidated Gold Fields, London, 1985.
3 Consolidated Gold Fields' annual report, 1979.
4 Interviews with British diplomats serving in South Africa, 1986.
5 *Evening Standard* (21 January 1980).
6 Author's calculation from the annual reports of the two group companies, Consolidated Gold Fields and Gold Fields of South Africa, together with reports from the individual South African operating companies for each of seven group mines in South Africa. The seven mines included in this calculation are West Driefontein, East Driefontein, Kloof, Libanon, Doornfontein, Venterspost and Vlakfontein.
7 For further information on the Driefontein super-mine see Cons Gold and GFSA, East and West Driefontein annual reports and Paul Johnson, *Gold Fields – a Centenary Portrait* (Weidenfeld & Nicolson, London, 1986), pp. 63, 64.
8 See A.P. Cartwright, *Gold Paved the Way* (Macmillan, London, 1967), p. 242.
9 See annual reports of Cons Gold and GFSA, 1979, 1980 and 1981.
10 The Deelkraal mine, the Leeudoorn extension to Kloof and the vast new platinum mine at Northam all proceeded in the 1980s on the basis of migrant labour. And while a vast financial reconstruction was undertaken at the richest mine in the world, Driefontein, this was for the benefit of Gold Fields' shareholders and business executives and the South African State, not the tens of thousands of miners who worked there and continued to live in grim, single-sex hostels.
11 *Sunday Telegraph* (29 June 1986).
12 Martin & Co, stockbrokers' report, Johannesburg, 1984.
13 Rudolph Agnew to the 1987 Consolidated Gold Fields shareholders' meeting. Reported in the *Guardian* (17 September 1987).

NOTES

14 Information confirmed by Gold Fields' press office, 1986.
15 Ibid.
16 For further information on the 1988 Local Government Act see anti-apartheid movement publications on this legislation.
17 Interview with Francis Wilson, Cape Town, 1986.
18 Merle Lipton, *Capitalism and Apartheid* (Temple Smith & Gower, Aldershot, 1985), p. 413, and *Optima*, vol. 29, nos 2 and 3 (Johannesburg, 1980), p. 33.
19 In his interesting book *The Emergence of Modern South Africa* (David Philip, Cape Town and Johannesburg, 1984), David Yudelman underlines that mining is a highly concentrated and monopolised business and may be significantly 'tougher' in its corporate behaviour as a result. He also underlines that social structure and corporate behaviour in far-flung corners of an empire are vital to any understanding of events in the metropolitan centre. See pp. 36–8, 272–80.
20 See William Plomer, *Cecil Rhodes* (Peter Davies Ltd, London, 1933), p. 13.
21 J.A. Hobson, *Imperialism: a Study* (James Nisbet, London, 1902), p. 68.
22 Brian Roberts, in *Cecil Rhodes – Flawed Colossus* (Hamish Hamilton, London, 1987), p. 13, states, 'Bribery of one sort or another was to play an important part in Rhodes' business dealings.' Further details of Rhodes's 'financial juggling' are given on pp. 121, 122. For details of Rhodes's generous financial arrangements with himself, founders' shares and guaranteed profit percentages see Cartwright, *Gold Paved the Way*, pp. 30, 33.
23 For scholarly exposition and analysis of the development of the British South Africa Company, see John S. Galbraith, *Crown and Charter: the Early Years of the British South Africa Company* (University of California Press, Berkeley, 1974), esp. pp. 310–39.
24 See Plomer, *Cecil Rhodes*, pp. 120, 121.
25 Ibid., p. 121.
26 John Burns, 'On the Trail of the Financial Serpent' (privately published, London, no date).
27 Robert Vicat Turrell, *Capital and Labour on the Kimberley Diamond Fields, 1871–1890* (Cambridge University Press, 1987), p. 85.
28 Details of the seizure of Matabeleland and the Jameson Raid are drawn from Galbraith, *Crown and Charter*; and from the neglected but most important book by John H. Harris, *The Chartered Millions* (Swarthmore Press, London, 1920), p. 117; and Elizabeth Longford, *Jameson's Raid* (Weidenfeld & Nicolson, London, 1982). The quotes from Lobengula are drawn from Harris's book.

29 Roberts, *Cecil Rhodes*, p. 153.
30 See Roy Macnab, *Gold Their Touchstone* (Jonathan Ball, Johannesburg, 1968), pp. 53–68 for an honest appraisal of Gold Fields' corporate involvement in the attempted coup and details of the subsequent trials, sentences and pardons. Macnab's well-researched and beautifully illustrated narrative is in marked contrast to the white-washing account by Paul Johnson. In *Gold Fields* Johnson applauds Rhodes's colonial rowdyism and regrets the failure of the illegal coup.
31 Plomer, *Cecil Rhodes*, p. 13.
32 Longford, *Jameson's Raid*, p. 10.
33 Plomer, *Cecil Rhodes*, pp. 130, 131.
34 Quoted in Galbraith, *Crown and Charter*, p. 68.
35 Meeting of the Consolidated Gold Fields company 1899.
36 Adèle Lizard, *Gold Blast* (Rich & Cowan, London, undated), p. 136.
37 Plomer, *Cecil Rhodes*, p. 69.
38 Matthew 16:26: 'For what is a man profited, if he shall gain the whole world and lose his own soul?'

9 Dust to Dust: Mining Companies and Environmental Catastrophe in the North Western Cape

1 Medical information in this and the subsequent chapter draws on the work of Doctors Irving J. Selikoff and Douglas H.K. Lee of Mount Sinai School of Medicine, New York. Their book *Asbestos and Disease* was published by Academic Press (New York and London, 1978). Other fine books on which I draw are Barry I. Castleman's encyclopaedic book, *Asbestos – Medical and Legal Aspects* (Prentice Hall Law and Business, N.J., 1990) and George A. Peters and Barbara J. Peters, *Sourcebook on Asbestos Disease* (Garland STPM Press, New York and London, 1990). In addition there is the majestic work of Paul Brodeur of the *New Yorker*. Brodeur published *Expendable Americans* on the subject in 1974 (Viking Press, New York) and returned to the subject with an overview of the asbestos tragedy in *Outrageous Misconduct* (Pantheon, New York, 1985).
2 The most recent estimate, quoted by Barry Castleman, *Asbestos*, suggests that there will be 131,000 deaths from asbestos-associated cancer in the United States between 1985 and 2009. The estimate is by D.E. Lilienfeld and other scientists and was published in the *British Journal of Industrial Medicine*, 45 (1988), pp. 283–91.
3 The author has made repeated requests to the South African State President F.W. De Klerk and his press attaché in London, Michael de Morgan, to return to South Africa to continue investigating the asbestos

tragedy. All requests for a press visa have been turned down without explanation.

4 Interviews with Emily and James Ebang for Granada's *World in Action*, 1981.

5 See annual reports of Eternit, Everite and Kuruman Cape Blue Asbestos for the company history.

6 See the manuscript of J.C. Wagner's PhD thesis, 'The Pathology of Asbestos in South Africa' (University of the Witwatersrand Library, Johannesburg, 1962).

7 Interview with Fritz Baunach, Johannesburg, 1981.

8 See Laurie Flynn, 'South Africa Blacks Out Blue Asbestos Risk', *New Scientist* (22 April 1982). This edition of the magazine was withdrawn from circulation in South Africa under pressure from the mining companies, who threatened the local distributor with legal action.

9 Lonrho still owned the mine in 1992. The company's South African subsidiary had temporarily closed the mine due to poor market demand but was planning to reopen it.

10 The British Asbestos Regulations were framed in 1931. The 1969 revision of the regulations effectively banned crocidolite or blue asbestos in Britain.

11 None of us was happy about the element of deception involved in making these and other films in South Africa in the 1980s. But the apartheid government had no love for British television reporters and was particularly hostile to those of us from Granada Television who were fascinated by and loved their country.

12 Interview with Ted Rushworth, Manchester, 1981. Mr Rushworth inspected British asbestos plants and other dangerous installations as a young factory inspector. He himself contracted an industrial disease and became a passionate and effective campaigner for enforcement of existing laws and more effective human rights at work.

13 Interview with Sister Seamaco, Bathlaros Hospital, North Western Cape Province, South Africa, 1981.

14 Interview with M.L. Newhouse, London, 1981. Molly Newhouse has been publishing research into asbestos and cancer since 1972. Her warnings about stopping production came after the disclosure of the scale of the tragedy at Hebden Bridge in Yorkshire.

15 Lewis Mumford is quoted in Anne Chisholm's *Philosophers of the Earth – Conversations with Ecologists* (Sidgwick & Jackson, London, 1972).

16 Wally Walters, GEFCO annual report and accounts, 1979.

17 The details of the murderous conditions at Central Asbestos were reported in *The Times* and the *Daily Telegraph* (23 June 1970). The historic House

of Lords judgment which set aside the three-year statute of limitations preventing miners and asbestos workers from suing for lung disease caused by their employment was given by Lord Reid and is reported as House of Lords, *Central Asbestos Company* v. *Dodd.*

18 Interview with Anthony D. Woolf, London, 1972.
19 See A.L. Hall, 'Asbestos in the Union of South Africa', Union of South Africa, Department of Mines and Industries, Geological Survey, *Memoir no. 12* (Government Printing and Stationery Office, Pretoria, 1918), p. 133.
20 Interview with London dockers, 1975. The Cape Mines annual reports confirm that the Koegas mine shut down after the Port of London's refusal to handle unsafe goods.
21 Interview with Dr Bertram Mann, Royal Infirmary, Halifax, 1981.
22 Interview with Dr Ian Webster, Johannesburg, 1981.
23 Cape Industries telex to Granada Television, 1981.
24 The Oppenheimer company Cape Industries finally succeeded in avoiding the jurisdiction of the American courts and has to date paid no compensation to its victims in Bloomington, Illinois.

10   Conduct Unbecoming: Mining Companies and the Suppression of Cancer Research in Southern Africa

1 See J.M. Tallent, W.O. Harrison, A. Solomon and I. Webster, 'A Survey of Black Mineworkers of the Cape Crocidolite Mines', in *Biological Effects of Mineral Fibres*, vol. 2, ed. J.C. Wagner. IARC Scientific Publications, no. 30 (International Agency for Research into Cancer, Lyons, 1980).
2 Interview with Dr Tallent, Mafeking, 1981.
3 Interview with Cyprian Gabetse, Bathlaros, 1981.
4 In his important but still unpublished paper 'Health Hazards of Foreign Investment in South Africa – the Case of Asbestos', Barry Castleman reports a 1971 House of Commons question from a then little-known British Labour MP, Neil Kinnock. Noting that the British-registered Oppenheimer company admitted 1,309 black workers had contracted asbestosis in the preceding five years, Mr Kinnock decried the lack even of financial compensation. He asked the British Foreign Secretary to support an investigation of the Cape Industries' record by the United Nations Human Rights Commission. The Foreign Secretary declined Mr Kinnock's request.
5 Interview with Dr Gerrit Schepers, Washington DC, 1982.
6 Interviews with government scientists in Johannesburg, Cape Town, London and Cardiff, 1981. The reforms were minimal. For the first time asbestos mines could be scheduled in South Africa.

7 Cape Industries' company secretary Anthony J. Penna repeatedly denied there was any connection between Cape and Associated Minerals of Lichtenstein. But company documents obtained by the author and used in the 1982 *World in Action* programme 'Asbestos – a Small Town Tragedy' proved that Cape owned many shares in the company with which it was 'unconnected'.

8 Dr R.D.W. Reid's statements were reported in the *Cape Times*, Cape Town (18 November 1981).

9 Carolyn Dempster's article appeared in the *Star*, Johannesburg (27 August 1984). Phillip van Niekerk's revelations appeared in the *Rand Daily Mail*, Johannesburg (19 July 1984, 1 August 1984, 8 August 1984).

10 See Phillip van Niekerk, 'Shock Figures Expose the Extent of Asbestos', *Rand Daily Mail*, Johannesburg (8 August 1984).

11 Interview with Dr C. A. Sleggs, Cape Town, 1981.

12 See J.C. Wagner, PhD thesis, 'The Pathology of Asbestos in South Africa' (University of the Witwatersrand, Johannesburg, 1962).

13 Interview with Dr J.C. Wagner, Penarth, Wales, 1981.

14 See *Proceedings of the Pneumoconiosis Conference, University of the Witwatersrand, 9–24 February 1959*, ed. A.J. Orenstein (J.A. Churchill, London, 1960), p. 381.

15 Interviews with South African asbestos scientist, Johannesburg, London and Cardiff, 1981. (Name withheld at the request of the interviewee.)

16 See South African Council for Scientific and Industrial Research, Pneumoconiosis Research Unit, 'Report on the Progress of the Mesothelioma Survey as at 30 April 1962', unpublished, Johannesburg, p. 3.

17 Ibid., p. 4.

18 Ibid., p. 2.

19 Interview with South African asbestos scientist, Johannesburg, London and Cardiff, 1981.

20 See Gill Reid et al., 'Mortality of an Asbestos-Exposed Birth Cohort', *South African Medical Journal* (1990), pp. 554–65. The figure of one death in a million from mesothelioma in a random population is Gill Reid's. (Personal communication with the author.)

21 Interviews with Dr Marianne Felix, Johannesburg and London, 1987 and 1989.

22 Dr Felix has now published a moving account of her work. See 'Risking Their Lives in Ignorance – the Story of an Asbestos Polluted Community', in *Going Green – People, Politics and the Environment in South Africa*, ed. Jacklyn Cock and Eddie Koch (Oxford University Press, Cape Town, 1991).

23 Interview with Dr Marianne Felix.
24 Paul Brodeur, *Outrageous Misconduct* (Pantheon, New York, 1985).

11 Endless Washing Softens the Stone: the First Steps towards Freedom in the Mines

1 Quoted in Baruch Hirson, *Yours for the Union* (Zed Press, London, 1990), p. 171. The 'political company' was a Chamber of Mines recruiting organisation set up by the mining houses to overcome that particularly unpleasant aspect of colonial history and its 'free market' – the labour contractor or tout, the private enterprise dealer in economically disadvantaged, and therefore rightless, human beings.

2 C.S. Goldmann, quoted in Sheila van der Horst, *Native Labour in South Africa* (Oxford University Press, London, 1942), p. 133.

3 George Albu, quoted in Norman Levy, *The Foundations of the South African Cheap Labour System* (Routledge & Kegan Paul, London, 1982), p. 23.

4 Albu, quoted in Levy, *Foundations*, p. 24.

5 See Sean Moroney, 'Industrial Conflict in a Labour Repressive Economy: Black Labour on the Transvaal Gold Mines', dissertation submitted to the Faculty of Arts, University of the Witwatersrand, 1976, p. 5.

6 Sol Plaatje, *Native Life in South Africa* (P. & S. King, London, 1916), pp. 70, 71.

7 Ibid., p. 129.

8 Charles van Onselen, *Studies in the Social and Economic History of the Witwatersrand, 1886–1914*, vols 1 and 2 (Longman, London, 1982).

9 See Dunbar Moodie, 'Mine Culture and Miners' Identity on the South African Gold Mines', in Belinda Bozzoli (ed.), *Town and Countryside in the Transvaal* (Ravan Press, Johannesburg, 1983), particularly pp. 188, 189. Moodie quotes one old miner on the nature of the bargain: 'If your children are starving and the only way across the river is on the back of the devil, then you choose the devil.'

10 See Luli Callinicos, *Gold and Workers – a People's History of Southern Africa*, vol. 1, esp. ch. 16, pp. 88–98. This author would like to acknowledge his debt to the remarkable work done by Luli Callinicos and her associates in History Workshop.

11 For an account of the experiences of Chinese mineworkers in South Africa, see ibid., pp. 64–70. For details of the 1913 strikes and the 1918 boycott and refusal to work unless increases were paid, see p. 91. For the 1920 events, see p. 92, where the statement of the President of the Chamber of Mines is also quoted.

12 For accounts of the 1922 Rand Revolt see John Lang, *Bullion Johannesburg:*

NOTES

Men, Mines and the Challenge of Conflict (Jonathan Ball, Johannesburg, 1986), pp. 207–27, and Callinicos, *Gold and Workers*, pp. 82–5.

13 See David Yudelman, *The Emergence of Modern South Africa – State, Capital and the Incorporation of Organised Labour on the South African Gold Fields, 1902–1939* (David Philip, Cape Town and Johannesburg, 1984), pp. 128, 165–211.

14 Stanley Greenberg, *Race and State in Capitalist Development – South Africa in Comparative Perspective* (Ravan Press, Johannesburg, 1976).

15 Dunbar Moodie quotes extensively from the Chamber of Mines spy reports in his work. My own examination of confidential reports from diamond and gold mines belonging to a variety of companies attests to the fact that they used spies widely and the purpose of the closure of the compound was to have total control. This involved the denial of freedom of voluntary association across the board, to churches and sporting groups as well as unions and political parties.

16 Dunbar Moodie, 'D.L. Smit and the Role of the South African State in Industrial Conflict' (unpublished ts in possession of the author).

17 Dunbar Moodie has written a fine account of the strike of 1946 and the events which led up to it: 'The Moral Economy of the Black Miners' Strike of 1946', *Journal of Southern African Studies*, vol. 13, no. 1 (October 1986). Dan O'Meara has also published an important account: *Journal of Commonwealth and Comparative Politics*, XII, 2 (1975).

For the history of socialist and communist activism in South Africa see Jack and Ray Simons, *Class and Colour in South Africa, 1850–1950* (International Defence and Aid Fund, London, 1983) and Edward Roux, *Time Longer than Rope – the Black Man's Struggle for Freedom in South Africa* (University of Wisconsin Press, Madison, 1978).

18 Ruth First, 'The Gold of Migrant Labour', *Africa South in Exile*, vol. 5, no. 3 (London, April–June 1961), pp. 7–31.

19 Interview with James Phillips, London, 1984.

20 Ibid.

21 E.S. Sachs, *The Choice Before South Africa* (Turnstile Press, London, 1952), p. 101.

22 See First, 'The Gold of Migrant Labour', Moodie, 'Moral Economy of the 1946 Black Miners' Strike' and Sachs, *The Choice Before South Africa* for further details of the miners' grievances.

23 Gold Fields' records, seen by the author, Johannesburg, 1986.

24 Simons, *Class and Colour in South Africa*, p. 576.

25 Interview with James Phillips.

26 According to John Lang, McLean's nickname was Mussolini McLean, *Bullion Johannesburg* (Jonathan Ball, Johannesburg, 1986), p. 375.
27 E.S. Sachs, 'The Natives and Trade Unions', *Manchester Guardian* (19 August 1946). On 13 September in an unsigned piece the paper's unnamed South African correspondent put the considerable weight of the *Manchester Guardian* behind the South African Chamber of Mines, gave unconditional support to the fantasy of a Communist plot 'to produce race riots and deaths on a shocking scale' and flatly opposed the right of migrant miners to form unions.
28 See Memorandum on the background to the recent strike of native mineworkers on the Rand, Office of the High Commissioner for the United Kingdom, Pretoria, 18 September 1946, PRO, London.
29 Ibid., p.2.
30 Michael Scott was a member of the committee formed to defend the African Mineworkers' Union from what he describes in his autobiography as the 'relentless attacks of the all powerful Chamber of Mines'. See Michael Scott, *A Time to Speak* (Faber & Faber, London, 1958), p. 115. Scott's 1949 statement to the United Nations on South West Africa contains a powerful attack on the migrant labour system both in South and South West Africa. See Michael Scott, *Shadow over Africa* (Union of Democratic Control, London, 1950). Scott is the subject of a good biography, *In Face of Fear* by Freda Troup (Faber & Faber, London, 1950) and a moving memoir by Mary Benson, *A Far Cry – the Making of a South African* (Viking, London, 1989), pp. 53–93.
31 First, 'The Gold of Migrant Labour'. *Africa South in Exile*, vol. 5, no. 3, April–June 1961.
32 Ibid., p. 17.
33 Dudley Horner and Alide Kooy, 'Conflict on South African Mines, 1972–1979', South African Labour and Development Research Unit, Cape Town, SALDRU Working Paper no. 29, Cape Town, June 1980.
34 Ibid., p. 1.
35 Ibid., p. 46.
36 Ibid.
37 Dennis Etheredge wrote an 'Early History of the Chamber of Mines: Johannesburg, 1887–1897' for his Master's Degree at the University of the Witwatersrand in 1949.
38 'Report of an Inquiry into the Disturbances on Anglo American Gold Mines, January 1975', Xeroxed report for private circulation only (Johannesburg, 1975), pp. 49–53.
39 The name of the agent is given in the report. I have withheld it because of continuing tensions in Vaal Reefs, the biggest mine in South Africa.

40 See 'Report of an Inquiry', ch. 4.

41 Ibid., p. 78.

42 Ibid., p. 92.

43 Inter-departmental inquiry into riots on mines in the Republic of South Africa, Johannesburg and Pretoria, 1975.

44 Ibid., p. 8.

45 Ibid., additional report of the ad hoc sub committee set up to comment on findings and recommendations, p.7.

46 'Report of an Inquiry', p. 98.

47 Quoted in Mark Green and John F. Berry, *The Search for Hidden Profits – Bureaucracy and Waste in the Modern Corporation* (William Morrow, New York, 1985), p. 69.

48 Quoted in 'Report of an Inquiry', p. 98.

49 Interview with Dunbar Moodie, Boston, Massachusetts, January 1991.

50 Ibid.

51 Desmond Quigley, 'Grim Report on Life of Black Gold Miners', *The Times* (13 May 1977).

52 See ibid. *South African Mining* (May 1977) carries a useful summary of the report. Moodie has also dealt with the impact of mining compounds on human sexual behaviour in a paper entitled 'Migrancy and Male Sexuality on the South African Gold Mines' (ts in possession of the author).

53 *The Times* (13 May 1977).

54 *South African Mining* (May 1977).

55 Harry Oppenheimer, quoted in the *Citizen*, Johannesburg (13 May 1977).

56 *Financial Times* (14 May 1977).

57 Figures taken from Merle Lipton, 'Men of Two Worlds', *Optima*, vol. 29, nos 2–3 (Johannesburg and London, November 1980), p. 114.

58 *South African Mining* (May 1977).

59 See 'Report of a Study of Black Mineworker Leisure Activities at Western Holdings', Industrial Relations Department, Anglo American Corporation of South Africa, Johannesburg, March 1977.

60 Ibid., p. 23.

61 See Chamber of Mines of South Africa Internal Report no. 5, 'A Human Resources Audit of Elandsrand Gold Mine following the April 1979 Disturbance'.

62 See Elandsrand Gold Mining Company and Anglo American Corporation press releases, April 1979.

63 See 'Human Resources Audit', esp. pp. 3, 23, 31.

64 The listing of problems takes up the whole of the report's Appendix 1, pp. 49–60.

65 'Human Resources Audit', p. 29.
66 Ibid., Appendix 3, pp. 65–8.
67 Ibid., p. 66.
68 Gavin Relly, quoted in Merle Lipton, *Capitalism and Apartheid* (Temple Smith & Gower, Aldershot, 1985), p. 128.
69 The complex methods by which the Oppenheimer family keep control of the Anglo–De Beers empire were charted by the corporate research and detective agency Kroll for Gold Fields during the 1989 Minorco take-over battle.
70 'Human Resources Audit', pp. 41, 42.
71 Ibid., p. 42.
72 Interviews with Chamber of Mines officials and Anglo executives, Johannesburg, 1986.

12   Conspiracy of Hope: the Rise of NUM

1 See John Lang, *Bullion Johannesburg – Men, Mines and the Challenge of Conflict* (Jonathan Ball, Johannesburg, 1986), pp. 455–74.
2 The account of events at Marievale relies on court records, conversations with Clive Thompson, the NUM lawyer who handled the case, and interviews with Mlungisi Nelani carried out in and around Johannesburg by my Granada colleague, Steve Bolton.
3 Transcript of a tape recording in the possession of Cheadle, Thompson & Heysom, attorneys to the National Union of Mineworkers. Transcript made by Granada Television, whose library has a copy of the tape.
4 Speech to the South African Institution of Race Relations by Cyril Ramaphosa, SAIRR press release, 31 July 1985.
5 This account of the rise of trade unionism in the mines is based on my own personal observations in 1981, 1986 and 1987 and many conversations with NUM leaders.
6 For fuller background on the return of independent black unionism after the repression of the 1960s see the *South Africa Labour Bulletin*, a consistently valuable source, Don Ncube, *The Influence of Apartheid and Capitalism on the Development of Black Unions* (Skotaville Press, Johannesburg, 1987), and Ken Luckhardt and Brenda Wall, *Working for Freedom: Black Trade Union Development in South Africa throughout the 1970s* (World Council of Churches, Geneva, 1981). For the emergence of NUM and an account of the 1981 and 1982 strikes, see Steven Friedman, *Building Tomorrow Today* (Ravan Press, Johannesburg, 1987), esp. pp. 355–92.
7 The situation at TEBA has been documented by the Agency for Industrial Mission. My account also relies on personal observations

and interviews with TEBA employees in Johannesburg in 1981, 1986 and 1987.

8 Putseletso Salae's account of events in 1982 is not seriously challenged by TEBA, an organisation which despite various changes is still profoundly authoritarian.

9 Interviews with Putseletso Salae, Maseru, Lesotho, July 1990.

10 Interviews with Cyril Ramaphosa in London and Johannesburg, 1986. See also profiles of Ramaphosa by Sheryl Raine in the *Sunday Star Review*, Johannesburg (28 September 1986) and David Beresford in the *Guardian*, London (14 August 1987).

11 Interview with Putseletso Salae, Maseru, Lesotho, July 1990.

12 For a fuller account of these events see Friedman, *Building Tomorrow Today*, pp. 362–4.

13 See the *Rand Daily Mail*, Johannesburg (6 July 1983).

14 Photostat copy of the TEBA docket in the author's possession.

15 *Rand Daily Mail*, Johannesburg (7 July 1983).

16 Miners' Bill of Rights, Johannesburg, National Union of Mineworkers, undated.

17 See Friedman, *Building Tomorrow Today*, p. 365.

18 The account of events at Vaal Reefs is based on the author's interviews with NUM officials in 1986 and 1987, and the joint NUM–Anglo American Corporation of South Africa study, 'Reaping the Whirlwind', Johannesburg, Anglo American, May 1986.

19 See Cyril Ramaphosa, 'Organising on the Mines', press release and report of a speech issued by the South African Institute of Race Relations, 31 July 1985.

20 Quotes from Dunbar Moodie, 'Alcohol and Resistance on the South African Mines' (ts in possession of the author). Moodie's work is to be published as a book.

21 See the *Sunday Tribune*, Johannesburg (3 November 1985) for a full account of how Malcolm Fraser learned of the disabling gas systems.

22 Ibid.

23 *Financial Mail*, Johannesburg (8 November 1985).

24 Quoted in 'Reaping the Whirlwind', p. 27.

25 Ibid., p. 28.

26 Clive Thompson, 'Labour's Challenge to the Mining Industry', Johannesburg, March 1986, pp. 2, 3 (ts in possession of the author).

27 Anthony Sampson, *Black and Gold – Tycoons, Revolutionaries and Apartheid* (Hodder & Stoughton, London, 1987), p. 240.

28 Interviews with Steve Brunt, Johannesburg, 1986. See also his report, 'A

South African Experience – a British Miner's View of the South African Mining Industry' (National Union of Mineworkers, Sheffield, 1987).

29 Ibid., p. 18.

30 Interviews with NUM officials, Johannesburg, 1987.

31 Quoted in the *Financial Times*, London (September 1987).

32 Quoted in ibid.

33 Cyril Ramaphosa and Marcel Golding, 'Horses and Hippos – Collective Bargaining at Anglo American Mines Before and After the 1987 Strike', Johannesburg, NUM, undated.

34 Figures from the NUM and the Anglo American Corporation of South Africa, press office.

35 Information from the National Union of Mineworkers press office.

36 Information from NUM's lawyers and press office. Rian Malan has put together a disturbing account of the circumstances in which violence comes to the mines in the section of his book dealing with Randfontein Estates gold mine. See *My Traitor's Heart* (Vintage, London, 1991), pp. 236–63.

37 Information from NUM press office, Johannesburg and Johannesburg Consolidated Investments.

13   Caution to the Wind: the Kinross Mining Disaster and the Evasion of Corporate Responsibility in South Africa

1 See J.D. McNamara, 'Contributed Article: Mining Safety', Gencor annual report and accounts for 1986, pp. 34–6. The 1985 report and accounts were equally misleading. In his chairman's statement on pp. 6–8 of the 1985 report and accounts which he signed on 3 April 1986, a few months before the Kinross disaster, Gencor's chairman Ted Pavitt wrote:

> Gencor also places a high priority on the creation of favourable conditions of employment for all its workers, with particular emphasis on the safety of the workplace. The mining sector has always performed well in the safety competitions of the Chamber of Mines and over the past five years has won approximately 60 per cent of all safety awards in the mining industry (p. 8).

2 See Gencor 1987 annual report and accounts.

3 For a brief report of the Ermelo disaster see *South African Labour Bulletin*, Johannesburg (Summer 1987). For the St Helena tragedy, see *The Sowetan*, Soweto/Johannesburg (2 September 1987).

4 See the 1987 Gencor annual report and accounts, p. 16.

NOTES

5 *Daily Telegraph* (6 September 1987).
6 Interviews with safety advisers, Johannesburg, October 1986.
7 All details from the report into the fire by the then Chief Inspector of Mines in Britain, H.S. Stephenson (HMSO, London, 1968), Cmnd 3657. A similar report on Kinross would be a major contribution to mining safety in South Africa.
8 See, for example, D.G. Wilde, 'Polyurethane Foam–fire Hazard in Mines', *Colliery Guardian*, London (August 1968), and a host of other Safety in Mines Research Establishment publications over the next few years. For the Chamber of Mines of South Africa digest of this information see Chamber of Mines of South Africa safety circulars, released to the press in the wake of the Kinross disaster and originally dated 21 October 1969.
9 See the British Health and Safety Executive, Safety in Mines Research Establishment film, *Assessment of Fire Hazards in Mines* (no date).
10 The details of the Sunshine Mine fire and the subsequent settlement were provided by Jack R. Ormes, the lawyer in Los Angeles who acted for the relatives of the deceased.
11 Interview with Jack R. Ormes, by telephone, October 1986.
12 For the Buffelsfontein and Vaal Reefs fires, see Jean Leger, 'From Hlobane to Kinross', Johannesburg, University of the Witwatersrand paper (1987), p. 3. The Gencor warning to its colliery companies was quoted in 'Death is Part of the Process', *World in Action*, Granada Television, Manchester, 13 October 1986.
13 Gencor press conference, Johannesburg, October 1986.
14 Con Fauconnier at the Gencor press conference.
15 Interviews with Dr Herbert Eisner, Johannesburg and Buxton, Derbyshire, October 1986.
16 See Michael Pollard, *The Hardest Work under Heaven* (Hutchinson, London, 1984), pp. 103–23, 178–81.
17 See De Beers' annual reports for 1888 and 1889 and Hedley Chilvers, *The Story of De Beers* (Cassell, London, 1939), pp. 75 et seq.
18 Quoted in Robert Vicat Turrell, *Capital and Labour on the Kimberley Diamond Fields, 1871–1890* (Cambridge University Press, 1987), p. 159.
19 Ibid., pp. 159, 160.
20 Statement to the Gencor press conference.
21 Danie Steyn, Minister of Mines, press release from the Department of Mineral and Energy Affairs, Johannesburg, October 1986.
22 P. W. Botha, quoted in the *Star*, Johannesburg (28 October 1986).
23 NUM press statement from Cyril Ramaphosa, 'The Kinross Verdict', Johannesburg, March 1988.

343

24 From the official transcript of: The State versus Kinross Mines and others, Regional Court of the Northern Transvaal, Witbank, October 1987. Lubbe Recordings, Johannesburg, 1987.

25 Information drawn from the official transcripts of the Witbank Court.

26 Information provided by Paul Benjamin, lawyer to NUM.

27 Minutes of the evidence of Johannes Vellema before the Chief Inspector of Mines, Klerksdorp, 30 January 1984. (I would like to thank Paul Benjamin for drawing this material to my attention.)

28 Interview with Paul Benjamin, London, 1990.

29 See 'Flashback to Hlobane's 1943 Nightmare', *Daily News* (16 September 1983).

30 The section on Hlobane is based on the inquiry, press reports of the inquiry and long interviews with Paul Benjamin and Dr Herbert Eisner, respectively legal adviser and technical adviser to the National Union of Mineworkers at the Hlobane inquiry.

31 Interview with Dr Eisner.

32 Before Hlobane, the last occasion on which injured black migrant miners or the widows of dead black miners were properly represented at South African tribunals of inquiry into mining disasters was in 1960 when Joe Slovo represented the Coalbrook victims. Between 1960 and 1984, the year of Hlobane, since unions were illegal there was no independent representation. Instead TEBA, the Chamber of Mines recruiting organisation, sent along a 'representative', who 'heard no evil, saw no evil, said and did nothing', as one Johannesburg attorney put it to me.

33 See 'Mine Official "Cut Out Gas Reference"', *Rand Daily Mail*, Johannesburg (8 February 1984).

34 Ibid. (11 and 14 February 1984).

35 See Union of South Africa, Mines Department Annual Report for 1910 and the Interim Report by the acting government mining engineer R.N. Kotze, including report by the Acting Inspector of Mines, Natal, for the year ended 31 December 1910 (Government Print and Stationery Office, UG 34, Pretoria, 1911), esp. pp. 118–22.

36 For further details of the fines levied after the 1984 Hlobane disaster see the *Daily Dispatch* (28 July 1984).

37 Quoted in ibid.

38 NUM press release, Johannesburg, undated, 1984.

39 The details of the deaths at Ermelo are taken from Jean Leger, 'Ermelo Disaster – the Growing Methane Menace', *South African Labour Bulletin*, Johannesburg (Summer 1987), p. 8.

40 Personal communication with the author, 1988.

41 *City Press* (Johannesburg, 6 September 1987).

42 Brian Steele, quoting a stockbroker in his Diagonal Street column, the *Sunday Times*, Johannesburg (24 February 1985).

43 Derek Keys became F. W. De Klerk's Minister of Finance in May 1992. His successor as Chairman of Gencor is Brian Gilberston.

44 For the background to the involvement of Afrikaner business in General Mining see Anthony Hocking, *Oppenheimer and Son* (McGraw-Hill, New York, 1973), p. 372.

45 See the *Sunday Times*, Johannesburg (1 December 1985).

46 See the *Sunday Express*, Johannesburg (10 March 1985).

47 See 'Secret Report May Lead to Sweeping Changes at Gencor', *Star*, Johannesburg (17 February 1986).

48 Print-out in author's possession.

49 Table from Leger and Zwi.

50 Interview with Dr Anthony Zwi, London, 1991.

51 See Chapters 9 and 10.

52 Information from Paul Benjamin, NUM's legal adviser.

14 Death is Part of the Process: Frank Bird and the Illusion of Safety in South African Mines

1 See the *Rand Daily Mail*, Johannesburg (10 December 1981).

2 Ibid.

3 The circumstances of the closure are set out in Anthony Sampson, *Black and Gold* (Hodder & Stoughton, London, 1987), p. 191. David Pallister, the *Guardian* journalist, has also covered these events carefully in his *South Africa Inc – the Oppenheimer Empire*, written with Sarah Stewart and Ian Lepper (Corgi Books, London, 1988), esp. pp. 269–74.

4 Quoted in the extraordinary article, 'It Can Be Safe Down the Mines' by Margaretha Goosen, *Rand Daily Mail*, Johannesburg (8 October 1983).

5 Tim Green, *The New World of Gold* (Weidenfeld & Nicolson, London, 1981), p. 53.

6 Anglo American press statement, 2 August 1983, 'World Record for President Brand'.

7 Calculations made from official Chamber of Mines of South Africa death figures by Jean Leger, University of the Witwatersrand, Department of Sociology, 1986.

8 International Mine Safety Rating System handbooks in the author's possession.

9 Personal communication with the author. I wanted to check these figures

with Gold Fields of South Africa during my visit in 1986. The company declined all co-operation.

10 Telephone interview from Johannesburg, September 1986.
11 I interviewed Dr Eisner for the Granada programme 'Death is Part of the Process', 13 October 1986. I also interviewed him in Derbyshire after the Hlobane disaster, and it is from this interview that these quotes are drawn.
12 Interview with Dr Eisner, Buxton, Derbyshire, 1985.
13 Interviews with Dr Eisner, Johannesburg and Derbyshire, 1986.
14 Anthony Hocking, *Randfontein Estates – the First Hundred Years* (Hollards, Bethulie, 1986), p. 224.
15 Ibid., p. 220.
16 All quotes from an interview with Dr Eisner, Buxton, Derbyshire, 1985.
17 Interview with Jean Leger, Johannesburg, 1986.
18 All figures from Chamber of Mines death and injury figures, computed and aggregated by Jean Leger.
19 For the early history of ERPM see the annual reports of the company.
20 See the Report of the Inter-Departmental Committee of Inquiry into Riots on Mines in the Republic of South Africa, p. 45. Copies of this secret report were leaked and one is in the author's possession.
21 *Financial Times* (16 August 1980).
22 I interviewed the former manager at ERPM on many occasions while writing this book. He is an honest witness, who asked me to protect his anonymity because he would be unable to work again in the industry if his identity became known.
23 This account of the disaster relies on the investigations undertaken by the NUM.
24 See Sheryl Raine, 'Rand Mines Concerned at ERPM's Death Toll', *Star*, Johannesburg (28 November 1985).
25 All quotes from interviews with Frank Bird at the Holiday Inn Hotel, Secunda, September 1986.

15 Blood on the Tracks: the History of Danger and the Danger of History in South African Mining

1 The photographic images to match the words were seen in my *World in Action* programme about Gold Fields, 'The Midas Touch', 24 November 1986.
2 Interview with Tsibela Mohape, Lesotho, September 1986.
3 The estimates of deaths this century draw heavily on the work of the NUM and Jean Leger.
4 Chamber of Mines of South Africa, press release, October 1990.

5 *The Economist* (12 February 1983).

6 Luli Callinicos, *A People's History of South Africa*, vol. I, *Gold and Workers, 1886–1924* (Ravan Press, Johannesburg, 1980), esp. pp. 22–53.

7 Geoffrey Wheatcroft, *The Randlords – the Men who Made South Africa* (Weidenfeld & Nicolson, London, 1985), p. 98.

8 See William H. Worger, *South Africa's City of Diamonds – Mine Workers and Monopoly Capitalism in Kimberley, 1867–1895* (Yale University Press, 1987), p. 216.

9 Ibid., p. 164.

10 *South African Press Bulletin*, London (3 December 1903).

11 See the entry for Edgar Rathbone by A.M. Cunningham, *South African Dictionary of National Biography* (Pretoria, 1990), p. 622.

12 For details of the Selborne Commission see Ambrose Pratt, *The Real South Africa* (Holden & Hardingham, London, 1913), pp. 151–3.

13 Callinicos, *Gold and Workers*, p. 77.

14 Quoted in Dr H.J. Simons, 'Death in South African Mines', *Africa South in Exile* (London, 1960), p. 47.

15 Pratt, *The Real South Africa*, pp. 153, 158, 159.

16 Ibid., pp. 160–2.

17 Ibid., pp. 164–5.

18 Randall Packard, *White Plague, Black Labour: Tuberculosis and the Political Economy of Health and Disease in South Africa* (University of Natal Press, Pietermaritzburg and James Currey, London, 1990), p. 93.

19 Ibid., pp. 72, 78, 177.

20 Adèle Lizard, *Gold Blast – Being the Romantic History of the Rand Goldfields* (Rich & Cowan, London, no date), p. 158.

21 Packard, *White Plague, Black Labour*, p. 166.

22 Ibid., p. 158.

23 For a fearsome list of negligence see the Marais Commission, *First Interim Report of the Commission of Inquiry Regarding Safety in Mines* (Government Printer, Pretoria, R.P. 21, 1963). See also the transcript of the court hearings of the joint inquest and inquiry held at Sasolburg in 1960.

24 The rest of the account is drawn from the pages of the *Rand Daily Mail* and *New Age* for the month after the disaster.

25 Dr Verwoerd, quoted in John Lang, *Bullion Johannesburg*, Jonathan Ball Publishers, 1986, p. 409.

26 See the Marais Commission, *First Interim Report*, paragraphs 1–23.

27 Ibid., paragraphs 39–42.

28 Jean Leger, private communication with the author.

29 Marais Commission, *First Interim Report*, paragraph 24.

30 See Simons, 'Death in the South African Mines', p. 41.
31 Ibid., p. 42.
32 Ibid.
33 Interviews in Johannesburg, 1981, 1986 and 1987.
34 Steve Bolton of Granada interviewed Dr Barry in Johannesburg in 1986 in preparation for the *World in Action* programme on Gold Fields, 'The Midas Touch'.
35 Shelley Arckles, *Permanent Disability in Mineworkers: Case Studies* (University of the Witwatersrand Press, Johannesburg, 1986).
36 Interviews with Dr Herbert Eisner, 1985 and 1986.
37 Interview with Jean Leger in Botswana, 1990.
38 Interview with Archie Luhlabo, Johannesburg, 1986.
39 Cyril Ramaphosa, NUM press statement, Johannesburg, 1989.

16 Resources for a Journey of Hope

1 Allister Sparks, *Daily Mail*, Johannesburg (8 August 1990).
2 Ibid.
3 Robin McGregor, *McGregor's Who Owns Whom* (Purdey Publishing, Cape Province, annually).
4 Julian Ogilvie-Thompson, *Daily Mail* (11 July 1990).
5 Information on Anglo/De Beers from: Robin McGregor, *Who Owns Whom* (Purdey Publishing); Greg Lanning with M. Mueller, *Africa Undermined* (Penguin, Harmondsworth, 1979); David Pallister, Sarah Stewart and Ian Lepper, *South Africa Inc – the Oppenheimer Empire* (Corgi Books, London, 1988); Duncan Innes, *Anglo American and the Rise of Modern South Africa* (Heinemann Educational Books, London, 1984).
6 'The Oppenheimer Empire – South Africa's Family Affair', *The Economist* (London) (1 July 1989), pp. 73–5.
7 Quoted in Bill Jamieson, *Gold Strike* (Hutchinson Business Books, London, 1990), p. 3.
8 Dr Anthony Barker, 'Community of the Careless', *South African Outlook* (April 1970).
9 Francis Wilson and Mamphela Ramphele, *Uprooting Poverty – the South African Challenge* (W.W. Norton, New York and London, and David Philip, Claremont, South Africa, 1989).
10 Alfred Temba Qabula, 'A Working Life Cruel Beyond Belief', quoted in *Learn and Teach*, Johannesburg, no. 5 (1989), p. 52.

Index

349

South African Asbestos Producers
  Association 200
South African Communist Party 132,
  206, 209
South African Congress of Trade
  Unions (SACTU) 304
South African Council of Churches 145
South African Council for Scientific and
  Industrial Research 196
South African Department of Mines
  194, 198, 269
South African Federation of
  Mineworkers 244
South African government 7, 31–2, 34,
  37, 83, 197–8, 247–8, 262, 263, 267,
  270
South African Institute for Medical
  Research 196
South African Institute for Race
  Relations 229, 241
South African Mining magazine 218–19
South African National Research
  Institute for Occupational Diseases
  189
South-West Africa Company 92
South-West African People's
  Organisation (SWAPO) 53, 55
Soweto revolt 215
Spamer, Johannes 227–9
Sparks, Allister 312
Sperrgebiet *see* Forbidden Zone
Spoor, Richard 134–40
Stauch, August 38
Stellenbosch University 48
Stephenson, H.S. 258
Steyn, Danie 5, 262
Stheeman, Willem Hendrick 105
Stilfontein gold mine 285
Storke, A.D. 92, 106
strikes 113, 133, 134, 143, 194, 205,
  207–9, 212, 227, 230, 240, 250
Sub Nigel gold mine 143, 208
Sullivan, Revd. Leon 147
Somers, Howard 7, 77
Sunday Telegraph 157

Sunshine Mine, Idaho 258–9, 260

Tallent, Dr Jennifer 189–92
taxes 105–6, 156, 157, 161
Taylor, Phil 288
Tchudi mine 98
TEBA *see* The Employment Bureau of
  Africa
television documentaries: 'The Case of
  the Disappearing Diamonds' 71–86;
  'Dust to Dust' 166–88; 'Asbestos – a
  Small Town Tragedy' 194 (note 7);
  'Death is Part of the Process' 263
Thabisis, Ntlebere Francis 14
Thatcher, Margaret 156, 157
The Employment Bureau of Africa
  (TEBA) 19, 135, 216–17, 230–33
Theko, David Theko 114–16
Thirion, Pieter Willem/Thirion
  Commission 55–6, 60, 62–70, 80–81,
  106
Thompson, Clive 228, 239, 247
Thompson, Julian Ogilvie 45, 312
Times, The 216, 217
Tjijenda, Peka 89–90
Todd, John 182
toilets 20, 43, 44, 49, 97–8, 100, 110,
  113, 116–18, 252
torture 141
tourism 51–4
trade unions: rise of 130, 203–24; Gold
  Fields and 121–2, 135–6, 139, 151; *see
  also* National Union of Mineworkers
Transformation Resource Centre 17
Trigger, Captain 207
Tsime haHlasoa village 12, 14
Tsukulu, Justice Sello 109
Tsumeb copper and lead mine 87–106
tuberculosis 296, 300, 307
Turner & Newall 177, 178
Turrell, Rob 35, 161, 261

Ulenga, Ben 87, 88–90, 96, 99
Union Corporation 19–20
United Democratic Front 244

INDEX